ADOPTION RESOURCES
FOR
MENTAL HEALTH
PROFESSIONALS

ADOPTION RESOURCES FOR FOR MENTAL HEALTH PROFESSIONALS

Edited by
Pamela V. Grabe

Project directed by
Paul D. Reitnauer

Transaction Publishers
New Brunswick (U.S.A.) and London (U.K.)

Originally published in 1986 by Children's Aid Society in Mercer County, 350 W. Market Street, Mercer, PA 16137, in conjunction with The Mental Health Association in Butler County, 124 W. Cunningham Street, Butler, PA 16001

Library of Congress Catalog Number: 89-5084
ISBN: 0-88738-7-934 (paper)
Printed in the United States of America

Library of Congress Cataloging-in-Publication Data
Adoption resources for mental health professionals / edited by Pamela V. Grabe.
     p. cm.
    ISBN 0-88738-793-4
    1. Children, Adopted—Mental health. 2. Foster children—Mental health. 3. Children, Adopted—Family relationships. 4. Foster children—Family relationships. I. Grabe, Pamela V.
RJ507.A36A38   1989
362.7′ 33—dc20   89-5084
                                                  CIP

Acknowledgement is gratefully made to the following copyright holders for permission to reprint from previously published materials.

(1) The Society for Research in Child Development
The University of Chicago Press
5801 Ellis Avenue
Chicago, IL 60637

(2) Child Welfare League of America
PERMISSIONS, CWLA Publications
440 First Street, NW
Washington, D.C. 20001

(3) Foster W. Cline, M.D.
Evergreen Consultants in Human Behavior
P.O. Box 2380
Evergreen, CO 80439

This publication has been prepared as a part of the MH/AT Project, under a grant with the Children's Bureau, U.S. Department of Health and Human Services. The content however, does not necessarily reflect official HHS/OHDS position or policy.

We must see the first images which the external world casts upon the dark mirror of his mind; or, must hear the first words which awaken the sleeping powers of thought, and stand by his earliest efforts, if we should understand the prejudices, the habits, and the passion that will rule his life. The entire man is, so to speak, to be found in the cradle of the child.

—Alexis de Tocqueville

Contents

Preface

A truly helpful mental health professional is not only one who is highly empathetic, caring, and skilled in problem solving. She/he is also knowledgeable about the life circumstances of individuals receiving help, the kinds of unique demands they have faced, and why and how they have learned to cope as they do. This text goes a long way towards providing critical knowledge about the experiences of a specific group of children—those who have lived in substitute care, who have moved from one substitute home to another, and who have struggled to survive repeated loss of contact with people they have trusted and loved.

Due to increased efforts now made to find permanent homes for these children, many more have been brought to the attention of clinicians, who work in mental health/mental retardation centers, family service and child guidance agencies, and those working in private practice. The background and problems of these children differs significantly from those of "typical" children—those who have not lost contact with their birth family, those who have not lived as "systems children." Professionals trying to assess children in foster care or adoptive situations using the same criteria they employ to evaluate the non-adopted will find their diagnoses misleading and their treatment unhelpful. These are the practitioners for whom this text will be particularly pertinent.

With the help of truly informed social service agency personnel, foster care can be an effective resource for children, and adoptive placements will succeed. Without the assistance of knowledgeable practitioners, these placements will—and have failed. Creating a stable and happy future for our children is dependent on the effective assistance from these individuals. *Adoption Resources for Mental Health Professionals* provides for much needed guidance in this effort.

Judith A. Martin, Ph.D.
University of Pittsburgh School of Social Work

Acknowledgments

In any effort of this magnitude, many "unsung heros/heroines" work to make it all come together. We want to offer our sincere "thank you" to the following:

Susan Sim Chrzan who brought to this project her experience and sensitivity gained through placing many challenged children, as well as her love.

Virginia Ramig who gave us her tireless efforts and valuable advice on English usage—above and beyond the call of duty.

Carolyn Schreiber who cheerfully and carefully typed and corrected footnotes and bibliographies.

Dr. Paulette La Doux who opened the magic doors of a computer search program to aid our work.

The Administration and Boards of Directors of the Children's Aid Society and the Mental Health Association who have offered us encouragement throughout.

Karen Wien, Child Specialist for Families in Transition, Parent and Child Guidance, Pittsburgh, PA, for working with some of the children on this project, and

The Children who contributed the pictures in this book. The drawings are from children who have experienced multiple separations and moves, and who now live in families. Their pictures vividly show that their experiences remain a part of how they view family life and circumstances.

Our Deepest Gratitude

xiii

INTRODUCTION

The Mental Health/Adoption Therapy Project had its beginnings in the lives of families in Western Pennsylvania who had adopted "special needs" children over the past decade. In their desire to parent older and physically-emotionally- and mentally-challenged children, families sought all types of supportive services.

Some services for these children, such as educational planning and medical services, were available. What was needed most, however, was most elusive: mental health professionals with a clear understanding of the impact of the adoptive experience on older children and the resulting chaos in many families. While most of the children adjusted into families with few or no complications, others did not. For them, and their families, the struggle was extremely painful. There were those who never succeeded. What the families identified as missing from their support network was a mental health system willing to address these issues.

A number of studies have shown that many children being treated in mental health clinics are adopted, the proportion far exceeding their representation in the general population. In a previous pilot project, a limited survey of community mental health counseling centers in Pennsylvania, it was also discovered that 20 to 30 percent of the families with children in therapy at most of the community mental health centers were foster/adoptive families. It was also learned that while therapists were aware that they were treating children who were in foster care or adopted, they attached no special significance to that fact. Less than 10 percent of the therapists had a working knowledge of counseling appropriate to modern adoption experiences.

It became evident that similar conditions prevailed in other areas. In a 1984 conference in Pittsburgh, 165 attendees from seven states spoke emphatically about the need for mental health professionals to learn more about the foster/adoption system and its impact upon the older adopted child, and to have training appropriate to the needs of these special children and their families.

This book, like the pilot project, is an effort by two agencies representing two different social services in two disciplines, in two counties to work cooperatively so as to improve services for the children we both assist. In a time of dwindling dollars and increasing need, we believe that such cooperation will make the most of the resources available.

The Children's Aid Society of Mercer, Pennsylvania, has a strong adoption placement program which includes special needs children and infants. The agency began its work in 1889. Its original purpose was to provide a home for dependent and neglected children. This mission continues today as a group residential facility for adolescent girls. Over the decades new programs were added such as those designed to assist parents in coping with problems and concerns of family life and child rearing. Most innovative has been the adoption work, which expanded from traditional infants to special needs children.

The agency is funded through the Mary L. Budd Fund and local United Way dollars. The Mental Health/Adoption Therapy Project is the second federally-funded project the agency has undertaken in recent years.

The Mental Health Association in Butler, Pennsylvania, is primarily an advocate for persons in the mental health system, both children and adults. The MHA is a voluntary, nongovernmental organization dedicated to the prevention of mental illness, the promotion of mental health, and the improved care and treatment of the mentally ill. It is funded through United Way dollars and private contributions. Since many of the children in the foster care/adoption system have no "natural advocate," the Association speaks for them as well.

In speaking to a coalition of mental health advocates in Massachusetts in 1983, Jane Knitzer, Ed.D., author of *Unclaimed Children,* spoke about the urgent need for coordinated mental health services for children. She cited the few programs existing in the United States that had proven to be successful, saying, "... the programs typically work intensively with children or adolescents in their own homes and communities, involve parents when they exist in treatment, show sensitivity to children's ages, developmental levels, strengths and weaknesses, and help children to move easily from one setting to another, by providing as a core treatment component advocacy with other agencies to ensure the children get the non-mental health services they are supposed to. They involve traditional mental health skills and sensitivities adapted to new ways." In short, there is close coordination between mental health providers and the other professionals who work in behalf of the children, the family is included in the treatment plan.

The Mental Health Adoption Therapy Project is part of the federal initiative encouraging state authorities to promote collaboration between the mental health system and the child welfare system so that the practitioners in both systems will work in concert for the benefit of children and their families. It is this commitment to such coordination and to reciprocal education between child welfare and mental health professionals that provides the impetus for the Mental Health/Adoption Therapy Project. *ADOPTION RESOURCES FOR MENTAL HEALTH PROFESSIONALS* is intended to offer a handy reference to counselors, family and individual therapists, psychologists, psychiatrists, and residential and group home staff members regarding the "system children" and their adoption experiences.

> *He drew a circle that shut me out—*
> *Heretic, rebel, a thing to flout.*
> *But Love and I had the wit to win:*
> *We drew a circle that took him in!*
> *—Edwin Markham*

OVERVIEW

In putting together the information in this book, several ideas resurfaced as each author discussed his/her own particular issue. Despite distance, time, area of adoption being discussed or the perspective of the author, key concepts were repeated over and over again. These are the essence of the following pages.

1. Children who have been adopted—or separated from significant family members, need to grieve their loss. They will grieve in good ways if helped by caring adults who are prepared to support the process, or in difficult ways. But grieve they will. This is true whether they were adopted as infants, toddlers, at latency age or as adolescents.

2. Adoptive families are like all families. Some are better prepared for the experience than others. They share a deep commitment to the concept of family and the impact that permanency and love will have on children. Sometimes that is not enough.

3. Children who have been through multiple placements have significant issues to work through that cannot be ignored. When they are, the adoption is in trouble—if not immediately than surely when societal pressures or family stress becomes an issue. Some children having been damaged by the system will not make it successfully in the adoption. We need to be prepared to help those children and families before the step of disruption is reached and afterward if disruption is inevitable.

4. All of the social services that assist special needs children must work together or else they only succeed in pulling apart the child and family who need help. A multi-disciplinary approach is vital to helping children and families make it together.

5. In removing children from their families, society has taken on a responsibility for their total care. That responsibility goes far beyond the simple needs of food and shelter. The system having determined that these children can no longer live with their families must begin to address the many

complex needs they have. The damage produced by the removal from family is too great, and too deep to continue to ignore. Waiting for the crisis of a disruption is also too late. If we are not prepared to help, then we too are adding to the damage and pain of an already vulnerable child.

6. The authors of the articles are clinicians and workers who have spent considerable time working with the special needs child. Their experience offers direction to us all.

Part I

1

The System

Pamela V. Grabe

We care for our children. At least we say we do. Daily, through television, newspapers, magazines, and nearly every way possible, we are told that "children are our most important national resource." However through the same television, newspapers, etc., we can see and hear that while the message is true for most children, there are some for whom there is a different message. They are our "hidden population," our "throw away children." They are the children who have become wards of the state because the adults in their lives could not, or would not, provide minimal standards of care. They live in the "foster care" system of this country. Unfortunately, though foster care began and continues with good intentions, the aware observer cannot help being impressed with the amount of institutionalized neglect and the confusion about ways to help children who can no longer live with their birth families.

History

During the 1950's, professionals took a serious look at the programs for the care of homeless children. Vast numbers of children were inundating programs that began as "temporary" until problems in the children's "permanent" homes could be solved. Many children entered at an early age and remained until they became adults. Through a variety of public policies and social changes we had created a program like a funnel: many children fell in, but few ever left. The emotional cost as well as the financial cost for these programs was staggering. In 1978 it was estimated that the foster care

3

programs in the United States were serving nearly 500,000 children at an annual cost of two billion dollars![1]

Children were brought into the foster care system for a variety of reasons: the increasing mobility of society which meant few extended family resources for families in trouble; the rising divorce rate, leaving many low income single women as heads of households; the rising number of unemployed parents who had no ability to support the family—or even provide a home in which to live; the overwhelming numbers of abused children being identified; the rising numbers of adults with addictions to drugs or alcohol who were unable to care for their children; the increasing number of people with mental illness who could not provide for their offspring; and the failure of public policies to pay for services that would reunite families. So while it was possible to pay for keeping children out of their families we would not pay for prevention or in-home services. The result was that by the late 1970's the United States was spending ever-increasing dollars to care for children in programs that many believed were seriously flawed.[2]

In the 1960's and 1970's the focus of many in the United States was on civil rights and human rights. The thousands of displaced children in foster care were among those to benefit from this movement. Professionals, parents, advocates, and others united to work for a national policy that would provide uniformity in the care of children rather than permit them to continue to drift through programs. Surveys that tried to present the full scope of the need reported that there were no clear statistics. Not only did we not have a national consensus on how to care for our children, we did not even have a system to track how many were in care, who they were, or where they were being placed.[3]

The passage of P.L. 96-272 in 1980 marked an important milestone in the treatment of children in the United States. This bill provided for the first time a national focus and direction for children and has come to be known by many as the "Civil Rights Bill for Kids." It grants them entitlement to certain safeguards and provisions of law. In order for states to receive foster care funding from the Federal government, they must make certain guarantees about the programs they provide. Active measures must be taken to keep children in their birth families, or if they must be removed, they should be returned as soon as possible. There must be specific plans and goals established for the care of foster children, with timely reviews of those plans —hopefully resulting in fewer moves for children while they are in care. Finally, there must be steps taken to work for permanent placements for children in care.[4] P.L. 96-272 has become one of the most significant pieces of legislation for children since the development of child labor laws in the early days of the twentieth century.

More Is Needed

It is clearly understood that infants and children need love and nurturance to survive. Traditionally we have accepted that love has been best provided by a family unit. Where alternatives have been tried, such as nurseries and/or removal to "safe" communities in time of war, significant developmental delays and problems have been documented.[5] Studies of children raised in orphanages and other institutions have shown that these children also have significant delays in their intellectual and physical development. Therefore the shift to family foster care was seen as being beneficial. It was not intended, however, to be a substitute for a permanent family.

Although children in care come from all social stratas many who enter the system have similar backgrounds. Studies through the years have cited basic characteristics: the families are typically of low economic, intellectual, and social levels; the children have experienced some form of neglect or emotional abandonment; and the parents have had severe personal or social difficulties.[6]

Although such conditions make a poor beginning for any child, most follow-up studies show that these children who were later adopted, that is, who achieved permanence in a family, went on to lead productive lives. So adoption came to be viewed as the ideal alternative to the impermanence of the foster care system.

Adoption is not always permanent, however. Recently a disturbing trend has risen among families who have adopted older "special needs" children. Some of them are returning the children to the child welfare system. This practice has forced many professionals to begin looking at the causes for these disruptions and to question the children and the parents.

Recent trends in the placement of older children have challenged much of the traditional social work thinking about adoption. The number of disrupted adoptions, though small, has also been a challenge. While it is not always certain why some adoptions succeed and others do not, this trend does illustrate that the solution to the problem of too many children living out their youth in foster care is not found by simply placing them for adoption. More is needed.

System Issues

We do know that children in the foster care system share certain experiences that are significant for later life and for their adaptation to adoptive homes. These are the experiences we call "system issues." We have called the children who experienced them "system children."

First: *These children have been separated from significant others in their early lives, probably several times*. Not only have they lost ties to their birth families, but they have also been attached to and separated from an average of 2.3 foster families before permanent placement for adoption.[7] In many cases, this number is significantly higher.

When children are born, their first and foremost task is to survive. To do so, they engage in complex interactions with the adults who care for them; these result in the close bonds and attachments upon which their very survival depends. Infants and young children are not critical of the adults who perform these vital tasks—as long as they are provided. It is society that judges whether or not the home is clean enough, or adequate enough, or if the emotional requirements are being met. It is society that decides a child should be moved—not the child. This may explain why he/she is extremely reluctant to give up the attachments he has made to his parents. The removal is an attack on his basic supports for survival.

These children grieve the losses of the people who were important to them. The child does not understand the concept of "temporary," particularly if he is under the age of eight. For him, the move appears to be permanent. He has lost his parent/s as effectively as if they had died. When that loss is repeated over and over again, by numerous returns to and separations from the birth family as well as foster families, the damage to the child can be enormous. This is particularly true, since until recently, the system has not recognized the importance of helping the child to deal with his grief.

These children also experience tremendous anger. It too remains largely unrecognized and unresolved. It is not hard to understand that anger at the loss of all that is familiar would be a salient feature of the child's entering foster care. And yet, a child has been expected to show gratitude and not to let that anger spill over into unacceptable behaviors. Worse yet, he has been expected to absorb the anger not only from the first move but from subsequent moves, perhaps many of them, and not always with advance warning or preparation. The anger is very often displaced onto the new mother he deals with, since he is most angry at the mother who permitted him to be taken away. It is also possible for the anger to turn inward, resulting in a depression that may be unrecognized far too long.

The process of being removed from home to home results in the loss of biological connectedness. These children lose their sense of belonging and their sense of personal history. It is not unusual for siblings to be placed in different homes, particularly if there are three or more. Sometimes, only the youngest children will be removed, the older ones remaining with the parents. This creates great emotional trauma for a child who must try to understand why he was given away but others were permitted to stay with the parents.

Boy, 14. Feeling sad.

When there are several moves it becomes difficult for the child to remember who belongs to whom, what history is his and what history belongs to others.

This sense of loss is exacerbated when minority children such as Black, Hispanic, and Native American youngsters are placed in foster care. In many parts of America this placement will almost always not be in the home of a family of the same race, but into a White home. Added to the loss of family for these children is also the loss of their cuture.

Children past infancy, who have been removed from their birth or foster families often exhibit developmental and intellectual delays of several years. The removal of a child from his family, especially without grief resolution, impacts on a child in many ways. Some will have cognitive delays, some will hang onto infantile behaviors just as an infant holds onto his security blanket. Seldom are removals from families or placements in new families planned to coincide with the academic year. Children move into and out of schools at all times of the year and lose much of the content of school programs in the process. Many times the child is tested for school placement shortly after his arrival in a new home. This is particularly true if his records have not followed him or been somewhat incomplete. The results of such testing reflect the inner turmoil, and many of the children test high with learning disabilities. Many will continue to have difficulties in school settings after being placed for adoption as well.

A disturbing truth for these children is that many of them have been sexually abused by someone in their past, either by birth-family members or by someone in the foster family setting. The abuser may have been an adult or another child, but the result is the same: These children have a precocious sense of sexuality. However, they may not distinguish their experience as abuse. The abuser, and even other family members, may have described it as being an acceptable way to show love. For some who have been abused over an extended period of time, there may even be an unconscious need to replicate the experience, since that is the only way they know how to express love. They need therapy and help in distinguishing between sexual love and the nurturing love of a parent. Many foster and adoptive families are poorly prepared for these children.[8]

In order to make sense out of their confusion, many of these children have developed "survival skills." They have decided that they, not adults, will be in control. Their experience has convinced them that adults are not able to keep the promises they make or to provide them with a sense of security. As a protection against the pain of continued loss they choose to rely only on themselves. They either remain emotionally aloof from the people they live with or become superficially attached to *everyone* they meet. They are not skilled at making the necessary adjustments for comfortable family living, i.e., sharing toys, clothing, or affections. On the surface, at least, they are survivors and loners, not joiners. It is this need to take while giving nothing in return that helps create the gulf between child and parents that eventually results in removal to yet another home.

Many of the children offer resistance to the concept of being adopted, particularly if little effort is made to help them understand the meaning of the new relationship and resolve the loss of old ties. For many children their fear of being "once more" rejected is so great that they will turn down the possibility of adoption just to protect themselves. The social worker must deal with this when preparing a child for adoption.

Once placed in foster care or for adoption, many children will behave badly to insure that they will be returned to the home or institution they came from.

In their eyes it is better to be thrown out by your own choice than be rejected by someone else's choice. This is a problem faced by parents and the therapists that they go to for help.

The Scope of the Problem

A child raised in an institution is not asked to make a commitment to anyone other than the group, or possibly himself. When the youngster becomes 18, he is on his own. The seeds of adult difficulties are planted when the system acquiesces to the child's desire to flee from commitments. The child who has not been committed to family living often has difficulty in supporting emotionally, even materially, the family he creates, and his children are the next ones to come into foster care. The child who has been abused consistently is often the next abusive parent—his children are the next victims of child abuse. The child who has not made the best of his education or been properly prepared for employment is the adult who is unemployed and unemployable, likely to join the ranks of the welfare or the adult criminal system. His children may follow in his footsteps.

The challenge for all professionals and parents who work with these children is to understand the scope of the problem that they face. Like many other social problems that the public sector attempts to provide a solution for, foster care was planned with compassion to meet the needs of children. But that compassion can do no good when we choose to fill the need as cheaply as possible. We are faced with the results of that policy. Far too many children live in out-of-home care. They grow up without the benefit of connection to family or history. When they become adults, they either return to the system via welfare or send their children back into it for care. If we hope to make a change in the lives of these children, the solution that we reach for should be a good one, not just an expedient one.

The real challenge for mental health professionals is to help the families that approach them to identify the conditions that are the outward manifestations of inner turmoil, that are a mask for confusion and lack of self-esteem. Once they are identified, it is essential to work for the reduction of those behaviors that isolate the child in the family and from the society as a whole. When we fail to do that, the child is in danger of acting out in more harmful ways, until he may well be in danger of losing his new family as well as the old one.

In the current social services system in the United States, a variety of agencies work independently of each other in providing services to children. Often they do not even understand what the other agency provides or ought to provide. The end result may be chaos for the child. Instead we should be developing programs that work together.

Author Quentin Rae-Grant summed up his recommendations:

> Intervention ideally should be the least intrusive, the least expensive, the least intensive, and the shortest in duration required to produce the needed restoration of competence to function and to grow productively. As children's and families' needs change with time, so the appropriate source to provide this continuing help and appropriate service also changes. The challenge facing all jurisdictions is the integration of a continuum of services.[9]

In 1982, in New York State, the results of the first (and perhaps only) project to provide psychoanalytically based preventive measures to the population of children who have just entered foster care were reported. The four year project sponsored by the National Institute of Mental Health (NIMH) was also one of the few to be based on the interaction of mental health professionals with a social service field. Their findings offer significant

Boy, 9. Repairing his snowman after someone broke it, and worried that it will happen again.

direction for those working with the foster care population today. In a time of shrinking fiscal resources, it is essential for the helping professions to work cooperatively to provide the best for our children. The report stated: "It is concluded that psychiatric diagnosis can have predictive value in the social system of foster care and that preventive psychiatric treatment has demonstrated clinical value for foster children. We recommend mental health agencies develop collaborations with local governmental social service departments to provide and further assess conjoint applications of clinical preventive services for foster children."[10]

If there is any additional concern raised by this study, it is the lengthy involvement of psychiatric services that is predicted as necessary. For a large population of children, it would be impractical as well as expensive. What they have learned, however, is an invaluable lesson for those who work with multiply placed children. While it raises some concern about the current trends in the social service field around placement of children, the study also points out a positive result when the two systems work together. After all, if children are our most significant national resource for the future, they deserve our collective best.

Notes

1. Persico, Joseph E. 1979. National Commission on Children in Need of Parents. *Who knows? Who cares? Forgotten children in foster care.* New York: Institute of Public Affairs, pp. 5–7.
2. *Children without homes.* 1978. Washington, D.C.: Children's Defense Fund.
3. Ibid.
4. Public Law 96–272. 1980. Washington, D.C. U.S. Congress.
5. Maas, Henry S., Ph.D. 1962. "The young adult adjustment of twenty wartime residential nursery children," given at Child Welfare League of American National Conference, New York City, New York, pp. 4–21.
6. Kadushin, Alfred. 1970. *Adopting older children.* New York: Columbia University Press, pp. 19–29.
7. Ibid.
8. Fahlberg, Vera, M.D. 1981. *The child in placement: Common behavioral problems.* Michigan: Michigan Department of Social Services, pp. 65–67.
9. Steinhauer, P. D. & Quentin Rae-Grant. 1983. *Problems of the child in the family (2nd ed.)* New York: Basic Books, p. 676.
10. Kliman, Gilbert, M.D. & Schaeffer, Harris M., Ph.D. 1984. "Prediction and prevention with foster children." Paper presented at the American Psychiatric Association, p. 5.

2

The Children

Pamela V. Grabe

Studies and Statistics

Children who move through the foster care system in the United States number in the hundreds of thousands. But we don't know just how many hundreds of thousands. In 1978, following closely on the heels of the National Commission for Children in Need of Homes, the Children's Defense Fund, a national advocacy organization focusing on children, published its study *Children without Homes*. They had spent nearly three years surveying children's services in the United States concentrating on seven states. From their study we were shocked to learn that over half a million children lived in out-of-home care. Even worse, neither the Children's Defense Fund nor anyone else was certain if the figures were correct—it was merely their best guess. The nation that prides itself on knowing where each and every wild horse roams did not know where its children were. Few disputed the accuracy of their claims.[1]

The CDF study looked at the child welfare agencies legally responsible for the care of children in out-of-home placement. It concluded that the results of state and federal policies could be summed up in three startling conclusions. 1) Families don't count. 2) Children don't count. 3) The children who count least are those in the care of the State.[2]

In trying to understand the failure of the state to care for the children in its custody, one need only realize that in most states the number of children in care is often not even known. It would be difficult to imagine that services could be adequately planned and followed if no one knew for sure how many children were in custody.

The late 1970's and early 1980's did see an effort on the part of state agencies that care for children to reduce the number of children in care by

13

aggressively recruiting parents for special needs children and making more efforts to maintain children in their birth homes before seeking to remove them. Most knowledgeable experts today would agree that the number of children in care has fallen closer to the 300,000 number. This is still an enormous population of children to grow up without consistent love and care.

Of that number perhaps 125,000 are free for adoption. Many more would be available if homes could be found (we don't know that number either). We do know that for many of the children and their families, adoption would be a much easier process if it were done early in the child's life or after fewer moves.

In 1982 a second work by the Children's Defense Fund documented an even stronger message. *Unclaimed Children* looked at mental health services and cited the "failure of public responsibility to children and adolescents in need of mental health services."[3]

This work also offered three conclusions. 1) Two out of every three *seriously disturbed* children and adolescents do not get any mental health services. Certain groups such as children in out-of-home care, the poor, and children of alcoholic or mentally ill parents are particularly unlikely to receive services. 2) Parents receive little assistance in seeking out services for their children. Often parents have no support or respite or other groups of parents to

Boy, 8.

talk with. Custody of children has to be given up in order to receive many residential services. 3) Only a few states have a policy focus on children within the Office of Mental Health, and even those who do often lack a budget sufficient to fund even minimal services for the children who need them.[4]

Adoptive families are not surprised when they read the summary of the Children's Defense Fund research. In many ways they know what those three conclusions mean in very real and human terms. The older children they adopt are often troubled, and parents turn to the mental health system for help— help that is not always available.

Many children will move into families with moderate success: Some will not. For those who will need help, it is essential that services be available when they are needed. When an adoption is about to disrupt it is too late to begin to develop the needed services. The time to begin that development is before the placement itself.

Examples

Tammy, Samantha, John and Scott are representative of the many children who are placed for adoption. Their stories do not reflect the best the system has to offer; neither are they isolated examples. Their experiences are real. Far too many of the children being placed have had similar ones.

Tammy

Tammy is the eldest of three sisters. She also has three brothers. Tammy and her sisters were often abused by their parents although their brothers had very little difficulty getting along and seemed to be loved and wanted. On one occasion, after being locked in the bathroom for nearly a week, Tammy was able to get out of the house and go for help. The authorities removed the girls, and also the boys for a short while; then parental rights to the girls were terminated and the boys were returned home. That was the last contact Tammy and the girls ever had with their brothers or their parents.

Tammy was six when she was removed from her parents. She spent the next three years in several different foster homes, sometimes with her sisters and sometimes alone. Her younger sisters got along well in their last foster home, stayed together and were finally adopted. Tammy was not.

Two more years of strenuous efforts were made by adoption advocates, who used agressive measures in an effort to find a family for Tammy. She was featured in various media presentations, and a couple with no other children was chosen from another part of the state. Tammy visited with them for one weekend before she moved to her new home.

Shortly after the placement, school started. Tammy began to have great difficulty. There were constant arguments with her mom over getting off to school on time and endless talks about completing homework. The school repeatedly called the mother to complain about Tammy's behavior both in the classroom and with the other students. She was disruptive and disobedient, and at times even threatened to hurt the younger students. She was especially difficult with the boys in her classroom, deliberately instigating problems and destroying their property. She was also caught stealing their lunch money.

Birth Sibs, 6 and 7. It hurts when you say, "I'm not your brother".

Tammy's new mom, who was feeling pressured on her job by all of the interruptions from the school felt that the school personnel had done little to work with Tammy. Their primary target seemed to be the mom as they repeatedly asked her, "What do you plan to do to improve Tammy's behavior?"

Tammy and her mom went to a counselor at the same agency that did the home study before the placement. Although not a part of the adoption program, the therapist has had some contact with families who adopted babies through the agency. He suggests that Tammy enter therapy for an extended period of time, and has been seeing her for nearly a year. Tammy's behaviors have changed little and she describes her sessions with the counselor as great "fun" since they play pool together quite frequently.

What appears to be the final blow to Tammy's chances for a permanent family came when she and her parents had a violent argument after Tammy threw a rock at the neighbor boy, hitting him in the head. On being sent to her room, Tammy put holes in the walls with her fists, and when her mom tried to stop her, she hit her mother as well.

Tammy has been in therapy for nearly a year, but may not last much longer in this family. The therapist has yet to talk with her about her anger at the boys that her parents never relinquished, or at her parents for giving her up. Nor has any effort been made to assist Tammy in learning to express her anger in more acceptable ways.

John and Samantha

John and Samantha were seven and ten when their mother brought them to the welfare agency for placement. Shortly before that their father had died, and despite her efforts Mrs. F. could not hold the family together. Her parental rights were terminated and a new family was sought to parent the children.

Since no home was available to accomodate both of the children, they did not stay in the same home. During the next year John saw his sister on short visits and not even for each holiday. Christmas was particularly difficult since the holiday marked the anniversary of their entry into the foster care system.

At one point the family who cared for John thought they might like to adopt him, but they did not want to consider taking on his older sister. In fact, they rather hoped that all contact could be severed, since visits with Samantha were usually followed by periods of disruption in their home.

The agency persisted, however, in looking for a family that could parent both children, and found one in a neighboring state. The children were told on one of their weekend visits that a new family, Mr. and Mrs. J. had been found. They appeared to take the news with great joy. On the surface at least, they were prepared to begin life with a new mom and dad.

The new parents-to-be had seen pictures of John and Samantha, and been told a great deal about them. However, the first meeting was arranged in such a way that the children could be seen and observed but would not immediately meet the family. The children were taken on an outing to McDonald's where the new parents "just happened" to be having lunch. After watching and listening to the children, they were told to give the worker a high sign to indicate that they wished to continue with the placement. Only after that step would they actually meet John and Samantha.

Looking good and on their best behavior for this treat, the children were accepted, and they met their new parents for the first time. The rest of the weekend was spent in touring the city, and taking a few pictures of their old home. On the following Monday the new family began the trek to a new home, a new city, and a new state.

When the children unpacked in their new home, it was discovered that much of what they had brought were broken toys, and outgrown clothing. They had no pictures of their lives before the ages of 8 and 11, and few school, medical or personal records. It was as if the children had suddenly been born as latent adolescents.

It did not take long for the family to experience problems. Mr. and Mrs. J. did not have other children, and they had spent nearly six years in the adoption process. They had looked forward to the day they would be able to begin doing things other families did. Their hopes and dreams for a family were certainly tied up in the children. Mr. J. was particularly pleased to have children of an older age who could do the outdoor type of things that both husband and wife enjoyed.

Both John and Samantha liked being in the out-of-doors, but were frightened when it became clear that overnight camping was part of the program. Plans would be made for a weekend together and then changed as first one and then the other of the children expressed fear and uncertainty. An entire summer went by, and not once did the family make it past the driveway.

John found it particularly difficult to be close to people. He refused to let either his mom or dad give him a hug or a kiss. Just casually brushing his shoulder would result in a flinching and withdrawal that left both parents feeling hurt and bewildered. Nowhere in the children's file had there been any record of physical abuse that might explain John's reactions to any efforts at intimacy. On the other hand, Samantha made new friends every day, constantly pointing out to her new mom other mothers who were more attractive, more sophisticated, less strict, etc. On several occasions Samantha would wistfully ask a girlfriend if her mother would like to adopt her! When she became angry at her parents, she was not above announcing that she did not plan to agree to the finalization of her adoption. (She knew that since she would be 12 by that time, she would be asked to sign the papers.) The legal phases of the adoption continued to move along, but both parents doubted that the day would ever come when they could feel that in fact they were a family.

The local agency worker met with the family the required three times before finalization. When the parents indicated that many questions about the children and their past remained unanswered, the worker hurriedly indicated that they would be good parents since they had been chosen for the placement.

When the children were invited to talk about their experiences, the dialogue was typically one word statements, few smiles, and little elaboration of their concern or feelings. The statement was often made that this was a "good" adoption for the family obviously needed no outside assistance. Placement had gone smoothly, the children had been transferred to the care of a new set of parents, finalization would be the next step and everyone would take pride in the new family created—almost the same as a birth family.

No mention was ever made of the rising uneasiness of the family that the children would not participate in overnight camping trips, or of John's obvious uneasiness with intimacy. Even Samantha's refusal to sign the adoption papers was brushed off as just a silly comment. However, the closer the day of finalization came, both Mr. and Mrs. J. wondered if they were going to be able to complete the finalization. Maybe another family would be better for these two. After all, the children are certainly being very verbal about their desire to have other parents.

Scott

Scott is one of four brothers born into a family whose success in American life was marginal. Both his father and his mother had a history of mental illness. Shortly after his second birthday, Scott and his next oldest brother were placed in foster care. Over the next three years, several attempts were made to return Scott and Frank to their home, but each time they would be returned to the foster family after a short time.

On one of the boys' visits home, their father was gone; on another their mom had moved to a new apartment. Shortly after that the older brothers were placed in residential care. When Scott was six, all visits with his mom stopped. Both boys were placed for adoption, but the placement disrupted after only a short time. Scott's older brother was placed in a group home, and a second adoption was pursued for Scott.

Due to the expanding national network of adoption exchanges, the adoptive parent chosen for Scott was not from his home area. He was to be placed with a single mom in another part of the country. Since the previous effort at adoption had failed, the agency argued that he should make the break with his past "cold turkey," so no letters or phone calls to his foster family were permitted. Even the request of the new mom for pictures of Scott and his previous six years with the foster family fell on deaf ears. It would be months before a few pictures and mementos of past achievements would be sent to Scott in his new home.

When Scott first arrived, he spent hours pacing and looking over every new item, even long into the night. He was restless during the day and quick to anger if thwarted in his desires. When school started two weeks later, he terrorized the classroom.

As events escalated and Scott had ever greater difficulties dealing with his day to day activities, his mom worried about his physical safety. On one occasion he put his hand through a glass window; another time he climbed out a second story window and threatened to jump. His behavior in school was so disruptive that the principal threatened to expel him, and finally recommended that Scott be placed in the psychiatric unit of the local hospital for evaluation.

With the diagnosis of "adjustment reaction," Scott began weekly visits at the local community mental health center. He was in therapy there for three years, and went through three therapists. He has since spent time in the newly developed adolescent psychiatric unit of the local hospital and time in a residential facility, had therapy with another psychiatrist, been in the custody of the child welfare system and the probation system, and spent time in a specialized foster care program. He has been placed in a special school for socially and emotionally disturbed (SED) children, and is currently in another residential group living experience. Scott is only fourteen.

Scott's mom does not want to stop being his parent, but feels frustrated and burned out. There appears to be so little help available for either of them. Her experience with therapy has been one of opportunities consistently missed. When she suggested to the therapist the possibility of working on a "life book," she was told that the counselor was too busy to read up on the subject. Three years later, another therapist thought it was a good idea, but never went very far with it. When mom suggested that perhaps Scott might need some help for his nightmares and firesetting, the therapist said that it would not be helpful unless Scott brought up the subject on his own. One night in a group session when Scott did bring up the subject of matches, the therapist said, "Not now, we're too busy." After three years, the mental health center had still not thought it important to work with Scott on the death of his foster father, the only father he had ever known. Scott had inadvertently found out about it on a call back to his foster family—they weren't going to tell him.

Even after the situation was explained to the therapist, he didn't find it important, for "that family is no longer the one Scott lives with."

* * * * *

Grief, anger, rejection, fear of yet another loss, connections to one's past; these are the essence of therapy with adopted older children. Their years as children are few. We are not only wasting the opportunity to offer help but through our negligence we are wasting their childhood and undermining their future.

Children Under Stress

It cannot be said often enough that older special needs children are children who have faced very stressful events in their lives. If the examples of Tammy, John, Samantha and Scott tell us nothing else, they show us the strains that accompany day to day living in the foster care system, and that follow the child into adoption.

Noted child psychiatrist Erik Erikson has described eleven separate fears that children face. They are: fear of withdrawal of support; fear of suddenness; fear of noise; fear of being manipulated; fear of interruption of a vital activity; fear of being deprived of a valuable possession; fear of restraint; fear of having no imposed controls; fear of being exposed, or inspection; fear of remaining small; fear of being left alone.[5]

When the experiences of children are placed against this list it is some wonder that any of them grow emotionally healthy. All children, even those who have never had to leave the safety and security of their birth families, will experience these fears. School, the largest task children face in their early years, presents nearly every one of these fears to children and expects them to learn to overcome their fears and to excell.

How very much more we add to their fears when we bring children into the foster care system. The act of removal alone exposes them to their worst fear: that of being abandoned. To it is added the loss of prized possessions; being inspected; failing at school subjects and relationships; and sudden changes in life style, daily rules of living, and family members. The list does not end there. We are fortunate that most of the children have the resiliency to overcome the experience of foster care and be able to continue on with their lives.

Recently researchers Thomas Holmes and Richard Rahe developed a chart for adults that listed stress events in one's life and assigned numerical values to each. This has been adapted for children, and helps to remind us that

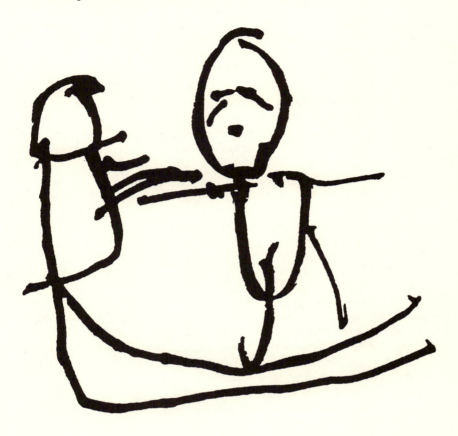

Boy, 7. After the anger — sitting on mom's lap.

children also experience stress in great measure.[6] That stress is greatly multiplied for children who have lived in a variety of homes.

The average score for low stress is 150, medium to high 150–300. Above 300 the child will probably experience some outward symptoms of the inner stress.[7] When the experiences of an older adopted child are placed against this list the total can quickly surpass the 300 mark. Complicating the situation is the fact that we seldom talk to children about stress, nor do we show them ways to handle that stress.

Life Event	Value
1. Death of a parent	100
2. Divorce of parents	73
3. Separation of parents	65
4. Parent's jail term	63
5. Death of a close family member, (i.e., grandparent)	63
6. Personal injury or illness	53
7. Parent's remarriage	50
8. Suspension or expulsion from school	47
9. Parents' reconciliation	45
10. Long vacation (Christmas, summer)	45
11. Parent or sibling sickness	44
12. Mother's pregnancy	40
13. Anxiety over sex	39
14. Birth of new baby (or adoption)	39
15. New school, classroom, or teacher	39
16. Money problems at home	38
17. Death or moving away of close friend	37
18. Change in studies	36
19. More quarrels with parents (or parents quarreling)	35
20. Not applicable to a child	
21. Not applicable to a child	
22. Change in school responsibilities	29
23. Sibling going away to school	29
24. Family arguments with grandparents	29
25. Winning school or community awards	28
26. Mother going to or stopping work	26
27. School beginning or ending	26
28. Family's standard of living changing	25
29. Change in personal habits, i.e., bedtime, homework, etc.	24
30. Trouble with parents—lack of communication	23
31. Change in school hours, courses, or schedule	20
32. Family's moving	20
33. A new school	20
34. New sports, hobbies, activities	19
35. More or less involvement in church	19
36. Change in social activities; peer pressures	18
37. Not applicable to a child	
38. Change in sleeping habits, staying up later, etc.	16
39. Change in number of family get togethers	15
40. Change in eating habits, diet or new way of cooking	15
41. Vacation	13
42. Christmas	12
43. Breaking home, school or community rules	11

In a survey asking children to list or draw pictures about what they found stressful, the following were recorded:[8]

Stressful Experiences for Preschoolers, Two to Five

toilet training

sharing

being disciplined, accepting "no"

separating from parents

not being understood when still learning to speak

being afraid of strange animals, people, noises, situations, routines being interrupted

starting school

cooperating

Stressful Experiences for Children Ages Six to Twelve

pressure to perform academically

being teased

getting angry

not being listened to

not being allowed to do things when the child thinks he can

being overworked (homework, after-school activities)

being excluded

being left alone

starting new things

forgetting (homework, chores)

failing

arguments with parents

pressure to conform to rules

being embarrassed

feeling jealous

being ignored

competition sports

fights with friends

responsibilities

making new friends

fear of death

being unable to fall asleep

Special Stresses for Ages Eleven to Thirteen

body changes (especially sexual development, height, weight)

the opposite sex

concern about what's fair

drugs and sex

peer pressure

self-consciousness

For the child who has been through multiple placements and is finally told that this is truly his last family, the stress factor could be enormous. Each day could have him facing any six or eight on the list, with few internal or external resources to assist him. Though children have astounding resiliency, and can recover from many of life's problems and disappointments, there is a limit to how often they can bounce back. At some point they will begin to suffer extensive damage, damage that takes ever greater amounts of time and energy to correct. Some will suffer damage that can never be repaired.

Notes

1. *Children without homes.* 1978. Washington, D.C.: Children's Defense Fund.
2. Ibid, pp. 5–7.
3. Knitzer, Jane. 1982. *Unclaimed children.* Washington, D.C.: Children's Defense Fund, p. 4.
4. Ibid, pp. 5–9.
5. Miller, Mary Susan. 1982. *Child Stress!.* New York: Doubleday Company, pp. 21–24.
6. Ibid, p. 24.
7. Ibid, pp. 26–33.
8. Saunders, Antoinette & Reimsberg, Bonnie. 1984. *The stress-proof child.* New York: Holt, Rinehart, Winston, p. 81.

3

The Parents

Pamela V. Grabe

The Parents' Experience

Adoption has been a part of human experience for centuries. From the time of the Pharoahs there is recorded evidence of society's desire to solve problems through adoption. Examples from ancient Roman and Greek history as well as primitive civilizations indicate that adoption served the primary purpose of providing a male heir to continue the family name and inherit the family property.[1]

In modern times that focus has changed from the concerns of adults to the concerns of the children. No longer is the emphasis on finding a child to serve the purposes of the parents, but rather on finding a family that can become a resource for a child in need of a home. This change in attitude is not always clearly articulated at the beginning of the adoption process and can confuse some families.

Approximately thirty years ago, the Child Welfare League of America challenged the traditional thinking of the social work field by espousing the idea that "no child is unadoptable." They became a leading voice for the concept that children who had hitherto been unplaceable would have homes if the proper recruitment of adoptive families were done. This philosophy laid the groundwork for the development of the special needs adoption programs of today. It is not uncommon for children who have multiple challenges— mental retardation, blindness, emotional disturbance and being of adolescent years—to find parents who want to bring them up in loving homes.

Attitudes towards Adoption

Many of our ideas about adoption are put forth by the society around us. These ideas have been shaped through the years by the books we read, the movies we see, the people we have met. If one were to take a quick sampling of children's movies, it would be readily apparent that adoption has a large part in the fantasy world that adults present to children.

Recent fare has included *Pete's Dragon* (an orphan boy taken in by a family who worked him very hard and physically abused him,) *Annie* (an orphan girl who was adopted by one of the richest men in the world,) *Escape to Witch Mountain* (two orphan children with magical powers who were chased by evil guardians,) *The Rescuers* (an orphan girl taken in by a wicked woman who wanted the child to locate a valuable jewel and then planned to abandon her,) and *Follow That Bird!* (an orphan bird who the feathered social worker wanted to send to live with a "family of his own kind"). And those are only a few. These are the fantasies helping to shape the ideas of the next generation about adoption.

The story lines of books and programs on television, from soap operas to mini-series, do not deal with the subject in much more realistic fashion. It is no wonder that the world around us describes adoption as something other than "normal," and submits parents to such fatuous comments as: "How wonderful you are to do this." "How lucky those children must feel!" Of course there are also those who say, "Well, you asked for it when you adopted that child. Don't talk to me about the problems you have. You knew what you were getting into!"

Even today, most adoptions are relative adoptions, in which the child is related by birth to the adult who is adopting him/her. But from the post World War II period through 1970 the number of unrelated adoptions tripled.[2] Since that period the difficulty of getting nationwide statistics has made the task of gathering accurate information nearly impossible. What we do know is that since the 1970's, the number of unrelated adoptions has continued to rise, and that the kind of children adopted has changed dramatically.

The profile of parents who seek to adopt has also changed. In the past the approved family had two parents, one a nonworking mother, and was educated, White, middle class, church attending, not overweight, nonhandicapped, home-owning, with a moderate income and a substantial savings account, preferably without a history of divorce and with a college education for at least one parent, and usually without children for whatever reason.

Today the picture has changed. An adoptive family can be White, Black, Hispanic, Native American, two-parent, single, male, or female, divorced, church going or not, middle income, low income, home owners, renters, or apartment dwellers. They may already have adopted other children, or have birth children—and in great number—or be infertile. One or both of the parents might be overweight or handicapped. The mother might be a working parent, who may or may not be able to take a limited leave of absence from her work. In short, there is very little similarity to the picture of only twenty years ago.

This acceptance of diversity has come about through at least three changes in the way the social work profession views adoption. First, social workers know that many of the children in need of homes can fit into a variety of different life styles—no one financial, cultural, intellectual, social status is necessarily the best. For example, a well-educated parent may not be the best resource for a retarded child. Secondly, social workers now realize that for many years agencies have overlooked the resources available in minority communities that could have been recruited for the placement of minority children. Since nearly half of the children who wait for adoptive placement are minority children, it is imperative that more emphasis be placed on expanding the resources available. Finally, they realize that many family strengths cannot be measured in material goods. As the adoptive candidates changed, so did the perspective of agencies who have begun to assess the hidden strengths of a family as they approve them for adoption. Workers are looking for extended family support, an understanding and acceptance of the problems that the child has, and perhaps the commitment to last through many sessions of therapy as they struggle with attachment issues and other such variables.

Parent Preparation

The preparation of parents also began to change as the agencies shifted from the old adoption home study which provided primarily a financial and social history, to a group process which gave expanded education to the family. This shift was particularly true in special needs adoptions, although sometimes it has occurred in infant placements as well.

One of the best known of these approaches was developed under the auspices of the North American Council on Adoptable Children in their TEAM TRAINING project in 1981. This project was modeled after the work done in Pennsylvania by Barbara and Bill Tremitiere and Tressler Lutheran Associates.[3]

In this approach the parents are regarded as a RESOURCE for the waiting child and a member of the adoption team. Emphasis is placed on the peculiar problems that come with a special needs child and the possible problems that the new family unit will face once the placement has been achieved. The family is prepared not only to recognize the child's problems when they are first presented—and before they become too much to handle—but also to identify the possible community resources that could help them. Families are made aware of mental health facilities, special education possibilities, pediatric, and other such resources.

When couples consider adoption, it is for a variety of reasons. Some have been unable to give birth to a child and are seeking to begin or expand their family. Unfortunately for such a family, the issues of infertility and the inability to achieve genetic connectedness to their past and future are seldom explored in the adoption process. This omission is often the root of problems many years later, when the adopted child becomes a teenager and unresolved issues around this subject again become very important to the family.

Other families decide to adopt because they have chosen not to expand their birth families, but are willing to parent a child who is already here, rather than to add one more person to the world's population. They are committed to the concept that children grow best in permanent families. Some parents have been touched by the plight of children they have seen on TV commercials or in church presentations. They want to reach out to someone less fortunate and offer to help.

Occasionally parents arrive at adoption from the wrong motivations. They have heard that the adoption of a child can save a failing marriage, replace a child who has died, or provide someone to take care of them in their old age. Surprisingly, a lot of people still have those old beliefs. But social workers, children, and parents who have already adopted, know they are not true.

Parent Characteristics

However diverse the motives may be, families considering adoption have several things in common. *First and foremost is the belief that the agency worker is trying to screen them out of the adoption process.* Therefore they will tell only the best about themselves. Families operating under this belief create future problems for themselves by not being able to openly evaluate their strengths and weaknesses and what they are best prepared to offer a child. As agencies have shifted to the team approach in the adoption process, this idea is not as powerful. However, the truth remains that the agency does have final decision over the placement of a child, and many families are too fearful to share their secrets—even small ones.

Families struggle with the discrepancy between messages they have received from well-meaning friends and the reality of the adoption process. "Don't feel too bad, you can always adopt." "There are so many children who wait for a loving home like yours. You will have a child in no time." While in essence those statements are true, the length of time between the beginning of the adoption process and the successful placement of a child will make it difficult for families to believe that the agencies are not just trying to "hide the truth" from them. There are children who need good homes, there are many children who wait, but the adoption process is a long and arduous one. Parents find it difficult to wait while the agency tries to match a child to the family who can be the best resource for him/her.

Families going through the adoption process experience stress and anxiety. This is due partly to the amount of waiting time, partly to the mystery surrounding the adoption process. Only in recent years have agencies encouraged prospective families to talk with experienced families to help eliminate the mystery and stress.

Adoptive families, unlike birth families, cannot predict with any accuracy the "preparation" time they will experience before they can become a family. There is no nine-month waiting period for them. A few may find that they actually "hit the jackpot" and have a child placed with them in six months. Others may have counted the endless days and months of two or more years. For most, the actual arrival may be as unexpected as a three-month premature delivery! The call may come at any time to announce the imminent arrival of a child in one to three days. The shock to the family may take weeks to overcome.

Families have little real, in-depth understanding of the unique problems they are undertaking. For that matter, neither do many of the workers who place children with them. This is true partly because the families' fantasy

to Mom

I love You Mom

Girl, 7.

thinking is working overtime—they are hoping that the long-awaited child will quickly become a full-fledged member of their family. It is partly true because few people, professionals or other experienced adoptive parents, really "tell it like it is." Prospective adopters may find that they are either defending their choice to an extremely negative person, or are being overwhelmed with wonderful stories of living happily ever after. The reality is between. Some agencies have begun to take innovative approaches to this problem by insisting that prospective families become active in the adoptive parents' group in the area, or become "respite" parents for adoptive families needing a weekend off. Some agencies are assigning old and new families to a "buddy plan" permitting new families to spend time with a family having a child of similar background to one they would like to adopt. It would be helpful if more of that were done.

There is often little specific direction offered to a family on integrating a newly adopted child into the family—particularly an older child. The rituals that accompany the birth of a child (or even the adoption of an infant) seem out of place with a ten year old. And yet the establishment of such connections may be even more crucial than for younger children.

Extended family members often ignore the arrival of a new family member, particularly if he happens to be one with obnoxious behaviors. Claiming rituals are helpful in creating a sense of belonging and common history, but for families who do not have other adoptive families as resources, support for a claiming is not readily available. In some instances, in fact, well-intentioned family and friends erect barriers to claiming when the child who arrives creates unexpected difficulties for the family.

Adoptive families are often poorly prepared for the reality that a system child brings with him. Parents are not given specific training in recognizing and understanding grief reactions, and often add to the child's burden by refusing to talk about the past. In their rush to become a family, there is a danger that they may close off the very discussions that will strengthen their bonds to the new child.

Because parents feel vulnerable when challenging the adoption agency, they often will not insist on full disclosure of the child's background for fear that the agency will not place a child with them. They have learned that in the adoption game it is the agency that makes the rules and they are wise to abide by them. Thus they acquiesce to plans of blind meetings and rushed placements with older children, leading to further trauma that jeopardizes the placement.

On the bright side, adoptive parents who chose a child with a physical or mental handicap, do not bring the added burden of guilt into the relationship. Having chosen to accept a child with a handicap, they do not experience the initial shock of guilt and denial that birth parents face. Without that complication it is easier for them to learn how to cope with the handicap. Most are capable of becoming strong advocates on behalf of the child for the special services that he might need in school and the community.

* * * * *

Adoptive families are not unlike nonadoptive families. They have the same risks of illness, car accidents, poor parenting skills, job changes, unemployment, and other hazards of life as other families. It is not important or practical to look for perfect families who have some magical guarantee of happiness. For the waiting children, it is only important to find committed, loving families who have the openness to seek help, and room for one more.

Notes

1. Kadushin, Alfred. 1970. *Adopting Older Children.* New York: Columbia University Press, pp. 1–3.
2. Ibid, pp. 3–4.
3. Tremitiere, Barbara & Tremitiere, William. 1981. *Team training manual.* Washington, D.C.: North American Council on Adoptable Children.

4

The Therapy

Pamela V. Grabe

In any discussion of therapy that can be effective with the "special needs" child and his family, it is important to remember the issues presented earlier: the impact that the "system" has had on the child being brought to the therapist, and the impact of the adoption process on the family. It is also important to remember the words of one of the earliest proponents of the placement of older, at risk children, Alfred Kadushin, in talking about therapy with these children:

> The behavior itself is purposive and beyond rational control, simple reeducation, exhortation or persuasion since the individual is motivated to act in this way in response to a conflict which he cannot resolve because its nature is not fully available to conscious awareness. Changes in behavior may be achieved, but unless the basic conflict is resolved, other, equally disabling, symptoms may be substituted for the symptom which is no longer manifested.

> It would be futile to seek to change behavior and/or relieve symptoms without attempting to trace and resolve the conflict, the "real" problem, from which the symptoms originate. It follows then that effective therapy is directed not toward changing behavior but toward achieving understanding,....[1]

Views of Therapy

Reaching out for the services of a mental health facility is not something that a lot of people want to do. Instead families and individuals go to other less intimidating sources of help, such as ministers, doctors, teachers, and social workers. Only when families feel overwhelmed and desperate are they likely to seek a mental health expert.[2]

For too many Americans, the concepts of psychotherapy, mental illness, counseling, etc., carry images of bizarre individuals, the substance of many television movies or nightly news headlines. Despite the efforts of advocates in the mental health professions, the view of an emotional problem as "mental illness" and the stigma attached to "mental illness," are still significant. Adoptive families who need help with special children are no different from others in this regard.

Prior to the late 1960's and early 1970's, adoptions were generally done for the healthy, same-race infant. Agencies seldom called in a mental health professional except to qualify the prospective parents or possibly the mental health of the child. Efforts were not made to prepare families for the unique challenges of the children being placed with them, or to develop services that might help the family in the future. The possibility of providing therapy services was not considered.

In the early days of special needs adoption, it was thought that little more than "lots of love and a permanent family" would be enough to solve the problem of the growing number of unwanted children. Adoptions of older children, physically and mentally handicapped children, and sibling groups used the same routine as adoptions of single healthy infants. The placing agency recruited a family, made certain that they met the agency standards, and placed the child. What happened after finalization of the adoption was not their concern.

Disruptions in Adoptions

It was not long, however, before the sad results of this policy process began to appear: Many adoptions disrupted. Where once the return of a child to the system was a rarity (perhaps 3% nationwide), the experience was becoming all too frequent. A recent study on disruption indicated that the rate for older children may be as high as 25% although the average for all ages is closer to 13%—still too high for something we all once took to be permanent.[3]

Disruption sometimes varies in definition, depending on who uses the term. In research done in the early 1970's it was defined by Kadushin and Seidl as "the return of the child to the agency at any time, for any reason, following placement and before legal adoption."[4] That is still the basis of the definition, although it is true that some children are returned to the system after the legal finalization of an adoption as well. Whatever the definition, the suffering of the child, the family, and the worker, and the desire of professionals to alter the situation, have forced a reconsideration of the various parts of the adoption process.

It was determined that the first line of attack on the problem should be the make-up of the adoption home study and what it offered to the prospective parents. If part of the disruption puzzle lay in the failure of the adopting parents to understand the reality of this adoption, then it made sense to restructure the home study process to address that issue. Instead of the simple social and financial history of the family taken by the adoption agencies of the past, a new educational process began, done in groups. It was hoped that this more extensive preparation would help to eliminate later problems.

Many social work professionals believe (and parents would agree) that adoption failures are often caused by the lack of post placement supports. Therefore to begin to address this issue, experienced adoptive families and new adoptive families were brought together. This was most often done through an adoptive parents group. Unfortunately, not every family was fortunate enough to be in an area where such a group existed. Too, the strength of the parent groups varied widely from place to place and time to time. In some areas groups might exist one year but not the next. A group might exist for social support only, and not be available to offer the more substantial help that a family with difficult children might need.

As families continued to live with great stress and disruptions continued to rise, other professional resources were tapped. It was not always clear, however, that these service providers understood the complexities of the modern adoption process today.

Girl, 8. Mixed feelings.

A Family in Trouble

When adoptive families gathered together, at national conferences as well as at local and regional ones, it was not uncommon to hear the following scenario, one that could be repeated over and over again:

An adoptive family having already successfully adopted three children are asked by the agency if they would consider two siblings, aged seven and eleven. The boys have been in multiple homes prior to this placement but were not always able to stay in the same home. Therefore they have not always thought of themselves as a family, although they have often talked about how important it is for them to stay together.

Some time after the placement of the children, the parents begin to suspect that there has been sexual abuse in their background, although that was not information given to them at the time of their placement. After talking with their caseworker, they seek an appointment at the local community mental health center. At the initial intake, the worker asks for much information that is unavailable to the family, since the children's medical records and developmental history are scattered and incomplete. The worker also takes years of history on the adoptive family, both marital and parental, though the children have been in the home for only the last seven months.

When the family returns for an assessment of their situation and direction for therapy, they are met with an astonishing set of conclusions:

1. These children have such problems that they probably should not have been adopted in the first place. They should be sent back to foster care. Adoption has been painful for them.

2. The other children in the family are culpable. They have not accepted the new children and are just trying to make trouble.

3. The parents, despite having raised three other children who have been successful in school and the community, are lacking in parental skills and should take parenting training.

4. The children should embark on a lengthy (and possibly expensive) series of evaluations and individual therapy sessions. Being individual sessions, they will not include the family because of confidentiality constraints.

5. There would be no mention of the multiple moves made by the boys prior to placement with their new family, nor of the explosive anger often expressed by the boys towards their new parents, particularly the mom.

6. There would be no discussion of the possibility of past sexual abuse, no help for the boys in exploring what has happened to them and providing resolution for their confusion.

Generic Therapy

The problem for this family is that they expect the therapist to know, understand, and provide guidance for them in the situation they face much as they would expect direction from the family doctor if their son had an appendix that needed to be removed. Many families, adoptive and nonadoptive, regard "therapy" in the generic sense, much as they do generic prescription drugs: It is always possible to substitute one qualified therapy for another.[5]

But such is *NOT* the case. Therapy, as everyone in the mental health field knows, is very specific. One form can vary widely from another. A variety of options should have been explored with this family, who could have been seen as resources for their new children, rather than being put off and discouraged. It becomes frustrating to all parents when they are ignored in the therapy setting. This is especially true of families who have gone through the team home study, for they have already been a member of a successful team approach. The resulting conflicts can contribute to the failure of the therapy. In a survey of 75 adoptive parents done two years ago, several conclusions were drawn concerning adoptive families as they have experienced the therapy process:

1. Though they usually don't understand the therapy process, families are too intimidated to ask about goals or even how long the therapy is expected to last.

2. Triangulation between parent, child, and therapist can occur, with devastating effect, when the therapist does not include the family in the treatment process.

3. When presenting behaviors are ignored or not resolved, parents feel that the process is a failure. When kids are not "cured" or families feel threatened, they leave therapy.

4. The nondirective approach does not work with foster/adoptive issues, nor does an approach that excludes the family, that does not see the family as a resource, or opts for confidentiality. Much of the potential of a therapy session is lost if the family cannot continue to reinforce the issues during the next week.

5. Information vital to working successfully with children is scattered around the country. The mental health system, the child welfare system, and any others that might be involved must work together for the child's benefit.

6. The community mental health center is one of the most affordable of the mental health resources available to families. Yet a great number of families report dissatisfaction with them as a resource for their child. Since nearly all foster children are seen by this system, this trend is alarming as families will either resist the therapy process or withdraw entirely and fail to receive necessary help.[6]

A Therapy Approach for "Systems Children"

When a child is brought to a mental health professional for evaluation, he/she is usually perceived in one of three traditional ways: the child is ill, the family is dysfunctional, or there is a faulty family structure. If this is an adopted older child, foster care "system" influences are there but will probably be overlooked. The multiple separations which have generated

Girl, 9.

anger, and unresolved grief, will probably be ignored. Perhaps what needs to be added to the three perceptions is a fourth one; The child is not ill, but rather is a "system child."

Children who have spent years in impermanent family settings arrive with entirely different issues than those who have had long term attachments to caring adults. These "system kids" have developed sophisticated internal coping mechanisms that could be called "survival skills."

Improper attachment, poor disengagement techniques, lack of separation messages, movement from home to home, lack of attention to grieving needs, developmental delays and a host of other problems can be seen in these kids. In the absence of committed, involved, and permanent parents, they have been forced to develop for themselves an alternative protector. They have, *in effect, become their own parent.* Their survival skills are often inconsistent with comfortable family living, although the skills may have enabled them to cope with the system that had custody of them.

One of the concerns of child advocates who work with these children is to find a way to discriminate between problems imposed by the system, and a more serious mental illness. For on the outside, many of the behaviors look similar. Of particular concern is our knowledge that placing a child for adoption asks him to make fundamental changes in his established survival pattern. The conflict within him as he struggles to adapt may create more severe problems than anticipated. To ease that struggle, caring adults must help him to find the best path into a family.

Too often, children who have become self-parenting present behaviors that push the family away rather than encourage inclusion. Although an urgent part of the child may want to be a full-fledged member of the family, his terror of losing them makes him afraid to trust their permanence in his life.

Many of these children do not need long term mental health care. One of the dangers may be that in trying to help them in traditional centers, we will prolong needlessly their involvement in an expensive and intrusive system. But if we fail to work with the root causes of his behavior—grief and anger— we may push the child into more deviant behaviors.

This then is the child that is brought to the attention of the mental health professional by the adoptive family. What is happening to the family system is important to look at as well.

Adoption Creates Families

The adoption process has always been a stressful process for all of the parties involved. The child has to accept the loss of birth family, relatives, and genetic history at whatever age he/she cognitively begins to deal with the reality of adoption. If the adoptive parents (occasionally a single individual) have arrived at adoption through infertility, they must come to grips with the reality that they will not have the opportunity to bear a child of their own genetic heritage. All adoptive parents must deal with the unknown past of the child they have chosen to adopt.

There may be other factors to consider. The child might be the victim of abuse and neglect, or afflicted with severe and multiple handicaps. He/she must accept the loss of the ''normal'' growth and development expected and experienced by most children. The adoptive parents might have thought they could accept a particularly challenging child, but if they have difficulty, they must deal not only with the reality of the child in their midst, but also the loss of their idealized fantasy child.

When families recognize that they are in trouble with their adoption, they must work through some problems. For example, the parents have been "survivors" themselves. They have made it through the adoption process, which is not only long (often two years or more), but also expensive and filled with stress. They have received the agency's stamp of approval—with the message that, of course, they will be excellent parents since they have passed the test.

If they were experienced parents, they thought they knew about raising children, particularly if their kids are doing well in school and the community. What has not been expected is the damage that the system child brings to the family. Parenting a child who has had multiple placements often requires parents to reach beyond their own experiences either as a parent or a child. At times the process asks them to reach beyond their own maturity level, which may have remained untested by their birth children.

When parents come to the mental health professional they feel lost, buffeted, and in need of some direction and assistance. What had begun as an exciting adventure has turned into a nightmare. The child they had thought they would help by offering him a family has become the focal point of family anger, dissension, and constant irritation. Oftentimes they do not even recognize themselves, as they react to this child in ways unlike their past performance.

In these cases, adoption did create a family—but what a family! Instead of the wished-for picture of smiling faces and a child happy in his new home, they see disillusioned adults and fearful and angry children. If the family has struggled with the situation for very long, they are in need of validation of themselves as parents, their adoption as a caring and still potentially helpful act, and concrete assistance in maintaining their sanity until some help can be brought to change the situation.

Short-Term Adoption Therapy

Adoptive families who seek help from mental health professionals often come when behaviors have reached a point of being intolerable. They are looking for some immediate relief in their day to day lives. Too often they fail to receive attention for those immediate needs and the seeds of failure in the therapeutic process can begin at the initial stages of the intake procedures.

The community mental health movement which received its impetus from the commitment of President John Kennedy in the early 1960's was based on the premise that many who experienced mental health problems could be helped within their own community. This directive coincided with the shift of many mental health practitioners away from long term psychotherapy to short term methods. Federal dollars were poured into communities to help build both the structure and the staff of these facilities in order to turn the dream into a reality. Children were to be included in the services provided, but years later are still far behind in the number of programs available.

Short term therapy is defined by professionals as involving the client with the therapist in anywhere from six to twenty sessions, depending on the type of therapy approach used by the therapist. Two early practitioners of short term therapy, L. Bellak and L. Small, provided an outline of the steps for brief therapy in the following way:

1. identifying the problem
2. taking a detailed history
3. establishing an understanding of the relation between the history and the presenting problem
4. selecting and applying appropriate intervention
5. working through the problem from differing perspectives
6. termination[7]

Such an approach appears to be suited to the adoptive family and the experiences of the child in placement.

By clearly following the steps indicated by Bellak and Small the therapist would quickly be able to engage the family and the child (particularly latency-aged or adolescent) in assisting in the development of a therapeutic plan. As was seen in the adoption field, when the family became invested as a member of the team, the placement had a greater chance of success. Similarly, if the family becomes invested in the treatment plan, understands and accepts the goals and strategies, therapy stands a greater chance for success.

Beginning with the identification of the problem (step 1), the history of the child (step 2), and establishing an understanding of the relationship between that history and the presenting problem (step 3), the process of short term therapy can impact quickly on the family system.

However, the experience of families has often been that such success does not occur. Perhaps it is because the history of the child is difficult to obtain and the family history is immediately available. It becomes easier for the therapist to concentrate on more conventional approaches to working with families. Perhaps this is true also because the presenting behaviors appear to be the same for system children as for many children who have lived all of their lives with their birth families. Whatever the cause, it is important to find a solution.

The therapist must understand that the first few sessions of the therapy are critical. The initial session is not the time to question the family's commit-

Girl, 16. Feelings of living in her blended family.

ment to this specific child (who after all arrived with problems), or to question the size of their family (it exists), or even to suggest that they may want to return the child to the system (that may yet happen). It is not the time to say that the child is too young for therapy, or that the therapist needs a year of playing Yahtzee with the child to gain "rapport" (as actually happened to one family). Rather, this is the time to offer some initial relief (however small) that will help the family hang together until substantive improvements in the relationship can be achieved.

Everyone finds the disruption process a painful experience. In the adoption field it is an admission of failure which makes the agency worker question her ability, the family feel that it has betrayed its commitment to their child, and the child believes that once again the adult world has failed to care for and protect him. It is a vicious cycle that makes finding a permanent home for the child increasingly difficult.

For the mental health professional, disruption must be an admission that the key to finding help for this family unit was missed. The original family, however, will survive. The child may not. He is in jeopardy. He needs the best efforts we have to offer.

Groups for Adults

One of the therapy strategies that can be emphasized by mental professionals is the effective use of groups in working with adoptive families and/or adopted children. Many adoptive families have been prepared by the group home study process and are familiar with the concepts. Family therapy is also an excellent option, utilizing the primary group—the family. In working from this approach, the therapist can utilize the input from various members of the family unit.

Participation in groups of individuals who share a common bond, such as parents of retarded children, mothers of twins, weight watchers, alcoholics, etc., has proven to be very beneficial. Adoptive families find value in groups as well. When adoptive families come together they can benefit from each others experiences and offer constructive suggestions.

Over the last eight years, a small parent group in Western Pennsylvania, Parents and Adopted Children Organization-Midwestern (PACO-Midwest), has had a unique approach to the group therapy concept. The parent group contracts with a therapist for a specific number of sessions each year. Parents indicate the subjects they wish to have covered whenever the therapist wants to use a part of the two-hour session as an education time. Parents pay a small fee ($2.00 per family per session they attend) to the adoptive parent group.

Attendance at these sessions is not mandatory, and is often affected by the behaviors erupting in the family. When someone feels the need for help, they come—sometimes for one or two sessions, sometimes for more. The sessions are a combined education forum and a therapeutic question and answer period. The family may describe a particular incident or series of incidents and receive feedback from the therapist. The other families attending can offer suggestions from their experience for both the family and the therapist to consider. The amount and value of the support received in this way is amazing.

The decision to speak out in these sessions is left to each family. Obviously the information shared is not to be spread around the community—the usual rules of confidentiality apply. The local adoption agencies have taken advantage of this resource by sending prospective adopters into the sessions to hear about the problems that experienced adopters are facing and the solutions offered. Through the years, the expertise of the therapist and the families who have attended has increased greatly. The benefits extend far beyond the immediate session, since the families can turn to each other between sessions for help and suggestions.[8]

A family with problems, that can't be adequately dealt with in the group sessions, is free to continue with the therapist in private sessions paid for by the family. But the initial steps, usually the hardest, have been taken in a supportive setting.

The advantages of this program in addition to the ones just mentioned, are many:

1. Mental health therapy is affordable to a family. They need not make decisions about ''buying groceries or going to a therapist'' to find out whether they have a problem that can be helped. Indeed they may find a solution while in the group.

2. The years of experience with the group have given the therapist a unique expertise in adoption dynamics, an expertise not found in many mental health

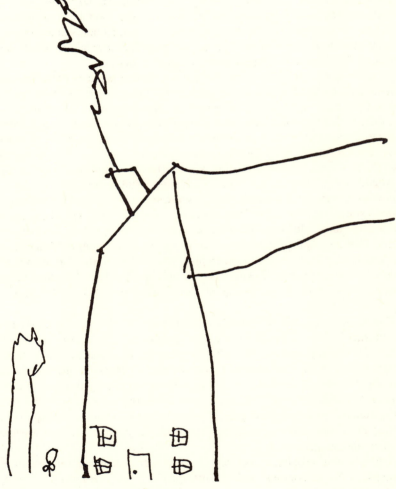

Boy, 7. Our house - a happy house!

professionals. As part of the "burn out" process, families cite the number of professionals they have had to deal with, repeating each time the entire history of the adoption from the beginning, only to discover that this therapist too has no solutions for them.

3. The concrete suggestions of other families as well as the empathy shown in the sessions helps families to know that they are not alone. Families who have lived through similar experiences tend to offer practical suggestions of how to "tough it out." Seldom does a family feel that this group is critical of their parenting, since their expertise comes from having been through the same experiences.

4. The network of family support that follows throughout the year offers a backup to the therapist. When the professional is unavailable another family can be of some help, at least on a temporary basis. Such help may be enough to stem a crisis until the next therapy appointment.

5. The group experience offers everyone the opportunity to recognize a problem while it is still small, and perhaps get help before the point of a disruption is reached.

6. The therapist notes that by offering help to the parents in this way, there is less need to bring the child into formal sessions. Once the parents are aware of the significance of their child's troublesome behaviors and are united in their response, they bring knowledge and confidence to the task of changing the child's conduct.

In recent years, agencies that work exclusively with special needs adoptions have begun to offer similar group therapy sessions, or to enlist the aid of a mental health professional early in the adoption process. Some have begun to make post placement therapy an integral part of the adoption process. The kind and extent of support varies from agency to agency. Most families, looking for help, however, will find themselves working with a mental health facility.

Groups for Children

Another beneficial group approach brings adopted children of similar ages together. This concept has great potential for both child welfare agencies and community mental health facilities. These two agencies work with large numbers of children (those from the foster care system, many of whom will eventually become the older special needs adopted children).

In a pilot program funded through the National Region III Adoption Resource Center in 1984, two groups of adopted children met with a local psychologist who had done some advance study in the area of adoption. The groups were divided by age into the A-group of 9–12 year olds and the B-group of 13–15 year olds. The sessions were informal and kept strictly to the scheduled time of one and a half hours. The groups met for six consecutive weeks.

The format for the two groups was the same, featuring six questions that could be readily answered by the children. The activities were all designed to give the children an opportunity to express their views in a supportive and non-threatening environment. The questions developed were:

1. "Who am I?" (Get Acquainted)
2. "Who am I in my family, and how do I feel about it?"
3. "Who am I in school?"
4. "Who am I in the system?" (foster, birth, etc.)
5. "Who am I going to be?"
6. Final questions, wrap-up

Activities for each group included crayoning, writing, drawing, playing games, discussions, and question-and-answer. There was also some social time as well.

Comments from the children and their parents indicated that both felt the groups had been helpful. Two of the families finalized adoptions of older children during the six week period; they indicated that the sessions had been particularly useful for their children.

Comments from the children included, "It's nice to be with other adopted kids and hear how they feel about being adopted." and "Can we do this again next year?" Many of the kids had initially been reluctant to attend the sessions, but after the first night were excited about returning.

One child was extremely reluctant to attend the sessions, saying that he would refuse to talk during them. He kept his word and uttered not one sound during the session. But, after it was over he cornered the therapist and talked for 15 minutes! He gladly returned, for the second session, even stopping to talk to some of the waiting parents on his way in. During the rest of the sessions he had much to offer.

The psychologist who ran the sessions also felt that much good had come out of the sessions. He particularly mentioned the surprise of the children as they heard the stories of the rest of their group. They were relieved to hear that the other kids shared their feelings, and did not look down upon them for having such concerns.[9]

The value of this approach is evident:

1. The children found the atmosphere comfortable, similar to the school setting with which they are familiar.
2. The children repeatedly expressed pleasure that their families found them "important enough" to pay a therapist just to talk with them.
3. For recently placed children, the group experience helped to ease their feelings of being different and alone in the adoption experience.

4. The families had an inexpensive way of helping their children receive some help. Once again, the parent group bore the expense of the therapist. Each family paid $12.00 for the series of six sessions (or $20.00 if there was more than one child involved).
5. The children found that they were helped to accept themselves in a more positive light.

* * * * *

Whatever the approach, whatever the tools, it is essential that therapists and parents, and children work together in order to maintain placements. Families and children coming together have a responsibility to each other. Families must learn to share what they have with the new individual coming into their home, and the child must offer to give something back in return. If the child's ability to give is fragile and damaged, then it is essential that helping professionals give guidance to help him learn how to give. When families burn out and children are too hurt to "try once more," then disruptions occur. That price is too high.

Notes

1. Kadushin, Alfred. 1970. *Adopting older children*. New York: Columbia University Press, p. 226.
2. Steinhauer, P. D. & Quentin Rae-Grant. 1983. *Psychological problems of the child in the family*. (2nd ed.) New York: Basic Books, p. 665.
3. Tremitiere, Barbara. 1984. *Disruption: A break in commitment*. York, PA: Tressler-Lutheran Services, p. 9.
4. Kadushin, Alfred & Seidl, Frederick W. July, 1971. "Adoption failure: A social work postmortem." *Social Work* 16, p. 32.
5. *A common sense approach to therapy options for families*. 1983. Butler, PA: Parents and Adopted Childrens' Organization.
6. Reitnauer, P. & Grabe, P. 1984. *Focusing training for mental health professionals*. Mercer, PA: Mercers Children's Aid Society, pp. 17–19.
7. Bellak L. & Small, L. 1978. *Emergency psychotherapy and brief psychotherapy*. New York: Grune & Stratton.
8. *Adoption is a group affair*. 1982. Butler, PA: Parents and Adopted Childrens' Organization, pp. 3–4.
9. Mellinger, George, Ph.D. 1984. Report to Region III Adoption Resource and Training Center. Richmond, VA.

5

The Definitions

Pamela V. Grabe and Susan Sim

Many of the terms that are used in the adoption field have acquired special definitions and usage. Like any other discipline, terminology has grown through time to have particular meaning when applied to specific situations. Adopted children and families are accustomed to hearing the terms as they understand them through the adoptive experience. Being familiar with them will also have some value to the mental health professional who works with the adopted child and his family.

ACTIVATION THERAPY. A unique form of therapy used in the treatment of a severely disturbed child. This therapy utilizes the belief that through restraint, a child can confront his rage and learn to attach to adults—the step of development denied him by his earlier chaotic upbringing.

A major component of activation therapy is a technique known as "holding." Holding involves a trained therapist's holding the child on his/her lap for a sustained period of time and limiting the child's movement. The therapist may utilize his/her own legs to prevent the child from kicking out or may employ the assistance of other adult individuals to help hold the child in the position. The therapist allows for interaction with the child by use of verbal, facial, non-verbal, tactile, and/or eye contact with the child.

The essence of containing a disturbed child in this manner is the belief that when rage is confronted, "firm and loving control will lead to a sense of trust." (Foster Cline) Once a child feels trust towards an adult, he or she is capable of moving on in his development. Dr. Robert Zaslow, one of the early developers of this method, describes his theories (he calls his the Z-Process) as a "holding technique for the purpose of handling anger, rage, and resistances that block progress in the areas of therapy, education, and new growth experiences."

The same anger, rage, and resistance that Zaslow describes is what is seen in "system" children. Lack of bonding to a significant adult, imperfect attachments to a family, and poor or no reconciliation to separations from loved ones from their past all result in rage. When left untreated, this rage prevents the child from becoming firmly rooted in a new family. Even though temporarily suppressed, the rage will erupt into other disruptive behaviors and the placement may be jeopardized. Disruption may result, if not early in the adoption, then possibly when the adolescent emerges.

Further Reading: Foster W. Cline, M.D., *Understanding and Treating the Severely Disturbed Child,* Evergreen Consultants in Human Behavior, Evergreen CO., 1979.

Robert W. Zaslow, *The Psychology of the Z Process: Attachment and Activation.* California: San Jose University, 1975.

ADOPTED-CHILD SYNDROME. A term used to describe a set of antisocial traits and behaviors in a small number of adopted children. Usually included are conflicts with authority, pathological lying, stealing, and lack of impulse control.

Several cases of adopted children who have committed murder or other serious crimes against individuals have recently hit the news headlines. Usually these are sensational trial cases accompanied by much publicity, exaggeration, and speculation by the media (David Berkowitz, "Son of Sam;" Kenneth Bianci, the "Hillside Strangler;" Joseph Kalinger, the "Philadelphia Shoemaker,"). The result has been that many people from a wide variety of disciplines and professions have become concerned about adoptive placement and its impact on children.

The term itself was coined by child psychologist David Kirschner and psychiatrist Arthur Sorosky, both of whom have done years of clinical work with adoptees. They argue that this syndrome contributes to the psychotic rage felt by the child or adult at the time he/she commits the crime, or during the time preceeding the crime. While these behaviors can be found in nonadopted children, in the adopted child they are linked to the feelings of abandonment and rejection that an adoptee experiences.

The message is very clear for everyone who works with the adopted child: Problems that remain unresolved over the years can explode into far greater difficulties later on. The person experiencing the adopted-child syndrome may be the best evidence of the failure of the system to find responsible solutions to a difficult problem.

Further Reading: Betty Jean Lifton, "How the Adoption System Ignites a Fire," *New York Times,* March 1, 1986.

ADOPTION. A legal proceeding in which an adult and a child enter into the relationship of parent-child. Thereby the adult acquires the rights to and responsibilities for that child.

The adoption process is controlled by laws which have protection as their purpose: protection of the child, the birth parents, and the adoptive parents.

Two types of adoption are recognized in the law of most states—gray market adoption (private adoption) and agency related adoptions.

Adoption provides the permanence of a home and a family to a child who for whatever reason is not able to live out his or her childhood with the parents that gave birth to him. The adoptive parents are enabled to have a child/children in their family, and a child has a chance to receive love, caring and the emotional and physical support needed for his growth into an adult.

Unlike foster care, adoption gives the parents complete legal responsibility for the child. It is commonly stated that adoptive parents must provide for the adopted child in every way (as if the child was born to them.) Adoptive parents are not paid to care for the child coming into their home as are foster parents who receive a monthly payment. Occasionally, however, a child with special challenges like a developmental disability, or a family group of several children, will receive an adoption subsidy from the state placing the child/children. This payment is given to insure that the particular needs of the child will continue to be met until the child is eighteen, or 21 for some handicapped children.

Adoption presents for all of its participants a unique set of circumstances that surface and resurface throughout the life span of each of the members. For those helping professionals assisting the adoptive family, specific information, material, and research addressing the complexities and unique features of adoption are essential in developing services and programs to better serve the needs of the adopted child.

Further Reading: Claudia Jewett. *Adopting the Older Child.* Harvard Common Common Press, 1978.

————, *Adoption Fact Book.* Committee for Adoption, 1985.

Children without Homes. Children's Defense Fund, 1978.

ADOPTION DISRUPTION. The breakdown of an adoptive placement prior to finalization. The child returns to foster care with a child welfare agency. Disruption occurs for a variety of reasons, some more easy to understand than others. Disruption brings confusion, hurt and pain to all parties, even when the removal of the child has come about through careful planning.

Many adoptive parents do not receive adequate preparation before an older child is placed in the home. The actual presence of a child experiencing significant adjustment to a new family and separation from old ties creates an enormous task for the parents.

In many cases, disruption occurs when the newly placed child had not been sufficiently prepared for the move. Old struggles, past moves, multiple losses, and grief come to the surface, interfering with the child's ability to cope with the new demands of yet another home and family. The child needs guidance and help in moving toward accepting a new family.

All too often, the support of someone willing to prepare the child for an adoptive placement is not there, or the person hesitates to review the child's past because of the pain and confusion they feel it may cause the child. However, the child already knows these hurts; and when the child's past life experiences are not addressed, the possibility of his/her succeeding in an adoptive placement is less.

When faced with day-to-day turmoil and upheaval from an angry, confused child, the adoptive parents may begin to question their commitment and purpose in the child's life. Disruption becomes more likely when the child senses, "They are not going to keep me." He may hasten the move by increased acting-out, so that in essence the child is taking control. "I'll move now, when I say so." Older adopted children have had to learn how to survive in a system where losing out is an all too often occurrence.

It is at this time that the parent support system plays its greatest role. The support of other parents who have been in similar situations, and understand the feelings of these new parents is critical. Many times all that is needed for parents to "make it through" is to have a sympathetic ear and an understanding friend. Disruptions do not tend to occur when parents understand that others have heard the same hurtful comments from their child, lived through tough times together, and survived to become a loving, caring family.

The inability of some children to adjust initially to family living causes some adoption disruption. If a child has had multiple moves or is just coming out of residential living, the skills needed to function within a family setting may just not be in place. Some children learn from one disruption what went wrong, how things can be different, and so move into another placement with a clearer idea of what their role in a family setting will be.

Further Reading: Vera Fahlberg, *Attachment and Separation,* and *Helping Children When They Must Move,* Michigan Department of Social Services, 1979.

Kathryn Donley, *Looking Back on Disruption.* Spaulding for Children, 1976.

ADOPTION SUBSIDY. A monetary stipend or access to medical assistance provided by the state (or federal government) for a child with special needs, paid monthly after the adoption has been finalized. To receive a subsidy, the child must meet certain requirements set by the state, i.e., age, ethnic background, handicapping condition, etc.

Only recently have agencies and states begun to offer subsidies for children being placed for adoption. Prior to the late 1970's, a monthly stipend was seen only as a payment to foster parents for the care of the child. Alarmed by the growing number of children being raised without permanent families social work advocates sought change in this traditional thinking.

Rather than letting financial hardships get in the way of providing a permanent, loving home for a child, advocates developed the concept of an adoption subsidy. Determined by the needs of the child, an adoption subsidy is not considered a payment to the adopting family. Rather it is a fiscal entitlement for the eligible child to assure continuing care for his needs after final adoptive placement.

Criteria for the conditions and guidelines for the amount of subsidy are found both in various state laws and the federal law PL 96–272. Adoption subsidies cannot be higher than the day rate for foster care and continue only as long as the child is legally a member of the adoptive family or reaches the age of 18 (or 21 for certain handicapping conditions).

Further Reading: P. L. 96–272

BIRACIAL and INTERRACIAL. Terms that apply to children and families of mixed racial heritage. Biracial applies to one person who is the product of two different cultures, such as a child with one Native American parent and one Black parent. Interracial applies to a couple representing two cultural backgrounds, such as a prospective adoptive couple one of whom is Black and the other White.

Although children of mixed racial heritage, have been considered for years as being non-white, recently the term "biracial" has been the term applied in the adoption field. Biracial is most frequently heard in social work circles to describe a child of Black/White heritage who is adopted by White parents. Although social work agencies have coined the term biracial, it is not a term society recognizes to describe a race of people: The same child adopted into a Black family would be described as a Black child.

For the child, the biracial label can be misleading unless accompanied by a clear understanding of how our society views ethnicity. The child of mixed heritage must be offered the opportunity to know and understand his different cultures and also must be helped to develop the coping skills to live with the prejudice and racism still prevalent in society.

The preferred placement for a child born of African/American background is often an interracial home, where parents and siblings are available to offer identity and cultural exposure to both parts of the child's heritage.

The issues presented by the ethnic heritage and background of a child become extremely complex for families and agencies when the background of a child is not clear. Often the decisions made reflect the consistently inadequate attempts by agencies to provide for the recruitment of adequate numbers of minority families of all backgrounds to provide homes for minority children.

Further Reading: J. Kunjufu, "Developing positive self-images and discipline in Black children," *African-American Images.*

Azizi Powell and Frank Jones, *Racial Terminology in Adoption,* 1985. Ms. Powell can be reached at Three Rivers Adoption Council, Pittsburgh, PA.

Ruth McRoy and et al., "Self-Esteem in Transracial and Inracial Adoptees." *Social Work,* Vol 27, No 6, 1982.

BIRTH ORDER. The place within a family structure which a child holds by virtue of order of birth: the first, third, fifth, middle, youngest, or only child.

An individual's personality development is strongly influenced by the experiences gained from a particular position in a family setting. Specific strengths and weaknesses attributable to differences in early development as a result of birth position are among the many variables to consider when assisting families.

When an older adopted child is placed with a new family, there is a restructuring of family positions. The family, much like a mobile, begins shifting and searching for a new balance.

As a new member of the family, the child begins to look for his/her place within the family structure. Frequently the child tries to take over an already established position, i.e., the mother role or baby of the family. Helping the child to become settled in his own special place and all members to become comfortable with the changed positions is sometimes necessary.

A significant change that occurs for birth children or previously-adopted children is the move from a birth/family order which they have held for considerable time. There has been sufficient study of the experience gained from an individual's birth order for us to know that attention must be given to the effects on siblings when their birth order is being changed. For some children, the readjustment is met with little difficulty; for others, time, professional help, and understanding are often needed.

Older adopted children have experienced numerous moves in and out of families and are likely to be more flexible than birth children in adapting to a different sibling position. However, it is important to prepare an established member of a family to understand that a child coming into the family will also be receiving hugs, kisses and love from the parents. When parents offer their love to a new child this does not diminish the love they have for others already in the family.

When parents see that children to whom they have an attachment and bond are threatened by the presence of an older special needs child, the placement is at risk. The placement is jeopardized as parents attempt to protect that first attachment and commitment and often feel at a loss as to how to help each child feel a part of one family.

Further Reading: Dr. Alfred Adler, *What Life Should Mean to You* (New York: Capicorn, 1958).

J.H.S. Bossard, *The Large Family System: An Original Study in the Sociology of Family Behavior* (Philadelphia: University of Pennsylvania Press, 1956).

Lucille Forer, Ph.D., *Birth Order & Life Roles* (Springfield, IL, Charles C. Thomas, 1969).

BONDING/ATTACHMENT. A process between infant and parent as the child's needs are met, and between older child and parent as needs are reciprocally met.

The parents' attachment to the infant increases as a feeling of their emotional connectedness emerges during the caretaking. For the infant, the bonding can be strengthened and enhanced only if the caretaking is predictable and continuous.

For the child removed from this first bond, attachment becomes an even more complicated process as they move through the stages of childhood. The adults in his life must aid the child in making new attachments. A prerequisite for a new tie is grief-work for the loss of former bonds. Thus, children must be given help in working out their feelings of loss and grief. The attachment process between a parent and older child is much the same as between parent and infant. The dynamics and psychological forces inherent in bonding should be strengthened and supported in every way possible.

In an adoption, this newly created and vulnerable parent-child attachment comes under enormous pressure as the child enters into the testing stage following the honeymoon. Feeling close to an adopted parent may cause ambivalent feelings to arise. Because all past relationships with adults have ended in separation, the child is fearful of getting too close, fearful of losing this adult as well. During this stage, older adopted children distance themselves from the parents by using abusive language, refusing to make eye contact, fighting, lying, and other negative behaviors. The adoptive parents must be aware that what is happening is the child's attempt to understand his place in the family and his new environment. It is necessary to help the child gain a sense of truly belonging to the family, not just a sense of warmth and comfort between the adults and a child.

Some older children available for adoption have experienced a tremendous number of broken attachments; it is very hard for them to feel that they belong to the next family. The unattached child has been damaged emotionally to such an extent that he exhibits no conscience and shows no remorse for acts of bad behavior. It is lack of conscience and lack of the wish to belong to the family that most often brings parents to the point of returning the child to the child welfare system and disrupting the adoption.

Further Reading: Frank Bolton, *When Bonding Fails.* Stage Publications, 1983.

Vera Fahlberg, *Attachment and Separation.* Michigan Department of Social Service, 1979.

Claudia Jewett, *Helping Children Cope with Separation and Loss.* Harvard Common Press, 1982.

CANDLE CEREMONY. An activity that provides a visual image around which love and loving can be discussed. The candle ceremony is used to help children create a bridge between their past families, the love they've felt in some of those homes and the potential for love in their new adoptive family.

Candles are placed in a row, beginning with the child's birth family and continuing for each successive home the child has lived in. A candle is placed at the end of the row for the new adoptive family.

A candle is then held by the helping professional. This candle represents the child and his/her ability to love, and is lighted first. It is explained to the child that being able to love is a gift we are all born with. Next the birth parents' candle is lit, with comments like, "This was your first family, the family you were born to, and while you lived with them your love for them grew." The candle ceremony proceeds in this manner, lighting a candle for each family the child has loved and pointing out that the light in the first, second, third, etc. candles did not stop burning, just as the love the child felt for these people did not have to stop just because he was no longer with them. Candles are not lit for those families to whom the child felt no attachment.

After the candles are lit, it is explained that love for the birth family did not stop when the child was moved to the second family: "See, the candle is still lit." The professional moves on, pointing to each candle, talking a little about the families, their names, bringing back to the child the good feelings he felt while living there. When coming to the adoptive family's candle, the professional comments, "See, the love you felt for these other families doesn't have to stop because you're with your adoptive family now. You can love your adoptive family and still feel love for the people you once cared for. We can love lots of people and in different ways at the same time."

Before extinguishing the candles it is important to say, "We're going to blow out the candles now, but I want you to remember that the candles are only a way to show you and talk with you about loving. Blowing out the candles doesn't end that love. The candle ceremony has just helped us to talk about these things.'' Then the child is asked if he's ready to blow the candles out.

The candle ceremony can be used prior to a child's move into a new adoptive home or afterward, with the adoptive parents present. Permission from the other families for the child to move on will enhance the value of the candle ceremony. For example, a foster family can tell the child, ''We want you to have a family. We will miss you, but you need your own family right now.''

It is important for adopted children to continue believing that the love they have for previous families and individuals in their past is real and does not need to be discarded. The child's belief that his love continues lets him believe in the continuity of others' love for him, thereby, building a more positive self-image.

In years gone by, children about to be adopted were given no encouragement to share their positive feelings for the former families they had lived with. When entering a new adoptive family, children became silent about the others they had known in their life. Much self-esteem can be provided for the child if permission is given to remember and love those from the past.

Further Reading: Claudia Jewett, *Adopting the Older Child.* Harvard Common Press, 1978.

Vera Fahlberg, Video Presentation, Pittsburgh Conference on Permanency in Adoption: A Mental Health Concern, April 30, 1982.

CLAIMING SKILLS. The traditions, rituals and ceremonies parents participate in to demonstrate a belonging or claiming of a child as a part of their family.

Adoptive parents generally have no direction as to what, if anything, they can do to say, ''This is now our child.'' Adoption announcements and baby books that allow for events around the adoption to be recorded are available for families adopting infants. Claiming behaviors for parents of older adopted children are not as clearly spelled out.

Assisting an adoptive family and their recently placed child to find ways to demonstrate their ''togetherness'' not only to themselves and the child but to extended family, friends, neighbors and the community will strengthen the chances for a successful adoption.

Taking pictures of the child and family together and putting these with the child's life book, as well as adding pictures of the child to the family's picture albums enables all of the family to participate in the process of becoming one unit.

Welcome to the family gifts given by close friends and family help the parents and the child, who often has few personal possessions or clothes.

The candle ceremony explained previously conveys the message to everyone that love is infinite and that permission is given to love more than one person or family.

Planting a tree is another way of making a symbolic statement that a child's arrival is special. Having a concrete, tangible comparison allows the child to see that they do belong.

By utilizing the child's placement date as an anniversary to be acknowledged in a special manner (i.e., a cake, an outing or a week-end trip) year after year permits the parents and child to come together to acknowledge the time that they began to form a family.

For the child, the challenge of claiming a new family as their own is difficult and most often a confusing experience. The child comes into a family with no common history, no ideas as to the ways in which this family goes about not only the day to day activities, but also holidays, birthdays or vacations. Since many foster children have had to be replaced when the foster family went on vacation, this worry can take on paramount proportions.

Letting a child contribute something they've done in the past for holidays to the family's already established traditions brings the child's past world into their present one. And giving a child a choice in their room decorations removes the worry about, "What does he like?" and brings the child into active family decision making.

The passing of time, time and more time lets the older child establish experiences that gives them a history and a connection to the new family. When the child can say, "I remember when we did..." then a feeling of "I belong here" is easier to hold on to.

Further Reading: Margaret Ward, *Parental Bonding in Older Child Adoptions,* Child Welfare League of America, Vol. LX, 1 January, 1981.

DEVELOPMENTALLY DISABLED. A term applied to a severe chronic disability that results from mental and/or physical impairment. Developmental disabilities are defined as being present before the age of 22. They significantly impede development and functioning ability.

For the older adopted child with developmental disabilities, the experiences of foster care and adoption are complicated by the presence of a disability. Children with significant disabilities or handicapping conditions are vulnerable to abuse and neglect and subject to multiple moves and introductions to new families. They are the least able to speak out and make their victimization known. With the rise in the number of developmentally disabled children coming to the attention of child protective services, the move towards deinstitutionalization, and the goal of permanency, more children with these very special needs are being placed for adoption.

If such children are going to remain in their new families, they must be given services that view the disability, not the child, as the problem. Those programs that help the disabled child to reach his/her fullest potential best serve the child and his new family. The physical, emotional, and social ramifications for the family and the child with a developmental disability are far-reaching; they enter into every aspect of family life. A multidisciplinary approach that provides a comprehensive view of the disability and the adoption experience has proven effective and enhances the chance of success for both child and family. When parents are viewed as part of the team and seen as an essential resource, there is less need for parents to take the confrontational approach with agencies in order to get desired services.

Adoptive parents of the disabled child do not begin with feelings of guilt for "causing" the disability; but they do experience guilt when they have hostile feelings toward the child or when they think, "I wish I had never adopted this kid." Such feelings are likely to occur when parents are directing enormous amounts of time and energy toward the child's wellbeing. It is at those times that parents need support and understanding of the challenges they face as parents of a developmentally disabled child.

Further Reading: Parent Professional Partnerships in Developmental Disability Services. (Eds. James A. Mulick & Siegried M. Pueschel) Academic Guild Publishers, 1983.

Ronald C. Huges & Judith S. Rycus, *Child Welfare Services for Children with Developmental Disabilities.* Child Welfare League of America, 1983.

Ann Coyne & Mary Ellen Brown, *Relationship Between Foster Care & Adoption Units Serving Developmentally Disabled Children.* Child Welfare League of America, 1986.

FAMILY COMMITMENT. The decision by a family to build their family through the adoption of a special needs child. For most parents who express this commitment, there is a basic belief that children grow best in families and that to grow up without a connection to a family creates problems for the child as an adult. Their commitment is to the concept of the inclusion of a child into the family circle, not just to a known child. Many families have made this commitment long before the placement of a child to be adopted.

In the adoption process, especially where group studies are done with an educational component, parents are exposed to the variety of problems that children may have. Parents are also involved in the selection of the specific child that will become a member of their family. When they are members of the team in this way, their belief in their ability to work with a child and their faith in their future as a family is much stronger.

However, during the adoption process not all families are given a full understanding of the potential problems faced by their child. They are left to discover them after the child's placement in their home. And some families have not clearly understood the importance or depth of problems described to them by a worker. In these cases, adoptive families need encouragement to understand the significance of making this commitment.

For families who believe in the concept of the family, the conflict arises when the child placed in their home is a "system survivor." This child does *not* have a strong belief in the support a family can provide. His experience has proven that families disappear—they cannot be counted on.

Asking this child to make a commitment to a family brings him into conflict with the internal controls that he has developed for survival. He will experience fear, even terror, which then erupts in ever wider circles of disruptive behavior: first in the family, then the school, and finally the community. He is seeking to return to the system (ie. foster care, shelter, group home) that does not ask him to make a commitment to a family.

The child's rejection of the family shakes their belief in their own commitment. They are particularly vulnerable when others suggest that another family may be more appropriate.

Further Reading: Patricia J. Kravik. *Adopting Children with Special Needs*. North American Council on Adoptable Children. 1981.

J. W. Corrigan, *"Family Advocacy Council Won't give up on Tough Kids." Youth Forum* Vol 4, No 3. 1980.

Eleanor H. Green, *Gregg's Case*. Family Defense Fund, 1986.

FAMOGRAPH. A tool to help children understand what has happened in their lives and place it against the history of their new family.

An older child coming into a family does not have a common history with this family. He or she does, however, have a history. Using a famograph, the child can come to understand how to blend knowledge of his past into knowledge of his new family. This allows both family and child to find some common ground. Unless such connectedness is developed, it will be at least one year before the child has shared anniversaries with his new family. Without shared happiness, there is increased chance of distancing and separating one member of the family from the rest.

Developed by Josephine Anderson in her long experience with foster children, the famograph is:

1. A pictorial representation for the child of where he has been.
2. A tool to identify people out of the child's past.
3. A way to pull together concurrent events from a variety of families who have had impact on the child's life.
4. By using a variety of colors to differentiate families, it helps the child (particularly a young one) to remember relationships.

Like other such tools, the famograph helps the child begin to make sense out of an otherwise chaotic existence. Adults often forget that children have short attention spans and poor cognitive skills. Children thrive best on continuity and structure; but these children have been the victims of stress, lack of continuity, continual separations and losses and a total lack of structure.

The following is a sample of a famograph done with a nine year old illustrating her life and the concurrent history of her adoptive family.

* * * * *

The center line represents the child herself, "S," and begins with her birth. The dotted lines prior to her birth connect visually the births of the two older boys in her adoptive home. The lower line represents the adoptive family's major life events.

Although her birth father was never in the home, she did spend the first four and a half years with her Mom, moving frequently in and out of a series of apartments. When "S" was 4 1/2, her mother was sent to a mental institution for an extended period of time, and "S" went to live with an aunt and her family. While there, "S" was physically abused and placed in a foster family by the local child welfare agency.

On her sixth birthday, "S" was placed with the family that eventually adopted her. She continued to have visits with her birth mother for two more years until it was decided that termination of parental rights and placement for adoption would be the right course for her. Sometime later the family adopted a sister, who just happened to have spent time in the same foster family, although at a later time than "S."

A technique such as the famograph takes the confusion out of the past for a child. It enables him to connect the pieces of his past with his current life, and begin to move forward into a common history with his new family.

Further Reading: Josephine Anderson, *Handouts at Chicago NACAC Conference,* 1984.

GENOGRAM, ECO-MAP. Techniques used to illustrate family relationships and help families understand the dynamics of both internal and external interactions with others.

The genogram can be used to illustrate the intrafamily connections over three or more generations. It provides an easy-to-read illustration of significant dates and events, i.e., births, marriages, deaths, jobs, and moves, that shaped the family.

A genogram used in post-adoption services facilitates a better understanding by the parents of their connections with their own parents and the emotions and events that affected their childhood. A genogram provides a tool to help increase an older adopted child's sense of his/her new family history

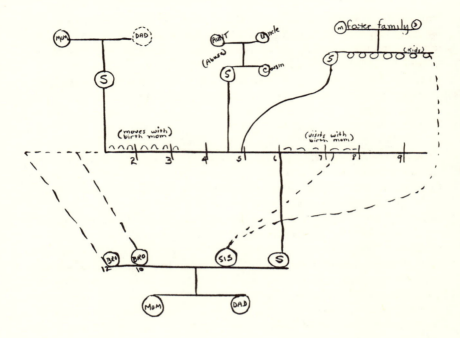

and his connections to his family of origin. When the adopted parents and child work on their genograms together they each have the opportunity to hear and learn about their respective experiences. The child has the opportunity to see the birth family in a constructive manner and is introduced to his new family and its extended members. This process helps him to learn about the people who will have some connection to him in his new family, making them no longer strangers.

An eco-map is a visual representation of a family's interactions with each other and their involvements with the world outside of the home. It can be drawn with paper and pencil or a "structured form" can be used; the latter has the advantage of being easier to use and less time consuming.

For the adoptive family, the eco-map reveals the areas where there are support and resources and those where weaknesses and stress are causing problems for the family. Changes that have occurred for the family since the arrival of the child become apparent.

Taking in a new family member is so great a task that parents can forget to make time for themselves. Having no real time to be together or to enjoy hobbies that foster their own sense of wellbeing adds to the stress parents experience. A visual reminder provides a focal point for discussing ways to help the family reestablish a sense of balance.

Further Reading: Ann Hartman, *Working with Adoptive Families beyond Placement.* Child Welfare League of America, 1984.

Eileen Pendagast & Charles Sherman, *"A Guide to the Genogram Family Systems Training." The Family,* Vol. 5, No. 2.

Ann Hartman, *Finding Families: An Ecological Approach to Family Assessment in Adoption.* Sage Publications, 1979.

GRIEF WORK. The process of reconciling the loss of a loved one with the reality of living day to day without that individual.

In recent years mental health professionals have offered specific steps to help adults working through a grief process. It has been suggested that two years are necessary for individuals to adequately work through the stages of grief: anger, denial, guilt, and acceptance.

Children who have lost a parent through death pass through similar steps as they also resolve their grief, although our society does much to insulate children from thoughts of sadness. However, seldom is recognition given to the pain and grief that is experienced by children who lose their parents through the process of termination of parental rights and subsequent adoption into another family. A "system child's" reaction to this loss is intense, and until recently was rarely given full attention by the adults attempting to help.

Most children who are adopted as "older, special needs" children, (over the age of four) have some remembrance of their birth families. For many it may be very extensive and full of good memories. Even for those children who have experienced abuse, their family ties represent all that is familiar.

The adult world, however, sees removing a child to the foster care system as a positive step, "saving" him from neglectful or inadequate parents. Little time is given to explaining the loss or helping the child to grieve that loss.

Creating even more difficulties, the system often adds a series of foster families to the emotional mix creating confusion in the mind of the child. Not only did he/she lose one set of parents, he must now accept the loss of at least one more. It is no wonder that the process of attaching to a new family is fraught with difficulties. When children have made inadequate separations from the adults of their past, they cannot begin to make strong attachments to a new family. It is too painful. What system children have learned is that when you permit yourself to love someone, it hurts. The adult world has given no assurance that this new set of parents will remain—they too may be lost. Better to remain insulated from the new pain and hope that somehow the opportunity will arise to return to a family from the past.

The effects of unresolved (or unreconciled) grief go beyond the process of attachment to a new family. Long term effects are also seen in the slowed emotional development of some children. Many of them also suffer from learning disabilities that impact in the school setting. And for many, their failure to understand and accept their grief leads to continual problems in the new family—ultimately to disruption.

Further Reading: Claudia Jewett, *Helping Children Cope with Separation and Loss.* 1982, Harvard Common Press, Boston, MA.

Bonding and Attachment, Ann Coyne, *ADOPTALK* July/August, 1983.

Alan Wolfelt, *Helping Children Cope with Grief.* Indiana Accelerated Development, 1983.

HONEYMOON. The period of time, after the placement of a child into an adoptive home, when "everything is absolutely perfect". This period is similiar to the period usually experienced by newlyweds. A honeymoon can vary in duration from a few hours to a few days, weeks, or months. The honeymoon period is a time when the child and the family are building their relationship with each other; during which the child, who is eager to be accepted, is polite, cooperative, and seemingly happy. The adopting adults also want to make a positive impression on the child, and therefore, often tolerate behaviors or activities that violate common sense or accepted values.

During the honeymoon the child strives to be the perfect son or daughter and parents may attempt to make up for all the child has missed. The stage is set for unrealistic expectations by everyone. But as the task of getting on with living together proceeds, the child will begin to reveal through his actions and behaviors, the areas where he needs help.

The honeymoon is over when the child begins to test the family system and the adults begin to discipline poor behaviors and to teach the child the family rules. The reality of just how much work needs to be done in order to become a family and how much "settling in" time the older adopted child needs quickly becomes apparent to the adoptive parents. It is not uncommon for adoptive parents to have a feeling of sheer exhaustion at this time.

The newly adopted child is under enormous pressure to find favor with the parents, establish brother/sister relationships, and also to cope with the loss of people who cared for him in his previous families. The child's stress coupled with the adoptive parents' questioning of their parenting abilities can place the adoption in jeopardy. Problems that arise and remain unresolved at this time will continue to surface and cause difficulties for both the child and the family until they are dealt with. Time is important to allow for all the pieces of this adoption puzzle to fall into place. However, time can become a hazard when families try to continue living with separation and grief issues that have not been reconciled.

Further Reading: Vera Fahlberg, *Attachment and Separation,* 1979, Michigan Department of Social Services.

Claudia Jewett, *Adopting the Older Child, 1978,* Harvard Common Press.

INTER-COUNTRY ADOPTIONS. The placement of foreign born children into a transracial adoptive family setting. Placements of the foreign born child have included children ranging in age from infancy to adolescence.

A significant number of intercountry adoptions are of very young children. With the decline in adoptable infants in this country, many couples have turned to foreign adoptions as a way to build their families.

Inter-country adoptions are regulated by the U. S. Office of Immigration and Naturalization and the states' Departments of Public Welfare. Inter-country adoptions involve considerable cost and time on the part of the adopting family.

As in all adoptions with a difference in race between child and parents, the family faces adjustments to their differences. For the parents who have taken this step for the first time, it is coping with the stares of people when they go out. For the child, it is learning to cope with the pervasive prejudice of Americans for people of other ethnic races. It is also the loss of cultural continuity and sense of belonging.

The majority of inter-country adoptions in the United States are of children from Korea. The growing antagonistic sentiment this country demonstrates toward Asians poses grave concern for these children being raised in predominatly white, middle-class families.

Families are often ill prepared for the lifelong ramifications of integrating their family. For example, they often believe, wrongly, that Asian and other foreign born children will not have to face the intense prejudice that Blacks and other minorities do. The problems of prejudice are frequently delayed until the child enters school. They continue to grow as the child enters adolescence and dating becomes a factor.

For the inter-country placements, adoptive parent support groups, mental health services, and continued post-placement services from the placing agency are vital resources to be developed and sensitized to the concerns and needs of these children and their families.

Further Reading: Hei Sook Park Wilkinson, *Birth Is More Than Once.* Sunrise Ventures, 1985.

Francis Koh, *Oriental Children In White Homes.* East-West Press, Inc., 1981.

LIFE BOOK. A technique for helping a child in the foster care system or in adoption to come to terms with the past and begin preparing for the future. It is a scrapbook collection of memorabilia from the past, i.e., photographs, drawings, awards, school report cards, and written narratives about the child and the experiences which he or she has had.

The life book is a valuable tool in helping a child integrate his past in a rational, realistic, and understanding way. A child who remains with his birth family can review family photographs and listen to family members recall their history and talk about the child's beginning. Most children in foster care and older children placed for adoption have a fragmented understanding of their own history, some not knowing where they were born or who they have lived with over the years. Emotionally, many feel as though they have no past and therefore have no sense of being connected to anyone.

The life book can help:

1. Organize past events in chronological order.
2. Aid in ego development.
3. Increase self-esteem.
4. Develop a tangible history that can be read at the child's own pace.
5. Share the child's past in an orderly fashion with selected others.
6. Build a sense of trust with the worker who aids in compiling the book.
7. Gain acceptance of all facets of the child's past and his current life.
8. Facilitate bonding.

Utilized as a therapeutic tool, the lifebook goes beyond being a mere scrapbook. While developing the information page by page with the therapist, a child has the opportunity to vent dismay and anger and learn appropriate ways to handle those feelings. With a mental health professional, the child can explore his sense of grief and come to an understanding of how to cope with the loss of his birth family. A therapist can also help the child to move past that loss and accept his new family and its traditions.

For many children who have spent time in the foster care system, the lifebook can be a bridge from their past to their future. It offers assurance that the child is worthy of belonging to his new family because he has belonged and continues to belong to his past.

Ideally, a lifebook is prepared as a child enters foster care and is updated regularly as changes in family occur. At the very least it should be prepared with a child before he/she is placed for adoption. Unfortunately this is not done for many children, and they arrive in a new placement with much confusion and very little concrete information about their past. It becomes very difficult for them to attach to a new family with so much of their past unfinished. Certainly, if we hope to help the child and his new family, it is essential that someone begin to work through these issues with the child.

Further Reading: Vera Fahlberg, *Helping Children When They Must Move.* Michigan Department of Social Service, 1979.

Candace Wheeler, *Where Am I Going?* Winking Owl Press, 1978.

MAGICAL THINKING. The process of idealized thinking about a family, a trait which is shared by both adoptee and adoptive parents. This appears also as a stage of child development of toddlers and later of teens.

Children who are placed for adoption often indulge in fantasies about their birth parents and origins. It is not uncommon for children to describe their birth parents as the "good, wealthy, attractive, caring" people who want to care for the child but are just not able to do it adequately at the moment. This fantasy can even extend to abusive parents whose neglect and mistreatment led to the removal of the child from the home.

Adoptive parents also fantasize about the child they hoped to have who was to help them become (or expand) a family. As with children, adoptive parents' magical thinking can be far removed from the reality of the child. An experienced set of parents who have already raised three children to teen-age years can be dismayed at their lack of success when confronted with the reality of their new adoptive child, who has been in three other homes, and does not have the skills to live in a family but instead has finely tuned survival skills.

There are times when the magical thinking of family and child can come into conflict. Adopting parents sometimes try to explain the reality of the child's past without allowing the child to retain a sense that the birth family had value and worth. In destroying the fantasy it is possible to destroy the child's sense of self-esteem and feelings of self-worth. While it is important to help the child recognize and understand the reality of their earlier experiences, it is equally important for parents to have a balanced approach to the subject, allowing the child to feel good about his origins.

The young child perceives the world in the only way he can at this age— "I did this and then this is what happened. I was so bad, Mommy left me." The magical thinking of the young child can create feelings of guilt and cause years of misunderstanding. For a child in treatment whose first loss occurred during this stage of development, it is crucial to figure out the child's unique form of magical thinking—how he perceived the cause of his loss. By holding onto the magical thinking and self blame, the child is able to keep a feeling of control over his emotions and the world in general. Children who are locked into self blame need help to see themselves in a more positive manner and to develop an accurate understanding of their losses.

Further Reading: Selma Fraiberg, *The Magic Years.* Charles Scribner's Son, 1959.

PARENT SUPPORT GROUP. An organization, formal or informal, that offers support to families in the adoptive process.

In the past, groups of parents who had adopted from an agency were occasionally formed together for the purpose of helping to raise money for the continuing work of the agency. But in the early 1970's, with the advent of older, special needs adoptions, parents began to form themselves into groups to support their children and each other.

Others who have shared the same experiences often are very reliable when offering ideas and help to a newcomer. There is a great lesson to be learned from people who have gone through the experience before you. Just the idea that someone will listen sympathetically to your experiences helps to make the task easier. Certainly, other adoptive families are a gold mine of ideas about "what to do when ...." For, while the adoption worker is a resource for some situations, she does not really know what it is like to live with this problem child from morning to night. Nor can she always be available. Support groups can offer help at all times of the day and night, on weekends and holidays, for the network of families in support groups means that there is more than one to draw from when emergencies arise.

Support groups offer transitions for children as well. When older children are placed into a family, it is comforting to meet other kids, perhaps near their own age, who can share the adoption experience. In the school setting the adopted child may be one of two or three, and is probably the only one who arrived in his family just this month. But in the adoptive parent group, the same child may be one of fifty other children who came into their families by the same route—and some only last week!

Through recent years adoptive parent groups have spread all across the United States. They share some similarities, although they are also very individualistic. A partial list might include the Council on Adoptable Children (COAC) and its affiliates; Organization for a United Response (OURS) and its affiliates; Council of Adoptive Parents (CAP), which went on to develop one of the first photo listing services for children; Parents and Adopted Children Organization (PACO) and its affiliates; the Latin American Parents Association (LAPA); and many others.

Both OURS and the North American Council on Adoptable Children have grown to have a national influence as well, attempting to represent the parent presence in their advocacy for the children who wait for homes.

Adoptive parent groups provide a range of services. Each group decides individually what they can or want to offer in their geographic area. They might offer:

monthly social meetings
telephone reassurance networks
newsletters
community recruitment
buddy families to new families

purchase of listing books
advocacy
family get-togethers
therapy support
low/no interest loans

Parent support groups are the first line of defense against an adoption disruption. Wherever they exist, their support is invaluable. Often they can help to smooth out the rough places before more professional help is needed— or direct a family to help before the problems become too engrained.

Further Reading: Paco, Adoption Is a Group Affair. (Ed. Pamela V. Grabe) Parents and Adopted Children's Organization, Butler, PA. 1981.

NEWS OF OURS, Organization for a United Response, 3307 Hwy 100 North, Suite 203, Minn. MN 55422.

PHOTOLISTING BOOK. A picture listing of children waiting for adoptive homes, developed by agencies as a way to make the community aware of specific children in need of adoption.

Photo books of infants in need of adoption were used in the very early days of adoption, as a way of permitting prospective parents to look through the available candidates. The emphasis in those days was on the needs of adoptive parents, who wanted only healthy children. These albums disappeared as agencies began to focus on the child as the client for adoption.

With the advent of special needs adoption, a new approach for the photolisting book was utilized. Too often children were left without adoption prospects because the description of the child sounded rather formidable. The use of a picture helps to bring the child into focus as a real child and not just scary words on paper. The primary purpose of any such listing service is to match waiting children with existing homes that are interested in adoption.

Nearly every state participates in a photolisting of some kind. Usually it is a somewhat sophisticated presentation of children's pictures and a sensitively written description of the child and his/her special needs. Occasionally a state has only written descriptions of children, although that approach has not proven very effective. Some states cooperate together to form regional exchanges to facilitate the process.

The federal government has seen the value of the services and funds a National Adoption Exchange which is housed in the National Adoption center in Philadelphia, PA. This program has an extremely ambitious and sophisticated approach using computers, and has found its ability to match children with families to be very effective. Because the program is able to cross county, state and regional boundaries, children have increased opportunities to find permanent, loving homes.

POST PLACEMENT SUPPORT. The process of offering additional services to the adopted child and his family after the placement and the finalization of the adoption.

In traditional adoption, the agency considered that its role was completed after the legal finalization of an adoption. Even after the placement of a child, their involvement was usually limited to the three post-placement visits required by regulations. During this time the agency was sometimes seen as intrusive, and many parents wished that even this involvement did not have to exist.

With the advent of "special needs" adoption, however, and the increasing number of disruptions, a growing concern among professionals led to the belief that the agency's responsibility to the child and the new family formed by the adoption did not have to stop after the legal papers were signed. Some adoption agencies have extended their role to include services such as:

Parent Group: the support and maintenance of the parent group by the agency itself, thereby insuring that it will continue to exist as a resource for new families through the years.

Counseling: the development of a specific expertise in family counseling with a recognition of the issues unique to the adoptive family. This can be done through either staff development or liaison with a community provider.

Bridge/Respite Families: the network of families that can be used as short term placements for a child disrupting from one home; or be offered to a family who can benefit from a short vacation from the behaviors of a difficult child.

Newsletters: a communication tool that allows the agency to keep in touch with families. Newsletters can provide families with information about what is going on in other families and in the field of adoption, and can also provide the agency with resource families for future adoptions.

Reunion Services: assistance to adoptees and their adoptive families in facilitating reunions between adoptees and their birth families. In some states this can be done through direct contacts, while in others the agency can become the petitioner to the court system on behalf of the adoptee. The agency could also serve as the intermediary for initial contacts between adoptee and birth family.

Further Reading: Ann Hartman, *Working with Adoptive Families beyond Placement.* Child Welfare League of America, 1984.

SEARCH. The desire on the part of an adopted individual to seek out birth parents and/or birth relatives. This is usually done after the adoptee reaches adulthood, though it may be earlier.

The involvement in search varies according to the adoptee. It may include meeting and establishing an ongoing relationship with both parents as well as other related individuals.

Typically, older adopted children have lived part of their lives with the birth family. Unlike individuals placed as infants, older children have a name and history that connects them to the family of origin. Search at some point in their life is more likely than for an adoptee whose every thread of identifying birth information is contained in sealed court records.

After moving into adoptive homes, some older adopted children can benefit from the reassurance, "at some point in your life, after you're 18, you may want to go back and contact your birth family." Knowing that if they do wish to search, someone (family, therapist, or placing agency) will be there to assist them helps the child put to rest some of the feelings of loss and allows him to go on with the business of being a child.

Search issues frequently arise at specific developmental stages in a person's life. As a child reaches adolescence, both the typical teenage thoughts of rebellion and awakened interest in sexuality add new meaning to the thought of searching for birth parents. As a child reaches adolescence, the compelling need to know "who I am" propels many adopted teenagers to search. This preoccupation with their birth connections places them at particular risk for identity conflicts. It is not uncommon for adoptees to use a search for their "shadow family" as a way of rebelling from family rules and traditions and establishing their own sense of identity.

Search questions raise some fears and reawaken a sense of loss for adoptive parents as well. Discussions of birth parents are a reminder to the entire family that the adoptive parents are not the "real" parents of the child and that strangers may begin to have an impact on the child's life. In addition, for infertile couples, search is a reminder of loss of the ability to reproduce. For many parents the issues of infertility were poorly resolved; and resurface at this time creating added difficulties between parents and teens.

Further Reading: Arthur D. Sorosky, Annette Baran, and Reuben Pannor, *The Adoption Triangle,* Doubleday, 1978.

Betty Jean Lifton, *Lost and Found,* Dial Press, 1979.

TIME LINE. A treatment tool that records significant events in a child's life. One method for utilizing the sequence of time is to have brief accounts of the child's life experiences written on note cards, placed in order, and then pinned to a string or clothes line. Time lines allow for a "story" to happen highlighting the dates and events that shaped the child's present life.

There is a part in every older adopted child that remembers when he or she was separated from first parents, when a significant event such as a divorce or death occurred, or when a sibling was moved out of the home. These traumatic events remain within the child as an "anniversary date." As the child moves closer to the season or month these events occurred there is an internal clock that sets off feelings of confusion and hurt and perhaps "acting out" behavior.

A time line not only helps to identify the events but allows feelings to be associated with experiences. By helping a child to see and hear the important facts surrounding the loss and hurt, distortions can be corrected that the child may have invented with the passing of time. Children often are not told all the facts, or may have created misconceptions due to their developmental/ emotional age at the time of the events. A preschooler abandoned by parents will likely believe he or she was "bad," "so bad that Mommy and Daddy didn't want me any more." Without the facts the child will probably go through all the stages of childhood with this underlying thought influencing all his development.

Many children moving through the foster care system have records about their past in many different agencies, sometimes spread across several counties or states. Information about their past is often in a piecemeal state that requires a diligent search for the information. Fitting the events and life experiences together will take time, but the rewards are great for a child who will then have a better chance to resolve doubts and concerns about his past. Laying to rest misinformation often held on to by a child over the years, can allow for the development of more normal relationships with a new family.

A time line is an inexpensive, readily available tool, easily used in therapeutic treatment with children.

Further Reading: Claudia Jewett, *Presentation at workshop for Three Rivers Adoption Council,* PA, 1985.

TRANSRACIAL ADOPTION. Placement of a child of one race into a family of another race.

In the late 1950's a recognition that large numbers of minority children were languishing in the foster care system led professionals to consider the placement of Native American Indian children with Caucasian families. This practice was extended in the late 60's to include Black and biracial children who were placed cross-culturally. Since the Korean War, large numbers of Asian children have been placed with White families. More recently, Vietnamese and South American children, have been added to the list.

Some transracial placements do take place today. However, the practice has slowed, except for children with multiple handicaps, children whose ethnic background is in question, and foreign born children. A transracial family seeking treatment may need to have their uniqueness and differentness addressed. A Korean child whose behavior is disrupting the Caucasian, blonde, fairskinned family has lived a life of feeling/looking different. The family stress needs to be viewed not only from the acting out behavior but also from the obvious physical/cultural difference.

The commitment of a family to accept a child or children of another race is not a single decision but a life-long acceptance of change in family orientation. The successful family is one that offers a variety of life/cultural experiences to all of its members, not solely to the child of the minority background. Current research indicates certain factors which help a transracial family to succeed: living in an integrated neighborhood, having more than one child of the different ethnic background, developing close social ties across racial lines for all the family, exposure to a broad continuum of experiences from both cultural backgrounds.

Despite the trend away from transracial placement, the existing families need support, as do children and families who are just entering the process. Children grow better in families, and where family members have different ethnic origins, it is essential to continue to provide constructive suggestions to help them succeed.

Further Reading: W. Feigelman & A. Silverman, *Chosen Children.* Praeger, 1983.

J. Ladner, *Mixed Families: Adopting Across Racial Boundaries.* Anchor Press, 1979.

Part II
The Articles

6

Grief Issues in Counseling Adoptive Families

Josephine Anderson

The commonly held opinion regarding grief and adoption has been that grief ends when a child is placed. The adopting adults are no longer childless, the child is no longer parentless, and the birth mother is reconciled to her choice. Under this rainbow of accomplished goals, the opinion goes, life for all concerned can be unencumbered by the past.

Unfortunately, the opinion and the facts are far apart. In 1962, Povl Toussieng of the Menninger Clinic wrote of the observation that a disproportionate number of adoptive children were being treated in the Child Guidance Center.[1] Subsequently, other studies have been conducted based on the same observation. In the past decade some counties have become alarmed by the number of adoptive families petitioning the court to terminate parental rights to their adopted children.[2] Yet, agencies seem to be reluctant to address what I believe to be the basis of this phenomenon.

It is my opinion, based on twenty years of experience in adoption, that grief is the dominant unique factor in adoptive family life; further, that grief issues have been neglected, misunderstood, and sometimes misinterpreted by professionals. Losses are felt (or feelings are denied) by all participants in every adoption.

This article addresses those issues in the traditional in-race, infant adoptive placement where infertility is the reason for adoption. Prior to 1970, the traditional adoption dominated the field. Those infants are now children between 15 and 18 and young adults, some of whom are in trouble with themselves and their families.

In this article I will present the adoptive family issues, offer an opinion on their impact in counseling, and make some suggestions for treatment. The birth parent's (or parents') challenge is appreciably different and will not be developed here.

Grief Issues

Dominant throughout the adoption experience is the loss of genetic tie. That loss not only exists for all participants but also has been reinforced by the legal system. In the 1960's and early '70's there was either a comprehensive avoidance of the importance of genetics or a deliberate attempt to "match" physical features and intelligence projection. In either case the mistaken premise was that, while a child may inherit intelligence level and physical features, characteristics and personality traits are entirely developmental, therefore environmentally dictated. Additionally, there was a tendency to ignore the genetic loss because it simply can not be resolved—it is the basis of the adoption phenomenon.

Without doubt, loss of fertility is the paramount grief for the adopting parents. Emotionally, infertility represents loss of an unborn child—a child anticipated as thoroughly as in pregnancy, a child often desired more intensely. As friends become pregnant, parents make references to desired grand-parenthood, and the couple is bombarded with loving children through the media, the pain of being unable to conceive increases. The foundations of biologic being and, in some instances, of the marriage contract which anticipated genetic reproduction are under attack. The unborn child then becomes the symbol of imperfection as well as the unconceived desire. All of these levels of grief and guilt are carried into the parents' life with the adoptive child in many subtle and not so subtle ways.

At the time of the adoption process the family's experience was likely that the emphasis on infertility was made in terms of medical proof, responsibility, and resolved feelings. Little, if any, attention was given to facilitating shared grief. In fact there was always the question of what the worker would deem appropriate. For instance, if the applicant allowed the grief to show, would the worker accept it as "normal" or interpret it as "not having resolved grief feelings?" Not infrequently, where a medical reason existed, the potentially fertile partner felt a need to protect the spouse in an effort to shore up defenses. For the applicant, the safer way to go was with control. Hence, the pre-placement process usually tended to inhibit expression of this profound grief.

As the family shared the joys, sorrows, frustrations, challenges, and nuances of daily life, an underlying, usually dormant but sometimes dominant parental grief was in the fact that this child was not born to them. Again grief was connected with infertility and genetic loss, but with a difference: the child had become a reality and was a family member. With troubled families a probable complication, sometimes unverbalized, sometimes explicit, was jealousy and resentment that s/he was born to someone else—someone who had no business having a baby, according to the middle class morality of the time. During the adoption process most applicants were aware that they should feel compassion for the birth mother, and usually they did. But that was before there was a child who became theirs in every sense of family relationship. Not infrequently the birth parent had become a malignant mystery rather than a benign donor, especially if the child was rebellious.

The child's grief centers on the loss of birth parents whom s/he never had a chance to know. Because grieving is alien, sadness is painful, and parental help is often unavailable, the child avoids grief by denial or fantasy. While fantasy can be useful in working out the meaning of facts, it can also become a separating factor in the adoptive family life when unshared. Even when shared, parents sometimes have misinterpreted the motive due to their over-sensitized preoccupation with the birth parent(s); and sometimes the child has used the fantasy vindictively. However, the sharing is usually beneficial to both child and parent. Always it is an opportunity for bonding and healing.

The child also shares the wish that s/he had been born to his/her parents—the only "real" parents s/he has known. The grief in that issue is somewhat obscure, especially to the child; it is the grief of being "different" and of having an additional complication in growing up. This is an unfairness in the child's life.

The Family in Trouble

As the child has gained a factual understanding of adoption, it becomes obvious that very important decisions were made by the adults at the time of the placement which had impinged directly upon the child. S/he had no say in them, creating some unfinished business of decision-making for the child. Meanwhile, the parents may be unaware of the child's need to confirm their original decisions, and may be raising their own questions regarding the decision they made years ago.

* * * * *

Unfortunately, the parents' and child's emotional needs of each other usually have been in conflict for some time. As they pertain to the adoptive situation, the conflicting needs show up this way:

Parent	*Child*
Confirmation of parenthood	Appraisal of decisions made for him/her as an infant

Continued denial of grief	Permission to grieve
Positive reflection of family in community	Withdrawal to reassess: sometimes acting out in community
Social & professional priority	More parent time for adoption issues

Another factor inhibiting adoption grief is the "let sleeping dogs lie" attitude which gives a non-verbal "off-limits" message. Interestingly, that can come from the youth as well as from parents; frequently, it is one aspect of the situation that is shared! As this has gone on over the years, secrets have developed resulting in super-sensitive defensiveness, unshared fantasies, and the diversion of unreconciled griefs onto extraneous differences between parent and youth. Often the diversion of unreconciled grief is onto real or imagined differences in genetic heritage, as well as hostility toward the placing agency. In the majority of cases the avoidance and diversion of grief issues has had a good deal of practice throughout the family's life. Always these complications are carried into the counseling situation.

Counseling the Family in Trouble

At this point it is important to explain the semantics of my use of "reconciliation" and "resolution." The difference is as much a frame of reference as it is a dictionary definition. *Resolution* is used here to describe *an act of appraisal and decision-making,* while *reconciliation* is referred to as *a process of reappraisal and acquiescence.* Resolution implies a time-oriented accomplishment; reconciliation implies recurrence and review.

The importance of that differentiation is specific: *grief cannot be resolved.* If the goal is resolution of the feeling of grief, and that goal is considered to be accomplished with or without help from others, then recurrence is not anticipated. Yet grief for any loss has a way of resurfacing with external or internal stimulus, sometimes years later. If one is not prepared for that, the inappropriate and unhelpful responses of denial, bewilderment, betrayal, and even fear can result. The effects of this in the adoptive situation have been discussed.

If, however, the goal of "grief work" is reconciliation, then there is acknowledgment that review and reworking will be part of the adoptive family's life together. For example, some accomplishment of the child can be a poignant reminder of the loss of genetic tie. Instead of becoming added emotional baggage, such resurfacing of grief can offer new possibilities for reappraisal and reconciliation.

My experience is that social workers and counseling therapists are encouraged and trained to think in terms of resolution. This is especially true in the recent emphasis on short-term counseling. In the initial interactions with the adoptive family, if the counselor's mind-set is toward resolutions, an opportunity to open the gates inhibiting grief reconciliations will be missed. If, however, the approach is toward reconciliation, there is a greater possibility that realistic and useful therapy can be accomplished.

One other aspect of reconciliation/resolution is important. Reconciliation is individual; therefore each family member will be *separately* reconciling his/her own griefs. On the basis of individual reconciliations, *shared* family resolutions of immediate and long term problems can be addressed.

I believe that counselors must understand the grief areas themselves and be committed to the need for a grieving process. Generally the family members are unaware of that need and often have taken their respective stands in the context of what I shall call "family denial:" The prevailing attitude, if not specification, is that "this is not our child" and "these are not my real parents." If the counselor can see the hurt in that presenting hostility and can steer the family in the direction of reconciliation, the barriers of anger and hostility may be lowered, making direct confrontation of the "problem" unnecessary.

Case Example

Mr. T. dropped into the office of the agency that had placed his daughter Suzie 13 years earlier, to make an appointment for family counseling. He made it clear that he had no confidence in counseling, having been to five resources previously in an attempt to resolve the problems presented by an older son who had recently died.

When the family came in, the hostility level was impressive. Mr. T. stated that Suzie apparently no longer accepted them as her parents; hence, finding out who the "real parents" were might be the final act of their parental commitment.

Suzie had no questions about her birth parents and the detachment she came with looked more and more like fearfulness as they talked. When the detachment was pointed out to Mr. T., he was genuinely surprised. Further exploration uncovered a recent confrontation in which Suzie had responded venomously to a social restriction by her parents. In addition to forbidden foul language, she had shouted that she wished they'd never adopted her or her brother either.

In discussion of the son's death it was learned that Mr. and Mrs. T. had grieved that loss together but had purposely excluded Suzie, being afraid that grieving with them would prompt her to follow in her brother's footsteps. Suzie's grief response in the counseling session was the beginning of a sharing of fears, hurts, griefs, and concerns. Over the span of four sessions, each came to a reconciliation. They were now able to approach resolution of their group problems, which they accomplished alone.

While much of that process is established generic counseling, the way that the family members "used" adoption issues, combined with the unique vulnerability of each family member, can exist only in the adoptive family.

Not infrequently, the fact of adoptive status is not acknowledged at intake. How and when that fact becomes known is important in subsequent dealing with it.

Case Example

The presenting problem in the F. family was what to do about the runaway 16-year-old girl and her influence on a 14-year-old girl still at home. Also their 17-year-old boy's lack of motivation and goals was discussed. After three sessions geared mainly to helping the parents make and articulate some firm decisions, the counselor interviewed the son. He was reluctant, but in his first sentence he referred to his "foster parents ... well, I mean, adoptive." It was his evaluation that his parents had always been "wishy-washy about important stuff" (including adoption explanations) and "killers about manners, and like that." He knew nothing about his birth parents and couldn't care less ... his sister was "dumb" to be out there looking for hers.

These revelations changed the direction of counseling. The young man and his 14-year-old sister became interested in looking at the issues that were not being addressed at home. The parents were willing to have the children join a group of adopted adolescents, but were not interested in their own exploration. They felt that encouragement to define firmly the family relationships and expectations had been helpful, but they were not ready to engage in a reconciliation process.

The child's knowledge of the facts of adoption can be an obstacle to the reconciliation process. Somehow the expectation is that if the child knows about it, then s/he shouldn't have to have feelings.

Case Example

Mr. and Mrs. C. with their 16-year-old daughter Amy were "not quite sure why" they had come for counseling. The parental concern was centered on Amy's increasing withdrawal from family and general social interaction. They described a "change in personality" which sounded to the counselor like a mild depression. Amy was certainly detached during the first interview.

In an individual session, the difference in affect was dramatic. Amy had brought a book on adoption with her and was full of generalized questions. When the counselor tried to personalize them, Amy reverted to detachment. A comment pointing that out was met with, "I know all about my other parents. This has nothing to do with me." The counselor disagreed and allowed the disagreement to stand while Amy talked about school matters.

When Amy returned to adoption via the book, the counselor gently removed the book and suggested that she unload whatever burden she was carrying. Through tears, the strongest message was that she *mustn't* feel so confused ... it wasn't fair to her Mom and Dad. They had been honest with her and had shared all the facts they had; therefore, she felt disloyal to her parents in asking questions about her birth mother.

Further sessions included all family members (three younger adopted children). Sharing and healing were spontaneous, and the family was reaffirmed.

Adolescence precipitated Amy's need to review the meaning of adoption as she was relating to her own sexuality and reappraising all her relationships. The presence of sensitively aware parents who were willing to share the experience of Amy's reconciliation with the entire family was a tremendous bonus to all.

The process of grieving and reconciling is one that often needs *practice*. It usually is helpful to use the concept of practicing, since whether it is in music, sports, homemaking skills or whatever, everyone knows what it means: first attempts may be awkward and embarrassing, perhaps even painful. The counselor needs to be aware that the line between awkwardness and avoidance is very narrow. With a goal of full exposure of the adoption grief issues, that line becomes quite important.

Coming back to the definitions of reconciliation and resolution, it is urgent in this kind of counseling that reconciliation be the goal. Resolving most of the chronic or immediate problems of family interaction can be done more quickly and easily if reconciliation to the emotional implication of adoption is accomplished first.

Sometimes the counselor is used for the resolution process and, if so, the ordinary family counseling modes and methods can be employed. Often the group situation is preferred, especially if there is a group of adoptive parents or youths. Appropriateness of inclusion in a generic group would depend to some extent on the success in reappraisal and reconciliation of the adoption issues.

Regardless of how the resolutions are accomplished, reappraisal for the adoptive family should include consideration of the birth parents as a recurring aspect of family life with different meanings to each individual and with fluctuating importance according to age and stage of development. The coincidence of parental vulnerability and adolescent rebellion is generic; the fact of birth parents, how they fit into biological awakening, and how that threatens the cohesiveness of the family is unique.

Summary

All members of many adoptive families are particularly vulnerable to the child's adolescence. The seeds of the vulnerability lie in the adoption process prior to the infant placement, and are nurtured by denial of grief, defensiveness, and fantasizing as the child matures. Finally, the fact of adoption is misused by both parent and child as a barrier to genuine family ties.

Some tasks in counseling adoptive families are unique. These need attention before the behavioral problem is treated. Reconciliation of griefs, review of the meaning of birth parents, sharing fantasies and facts are basic aspects of the unique dimension of adoptive family life. If the counselor can encourage and empower the family to grieve losses and share hurts, s/he has provided the basis for ongoing growth and permission for recurrent reconciliation. Subsequent resolution of problems may or may not need the counselor's attention.

Notes

1 Toussieng, Povl: "Thoughts Regarding the Etiology of Psychological Difficulties in Adoptive Children." *Child Welfare;* 41 (2), Feb., 1962
2 Racine County (WI) Human Services Department Adoptive Family Research Project: "Making Permanent Planning Permanent." 1981

7

Holding Therapy: A Way of Helping Unattached Children

Josephine Anderson

If ever you hear it said, referring to an older child candidate for adoption, "All this child needs is a lot of love," my advice is to be very skeptical. Increasingly, the older children being placed are disturbed kids who have little or no foundation within themselves to understand or accept love as it is defined in normal family life. Many of them are "unattached children."

The Unattached Child

The first few years of the unattached child's life have been fractured by abuse, neglect, and/or multiple moves. When he desperately needed to he could not trust relationships with adults. As the years passed, usually with repetition of fracturing, he has become convinced that no adult can be trusted; hence, he has become self-parenting.[1] There are more unattached boys than girls, explaining the use of the masculine pronoun throughout this article.

The chief characteristic which devastates the stable, caring adoptive family is the child's lack of conscience. The "lying-cheating-stealing syndrome" we all know is only one manifestation of having no conscience. Inflicting pain without remorse and lacking regard for all "rules" of intrafamily life are harder to live with. Furthermore, the child sees himself as always right; consequently, he has no reason to change anything about himself. He understands neither obligation outside of himself nor logical consequences. This leaves the parent with no effective approach to discipline.

Additional characteristics include indiscriminate demand for affection with none forthcoming from himself; social retardation, causing poor peer relationships; impaired conceptual ability, especially regarding time and space; poor impulse control; and a short attention span. Another fairly common symptom is lack of awareness of body messages. This can lead to gorging of food until nauseated, nondifferentiation of elimination need signals, and insensitivity to temperature changes and pain. Some unattached children exhibit all of these symptoms. Others exhibit fewer, and still others have unique symptoms.

The behavior symptomatology (with DSM III classification) usually falls into these diagnostic classifications:[2]

Conduct disorder, unsocialized, aggressive	—312.00
Oppositional	—313.81
Schizoid disorder	—301.20
Narcissistic personality	—301.81
Histrionic personality	—301.50
Borderline personality (mostly girls)	—301.83
Attention deficit disorder	—314.00

Not infrequently there will also be mixed developmental disorder (315.50) and identity disorder of childhood (315.90), which I believe to be the diagnoses of more tractable and therefore not truly unattached children.

As the unattached child enters the adoptive family a malignant water-and-oil situation is created. The easiest way to describe it is by contrasting columns. Hence, we have:

Adopting Parents	*Child*
Eager to parent	Self parenting
Self confident	Used to failure, low self esteem
Functioning as stable integrated unit	Outsider dedicated to maintaining chaos
Trusting of others	Untrusting, sneaky, devious
Socially extended	Little sense of social relatedness
Usually proper	Little knowledge of propriety
Do not accept abusing others	No remorse regarding infliction of pain
Affectionate	Fear of physical contact, or else clinging
Anticipate joyfully	Anticipates with fear and/or resentment

What I have described is a child nobody can like—unless he has decided to "con" the therapist or other infrequently encountered adult. Furthermore, it is very hard to love a child—who is terrorizing the siblings, creating chaos at school, disregarding all rules, showing affection anywhere and everywhere except in the family, and always figuratively, sometimes literally thumbing his nose at your love. Unfortunately, too often foster and adoptive parents wait quite a while before they seek therapy.

I have been aware from placing older children for adoption that the traditional child therapies are usually not effective with these kids. Many children are either purposely or developmentally non-verbal, most are capable of oozing great charm if there's something to be gained, and their only care about a relationship is how it can be manipulated and controlled. A surprising number of unattached children have had years of therapy with little or no change in how they approach relationships. One of the most frequently encountered aberrations in therapy is the assumption that what's wrong is that this family just doesn't accept this unfortunate child—"all he needs is love." It may be true that by the time the therapist is involved the family *doesn't* accept the child—they certainly *mustn't* accept his behavior. It is not true that *all* he needs is love.

Obviously, if neither the traditional therapies nor traditional parenting techniques is going to work, something else is needed. My belief is that holding therapy may be a very fruitful "something else."

However, specific parenting techniques lay the groundwork for the therapy and should be comfortably in place before holding is used. The purpose of these techniques is to desensitize the parental stress and create an environment in which conscience can develop.

Love, the Foundation

The foundation for everything which follows is unconditional love. By this I mean *steadfast caring regardless of behavior.* With my unattached foster children I often said, "No matter what you do, you are loved because you are a child of God—and that *you* can't change." It was often the only way that child could be loved!

Conscience Development

The tools I found to be helpful are:

1. neutralizing language
2. insisting on eye contact with every exchange, especially a directive
3. using cue words
4. avoiding argument
5. being relentlessly consistent in the face of relentless provocation
6. setting behavior expectation priorities
7. using physical restraint

As I write them I think "Well, that's easy—so what's the big deal?" Living with a relentlessly provocative child teaches one how difficult it is.

We don't realize, until faced with the need to observe, how full of judgments our parenting language is. Moralizing and reasoning—even lecturing, sometimes—work with the child who can feel guilt at appropriate times. With the child who has no moral base and usually no logic perception, those methods don't fly. Neutralizing language is fun and all family members can participate. Some useful neutral words are *appropriate and inappropriate, tolerable* and *intolerable, options, agenda, penalty situation, accountable,* and various forms of *provoke*—there are lots of good ones. Foster Cline's *Understanding and Treating the Severely Disturbed Child* is a gold mine of one-liners.

One of the most important tools in dealing with the self-parenting child is eye contact. The kids hate it, strongly resist it, and become really annoyed with insistence, because eye contact demands interaction. Gentling and humoring them into it works better than bullying (although the child may leave you no choice). But however it is done, *achieving* eye contact *with every important communication* is the goal.

Cue words are exceedingly helpful. One child chose "butterfly" as the word his parents could use instead of "There you go again trying to say what you think I want to hear in order to get me off your back. You *know* I hate that and you're doing it just to make me mad." It was a light, almost humorous way to give a strong message—"I've got your number."

Every lecture or repetitious reasoning can have a cue word. It's amazing how useful that is in desensitizing as well as avoiding embarrassing public situations. I used "mushroom" with one of my kids to cover inappropriate behavior in public—in a store when he was pawing at and hiding in racks of clothing, in the neighborhood when he was playing *at* rather than *with* others, and at church when he was disrupting choir practice. From previous discussion he knew that he could then make the choice of continuing the behavior and taking the consequences, trying to regroup and change the behavior, or coming to me for help in self-control. As experience with the cue word is repeated and the child learns that choices *do* have consequences, he can believe in the fact that he *has* options.

Cue words can be used to intercept arguments, too. This is very helpful, for arguing with an unattached child is worse than useless. Argument offers him a sense of domination, regardless of the conclusion: He sucked the parent into his agenda, and that is a triumph. Many a time I have had to say ruefully, "There—you did it again, didn't you? You sucked me into your agenda," and then regroup. The regrouping after or avoiding argument can take the form of mentioning the choices and then asking the child if he wants to know your opinion. Likely he already does and won't want to hear it when it's on your neutral terms.

Another method of building conscience is by meeting relentless provocation with relentless consistency. I have learned that families whose lives are structured have more success with unattached children than those who prefer spontaneity. Consistency provides the cause and effect relationship on which *reasonable* expectation can be based. I emphasize "reasonable" because it is easy to get hung up on expecting a 12 year old to act like a 12 year old when his emotional age is 5.

As a way of meeting the challenges with an unattached child, I recommend that parents establish priorities in their expectations of behavior. I am not naive enough to believe that there can be a tidy progression in the child's compliance with the parents' priorities, but it is helpful to know where the priorities are as one deals with the multitude of challenges. It gives some opportunity to measure progress, especially when things get grim.

Sometimes physical restraint is necessary. When it is, it should be exactly that—restraint, not attack. It is most effective when it is a surprise.

Restraint can sometimes lead to therapeutic holding, which I believe to be by far the best treatment for the unattached child. I became interested in this therapy after attending workshops presented by Russ Colburn, Vera Fahlberg, and Foster Cline of Forest Heights Lodge in Evergreen, Colorado. Perhaps because I need to know what's happening and why, I have developed a procedure around those concepts which I started using with unattached children in placement. As I later got into foster parenting and learned through the kids what the unattached child *really* is, I refined and expanded the techniques. At first I worried about harming a resistant child by using confrontational and restraining methods. But that concern was allayed through consultation with a traditionalist.

Preparation

A parent can lead into holding by setting up a touching program to help the child accept physical contact that is reasonable and dispassionate. The sexually abused child will not understand and usually will attempt to sexualize any touching. It is important that such behavior be acknowledged and redirected to an appropriate response. If it is punished or ignored, an opportunity is lost and the child's past experience is reinforced.

Simultaneously the parent can help the child identify the feelings that have been associated with past experiences. It is easy to get bogged down in facts —did this or that really happen and in which home, etc.—but, at this point, helping the child with feelings is more important. Often it is confusing to the parent that this child truly does not differentiate appropriately among normal feeling responses—his ability to feel has atrophied. In that case, the parent must explain, using family examples, while urging the child to practice appropriate response.

Meanwhile the therapist must carefully explain to the parent what holding is, what can be expected, and why it is useful. I will start with "why" and go on to "what."

The most important value to this child is being in control—through creating chaos, through lying, through disruption, through false charm, through whatever means he can devise. *As long as he is able to control, he can deny and displace his rage and grief and remain unattached.* The purpose of this therapy is to break through his control barrier and get to the rage and grief, freeing him to attach and trust. He may not make it; he may make it through therapy and choose to remain unattached; but giving him the chance to learn caring is what we can do.

Holding

Therapeutic holding uses the infant nurture position. Choose a comfortable sofa or oversized chair—it could be a long haul. The right-handed person puts the child's right hand behind the adult's back. The child's head is cradled in the left elbow, perhaps with a pillow. The adult's left hand holds the child's left arm, leaving the right arm to control the body and the right hand on the child's chin to require eye contact. Sometimes a leg scissor-hold on the child's legs is in order.

If the child cannot be restrained by one person it is important to have back-up personnel. Usually the therapist and two parents, or parent and significant other adult, are sufficient. It is my opinion that using a sibling or other older child is *not* appropriate.

The therapy session should allow a minimum of one hour—often more time is needed. It should be uninterrupted, and should be private. It can get quite noisy. Others within ear-shot should be told in advance that the child will not be endangered.

If there is any doubt before a session is started that there is sufficient time or will, it should be postponed. If for any reason holding therapy is discontinued before the process is complete, it *must* be stated that "we will do it again," and then reinitiated within 48 hours. The purpose is to break into the child's control pattern. If he gets the message that he can control this too, then it has had an actively negative effect instead of the therapeutic goal.

Following or even during a holding session the child may regress in age-appropriate behaviors. Unless it is expected, such regression can be annoying and even frightening. Actually, it is part of the therapeutic process. Regression eventually allows the child to progress.

If the therapy is working, the child will resist in every way he can. He does this because he is aware that his manipulative control is under attack. He will fight physically, become verbally abusive, and resist eye contact. The forms of resistance serve the useful purpose of catalyzing rage; hence, with the exception of adult insistence on eye contact, resistance can be actively encouraged during the first three stages of the holding. Foul language should be welcomed, with acknowledgment to the child that these are his true feelings, even though displaced from earlier times.

Because this is a profound emotional experience, it is possible that some unreconciled griefs or losses in the adult's life could surface. My advice is to let it happen but not verbalize it at this time—later is much better.

My experience is that if the therapy is introduced to the child as being something good for him you can forget it. He *knows* that whatever an adult says is good for him won't be. Hence, while getting into the holding position, the adult can say, "This is for me. I need it in order to understand you better." This can be followed by comments such as, "There are parts of your life we didn't share, and I have sad feelings about that." If there has been abuse, it is appropriate to add, "I am angry about some things that happened to you." And, with further settling into position, statements regarding the therapy itself are in order, such as, "Someone told me about this way of getting to know you and I'm excited about it." If it is true (& *only* if it is), other feeling comments are useful: "I'm sort of scared and embarrassed, too. So we will be practicing together."

Since feelings are what we're after, as long as it isn't fake, it is well to say so. It is a fact that feelings are getting in the way of loving each other—his feelings and the parents'. This is not the time to list grievances—rather, it is the time for compassionate acknowledgement of internal hurts, fears, and anger.

Process

The following step-by-step progression describes the holding experience. Sometimes it moves in just this manner; sometimes it is mixed up. The time-consuming steps are 4, 5, 6. If the adult interrupts the exposure of feelings, either because of his own pain or because he wants to proect the child from pain, the value of the experience is limited. That point cannot be over-emphasized: *the child needs to relive the abuse/neglect/separation experience and have it come out differently with these parents.* The child needn't understand that, but he must feel it.

Child	*Parent/Therapist*
1. Non-plussed compliance, usually	Gradual insistence on eye contact
2. Resistance and anger	"You hurt, but it's inside." "You're hurting me." If you struggle, I hold—that could hurt some, but the real hurt isn't on your arm."

3.	Threats—"I've gotta go potty." "I'll throw up."	Acceptance—"Go ahead, we'll wipe it up later."
4.	Anxiety—physical, diversionary	Firmness; verbalize what's happening
5.	Fear	Reassurance—"The bad things won't happen again."
6.	Exposure of feelings	Calmness is urgent. There may be some memory of abuse. Do not be horrified, do not stop. Listen and make calmly reassuring sounds—words don't matter.
7.	Anger, impotence, grief, bewilderment	Cry with the child *if* you feel it; at least accept the anger, sadness, and confusion. Verbalize the unfairness.
8.	Relaxation	This is the bonding time. Cuddle for as long as it feels comfortable.

Case Illustration

A case description may help to clarify some of the material.

Bob was a 7-year old when he came to my home with his older brother, age 11. They had been born to a single mother who had given the brother four years of adequate, caring nurture. Mom had tried to abort Bob, and had resented him from birth. When Bob was 2 years old Mom began to get excruciating headaches due to scar tissue from a previous head injury. One night in terrible pain, she died. Bob denied any and all memory of his Mom.

The boys were then taken into the home of their alcoholic grandparents. There was frequent violence, repeated moving, and two short-term foster home placements. When Bob was six, the children were removed permanently and placed into a loving inexperienced foster home with two home-made boys, ages 5 and 7. Both Bob and his brother were viewed as undisciplined, devious, and mean. Bob was described as a terror. It is to their credit that these caring parents stuck with the boys for a year. During that time Bob's brother improved markedly in the stable environment. Bob, on the other hand, seemed to get worse.

Bob was top of the line unattached with all the trimmings. He was physically very appealing and intellectually at least average. Psychological testing suggested the diagnosis of schizoid personality with a bleak prognosis.

For him, eye contact was to be avoided at all cost. Early on, the cost was frequently loss of play time, often with physical restraint and his resultant rage. Disruption of all personal interaction not centered on him was his consistent style. Foul language, biting, spitting, and hitting characterized his peer relationships.

Neutralizing language was fun—he enjoyed the new words and slowly began to respond to and use them. But Bob frequently needed to be restrained as he attempted to injure other kids, himself, or me. Taking over his temper tantrums in order to direct them into constructive rage became a common though not always successful technique.

After about three months I began therapeutic holding. Most of the feeling exposure of the first three sessions had to do with fear and anger while living with his grandparents. Following each session Bob was calm, cooperative, and genuinely fun to be around.

The fourth session started as usual. (Incidentally, Bob always threatened to "pee" on me and to vomit. He never did.) As he was claiming that I was hurting him, the quality of the complaint changed—it became higher in pitch and much more intense. I explained that I was not using pressure, for he had stopped resisting. Suddenly he cried out, "My head, my head—I can't stand the pain in my head." Over and over the same phrase. Nothing I said penetrated.

However, when I quietly said, "You've heard those words before, Bob," he stopped abruptly and asked, "How do you know?" I told him that I knew what had happened to his Mom, whereupon he resumed the wailing. I am convinced that he felt the pain.

Gradually the wailing changed to sobbing and he repeated, "She left me. She left me. I sent her away. I was so bad she left me." He could not remember what he had done to send her away—obviously, the fact was incidental to the feeling. Bob cried profoundly for probably ten minutes while I rocked him, commiserating on the unfairness of death. When Bob was ready to get down, he slid off my lap and started to crawl. After a few "steps," he sat, looked at me, and asked, "Why am I doing this?" I told him that he was feeling like he was a baby still with his Mom. "Oh," he said. After a few more "steps" he asked, "How long will this last?"

"I don't know, but I'll make a deal with you. As long as you are here in the house with me, you can be whatever age you need to be. But when you go out the door you'll be 8, OK?"

"OK." And he did just that.

His teacher called two days later asking what had happened—Bob was compliant, cooperative, calm, and once even shared with another child. But when he came home he fell to the floor, crawled, babbled, wanted a bottle (I'd anticipated and borrowed one from a neighbor), needed to be helped with dressing, and did a lot of lap-sitting and curling up. This lasted, gradually diminishing, for about a week.

It was during that week that I told him he had helped me face an aspect of my father's death I had not reconciled. In that instance he was my "therapist"—an awesome and binding experience.

Bob's personality integration over the five months following that session was remarkable. He developed a captivating sense of humor and gradually my friends stopped cringing when he entered into one of our social gatherings. He will always be aggressive and competitive, and I expect he will be basically egocentric; but at age 12 he is now viewed as a normal loving youngster by his adoptive parents, who learned the holding technique before Bob was placed with them four years ago.

I believe that training in conscience development was a necessary antecedent for the success of holding in Bob's case. He and I had started some constructive vibes going.

The therapist will need to be very active when intrafamily relationships have hit rock bottom and everything is grim in order to prevent the session from becoming judgemental. When a child has demanded and taken with no return on the investment for months on end, resentment and anger can be strong enough to contraindicate parental participation in holding until some of feeling has been defused by conscience development techniques. If holding by the therapist during this time is effective, there may be momentum toward more constructive interaction. Eventually the holding can and should include the parents, since it is the child-parent relationship that needs enrichment.

Summary

The unattached child who comes into adoption is unable to respond constructively to stability or loving. He is addicted to maintaining chaos and shows skill and imagination toward that goal. Lack of conscience is the hallmark.

Traditional therapy has often been unsuccessful. Hence a unique approach is needed. Because lack of conscience cannot be tolerated, conscience development is urgent. There are techniques that can prove to be helpful.

When some positive interactions begin, therapeutic holding is in order. The goal is to erode the child's need for control in order to allow for reciprocity in the relationship. This is accomplished by requiring the child to share his hurt, rage, fears, and grief in order to establish trust. It requires unconditional love, and faith that it is worth doing. Whether or not the goal is reached, I believe that holding therapy is well worth the effort.

Notes

1. Bowlby, John. *"Attachment and Loss,"* Vol. I Attachment. Basic Books, New York, NY 1969
   Fahlberg, Vera. *Attachment and Separation.* Michigan Department of Social Services, Lansing, MI 1979
   Cline, Foster. *Understanding the Severely Disturbed Child.* Evergreen Consultants in Human Behavior, Evergreen, CO 1979
2. American Psychiatric Association *Diagnostic and Statistical Manual of Mental Disorders,* Washington, D.C. APA, 1980

References

Cline, F. W., *What Shall We Do with this Kid? Understanding and Treating the Severely Disturbed Child,* Evergreen Consultants in Human Behavior, P. O. Box 14, Evergreen, CO

Coleman, J. W., "Forgetfulness of Things Past," *Psychology Today,* October, 1981, Pg. 17

Corrigan, J. W., "Family Advocacy Council Won't Give Up on Tough Kids," *Youth Forum,* Volume 4, Number 3, Fall/Winter, 1980, Pgs. 3–7

Crook, W. G., *Can Your Child Read? Is He Hyperactive?,* 1975, Pedicenter Press, Jackson, TN

"Forest Heights Lodge: Philosophy and Treatment Program," 1982, Forest Hill, Evergreen, Colorado 80439

Forsythe, J. L., *With Family in Mind; Multi-systems Approach to the Treatment of Adoptive Families and Others.*

Freud, A., "The Writings of Anna Freud: Normality and Pathology in Childhood," *Assessments of Development,* Volume 6, International Universities Press, New York, 1965, Pgs. 180–81

Friedan, Driezen, Harris, Shulman and Schoen, "Parent Power: A Holding Technique in the Treatment of Omnipotent Children," *International Journal of Family Counseling,* Spring, 1978, Los Angeles, California

Haley, J., *Uncommon Therapy: The Psychiatric Techniques of Milton Erickson,* 1973, New York, W. W. Morton, Pgs. 214–216

"Hold That Tiger," November 1982, Workshop on holding therapy at the State Annual Conference of the New York State School Social Workers Association

"Holding Therapy: An Ethological Approach," *American Orthopsychiatric Association Newsletter,* April, 1983, Pg. 53. Article about the work of Jane Ferber, M.D., Andrew Ferber, M.D. and Leon Yorburg, M.D. as reported at the Annual Conference Two-Day Training Institute

Mengeot, S. W., "The Impact of Cumulative Trauma in Infancy: Some Treatment Techniques," *Clinical Social Work Journal,* Volume 10, Number 4, Winter, 1982

Napier, A. Y. and C. A. Whitaker, *The Family Crucible: One Family's Therapy,* 1980, Harper and Row, Pgs. 177–87

Nelson, G., "Repairing the Bond," Del Mar Psychiatric Clinic, 240 8th Street, Del Mar, CA 92014

Palumbo, J., "Critical Review of the Concept of the Borderline Child," *Clinical Social Work Journal,* Volume 10, Number 4, Winter, 1982

Saposnek, D. T., "An Experiential Study of Rage-Reduction Treatment of Autistic Children," *Child Psychiatry and Human Development,* 1972, Pgs. 3, 50–61

Spezzano, C. "Prenatal Psychology: Pregnant with Questions," *Psychology Today,* May, 1981, Pgs. 49–57

Swartland, H. M., "Supportive Controls," May 12, 1961. Unpublished paper.

"Temper, Temper, Temper," *New York Times Magazine,* April 12, 1970

Tingergen, N., *Autistic Children: New Hope for a Cure,* Alyn and Unwin Pub., 1983

Yorburg, L. and A. Ferber, *Holding, Hugging, Loving,* 1982. Unpublished book.

Zaslow, R. W., *The Psychology of Z Process: Activation and Attachment,* 1975, San Jose State University, California

Zaslow, R. W. and L. Breger, "A Theory and Treatment of Autism" *Clinical-Cognitive Psychology,* 1969, Englewoods Cliffs, New Jersey

8

Emotional Problems of Neglected Children

Margaret Beyer

Children who are abused or neglected are at risk of emotional problems because of the inadequacies in their early relationships. Children who are removed from home are at even greater risk: they have experienced losses which threaten their connection to the biological family. These emotional problems are the most significant issues in treatment for neglected children of all ages. Caseworkers and therapists who treat neglected children often feel they are in uncharted territory. Their work is made more complex by the need to appreciate both the consequences of early deprivation and the child's crucial process of making peace with the biological family.

The Importance of an Early Relationship with an Adult

To become successful requires at least one early relationship with a reliable, caring adult. Dr. Vera Fahlberg[1] has identified five ways this attachment is essential for the development of the child:

Developing a conscience

Children can only learn about right and wrong in the context of loving relationships. Caretakers let the child know what pleases and displeases them. The child's desire to please those he/she cares about and who care about him/her is the foundation of moral development.

Handling fears

Children normally have fears. If they are protected from the real dangers of the world by a reliable, loving relationship, most of their fears are relatively minor or imagined. By getting over these fears, they learn to manage more frightening situations as they grow up.

Understanding consequences

The idea that behaviors produce logical results comes from the experience of consistent, loving limit-setting. If a child is beaten one day and ignored another day for spilling milk, consequences do not form predictable patterns. Children who have not been consistently responded to when they needed something do not learn about predictability.

Coping with frustration

Handling disappointments or unanticipated obstacles is a learning process. Children learn to tolerate not getting their way by observing the adults around them manage their frustration.

Forming trusting relationships

Children can only learn the rules of friendship, the tolerance of anger and disappointment in relationships, and the meaning of affection through their connection to a reliable, loving adult.

Most children have had *some* relationship early in life. Consequently, almost every child has some of these five skills. But most neglected children lack significant parts of one or more of these crucial skills as a result of inadequacies in their relationships with adults in early childhood.

Symptoms of Early Emotional Losses

How do gaps in these five skills manifest themselves in neglected children? Ten year-old "Jerome" shows the symptoms of early emotional losses. His mother is an addict. He was born when she was 14. He was sexually abused in early childhood by a teenage uncle. His symptoms included:

Fear

Jerome was afraid of adults. He drew terrified drawings, pictures of children carrying clubs that were larger than their bodies. When he went into care his foster parents found that he stole knives and kept them under his pillow and insisted on sleeping with the light on.

School failure

Despite his tested high intelligence, at the age of ten Jerome was a chronic truant and was failing in school. What can explain the discrepancy between his intellectual capacity and his inability to read or do simple calculations? Because of the inconsistencies in his early care, he had great difficulty adjusting to the routines in school. He was impatient and easily distracted. His frustration in school and his mother's lifestyle as an addict were the source of the truancy.

Low self-esteem

How could a ten year old feel worthless? First, Jerome is embarrassed about his failure in school. Most youngsters' cycle of school failure and truancy starts with an intolerable feeling of not being good enough: they do not want to expose their incompetence and thus avoid attending school. Second, Jerome blames himself for the abuse and neglect he received as a child: he believes that he was being punished for being bad. Although they may not verbalize it, neglected children feel ''I wouldn't have been treated this way if I didn't deserve it.'' This belief is a major contributor to self-dislike, which may endure throughout life.

Chronic depression

How could a ten year old be depressed? Jerome doesn't look like a depressed adult. He is boisterous and mischievous, and he appears happy. His main symptom of depression is accident-proneness. He has many more injuries than the typical active ten year old. Furthermore, Jerome's acting-out is misdiagnosed depression. Most children who have experienced major losses are depressed. Their trouble-making gets people angry at them and meets their need for attention.

Uncontrolled anger

Jerome has temper tantrums, which can be terrifying for the people who take care of him because he is a large, aggressive youngster. His temper tantrums are not normal: they are frequent and violent. When Jerome becomes an adolescent, his temper is likely to subside into a confused anger/anxiety state which alternates between explosion and passivity. Jerome is angry at his mother and father for not taking care of him adequately. He has no other outlet for this anger. The hurt he has experienced builds up internally to form a large reservoir of anger. Sometimes as the result of an insignificant precipitating incident, anger flows out of the reservoir in young people like Jerome—terrifying anger that has built up from many rejections, losses, and hurts.[2]

Another influence on this uncontrolled anger is that Jerome grew up in a violent household. He has observed adults abuse each other and him. He has experienced violence as the primary way of handling anger. He has not seen anger talked out successfully. Jerome is not able to say, "I am angry at you. Don't borrow my bike again without asking." He has learned to handle anger by losing control of it and beating someone up if they borrow his bike.

The last aspect of this uncontrolled anger—and what bothers foster parents and child care workers so much—is that Jerome does not seem to have an adequate conscience. He never learned not to be hurtful. If Jerome had a temper tantrum and injured another child in the classroom, he would not understand it if we said to him, "You should not have thrown that at Tommy." His uncontrolled anger does not seem as wrong to him as it does to us.

Attachment and separation

Neglected children are abnormally afraid of losing important adults. Jerome had that fear long before he was removed from home and placed in foster care. He is afraid of loss because of the inconsistency of his relationship with family members. Consequently, he has an almost insatiable hunger for affection. At the same time, Jerome is terrified of trusting others. Many neglected children have an intolerable conflict between their desire for attention and their fear of getting close. Both arise from the losses they have experienced. Although it is a conflict Jerome would be unable to put into words, it consumes considerable emotional energy.

Children who have trouble forming relationships but are also hungry for nurturance are at high risk for substance abuse and early pregnancy. Many adolescents describe feeling high in the same way adults would describe a close relationship—it makes them feel good, it makes them not worry, it makes them feel that they belong. Youth use drugs and alcohol as antidepressants and a substitute for forming a relationship. Young mothers describe a similar sense of feeling good and belonging when they have a baby, at least initially. They feel that they have closeness without the challenge of relating consistently to a peer or an adult. Tragically, substance abuse and early pregnancy usually backfire for these youngsters.

Birth Family as the Lifeline

We have not appreciated the importance of the biological family to the child who has been removed. There is an antifamily bias in child welfare which has grown out of our anger at parents who fail to provide adequate nurturing for their children. Often we do not recognize that we do more damage to the child by punishing the birth parents. Treatment must take into account that removal has threatened the child's lifeline and will have longlasting consequences.

Parents who are immature, are overwhelmed by poverty, and/or are substance abusers can be dangerous to their children. Consequently, the children are removed. Optimally, this would be a short separation. Services would be provided to enable the parent to be more adequate. The family would be quickly reunited and the child would not suffer the damage of losing the parent. But children are typically removed for long periods. The parent often backslides and becomes dangerous again, and the child may be removed several times. These long separations are more complicated if the child has some emotional problems and does not settle down well in a foster family. Administrative reasons also may account for moving from one foster home to another. Thus, a child may experience a series of moves among family members and foster families.

These moves generally make the symptoms worse. Every move makes for more anger, more depression, and more feelings of worthlessness. Each time a child is moved, he/she trusts the next set of adults even less than the last. Having already experienced emotional losses from the inadequate parenting relationship, the child is further traumatized by repeated losses of the parents and other adults as a result of removal and multiple placements.

"Anita" is a young person who exemplifies what happens to the child's relationship with the birth parents as these separations occur. In her record are psychological evaluations of her parents when Anita and her siblings (all under five years old) had been removed as a result of abuse. These assessments indicated that both parents were mentally ill and could not meet the children's needs. Shortly after, the children were returned to the parents, then subsequently removed and put in foster care, and then returned again.

At 15, Anita now has a cycle: she stays two weeks at one group home, two weeks with her mother, two weeks at another group home, and two weeks with her father. One parent is an alcoholic and the other is in and out of a psychiatric hospital. The most recent court report on Anita impatiently asked, "When is Anita going to give up on her parents and settle down?"

Anita is too old for adoption; she has not adjusted well in care since her fifth foster placement broke down; and no family members can provide an acceptable home for her. Consequently, independence is the only option for

Anita. But Anita's cycle demonstrates that she is not doing well at separating from her family, which will impede the progress she can make in moving into independence.

What does Anita want from going back to her clearly inadequate mother and father?

The child's original family is his/her lifeline. The primary connection in life is to their biological family, no matter how limited it is.[3] Anita's family, with whom she has not lived a full year since she was three years old, is her lifeline. Her family is the source of her identity. Anita defines herself by her mother and father. They are where she came from, and her identity derives from who they are. Her sense of herself in the future is connected to her family. Furthermore, Anita's birth family has been a significant source of self-esteem. Her feeling of self-worth, limited as it is, comes from the connection to her mother and father. What she likes about herself are characteristics most likeable about her parents. Despite the fact that she hasn't lived with them for long periods of time, this connection is still her lifeline.

Anita's cycle is explained by her hope that childhood needs will finally be met when she returns to her parents. She can not articulate what she wants and is unaware that her goal is unrealistic, given her parents limitations. Both parents have loved Anita. It would be intolerable emotionally for her to say, "My mom and my dad are never going to love me as I need them to." To give up on that hope would cut off her basic connection. No one else's love will be what she imagines her parents' love to be.

Even youngsters with strong, enduring relationships with foster and adoptive parents have this lifeline to birth parents. The foster/adoptive parent is not inadequate. The relationship with a loving foster/adoptive parent is entirely different from the lifeline connection to birth parents from whom the child has been separated. Even the best foster/adoptive parents cannot replace what the child wants the birth parent to provide.

There is an undeniable continuing relationship with the birth parents when a child age seven or eight years is removed. That connection is there forever. Placing the older child in a foster or adoptive home does not undo this connection. The child prevented from contact with birth parents is more likely to run to them in adolescence when placement breaks down. The failure to help the child make peace with the biological family ultimately may cause disrupted placement. The adolescent search for an independent identity drives them to reassert the original connection, no matter how inadequate the biological parent or how loving the foster/adoptive parent.

In-Home Services

Children who are abused or neglected are at risk of emotional problems throughout their lives. The best treatment is to improve the birth family for the child, with services provided directly to remedy the weaknesses in the parent-child relationship before the emotional problems develop. If we want a child to have the skills to form relationships, if we want a child to know right from wrong, if we want a child to do well in school, we must improve the parent-child relationship as early as possible. We must take the debilitating pressures off the parents so they can be consistently nurturing. Additionally, when children develop depression, low self-esteem and uncontrollable anger, we must reverse these problems by strengthening the parent-child relationship and introducing another caring adult into the home.

In-home counseling services successfully provide both support to the parent and nurturing to the child. These are services by private providers of five to 20 hours weekly for six months to several years, teaching the parent to be more supportive, to establish consistent routines, and to set more effective limits. This relieves some of the pressure on the parent. The cost of in-home counseling is relatively low, comparable to foster care for two children. In-home services not only keep the family together but also prevent subsequent emotional problems in the children.

School failure may be the earliest signal of the emotional problems described above. Of course, there are purely academic causes for repeating a grade, but a neglected child's emotional problems are often the cause of school failure and truancy. These signs may be ignored by school staff, who know little about the child's home situation, and by social service and mental health staff, who know little about the school situation. In-home counseling services can be most effective if they are offered to the family by school and social service staff who have recognized early school failure as a symptom of emotional problems.

Treatment for the Child

How much of the early damage done to Anita and Jerome can be undone? Can Anita at age 14 learn to have a close, trusting relationship? Can Jerome at age 10 learn to control his anger, to recognize right from wrong, and to be less fearful? The treatment of these emotional problems in neglected children requires therapists, workers, and foster and adoptive parents to develop five techniques, which may be more active than traditional therapeutic approaches to which they were exposed in their training:

1. Treatment through teaching

Foster parents, child care workers, and adoptive parents offer primary treatment for many neglected children, through their consistent love and their roles as teachers. They recognize that they cannot undo the early damage that comes from having an inadequate nurturing relationship in childhood. They compensate for that damage by teaching young people like Jerome and Anita the skills they have lost or only partially developed.

The older youngster is taught anger management or relationship building skills in different ways than he/she would have learned them at home in childhood. This teaching occurs through daily activities as the child learns to deal with frustration without being terrified about another loss, to trust that he/she will be picked up at school on time as promised, and to overcome fears of the dark.

Foster and adoptive families will face a long, painful struggle in working with children like Anita or Jerome because of the emotional damage that has occurred. At the age of 10 Jerome is a time bomb: he is potentially dangerous and has shown the early symptoms of uncontrollable anger, depression and low self-esteem that are likely to become major emotional problems in adolescence. Anita denies her problems and is self-destructive. However, the teaching role is an effective way to help Jerome and Anita overcome their emotional problems.

2. Enabling the child to make peace with the biological family

Children like Jerome and Anita have a combination of rage against birth parents for what they did not receive and a tremendous protectiveness of their birth parent. The child cannot tolerate criticism of the birth parent which is implied by the foster/adoptive parent, who is in many ways the better parent. When the child still has not come to terms with the inadequacies of the birth parent, the foster/adoptive parents face a difficult (and unintended) competitive situation between themselves and the birth parents.

The foster/adoptive parents, workers and therapists provide loving and teaching in the context of the child's lifeline to their birth parent. They help the child understand why the parent was abusive or neglectful. They stop the child from blaming him/herself for abuse/neglect. They help the child form his/her identity around the strengths of the birth family while accepting its major limitations. The foster/adoptive parents encourage the child's relationship with the birth family. At the same time, they give the child permission to move beyond the birth family in their aspirations.

3. Helping neglected children improve their self-esteem

Neither Anita nor Jerome has been really good at anything. Survival alone has consumed most of their energy. They approach most situations feeling inferior, although they often cover their uncertainty with an image of "looking good." Their inexperience with competence and their expectation of being inadequate make them pessimistic about the future. No one has encouraged a talent in either that would hold out the possibility of future achievement.

In order to improve their self-esteem, Anita and Jerome must come to terms with racism and sexism. Being a young minority member in this society means feeling inferior. Therapists, workers, foster/adoptive parents, and child care staff must help young people see their own potential in a culture which continues to deny minorities access to success. Although oppression is a real obstacle, Anita and Jerome can have much more control over their own success than they believe.

Each young person needs to be successful at something, and needs support to pursue something long enough to become successful. Being good at something is the best antidote to low self-esteem. Being good at one thing, with support, usually leads to becoming good at several things. Gordon[4] suggests that for vulnerable students who have low self-esteem and are poor readers, who are depressed, alienated, passive, and who seek immediate pleasure in drugs, the key element of self-esteem building programs must be *action* of some sort: learning something new; being recognized for an accomplishment; helping someone more vulnerable. His approach emphasizes exercise and involvement. These active steps are especially needed to help youth give up their helplessness and think of themselves in the future[5].

4. Helping neglected children form trusting relationships

Some young people who have grown up in care would say that their lack of trust has been an important survival skill. They have not been permitted to depend on others to get their needs met consistently, and they are chronically hungry for the nurturance they missed in childhood. As adolescents they stubbornly resist closeness with anyone, fearing more disappointment in getting their true needs met.

As they mature, these vulnerable adolescents are presented with a double bind[6]. On the one hand they are expected to sever relationships. They are losing their foster families. They are losing their workers. They may be leaving school. On the other hand they are encouraged to establish new relationships, an artificial "adult support system." Most other adolescents are allowed to take some of their old family relationships into their new adulthood, which makes the transition much smoother. It is no wonder that adolescents in care are untrusting and ask, "Why risk getting hurt in a new relationship?"

Workers and therapists play important roles in the life of a neglected child by offering a continuing relationship. Making the commitment to an untrusting child requires tolerance of excessive dependency and unpredictable rejection. However, this sustaining relationship is crucial for the child's development, to "...ensure that these young people have substitutes for significant adults they may have had to let go of. ...One of the major challenges facing the caseworker is mustering the skills that are necessary in order to enable the youngster to deal with 'letting go' by 'holding on'. ...The work is demanding and time-consuming. ...The caseworker in many instances becomes the most significant person in the young person's life." (Anderson and Simonitch, p. 385)[7]

5. Giving permission to neglected children

Workers and therapists also play an important role in clearing the way for the young person to recuperate from the emotional damage of early neglect by giving:

Permission not to blame self for the hurt of the past
Permission to succeed (and not to view success as a criticism of the biological family)
Permission to accept the strengths and weaknesses of the biological parents
Permission to feel close to and separate from peers, parents, and other adults
Permission to feel conflicting loyalties about birth family and foster/adoptive families
Permission to feel anger and sadness without being out of control

Mental health theory and practice are far behind in addressing the special problems of children like Jerome and Anita which result from limited nurturing and the continuing emotional connection to their biological families. Few mental health professionals have specialized in this kind of treatment. Few staff in treatment facilities can tolerate the uncontrolled anger and relentless self-dislike of these children. Working with emotionally disturbed neglected children is extremely demanding. Attention must be given to the needs of foster/adoptive parents, caseworkers, child care workers, and therapists. They must have regular support for this draining work. When a child who has always been a victim gets permission to feel entitled to more, the resulting bitterness for a lifetime of deprivation may be taken out initially on caring adults. These adults need to get refueled to tolerate the ups and downs of the neglected child's struggle. Fortunately, children as damaged as Jerome and Anita do receive the love they need from foster/adoptive parents, caseworkers, child care workers, and therapists. They learn skills not developed in early childhood; they make peace with the past; their self-esteem improves; they form trusting relationships; and they get permission for their feelings, their conflicting loyalties, and their future success.

Notes

1. Fahlberg, Vera, M.D. *Attachment and Separation: A Workbook.* Project CRAFT-Adoption Training Project, 1979.
2. Viscott describes a child's anger over the death of his beloved dog: "Expressing anger over the hurt that causes it allows an emotional wound to close . . . the youngster naturally began to seek out objects he could get angry at: first, the driver of the automobile, then the automobile, and then even a little at himself . . . Next he shifted the blame from himself to his parents, and finally, much diluted by time, the anger was directed at the dog . . . If any loss is to heal in the best and most complete way, the anger it generates needs to be allowed full freedom of expression." pp. 82–3. Viscott, David, M.D. *The Language of Feelings.* 1976: Pocket Books, New York.
3. Littner describes the foster child's need to recreate their biological parents "to master the unacceptable feelings of anger at his own parents and his guilt about these feelings by reproducing the situation in which they first occurred, as a form of self-punishment to alleviate his guilt." p. 18. He refers to the child's concern that "loving his new parents implies disloyalty to the old." p. 13. Littner, Ner, M.D. *Some Traumatic Effects of Separation and Placement.* New York: Child Welfare League of America, 1976.

    Fernando Colon describes the need for "rootedness" for displaced children. "The child's experience of biological familial continuity and connection is a basic and fundamental ingredient of the sense of self and personal significance." p. 241. Colon, Fernando, "Family Ties and Child Placement," *Family Process.* vol. 17, 1978, p. 289–312.

    Suzanne Tiddy summarizes the contributions of family therapy research to understanding the importance of the biological family to the child in placement. She describes the dangers for children who have been emotionally cut off from biological parents. "The way . . . to finish the unfinished business is to maintain or establish some form of contact and enable the children and their parents to work through their intense pain and confusion. p. 55. She describes the child's creation of fantasy parents as a "natural defense mechanism to cope with the separation trauma. The result is the inability of the child to integrate into the foster family and gain from the corrective and remedial benefits of a healthier family system." p. 55. She concludes that "The adoptive or foster child is in reality experiencing life in two (or more) family systems. We cannot deny the existence of one or the other; the placed child carries the imprint of the biological family and it is basic to the child's identity. If we do not try to understand this, or if we suppress it, we . . . have the placed child enacting within the foster family the role—usually dysfunctional—that the child carried in the biological family.' p. 55. She goes on to discuss the anger of the child at the biological parent: " . . . the source of this anger is frequently beyond the child's awareness because it is usually too powerful to admit or deal with. It, too, is associated with the child's frustrating efforts to preserve loyality to the family: to become angry would further jeopardize their precarious position with their parents. It is thus displaced on others or deeply internalized." p. 57. "One way to break through these conflicts is to go beyond visiting, to involve the biological family in therapy sessions with the child and perhaps the foster parents . . . Both the child and parents are much relieved . . . In this process, we must carefully address the needs of the foster family, with compassion for their position. They probably have already received the brunt of the child's displaced anger—

especially the foster mother,'' pp. 58–9. She sensitively describes the case studies and the steps of involving biological parents.

    Tiddy, Suzanne, ''Creative Cooperation; Involving Biological Parents in Long-Term Foster Care,'' *Child Welfare,* Vol. LXL, Number 1, January-February, 1986. pp. 53–62.

4. Gordon described vulnerable teenagers as having poor self-images and feeling inferior, inadequate or insecure. He has concluded that vulnerable teenagers are the most prone to engage in irresponsible behavior which tends to be destructive and irrational. Gordon, Sol, and Kathleen Everly, ''Increasing Self-Esteem in Vulnerable Students,'' *Impact '85.* The Institute for Family Research and Education, Syracuse University.

5. Clark, Clemes and Bean emphasize the need for an adolescent to have power in order to raise self-esteem: ''Let an adolescent know he is responsible for what he feels, explain and demonstrate how he can take charge of the way he reacts to people and events. Show him that he does not have to be a victim of other people's words, attitudes, or actions. When he wants to blame others for his own difficulties, direct his awareness back to his own choices and possibilities in the situation,'' p. 59. Clark, Aminah, Harris Clemes, and Reynold Bean. *How to Raise Teenager's Self-Esteem.* Enrich: 1980, San Jose.

6. Schachter describes a return to the early childhood separation process from parent, acted out as greater closeness with child care staff evolves. ''A new sense of disappointment, disillusionment and rage is followed by renewed distancing . . . [which] reflects the resident's eternal yearning for the perfect, caring, symbiotic parent never experienced.

    The feeling of having been cheated out of one's legitimate entitlements persists through the years—sometimes dormant, sometimes acutely active,' p. 296. Schachter, Burt, ''Treatment of Older Adolescents in Transitional Programs: Rapprochement Crisis Revisited,'' *Clinical Social Work Journal,* Vol. 6, No 4, 1978, pp. 293–304.

7. This confusion of feelings is described by Anderson and Simonitch in an article on depression in youth moving toward independence: ''Reactive depression appears to be a common reaction to emancipation among the youths involved in the Independent Living Subsidy Program (Oregon) . . . Reactive depression of some degree is always a response to loss or disappointment. The reaction varies in intensity and duration, depending upon the young person's personality strength, reconstitutive ability, and capacity to compensate for losses and disappointments . . . Too much deprivation, misfortune, or constitutional lack of adaptive capacity can lead to an essential lack of personality strength and a tendency to collapse into a reactive depression when facing even the most ordinary losses and disappointments of living. . . .'' p. 385. Anderson, James L. and Brian Simonitch, ''Reactive Depression in Youths Experiencing Emancipation,'' *Child Welfare,* Volume LX, Number 6, June, 1981.

9

Parental Management of Anger and Emotional Anxiety in the Adopted Child

Earl T. Braxton

Adoptive and/or foster care children have the same basic needs as other children, with one additional factor. Children who do not grow up with their birth parents must struggle with questions about whether they are really wanted and whether the reason the original parents let them go was that something was wrong with them. The logic of wondering whether the parents had a problem is too sophisticated for young children, and only becomes a real possibility at a later, less egocentric stage of development. The feeling that the birthing parent did not want them becomes a wound to the ego, which may be repressed, denied, or defended against.

Children's perceptions in the present are inevitably influenced by their sense of personal history, making any child who has lost access to natural parents, for whatever reasons, subject to wondering about his or her own validity and worth. It is difficult to risk growing and moving on in life if there has not been some healing of the basic wound to the self. The child questions, "Why am I not with them? Who are they? What did I do to deserve being left like this? Does anyone out there know I am here, or even care?" This condition can be healed to greater or lesser degrees depending on whether and how soon the child finds a center in his life where a loving adult or adults provide a secure base from which the child can move and grow.

Joining a Family

This paper is concerned primarily with adoptions that occur at an age when the child is aware of the process. In that case the child is said to be joining a

111

new family system, a process which requires careful attention on the part of the adoptive parents.

Joining is a psychological and emotional process during which the child develops feelings of acceptance and belonging. It requires two separate mechanisms, both of which are quite demanding of the child and the family: (1) In order to separate, one must let go of something or someone, becoming free from the other party in order to reconnect. It requires the child to feel the loss and acknowledge the empty space left by the absence of someone or something. It requires an inner as well as an outer healing. (2) Joining, on the other hand, requires letting go of illusions of separateness and giving up a part of ones self in order to be a part of something greater. In joining a new family, each child, at some level, decides what part of himself to bring into the family system or to leave out. This unconscious and usually unspoken decision will be a major determining factor as to how long it will take for a child to make a healthy adjustment to the adopting family.

A child with any attachment to a previous family system or person will not readily give up that attachment, no matter how attractive the new system may seem. Since children's attachments are not based on logic or rational standards, but rather on basic levels of emotional gratification, the attachment can be to the peer group of an institution, if that was the primary source of emotional gratification in an otherwise empty world. The sense that forming new attachments is a betrayal of the earlier one may cause the child to withhold acceptance and to sabotage the joining process. He or she may do something to push the adoptive parents away each time they act to establish any connection or link. Since children are masterful at learning what will aggravate or anger an adult, it is not hard for them to behave in ways that alienate the new parents and cause emotional distancing. The sad part is that the bond with the previous parental object(s) is rarely a reality outside of the child's creation. What this means is that the adopting family needs to be sensitive to the child, recognizing that patience and love will provide the most important impetus to a child's completion of the transition from one system to another.

The way the family handles this transition or joining process sets the tone for working with later problems that may crop up in the child's relationships. Although adopting parents may feel the need for their new child to be healthy, happy, and well adjusted to their family as soon as possible, they may also need to face some of the symptoms of unresolved emotional conflict in addition to enjoying the pleasure of parenting their new child.

In some cases, a child will try to hide areas in which he or she is troubled by trying to merge with the new-found family, but it will only be a matter of time before his or her true feelings will surface. Some children do seem to become comfortable in a new setting rather quickly. However, adoptive and/or foster parents ought to be aware that there is often an early adjustment period sometimes referred to as the "honeymoon," during which things may go exceptionally smoothly. When they first begin living in a new situation, children do not know what to expect; so they hold themselves in check until they think they know the rules for "surviving" in this new environment. After that, each child tests the new situation in whatever ways fit his or her own personality, temperament, and relative security. When the testing starts, the honeymoon is over and parents may experience disappointment. However, the testing is inevitable, and new parents should be prepared for it. It is the "real" beginning of the joining process.

Sometimes children who have had destructive or painful experiences with natural parents, foster parents, or institutions try to obliterate them by disconnecting from them or denying that they ever existed. Children who behave in this manner should be gently encouraged to talk about their feelings, but should be allowed to maintain their illusions until their egos can absorb the reality that it is safe to make a new connection, and that one connection can exist without detracting from the other. Without the adoptive parents' patient persistence, the child's conflict may be prolonged until it becomes a full-fledged identity crisis in later years. In order for the child to become an uncompromised member of his adopted family, he or she must acknowledge membership in the family of origin and integrate the past with the present.

Expressing Anger

Separation and joining are accompanied by anger and anxiety in most people. I am referring not only to the child's anger, but also to the anger and anxiety generated throughout the family system. Anger in our culture is often treated as an undesirable emotion and either kept under tight control or unleashed inappropriately. The task for the adoptive family is to find ways to channel the anger and to deal with it effectively. Understanding its nature, therefore, is a necessary beginning. However, anger is not what it seems. Beneath it are more powerful emotions which the anger usually masks— feelings of (a) fear, (b) vulnerability, or (c) pain.

In our society, anger is considered unpleasant and a sign of being out of control. As a result, it is often kept under rigid control until a sufficient stimulus causes breaks in the control, leading to irrational, sometimes violent outbursts or periodic leaks of passive-aggressive hostility. However, for most people the underlying emotions are even less accessible than the anger. It is easier to express anger than any of the emotions underneath, because vulnerability also creates feelings of powerlessness. When a child feels insecure or powerless, he or she may demonstrate inner agitation through angry outbursts or reactive behavior such as withdrawal, or oppositional tactics. The difficulty parents face is that of helping children to verbalize the causative feelings in order to relieve some of the impetus to act out anger rather than express anger, in combination with fear, vulnerability, or pain.

Each family establishes its own standards for handling angry energy. The parents bring their own upbringing to the family and give their children messages about what is acceptable and what is not. They accomplish this through expression of attitudes and behaviors that set the family's standards. Each child then finds his or her place in the family system based on individual characteristics and environmental influences. The adopted child may already have a model for expressing anger or other feelings—a model that differs from that of the family which he or she is joining. Thus, the stage may be set for a difficult adjustment if the two models are too far removed from each other. Because of this complexity it may be helpful to examine the role of anger and its expression in the family per se, before going on to discuss its place in the joining process.

Causes of Anger

Anger is the emotion of separation, distancing, and differentiating. When a developing child is beginning to sense his or her separateness and difference from the parent, there is both the fear of loss of the nurturing object and the need to discover where the boundaries are between the parent and the child. In order to do this, children "push" and test the space between them and the parents. This happens early on, in the phase called the "terrible twos." The reason they are so "terrible" is that children during that period are highly oppositional and very testy in relation to the parent. They are trying to determine for themselves what the space is like between them and the parents.

Anger always accompanies separation. It brings vulnerability, pain, and the fear of loss, often expressed by the forceful push and the word "No"—the single most important word in the two-year-old's limited vocabulary. Anger is increased when parents try to restrict beyond what is reasonable or good for the child. The more a child has to struggle to get free from the feeling of fusion and enmeshment with the parent, the angrier and more oppositional that child becomes. He or she has to get separate and find his own space with the parent in order to reconnect as a whole person. That process may be blocked by parents who either (a) do not know how to give the child space without feeling their authority as parents is being eroded, or (b) do not know how to set limits without feeling that they're being too hard on the child. When that happens, children have difficulty developing a whole self with both their thinking and feeling capacities intact.

Anger, therefore, can also be an expected part of the joining process of a new family, since joining requires giving up some part of yourself in order to be a part of something larger. For some children it is also having to let go of past ties in order to allow the building of new ones.

In the joining process, anger, because it is a pushing emotion, becomes much more threatening. Due to an insufficient sense of connectedness, the newly adopted child may be reluctant to express that aspect of him- or herself in the early stages of the relationship. Parents ought to be suspicious of the child who complies with everything and presents no problems even after the normal honeymoon phase described above. Every child has a healthy, even necessary "No" buried inside, and if the child cannot find it, he or she may be giving up too much of the self to please the system, rather than risking assertion and learning who he or she is within that system. The need for the parents to set firm *but permeable* boundaries cannot be over-emphasized, and the willingness to engage the child's "No" without destroying it or capitulating to it is critical.

Dealing with Anger

Some children may begin expressing the angry feelings as a way of giving the message, "I'll leave you before you leave me." Others may invite the parents to put them out as a self-fulfilling prophesy, proving "You did not want me in the first place." A child who comes into a new family situation and immediately begins expressing anger or pushing-away behavior is giving the parents a signal that something is wrong. It may be a cry for help, a reaction to the fear of being rejected again, or a misdirected attempt to connect in the only way with which the child is really familiar. The invitation from the child is for the parents to react by becoming angry in return or by pushing back against the child.

Aside from holding the boundaries as a parent and giving a clear, firm, but supportive message about what the expectations are in the new system, the adopting parents should immediately confer with the child. They need to reassure him or her that this new experience he is having is a manageable one, and to try to discover what the fear is underneath the behavior.

Anger also takes other forms in the newly-developing parent/child relationship. Children who cannot have their own way and are discovering the limits in a new environment may attempt several different maneuvers. Splitting the parents, playing one against the other, is a common ploy which takes parents off guard. It results from a parenting pair's not having a good pattern of communication between them prior to the child's arrival. Parents must have a mutually clear understanding of what the working rules are for the house and a commitment to work together toward them. They must also recognize the differences between them, and acknowledge them openly so that children cannot exploit those differences for disruptive or manipulative purposes.

Splitting is one way a child who is determining how to join a new family and carving out a role can reduce the power of a healthy parental coalition and thereby enhance his or her own. However, it is a losing outcome all around. The child ultimately grows to resent the parents who let him win such a game, because the price for winning is the loss of parental security. The boundaries of the living environment are not safe, because the child has found the holes in it and is now at the mercy of his own uncertain and sometimes dangerous ego boundaries.

Sometimes anger takes the form of withdrawal: reduced communication, less interaction with people, or a pulling back from self-assertive action. Children joining a new family system may have already developed a way of handling angry and hostile feelings by cutting them off and refusing to feel anything. The child who cuts feelings off may be too frightened by such feelings. He or she may have rage that is too intense to tolerate, due to previous violations or abandonments. Often there is no indication of the problem until a crisis arises in which the cutoff is so dramatic that it cannot be ignored. These children are in serious trouble with themselves and are at risk. They need to be encouraged and supported in rediscovering their feelings and learning how to tolerate small doses at a time until they can own what is inside of them.

Anger may also take the form of depression: anger turned inward. In depression the child does not cut off feelings, but rather slowly chokes off the life energy that feeds all the emotions. This results in cutting off the life energy to the body, and the depression manifests itself as tiredness, listlessness, and loss of energy. Interest and concentration wane, and the child may show symptoms of loss of interest in taking care of him or herself. Depression can be intermittent, a steady decline, or have the quality of mood swings. In its extreme it can lead to suicidal or self destructive activities. Children who are depressed basically need access to their rage and their right to ask for what they want. As long as they have no inner access to their anger, they will feel powerless and helpless. Adopting parents ought to be sensitive to this condition; and if they suspect their child is suffering from it, take him for help right away. Drugs alone should not be considered adequate help, and if a pharmaceutical approach is used at all for depression, it should be short term and accompanied by therapy that makes the anger available to the child.

Angry children may also set parents up to pursue them by either running away or disappearing for brief periods of time. This behavior should be treated by the adopting parents as symptomatic, and the goal should be to get at the cause. Going after the child who runs early in a transitional family situation is very important. The child is sending a message by his running, and the parents are also delivering one if they don't pursue the child when they have the opportunity.

Other symptomatic behaviors may be: acting out in school; over-or under-eating; difficulty sleeping at increased agitation or irritation with peer group and/or with parents; getting into fights; stealing; lying. If the adopting parents treat these behaviors as symptoms, they can discover what the causational feelings are underneath the behavior.

Much of what sends children into acting-out behavior has to do with the emotional turmoil or anxiety they experience inside of themselves. Adults too frequently fail to recognize that the more children are hurting inside, the greater the propensity for symptomatic and acting-out behavior. The child may wish to inflict on others that which he or she experiences inside of themselves, and they frequently choose those closest to them as targets.

Security

Children joining a new emotional system are very concerned with the safety of that system. If their own impulses are not sufficiently under control or there is any turmoil in their own inner space, they need to know that the family system can provide some reasonably firm limits within the context of a caring and nurturing environment. It is inevitable that children will test those boundaries—so parents ought to be prepared for the testing. Too often the parent takes the testing personally and fails to recognize such pushing as a normal part of the joining experience.

Children, in order to be free to express their differences, must feel sure that the parents will not be threatened and disappear (no boundaries or limits) or become authoritarian and dictatorial (too many nonnegotiable and rigid boundaries). The parental skill that incorporates healthy boundaries is *negotiation*. Parents need to be clear enough to delineate limits but flexible enough to give some leeway to encourage responsibility as growth in the situation merits it. It is a fine line, and the risk is to err on either side. Yet, teaching children how to negotiate can provide them with a sense of both freedom and responsibility. There should be no negotiations until children learn the meaning of responsibility and take it seriously. Only then does the freedom become meaningful enough to expand the boundaries in the family system on their behalf.

Case Study

Debbie was an attractive fourteen year old White female who had lost both parents in a recent flood disaster in her home community. After she had stayed with relatives for a short time, her behavior deteriorated until they felt they could no longer manage her. She began having bad dreams, acting out in school, and drinking to the point of being totally dysfunctional. She also had episodes during which she threw things and was verbally violent. This was relatively new behavior for Debbie, so it was surprising to the relatives. The final blow for them was that she began dating members of ethnic and racial groups of which they did not approve. Hence Debbie was placed in a group home.

The group home parents were comfortable with Debbie, until she began to express her anger. Then she appeared hyperactive, talked incessantly, paced the floor when she became agitated, and easily exploded into impulsive attacks with little warning. At such times she would pick up anything she could easily throw and launch it in any direction. She did not necessarily aim at a person although that was unpredictable. Debbie had also been suicidal. She had taken an overdose of sleeping pills and made numerous other suicidal gestures. The group home parents were frightened.

The therapist assigned to the home established a relationship with Debbie by making it clear that she (Debbie) was wanted and that, although they were there to insure she did not harm herself or others, she had a perfect right to be angry. She discovered by spending time with Debbie that whenever the loss of her parents and the experience around the flood came up, Debbie would refuse to talk and would either leave or threaten violence if there was any prodding.

The therapist first worked toward getting Debbie's trust. She found small ways to connect with Debbie. They discussed areas of common interest, such as Debbie's relationships with boys, with which she seemed obsessed. At this time she was choosing abusive young men, with whom she would fight. Clearly they represented self–destructive relationships and potential disapproval of the house parents.

The therapist made herself available to listen and provide a nonjudgmental but nevertheless parental viewpoint. She emphasized how much more deserving Debbie was of respect and appreciation than what she was getting. She also made it clear that she was not afraid of Debbie's anger, and on at least one occasion talked her out of a potentially explosive episode.

The therapist spent time with the parents helping them remain firm about the rules and standards for the home while giving Debbie alternatives and choices for working on her anger. The hardest part of the experience for the house parents was dealing with their own wish to control Debbie's anger by punishment and withholding. The therapist had to help the parents recognize that most of the behavior they were seeing in Debbie was aimed at defending herself from the intense pain she felt around the loss of her parents.

The therapist realized that Debbie had internalized the feelings, "What is wrong with me that my parents had to leave me like this?" and "What did I do wrong to deserve being left?" She was inviting other people to punish her, she was punishing herself, and her anger was related to the sense of abandonment by those who were close to her. The therapist therefore encouraged Debbie to express the anger more directly, to connect it with the losses in her life, and to still feel accepted and loved by those charged with her welfare. Yet the rules had to be clear, and Debbie had to be held responsible for her behavior when she broke them. Otherwise, the environment would not feel safe to Debbie. By the therapist's being comfortable with Debbie's anger, she could help the parents work on their discomfort with it.

When Debbie discovered she could trust the adults not to run away or use punishment to control her inappropriately, she was able to work on the real source of her problem, the pain of loss and the feeling of abandonment. It is important to note that Debbie damaged the home, stayed out with strange men, and cursed out both the therapist and the parents numerous times before she was willing to face her own inner pains. It is equally important to note that when this began to happen, the therapist as well as the new parents were there to offer friendly hands—the same hands Debbie had bitten more than once previously.

When sufficient attention is paid to the joining process, the parents will see clues that will point to the child's adjustment in the family. Incidents of boundary violations will gradually subside and the child will eventually settle into behavior with fewer peaks and valleys, allowing the parents to take on their parenting roles with him or her.

This does not mean that problems will cease. On the contrary, it may mean that the child, once having discovered that he has a reliable backstop who will not abandon him when he pushes, can begin to let parents see who he really is and trust that they will help him and not be put off by him. It will free him up to show more of his vulnerable side.

Each child will give and take the love offered within the limits of his own personality and inner resources. If the adoptive parents can accept their new child at whatever level they find him/her, they will be able to forge a parent-child relationship which respects the integrity of both of them, enabling them to take up their respective roles with increased responsibility and showing that the child can handle increased freedom or autonomy. The parents can then enjoy the difficult but rewarding experience of having provided a place of love, with structures to match, and the satisfaction of knowing they have helped their family to face the challenge of absorbing a new member.

References

Braxton, Earl T., *Structuring the Black Family for Survival & Growth; Perspectives in Psychiatric Care,* XIV 1976, 165–173.

Fogarity, Thomas S., *On Emptiness & Closeness: The Family,* Part I, Vol. III (2) 1984, 3–12.

Riese, Hertha, *Heal the Hurt Child,* Chicago, University of Chicago Press, 1962.

Tavris, Carol, *Anger: The Misunderstood Emotion,* New York, Simon & Schuster, 1982.

Another factor that may be implicated in the adjustment problems of adopted children is the role of attachment relationships to adoptive parents. Research with nonadoptive families has shown that the development of a secure, emotional attachment to caregivers (usually parents) is important for healthy psychological adjustment, not only in infancy, but in later childhood as well (Arend, Gove, & Sroufe, 1979; Lewis, Feiring, McGuffog, & Jaskir, 1984; Matas, Arend, & Sroufe, 1978; Sroufe & Waters, 1977; Waters, Wippman, & Sroufe, 1979).

Recently, Brodzinsky (1985) has argued that secure attachments in adoptive families may be undermined by the complications and problematic nature of the transition to adoptive parenthood (see also, Kirk, 1964). For example, infertile couples who have not adequately resolved their feelings about their biological condition may begin to resent one another and/or their adopted child, and in so doing create a family atmosphere that hinders the emergence of basic trust and security. A second hurdle in the transition to adoptive parenthood and the establishment of a secure parent–child relationship is the uncertainty and anxiety surrounding the timing of the adoption process. Unlike biological parents who know, once conception has occurred, when the baby will arrive (give or take a few weeks), adoptive parents often have to wait years for a baby to become available for adoption. Moreover, those individuals who adopt through sanctioned agencies must also undergo a rather extensive evaluation by agency personnel—a process that most parents find highly intrusive and anxiety arousing. It has also been suggested that adoptive parents have fewer appropriate role models for parenthood than biological parents, and are less likely to receive wholehearted support for adoption, as opposed to giving birth, from significant others—extended family, friends, neighbors, and so on. These experiences may make the transition to parenthood somewhat more difficult for adoptive parents by undermining their confidence in their ability to handle the normal problems associated with adoption. In turn, this could very well disrupt the parent-child attachment process. Another factor assumed to affect the adoptive parent-child relationship is the child's preplacement history. In cases where the child has spent a considerable amount of time with the biological parents prior to placement (and hence has become attached to them), and/or when the child has experienced a series of foster homes (and hence has not been able to establish a consistent relationship with any caregiver), the development of a warm and secure socioemotional relationship with adoptive parents may be jeopardized. Furthermore, to the extent that immediate post-delivery contact between the infant and its parents is important for their later attachment relationship (Klaus & Kennell, 1976), adoptive parents and their children should be at a disadvantage because they do not experience such contact. Finally, in cases of interracial adoption, parents may find it more difficult to identify with their children because of the obvious dissimilarities between their own physiognomic features and those of their children. Interracial adoption also is likely to be associated with decreased social support by significant others.

To date, only two research studies on the attachment relationships of adopted children and their parents have been reported, both of which involved longitudinal examinations of young children separated from their parents and subsequently reared in adoptive homes. Yarrow and his associates (Yarrow, 1965; Yarrow & Goodwin, 1973; Yarrow, Goodwin, Manheimer, & Milowe, 1973) found that socioemotional difficulties following separation from biological parents were quite common among adopted infants. In fact, these researchers reported that all infants separated after 6–7 months of age showed evidence of social–emotional maladjustment. In addition, in a 10 year follow-up study, many of the children separated after 6 months were still showing some signs of psychological problems, especially in their "capacity to establish different levels of relationships with people."

A second line of research has been reported by Tizard and her associates (Tizard, 1977; Tizard & Joseph, 1970; Tizard & Rees, 1974, 1975). In this case, the research focused on the impact of institutional rearing and subsequent restitution with biological parents, or adoption placement, on the adjustment of children. Tizard found that 2-year-old children from institutions were more clinging and more diffuse in their attachments than children reared from birth by their biological parents. At 4 years of age, the institutional children were still more clinging and had more difficulty establishing deep social attachments. They also tended to be overly friendly and attention seeking with others. Similar patterns of behavior continued to be evident at 8 years of age, especially in school.

The findings reported by Yarrow and Tizard suggest that at least under some conditions (particularly placement beyond the first 6–12 months), adopted children may manifest problems in the establishment of secure social-emotional relationships to caregivers and other significant figures in their lives. Although these studies provide useful insights into the issue of separation effects in adoption, they leave many questions unanswered, primarily because of their methodological limitations. The Yarrow studies, for example did not include a control group of nonadopted infants. Thus, the research provides no basis for determining whether there is any difference between adoptive and nonadoptive families in the quality of their attachment relationships. In addition, Tizard focused on a very select group of subjects— children initially reared in institutions and then adopted in later childhood (or returned to biological parents). Since most children who are adopted do not experience this form of rearing, it is questionable whether the results of this research can be generalized to the larger population of adopted children.

The present study combines data from two samples of adopted infants in order to address four specific questions. First, to what extent is the quality of mother-infant attachment in adoptive families comparable to that found in nonadoptive families? Second, is the quality of attachment in adoptive families related to the racial/ethnic similarity between mother and infant? Third, how does the timing of the adoption placement influence the development of attachment between infants and their mothers? Fourth, do mothers of adopted infants receive differential amounts of caretaking and emotional support from their husbands, extended family, and friends than nonadoptive mothers, and if so, does this affect the quality of mother-infant attachment?

Method

Subjects.   The present sample combines subjects who were observed in two recent Ph.D. Dissertations (Singer, 1983; Steir, 1982). Singer's sample consisted of 36 adoptive and 20 nonadoptive families from the suburban New Jersey/New York City area. Subjects from Steir's sample included 10 adoptive and seven nonadoptive families recruited from the metropolitan New York City Area. The latter 17 families were included in the analyses reported below in order to increase the power of statistical comparisons between adoptive and nonadoptive samples. Overall, the families were predominantly from middle-class backgrounds.

The total sample consisted of 27 nonadopted infants (12 girls and 15 boys), 27 intraracial adopted infants (12 girls and 15 boys), and 19 interracial adopted infants (14 girls and 5 boys). All of the nonadopted infants and their parents were Caucasian. With two exceptions, the intra-racial adopted infants and their parents also were Caucasian. The two exceptions involved a black infant living with black parents and an Oriental infant living with Oriental parents. The inter-racial adopted group was composed of 12 Oriental and seven Hispanic or Latin American Indian infants, all living in Caucasian families. All of the infants were only children, between 13 and 18 months of age, and were from intact, two-parent families. Infants were rated by their mothers as being healthy at the time of the study.

The adopted infants were placed for adoption between 3 days and 10 months following birth, with a mean age of 1 month, 9 days for the intraracial group and 3 months, 25 days for the inter-racial group. Twelve of the infants in the intraracial group were placed for adoption within the first month of life, 9 between 1 and 3 months, and six between 3 and 6 months. In the interracial adoptive group, two of the infants were placed within the first month, five between 1 and 3 months, 10 between 3 and 6 months, and two between 6 months and 1 year. All of the adopted infants had been living with their adoptive parents for a minimum of 4 months at the time of observation (M = 11 months, 29 days).

Preliminary analyses indicated that the three groups of infants did not differ significantly with respect to infant's age, parental education, father's age, and family SES. The only difference in demographics between the groups was that adoptive mothers were older than nonadoptive mothers—a finding that is very common in adoption research (see Table 1).

Adopted infants were recruited through adoption agencies, adoptive parent organizations, newspaper advertisements, and by word of mouth. Nonadopted infants were recruited through newspaper advertisements and by word of mouth.

Procedure. Individual differences in quality of attachment were assessed using the Strange Situation paradigm, a standardized procedure that has been validated extensively (Ainsworth, Blehar, Waters, & Wall, 1978; Waters et al., 1979). On the basis of videotape recordings of the Strange Situation behavior, infants were assigned to one of three attachment groups: (A) avoidant, (B) secure, and (C) ambivalent. Avoidance involves turning, looking, or moving away from or ignoring the caregiver upon reunion. Secure

TABLE 1

A Comparison of Demographic Characteristics for the Nonadopted, Intraracial Adopted, and Interracial Adopted Groups

	Nonadopt	Intra/Adopt	Inter/Adopt
Infant's age[a]	14:24	14:09	14:18
Mother's age[b]	30:01	30:03	33:03
Father's age[b]	33:09	33:11	33:06
Mother's education[c]	14:90	15:60	15:50
Father's education[c]	15:20	16:10	16:10
SES[d]	2.55	2.56	2.95

Note.--Nonadopt = nonadopted group; Intra/Adopt = intraracial adopted groups Inter/Adopt = interracial adopted group.
[a] Months:days.
[b] Years:months.
[c] Years.
[d] Hollingshead's socioeconomic status (1 = highest, 5 = lowest).

attachment involves positive interaction and contact-seeking upon reunion and the ability to be easily comforted by the caregiver following stress. Ambivalence involves a mixing of contact-seeking and resistant behavior upon reunion, and difficulty in being comforted by the caregiver following stress. Strange Situation classifications were assigned without direct knowledge of any subject's adoption status. In order to minimize the extent to which ethnicity might be a clue to adoption status, the video records were viewed in black and white and observers who had met the family members did not contribute to the classifications. It is acknowledged, however, that in some cases of interracial adoption, it was obvious to the rater that the infant was adopted. Reliability of Strange Situation classifications was 83% for a subsample of 18 mother-infant pairs.

Information about the number of foster placements the adopted child had experienced and the age of the child at the time of adoption placement was obtained from each adoptive family. For the Rutgers sample only (N = 56), the Bayley Scales of Infant Mental Development (Bayley, 1969, Rothbart's (1981) Infant Behavior Questionnaire (a recently developed, standardized measure of infant temperament), and a 12-item social support questionnaire were administered to each family.

The social support questionnaire focused on: (1) the extent (in terms of hours per week) that the husband, relatives, and non-family members take care of the infant; (2) the mother's degree of comfort in having her husband, relatives, and non-family members care for the infant; and (3) mother's perception of her husband's, relatives' and non-family members' emotional support regarding the decision to adopt a child, both before the baby was placed in the home as well as currently. A similar questionnaire was filled out by nonadoptive mothers, the only difference being that nonadoptive mothers were asked to rate the social support they received from others for giving birth to a baby rather than adopting one. Each question was rated using a 5-point scale—higher ratings indicated more involvement by others in caregiving, greater comfort on mother's part regarding the caregiving provided by others, and greater amount of emotional support offered by others.[1]

Results

Preliminary analyses indicated that nonadopted infants (N = 20) did not differ from intraracial adopted infants (N = 20) or interracial adopted infants (N = 16) in Developmental Quotient (M = 119, 118, and 119, (respectively) or on any of the six subscales of the Rothbart temperament measure. Furthermore, no relationships were found between attachment classification and Developmental Quotient or temperament.

Quality of attachment. Table 2 presents the frequency distribution by adoption status of infants' classification in the Strange Situation. In the absence of specific hypotheses about differences between A and C infants, these groups were combined to comprise a group of insecurely attached infants. Whereas only 7 of the 27 (26%) nonadopted infants were classified as insecurely attached, 22 of the 46 (48%) adopted infants were so classified. Although this difference approached significance, x^2 (2) = 3.41, p<.09, it has to be viewed in light of the fact that interracial adoptions accounted for a disproportionate number of anxiously attached infants. Indeed, the difference between non-adopted infants and interracial adopted infants was significant, $x^2(1)$ = 4.79, p<.05. Eleven of 19 (58%) interracial adoptees were insecurely attached, as compared to 7 of 27 (26%) nonadoptees. No differences were found between nonadopted and intraracial adopted groups, or between intraracial and interracial adopted groups.

Maternal social support. A 3 (adoption status) x 2 (attachment status) multivariate analysis of variance (MANOVA) was performed on the 12-item social support questionnaire. Whereas the main effect for adoption status was significant, $F(24,72) = 2.01, p < .05$, the main effect for attachment status and the interaction between these two variables were not significant. Separate univariate analyses of variance for adoption status indicated a significant difference between the groups for the following items (see Table 3): mother's comfort with the caretaking provided by extended family and non-family members; emotional support from friends prior to adoption/birth; current emotional support from husband, extended family, and friends.

Duncan's multiple-range tests indicated that mothers of interracial adopted infants were less comfortable than mothers of nonadopted or intraracial adopted infants in having extended family members care for their baby. Mothers of nonadopted and interracial adopted infants also were less comfortable than mothers of intraracial adopted infants in having non-family

TABLE 2

Frequency Distribution of Infants' Attachment Classification As A Function of Adoption Status

	ATTACHMENT STATUS		
ADOPTION STATUS	A	B	C
Nonadopted.............	4	20	3
Intraracial adopted....	7	16	4
Interracial adoptd.....	6	8	5

members care for their baby. A significantly lower amount of emotional support from friends prior to adoption was also perceived by mothers from the interracial group in comparison to mothers from the intraracial group. By contrast, mothers from both adoption groups rated their current level of emotional support for husbands, extended family, and friends higher than nonadoptive mothers. In fact, with only a few exceptions, adoptive mothers consistently rated their current level of emotional support as extremely high.

Preplacement history.—Separate 2 (adoption status) x 2 (attachment status) analyses of variance were performed on the two pre-placement history variables; number of foster placements and age of child at the time of adoption placement. Significant main effects for adoption status were found for both variables, indicating that interracial adoptees experienced a greater number of foster homes, $F_{(1,42)} = 15.30$, p< p<.001, than intraracial adoptees. The only other significant effect was the adoption status x attachment status interaction for placement age, indicating that securely attached interracial adopted infants were older at the time of adoption placement than the other groups of infants (see Table 4).

Discussion

The results of the present study indicate that, overall, the quality of mother-infant attachment in middle-class adoptive families is similar to that found in nonadoptive families. This is especially true for families that adopt infants of the same racial/ethnic background as themselves. These results suggest that lack of early contact per se does not place middle-class adoptive families at risk for the development of anxious mother-infant attachment relationships. Whether this conclusion can be generalized to lower-class adoptive families—who make up a rather small percentage of those families adopting infants (Kadushin, 1980)—is not known at the present time. Our findings also suggest that it is unlikely that the higher incidence of psychological and academic problems among adoptees in middle childhood and adolescence (see Brodzinsky, Schechter, Braff, & Singer, 1984) can be explained in terms of insecure family attachment patterns in the infancy years. Of course, the results do not rule out the potential importance of insecure or disrupted postinfancy family relationships as a basis for the adjustment problems of the adoptee. Brodzinsky, Singer, and Braff (1984) and Brodzinsky et al. (in press) have noted that as school-age children begin to understand the implications of adoption, including the reality of being relinquished by biological parents, they often feel confused, uncertain, and insecure regarding their current adoptive family relationships. In turn, these feelings may play an important role in the manifestation of socioemotional and school-related problems during this period.

Although the overall comparison of attachment in adoptive and nonadoptive families was reasonably similar, the results of our study did indicate that interracial adoptive mother-infant pairs were more likely to manifest insecure attachment relationships than nonadoptive mother-infant pairs. One possible explanation for this finding is that families who adopt children of a different race than themselves are less likely to receive whole-hearted support from extended family, friends, and neighbors than are families who adopt children of the same race, or families with nonadopted children. In turn, decreased support would then be expected to undermine the parent-child socioemotional relationship. Although our results do provide support for the hypothesis that mothers of interracial adopted infants are less comfortable having others care

TABLE 3

Mean Level of Perceived Social Support for Nonadopted,Intraracial Adopted,and Interracial Adopted Groups

| | ADOPTION STATUS | | | | |
	Nonadopt	Intra/Adopt	Inter/Adopt	F(2,50)	p
Type of child care:					
Husband	1.40	1.85	1.75	...	N.S.
	(.75)	(.75)	(.68)		
Extended family	1.10	1.15	1.06	...	N.S.
	(.30)	(.49)	(.25)		
Non-family	1.30	1.45	1.25	...	N.S.
	(.80)	(.69)	(.58)		
Mother's comfort with type of child care:					
Husband	4.65	4.70	4.75	...	N.S.
	(.75)	(.92)	(.45)		
Extended family	4.32[a]	4.52[a]	3.59[b]	5.54	.01
	(.93)	(.61)	(1.16)		
Non-family	3.74[b]	4.49[a]	3.40[b]	6.58	.01
	(1.19)	(.60)	(.93)		
Emotional support prior to birth/adoption:					
Husband	4.85	4.70	4.69	...	N.S.
	(.50)	(.47)	(.48)		
Extended family	4.60	4.70	4.31	...	N.S.
	(.68)	(.92)	(.79)		
Friends	4.56[ab]	4.85[a]	4.35[b]	3.67	.05
	(.58)	(.37)	(.47)		
Current emotional support:					
Husband	4.85[b]	5.00[a]	5.00[a]	3.71	.05
	(.48)	(.00)	(.00)		
Extended family	4.65[b]	5.00[a]	5.00[a]	3.96	.05
	(.67)	(.00)	(.00)		
Friends	4.30[b]	4.95[a]	4.81[a]	11.85	.001
	(.92)	(.35)	(.40)		

Note.-- Means with different superscript letters are significantly different from one another. Standard deviations are in parentheses.

for their babies and perceive themselves as having received less emotional support from others in their decision to adopt prior to the actual adoption than mothers of intraracial adoptive infants (and to a lesser extent, mothers of nonadoptive infants), this explanation is unsatisfactory for two reasons. First, both groups of adoptive mothers rated themselves as currently receiving higher levels of support from husbands, extended family, and friends than nonadoptive mothers. More important, though, is the finding that although social support was related to adoption status, it was unrelated to quality of attachment. In other words, no difference was found between mothers of secure and insecure infants in quality of support offered by others.

Another possible explanation for the greater degree of insecurity among interracial adoptive families is that this type of adoption may be associated with a more problematic preplacement history which could ultimately disrupt the attachment process. As plausible as this interpretation appears to be, however, it is not supported by our data. Although interracial adopted infants were exposed to a great number of foster homes and were placed for adoption later than intraracial adopted infants, these preplacement variables were not associated with an insecure attachment pattern. In fact, we found that

TABLE 4

Mean Number of Foster Placements and Mean Adoption Placement Age as a Function of Adoption Status and Attachment Status

Adoption and Attachment Status	Foster Homes	Placement Age [a]
Intraracial:		
Secure	.16	1:07
Insecure	.63	1.12
Interracial:		
Secure	1.00	5:13
Insecure	.88	2:133

[a]Months:days.

interracial adopted infants who were securely attached to their mothers were actually placed for adoption later than the other groups of infants. Individual differences in infant temperament and developmental maturity can also be eliminated as an explanation for our findings because these variables were unrelated to quality of mother-infant attachment.

How then are we to explain our findings? Why is it that interracial adoptive mother-infant pairs show a more insecure attachment to one another? The most likely explanation is that the finding represents an adaptational phenomenon. That is, adults who adopt infants of a different race may simply need more time to feel comfortable and secure in their parenting role. The unusualness of rearing a child from a different racial–ethnic background may temporarily undermine their self-confidence in their ability to handle the problems associated with this type of family life. The resulting uncertainty and anxiety that are likely to emerge would then be expected to disrupt the development of a secure socioemotional relationship with the infant.

Of course, we cannot be certain that the insecurity observed in the interracial adoptive families is only temporary. A longitudinal design is required to answer this question. Nevertheless, the hypothesis that early attachment problems in interracial adoptions tend to become less significant in later infancy and early childhood is consistent with evidence that the most common longitudinal change in attachment classification is from anxious to secure (Ainsworth et al., 1978; Connell, 1976; Vaughn, Egeland, Sroufe, & Waters, 1979; Waters, 1978). Furthermore, this hypothesis is supported indirectly by the bulk of the literature on the effects of interracial adoption on children. For example, if insecure attachment in interracial adoptive mother-infant pairs represented a robust and developmentally consistent pattern, we would expect that interracial adoptees would be at greater risk for psychological problems in later childhood than other adopted children. Yet the majority of studies on interracial adoption indicate; that these children adjust very well psychologically (Feigelman & Silverman, 1983; Gill & Jackson, 1983; Kim, 1977; McRoy, Zurcher, Lauderdale, & Anderson, 1982; Simon & Alstein, 1977, 1981).

In contrast to the results reported by Yarrow and his collegues (Yarrow & Goodwin, 1973; Yarrow et al., 1973), we found no evidence that timing of adoption placement in infancy was associated with specific patterns of socioemotional adjustment—in our case, quality of mother-infant attachment. One possible explanation for this result is that the range of placement ages, especially for intraracial adopted infants, was more restricted in our study than in the research reported by Yarrow. With a broader range of placement ages, particularly beyond 6 months, it is quite conceivable that we would have replicated Yarrow's results. However, even if our findings realistically portray the nature of the relation between adoption placement in the infancy years and quality of psychological adjustment, they certainly cannot be generalized to the effect of postinfancy adoption placement on children's adjustment. Fanshel (1972), Feigelman and Silverman (1983), Jewett (1978), Kadushin (1970), Kadushin and Seidl (1971), and Tizard and her associates (Tizard, 1977; Tizard & Hodges, 1978; Tizard & Joseph, 1970; Tizard and Rees, 1974, 1975) have all found that the older the child at the time of adoption placement the more likely he or she will display problems in socioemotional, behavioral, and school-related adjustment.

In concluding, our results can be interpreted as providing an optimistic perspective on the early adjustment of adoptive families. Like nonadoptive mother-infant pairs, most adoptive mothers and their infants develop warm and secure attachment relationships. The initial post-delivery bonding, as described by Klaus and Kennell (1976) and others, which is obviously not part of the adoption experience, does not appear to be necessary for the formation of a healthy family relationship. What seems to be more important is the emergence of caretaking confidence and competence on the part of parents, and a general caretaking atmosphere that is warm, consistent, and contingent on the needs of the infant. To the extent that adoptive parents develop these characteristics and provide this type of environment, there is little reason to believe their attachment relationships with their young infants will differ markedly from nonadoptive parents.

References

Ainsworth, M. D. S., Blehar, M. C., Waters, E., & Wall, S. (1978). *Patterns of attachment: A psychological study of the strange situation.* Hillsdale, NJ: Erlbaum.

Arend, R., Gove, F. L., & Sroufe, L. A. (1979). Continuity of individual adaption from infancy to kindergarten: A predictive study of ego-resiliency and curiosity in preschoolers. *Child Development, 50,* 950–959.

Bayley, N. (1969). *Bayley Scales of Infant Development.* New York: Psychological Corp.

Bohman, M. (1970). *Adopted children and their families: A follow-up study of adopted children, their background environments, and adjustment.* Stockholm: Proprius.

Bohman, M., & Sigvardsson, S. (1980). A prospective, longitudinal study of children registered for adoption: A 15-year follow-up study. *Acta Psychiatrica Scandinavica, 61,* 339–355.

Bohman, M., & Sigvardsson, S. (1982). Adoption and fostering as preventive measures. In E. J. Anthony & C. Chiland (Eds.), *The child in his family: Children in turmoil, tomorrow's parents* (Vol.7, pp. 171–180). New York: Wiley.

Borgatta, E. F., & Fanshel, D. (1965). *Behavioral characteristics of children known to psychiatric outpatient clinics.* New York: Child Welfare League of America.

Brodzinsky, D. M. (1984). New perspectives on adoption revelation. *Adoption and Fostering, 8,* 27–32.

Brodzinsky, D. M. (1985). *Adjustment to adoption: A psychological perspective.* Manuscript submitted for publication.

Brodzinsky, D. M., Schechter, D. E., & Brodzinsky, A. B. (in press). Children's knowledge of adoption: In R. Ashmore & D. M. Brodzinsky (Eds.), *Thinking about the family: Views of parents and children.* Hillsdale, NJ: Erlbaum.

Brodzinsky, D. M., Schechter, D. E., Braff, A. M., & Singer, L. M. (1984). Psychological and academic adjustment in adopted children. *Journal of Consulting and Clinical Psychology, 52,* 582–590.

Brodzinsky, D. M., Singer, L. M., & Braff, A. M. (1984). Children's understanding of adoption. *Child Development, 55,* 869–878.

Connell, D. B. (1976). *Individual differences in attachment: An investigation into stability, implications, and relationships to structures of early language development.* Unpublished doctoral dissertation, Syracuse University.

Fanshel, D. (1972). *Far from the reservation.* Metuchen, NJ: Scarecrow.

Feigelamn, W., & Silverman, A. R. (1983). *Chosen children: New patterns of adoptive relationships.* New York: Praeger.

Gill, O., & Jackson, B. (1983). *Adoption and race: Black, Asian and mixed-race children in white families.* New York: St. Martin's Press.

Jewett, C. (1978). *Adopting the older child.* Cambridge, MA: Harvard Common Press.

Kadushin, A. (1970). *Adopting older children.* New York: Columbia University Press.

Kadushin, A. (1980). *Child welfare services* (3rd ed.). New York: Macmillan.

Kadushin, A., & Seidl, F. W. (1971). Adoption failure: A social work postmortem. *Social Work, 16,* 32–38.

Kenny, T., Baldwin, R., & Mackie, J. B. (1967). Incidence of minimal brain injury in adopted children. *Child Welfare, 46,* 24–29.

Kim, D. S. (1977). How they fare in American homes: A follow-up study of adopted Korean children in U.S. homes. *Children Today, 6,* 2–6.

Kirk, H. D. (1964). *Shared fate.* New York: Free Press.

Kirk, H. D., Jonassohn, K., & Fish, A. D. (1966). Are adopted children especially vulnerable to stress? *Archives of General Psychiatry, 14,* 291–298.

Klaus, M. H., & Kennell, J. H. (1976). *Maternal-infant bonding.* St. Louis: Mosby.

Lewis, M., Feiring, C., McGuffog, C., & Jaskir, J. (1984). Predicting psychopathology in six-year-olds from early social relations. *Child Development, 55,* 123–136.

Lindholm, B. W., & Touliatos, J. (1980). Psychological adjustment of adopted and nonadopted children. *Pyschological Reports, 46,* 307–310.

Losbough, B. (1965). Relationship of EEG neurological and psychological findings in adopted children. *Medical Journal of EEG Technology, 5,* 1–4.

Matas, L., Arend, R. A., & Sroufe, L. A. (1978). Continuity of adaptation in the second year: The relationship between quality of attachment and later competence. *Child Development, 49,* 547–556.

McRoy, R., Zurcher, L., Lauderdale, M., & Anderson, R. (1982). Self-esteem and racial identity in transracial and inracial adoptees. *Social Work, 27,* 522–526.

Rothbart, M. K. (1981). Measurement of temperment in infancy. *Child Development, 52.* 569–578.

Sants, H. J. (1964). Genealogical bewilderment in children with substitute parents. *British Journal of Medical Psychology, 37,* 133–141.

Schechter, M., Carlson, P. V., Simmons, J. Q., & Work, H. H. (1964). Emotional problems in the adoptee. *Archives of General Psychiatry, 10,* 37–64.

Seglow, J., Pringle, M. K., & Wedge, P. (1972). *Growing up adopted.* Windsor: National Foundation for Educational Research in England and Wales.

Simon, R., & Alstein, H. (1977). *Transracial adoption.* New York: Wiley.

Simon, R., & Alstein, H. (1981). *Transracial adoption: A follow-up.* Lexington, MA: Lexington Books.

Singer, L. (1983). *Mother-infant interaction in adoptive families: A study of attachment.* Unpublished doctoral dissertation, Rutgers University.

Sorosky, A. D., Baran, A., & Pannor, R. (1975). Identity conflicts in adoptees. *American Journal of Orthopsychiatry, 45,* 18–27.

Sroufe, L. A., & Waters, E. (1977). Attachment as an organizational construct. *Child Development, 48,* 1184–1199.

Steir, M. E. (1982). *Patterns of attachment of adopted infants to their mothers.* Unpublished doctoral dissertation, Yeshiva University.

Stone, F. H. (1972). Adoption and identity. *Child Psychiatry and Human Development, 2,* 120–128.

Tizard, B. (1977). *Adoption: A second chance.* New York: Free Press.

Tizard, B., & Hodges, J. (1978). The effects of early institutional rearing on the development of eight-year-old children. *Journal of Child Psychology and Psychiatry, 19,* 99–118.

Tizard, B., & Joseph, A. (1970). Cognitive development of young children in residential care: The study of children aged 24 months. *Journal of Child Psychology and Psychiatry, 11,* 177–186.

Tizard, B., & Rees, J. (1974). A comparison of the effects of adoption, restoration to the natural mother, and continued institutionalization on the cognitive development of four-year-old children. *Child Development, 45,* 92–99.

Tizard, B., & Rees, J. (1975). The effects of early institutional rearing on the behavior problems and affectional relationships of four-year-old children. *Journal of Child Psychology and Psychiatry, 16,* 61–74.

Vaughn, B. E., Egeland, B., Sroufe, L. A., & Waters, E. (1979). Individual differences in infant-mother attachment at twelve and eighteen months: Stability and change in families under stress. *Child Development, 50,* 971–975.

Waters, E. (1978). The reliability and stability of individual differences in infant-mother attachment. *Child Development, 49,* 483–494.

Waters, E., Wippman, J., & Sroufe, L. A. (1979). Attachment, positive affect, and competence in the peer group: Two studies in construct validation. *Child Development, 50,* 821–829.

Yarrow, L. J. (1965). Theoretical implications of adoption research. In *Perspectives on adoption research.* New York: Child Welfare League of America.

Yarrow, L. J., & Goodwin, M. S. (1973). The immediate impact of separation: Reactions of infants to a change in mother figure. In L. J. Stone, H. T. Smith, & L. B. Murphy (Eds.), *The competent infant: Research and commentary* (pp. 1032–1040). New York: Basic.

Yarrow, L. J., Goodwin, M. S., Manheimer, H., & Milowe, I. D. (1973). Infancy experiences and cognitive and personality development at 10 years. In L. J. Stone, H. T. Smith, & L. B. Murphy (Eds.), *The competent infant: Research and commentary* (pp. 1274–1281). New York: Basic.

Yarrow, L. J., & Klein, R. P. (1980). Environmental discontinuity associated with transition from foster to adoptive homes. *International Journal of Behavioral Development, 3,* 311–322.

11

Understanding and Treating the Severely Disturbed Child

Foster W. Cline

In Evergreen, we have worked for fifteen years with children who have trouble in forming loving attachments to others. Such children show cruelty to themselves and others, an inability to give and receive gratification, extreme forms of lying, overt or passive resistance resulting in extreme control battles, and lack of long-term friends. We have become increasingly convinced that the usual modes of therapy are ineffective in working with this population of children. We feel that the first year of life issues must be re-worked for such children to make progress.

The following information and diagrams are excerpted from Foster Cline: *Understanding and Treating the Severely Disturbed Child,* available through Evergreen Consultants in Human Behavior, P.O. Box 2380, Evergreen, CO 80439.

Working with the Rage Filled Child is a two-hour audio cassette series with transcriptions of actual therapy sessions. The cassette series covers the etiology of attachment and bonding problems, and effective techniques of treatment. The tape series is accompanied by a 25-page booklet containing over 15 diagrams that help clarify the major issues present in working with this difficult population. The tape series is available through Cline/Fay Institute, P.O. Box 2362, Evergreen, Co 80439.

* * * * *

Theory of Therapy for Severely Disturbed Children—Onions

Before examining techniques of therapy for children with severe personality problems, it is essential to have a firm grounding in theory and familiarity with the developmental material covered earlier.

Children who have had problems in the first year of life usually have the history noted in the section on Lack of Attachment. Effective treatment involves leading or *forcing* the child repetitively through successful completion of developmental tasks not mastered during the first and second year of life. Thus, therapy is *regressive, forceful, loving and confrontive*. Therapy for little Onions has as its goal the development of Basic Trust. But Trust cannot be developed unless the child accepts Control. With younger children, the change is so dramatic that an observer remarked, "This whole process reminds me of an exorcism—the child enters with the devil himself and emerges loving, tender and responsive." The process itself may be diagrammed:

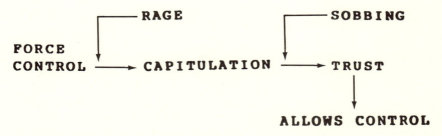

An untrusting child who is being forced to accept control will exhibit rage so intense that the therapist is unlikely to see its equal in any other therapeutic situation. Once the child capitulates and accepts control, however, this primordial rage—with its elements of anger and terror—converts to sobbing with elements of relief, thankfulness, and love. These feelings are reinforced by a tender therapist who holds the sobbing child and gives assurance of love.

For maximum effectiveness, therapy must ensure the expression of rage and total activation of the child. As control is formed in therapy, the child learns that neither he nor the therapist dies. He finds to his everlasting relief that both he and the therapist are happy. That a win–win position is possible! That a win–win position feels good. Out of such realizations, trust is born.

The Need for Touch

In working with severely disturbed children, therapists have emphasized the need for touch. However, it is not simply touch itself that is important. It is *when* it is given and *under whose control!* Often disturbed children insist on touch in their own controlling way. However, such touch is carried out on the child's terms and allows no opportunity for the building of Trust....

Although seriously disturbed children need more physical touch, and holding than the average healthy child, they present the therapist with a great number of difficulties. First, the child is often fairly unlovable: "Who wants to hold a brat like that!" Secondly, they do not easily accept touch and love when these are offered: "Don't touch me!" or, when a little older, "What are you, some kind of homo?!"

Severely disturbed children, then, are in a tremendous bind. The touch they need so badly is often seen as a potential means of control. A simple hug means terrifying containment. They have too little Trust; therefore, they ask for touch in aberrant and anger-provoking ways. If they are held, on the therapist's terms, they will usually go into a rage.

Rage is actually *anger* with strong elements of *hopelessness and helplessness*. A cat cornered by a dog exemplifies the rage state. If we simply saw the cornered cat, without perceiving the dog, the cat would appear ferocious and antagonistic. Once we see the reason for this rage state, however, we understand that beneath it all the cat is really afraid.

Likewise, a child in a rage state feels himself to be in a life-threatening situation. The rageful child being held appears ferocious and antagonistic—in fact, untouchable!

If we pick up a rageful cat and hold it, it will first go into a further fury. If, however, we continue to lovingly contain the cat, talk softly and pet it, after awhile it will settle down and begin to accept our love. A rageful child will do likewise. But how hard it is to love a furious cat or child! It takes an extreme amount of physical and psychological preparation to hold a child who desperately needs holding and at the same time resists holding. Also, this kind of intervention must be carried out by therapists who do not themselves have underlying anger. Therapists who have internal anger are uniformly frightened and threatened by the holding; they project their own needs and response into the child....

Contraindications to Regressive Rage Therapy and Containment of Children

A rageful child needing containment may easily trap the unwary therapist into a physical response that recapitulates the child's early, abusive, unhappy home experiences. Thus, there are specific contraindications for the therapeutic use of containment-holding in children:

1. *A child should not be held if the worker or therapist feels angry at the child.*

At times we may feel angry at an obnoxious child who forces us to grab him. Physical contact is thus initiated with the child in control. If the worker is irritated, frustrated or worn out, this is not the time for therapeutic containment.

2. *Holding for containment should not take place if the therapist cannot easily keep one hand free to control* the child's head and his possible biting. If the therapist cannot maintain one arm free, it means that the child is too large for a single person to contain or more help needs to be present to take care of the physical aspect of rage.

Early in her learning to use this technique, a surprised young therapist exclaimed: "Foster, this is hard work! You didn't tell me I would need three arms and an iron bra!"

3. *Holding for containment should occur only if there is enough time to work through the holding to a successful conclusion.* A residential treatment center may provide an appropriate setting. In the therapist's office, on an outpatient basis, appointments must be scheduled to allow plenty of time for the rage to reach its full fury. Activation is essential. Then time must be allowed for successful working through and resulting good feelings. The initial rage, when fully expressed, can generally be worked through to a state of quiescence—but this takes time and can rarely be rushed.

4. Containment holding *should not take place* in a school or around other children unless there are *other staff members* who *adequately manage the other* children. *The therapy itself should not take place the view or hearing of other children.*

The Technique of Activation Therapy

A fully activated child must be contained. Therefore, holding must take place if the therapist intends to use activation therapy. As previously explored in more detail, firm and loving control will lead to a sense of trust.

There are many nuances of this therapy that cannot be adequately explained by the written word. A grasp of the technique can be obtained from reading, but attempts to use this therapy without fairly extensive training almost always result in less than the desired outcome. The use of facial expressions, humor, optimal alternating ways of aversive and loving stimulation, and nuances of response pattern between therapist and child cannot be adequately conveyed on paper. They must be seen and personally experienced to be fully understood. A therapy session may last for several hours; however, the therapy is not "heavy" for the entire period. As the therapist works, he forces his rhythm onto the rigid patterns of the child. The child is forced to do things the therapist's way. The therapist uses smiles, eye contact and humor to force a win–win response. Then the win–win response is strongly reinforced and Attachment and Trust begin to lock in.

Proper positioning of the patient is very important. The child and therapist are going to be together for quite a while. When I work along with a child I choose a large, comfortable leather reclining chair with wide arms. If the therapist tries to work with a child who is too large, or does not attain a comfortable position, the therapy session degenerates into an endurance contest.

As I am right-handed, I lay the child across my lap so that his head is on my left with his body stretching out the right. The child's head is cradled in my left arm. I may hold the child's left arm up and around over the top of his head. Thus his own left arm forms a cradle for his head and restrains it, and this position leaves my right hand free to play "spider" or lovingly poke and tickle him around his ribs and tummy. One way or another the child's legs have to be refrained so that they cannot kick the therapist or other furniture in the room. This may take other people, or sometimes we can restrain their legs with one of our own. With my free right hand I can also open the child's eyelids, to force eye contact, or close his mouth when I don't like what he is saying.

Essentially, the therapist controls the placement and quantity of tactile stimulation with his free right hand, varying it from a fun little "spider" burrowing into the navel or subclavicular space to a somewhat abrasive, rubbing stimulation on the rib cage. When the child is not being worked with intensively through touch, his labyrinthine mechanisms may be stimulated by sitting him up, turning his head, etc. All of this varied, high-intensity stimulation is necessary to "break up" the child's habitually rigid and stereotyped responses. He is not allowed to use his usual repetitive auto-stimulatory mechanisms such as rubbing his lips, scratching himself, hitting himself, making repetitive vocalizations, etc.

Case Examples of Therapeutic Intervention with Character-Disturbed Children

The following case examples demonstrate varied aspects of regressive therapy and provide insight into a potpourri of therapeutic techniques. Each is written by a different author. On the surface, the experiences may appear to be surprisingly different, yet they all have a common thread of loving control which leads to rage and, finally, attachment.

—Ken's story is told by a therapist.
—Janet's surprising and unique response to body casting secondary to physical disaster is told by her social worker mother.
—Life with Eddie is written by an educated and intelligent adoptive mother.

—Bobby was an animal! An uneducated but "natural" foster mother wrote of changes brought about in his behavior.

—Eleven-year-old Paul tells his own view of rage therapy as he wrote it for a paper assigned in school.

—Finally, without editing, John Martin's typical evaluation with its poignant history and futile past attempts at therapy is given in full.

Although each of the case studies vary, it is possible to see the red thread of appropriate therapy running through each. This is the basic flow for treatment of a character disorder. And it is not always successful. But, whether it be in the Marines, by body cast (Janet), or in a residential treatment center, those cases which are successful must be treated with the following elements:

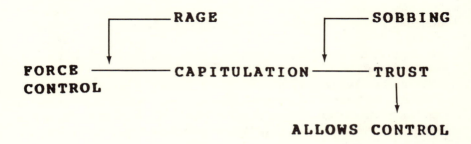

A Case Example—Ken

Ken is nine years old. He has a diagnosis of schizophrenia. He has a mixture of autistic, organic, behavioral and psychological difficulties that are difficult to separate. He is able to maintain eye contact, mirror another person with gross motor movement, and follow very simple, one-step requests. He has great trouble with speech but is able to say single words, with poor articulation and inflection. Most sentences, when he attempts them, are inarticulate mumbles. When he does attempt a sentence, Ken always ends with the word "now:" "I go now," "I sit up now," etc. Ken is very echolalic. He answers most questions with a parrotlike repeat of the question. At the time that Ken was first seen, he was able to dress himself, although he often dressed with his t-shirt backwards. Ken was toilet trained.

Early Therapy Goals with Ken

1. Maintenance of eye contact during periods of activation and high-intensity rage. Therapeutic expression of love and physical touch is essential. At this time attachment takes place.

2. It is essential to physically break up certain repetitive patterns by covering Ken's mouth when he:

a) Repeats questions with echolalic questions.

b) Ends every statement with "now."

c) Repeats words and statements with poor articulation and faulty inflection.

d) Repeats questions when asked to make a motor response; i.e., his response to "Close your eyes" is to say "clo ei."

3. Ken must learn to retain simple commands without the therapist having to repeat them over and over. He has to learn to retain: i.e., "Keep your eyes closed!" The retention of a simple command is extremely difficult for schizophrenic children, who may respond only momentarily. An example might be: "Give me the cup." The therapist points to the cup. The child heads off in the right direction and then "loses it," ambling past the original object and off into the distance. The importance of the ability to retain a concept cannot be overemphasized. Upon this simple cornerstone all planful thinking is built!

4. Ken must be taught to reciprocate interpersonal human emotional vibrations. (This automatically takes place between most mothers and children during the first year of life.) When a therapist kisses the child, the child is supposed to return the kiss; a smile is reflected by a smile; a loud voice from the therapist brings a rageful response from the child. Thus, the child's "biorhythm" is forced to fit, and to be responsive to, that of the therapist.

Ken is told to close his eyes. He is unresponsive at first. The therapist shouts his request and Ken blinks them closed, then opens them quickly. The therapist pats Ken's eyelids lightly: "Keep them closed—close them." Soon Ken gets the idea. Now he holds his eyes closed for perhaps three or four seconds. The therapist then calls upon his experience in working with many such children. He has a number of interventions designed to help Ken keep his eyes closed, and he varies these in ways that Ken can neither control nor anticipate. The therapist may use loud verbal commands, aversive tapping of the eyelids, occasional stimulation of the ribs, and strong positive remarks. Ken hates such control and resists with squirming, rage and general resistance. The therapist keeps on with this simple task until, after several hours of work, Ken begins to keep his eyes closed on first command, while not being restrained and not being reminded. At the end of the session, Ken is sitting happily on the therapist's lap. His response has been expanded to include his opening or closing his eyes—and mouth.

"Open your mouth, close your eyes—hold it that way—fantastic! I love you!" The therapist and child hug. The therapist says, "Yippee!" and raises his hands in the air. The child, maintaining eye contact, raises his hands in the air and yells, "Yippee!"

"Okay, great! Now let's get going again. Close your eyes and open your mouth. Good—fantastic—now open your eyes and close your mouth. Great!

Now open them both—open your eyes and your mouth. Really good!'' The therapist gives the child a hug.

This above sequence is carried off in a rapid-fire manner, with the power and pizazz of the therapist setting the rhythm within which the child must react.

A Case Example—Janet

The following is from a short biography written by a trained and competent social worker. It speaks for itself. Her perceptions cannot be dismissed lightly.

Janet was adopted from a South American orphange at age three years three months. There had been no pre-parental visits.

Because Janet had been the "pet" of the nuns, she had been given special consideration and, in contrast to the other children, had normal milestones.

When we first got Jan, her behavior could only be described as outrageous. She had daily screaming temper tantrums during which she would lie on the floor and kick. She bit me for no apparent reason a number of times. She went up to guests sitting in the living room and spat at them. She had nightmares in which she insisted that donkeys and other animals were under her bed. When food was set before her, she ate voraciously with her hands, without restraint. She grabbed glasses off of people's faces as late as six months after her arrival in our home. To hold her seemed an impossible task, for she never sat still and we got poked, kicked, hit, etc. in the process. She appeared to have no impulse control or response to commands. She often ran into the street or other dangerous situations. All women were "momma," and all men were ignored.

We moved to the U.S. when she was three years eight months old.

During the previous seven months in Ecuador, she had been cared for by a maid for two and three hours a day so I could have a rest from the constant hectic chores she presented. In the U.S. I had no such relief. I tried many things—severe spankings, bordering on abuse with loss of my temper—and nursery school. The spanking seemed to have no effect. Nursery school was good for me but Jan had trouble learning to share. Her attention span lengthened and her tantrums, biting and spitting largely dropped out. At five and a half, in kindergarten, she disliked school intensely. She attempted to dominate other children at all times with no give-and-take at all. Hitting, rock-throwing, breakage and clothing destruction were very common. She was not welcome in other homes in the neighborhood. She wanted our undivided attention so that entertaining, even talking on the phone, was difficult. Birthday parties and gifts for her sister were intolerable.

Suspecting that psychotherapy was indicated, the parents had the child tested by a Denver psychologist. The psychologist told the parents that Jan could not be expected to adjust to public school. A residential care center, a setting for the perceptually handicapped, was impossible for the parents to afford. The future looked very bleak. Then Jan was hurt in an auto accident. Both legs were fractured, and Jan was put in double plaster casts for six months.

While in the casts, Jan was completely under control for the first time. She was forced into a dependent position. She had to accept her parents' rhythms and accept what they had to give when they would normally give it. In short, Jan was controlled. The parents were able to sit by her, touch her and talk with her.

At age seven years ten months, almost two and a half years after the first testing, retesting was completed by a school psychologist. He noted that her emotional security level "was vastly improved as well as such factors as memory retention, attention span, impulse control." He said that he could hardly believe he had tested the same child!

Jan grew into a child who, with some difficulty, continued to attend public school. Now, at twenty-one, she is completing her second year of college. She has a B average, though she complains of difficulty with English composition, vocabulary and grammar. Her interpersonal relationships are good but not excellent. At times, she makes plans that lack follow-through.

All in all, the mother notes, "I feel that we really have seen a miracle."

A Case Example—Eddie

In a thoughtful and moving biography in our files, a mother talks about her Chicano child, adopted at sixteen months. At the time he was adopted, the parents had two natural children of their own—both girls—and they were overjoyed to have a boy. During the home study, Eddie appeared as an "affectionate, gorgeous, friendly little boy. He looked so healthy and happy we were bursting with joy to think he would be ours."

Things soon went wrong. "The honeymoon lasted until we got home, a twenty-minute ride. On entering the house he started running from the trash can, knocking it over and scattering trash, to the fireplace, where he pulled over the screen and crawled into the ashes. He tried to get into the parakeet cage, and on and on. For the first two weeks he ran constantly. I ached all over trying to keep up with him."

The mother then goes on to document the heartache and difficulty they had in finding therapy. Her child demonstrated the symptoms shown by an unattached child. All the therapy they tried was ineffective.

"By the time he was in second grade, he was incorrigible. He set fire to the house, he was stealing from everywhere and everybody, tearing up everything he could get his hands on, skipping school, starting fights, bullying the other kids and controlling our lives unmercifully. He had pulled the draperies down so many times that I lost count—molly bolts, plaster and all!

"One day he came home from school with $2.45 in his pocket. He said a boy at school had given it to him. I called the school and was informed that $2.45 had been taken out of his sister's teacher's handbag. The principal advised our seeing the school psychologist. I answered, 'No, we just went through a whole year of that and it didn't help. I read about a place where they treat children such as Eddie. If you know of that kind of place, I'll run; if not, I'm not going anywhere.'

The next night Dr. Cline called, and after talking with him for five or ten minutes I hung up and softly said to my husband, 'I think there is hope — he seems to understand what is happening.'

"After seeing him for an hour, during which he described Eddie and the attachment process, etc., we drove home in a state of elation. Eddie was scheduled for a holding session using activation therapy. The therapy was explained very carefully to us and, although it sounded drastic, we were desperate and relieved to discover there was something to try.

"Eddie's resistances became obvious within the first few minutes of the first session. During that session Eddie talked about how he was different from the other children. He felt different because he was adopted. Also he was mad that he didn't look like his dad. His intense feeling around these issues surprised me, as we had gone over his adoption very carefully.

"The session lasted four and a half hours, and at the end he came over, sat in my lap and snuggled in my neck like a baby does. I remember weeping with joy. It was the first time his love felt real to me. Afterwards I held him and rocked him twice a day for ten minutes at a time. Thus, I rocked him to sleep for the first time when he was seven and a half years old.

"His behavior improved dramatically. We did follow-up faithfully. We confronted old behavior patterns and were super supportive of behaviors we liked.

"Our lives as a family were as dramatically changed as Eddie. We began doing more and feeling better about it.

"We have been so encouraged we have adopted two more children.''

The Life and Times of Bobby

Donna is a tall, lanky blonde. Her fifty years on the farm have etched her face and bleached her long, unkempt hair. She looks like something that would sturdily grow from Kansas corn country. She and her husband have cared for literally hundreds of foster children. Donna is both our most experienced and our least formally educated foster mother. She sits in our office and reminisces about Bobby, a child she later adopted:

We took Bobby at two and a half years of age. He was to have been taken to the psychiatric hospital that same day. I picked him up from the medical hospital, and he was under sedation as no foster home would keep him. He was too difficult. He wouldn't talk. He screeched and screamed and hit and pulled hair and spit at people.... shucks, he didn't know how to play with the other children or toys. And would he ever break things—wowee, especially knobs off anything like the TV, coolers and that stuff. He would pinch, bite, kick and not leave the phone alone. He refused to mind anything he was told and would not allow no one to love him but would kick, stiffen like a board and screech and squeal in a shrill voice. When he could, he would pinch and pull hair to get away.

Mealtime was impossible with him screechin' at everything he didn't like. But he had an unbelievable appetite and ate like an animal. He was forever throwing his bowl and food on the floor. Same with milk or juice. He would mess his hands into the food and into his hair and all over and smear the person near him if he could reach 'em. He banged his head against things in his crib and rocked constantly. He didn't show no signs of happiness at all—only total confusion, frustration and wakin' up all night to fuss and shake his crib.

His nose ran constantly, and he whined because he didn't feel good. He had walkin' pneumonia for a long time. He was so constipated we looked at him and he strained until his face was deep red and passed hard, dark, knotted chunks and balls of stool. And he gagged on his food.

Now I'm happy to say Bobby is a happy, giggly, sweet little three and a half year old who can sit still when it is necessary. Often he comes up to me and puts his arms up and says, 'I wanta hug' or I wanta tiss.' He is learnin' to talk real well now. His nose don't run and he rarely whines and has checked out clear of pneumonia. He teases good-humoredly and laughs when he can get someone to chase him. He is in good control at the table and eats a normal amount of food. He doesn't bang his head against the crib or anywhere. Rocking back and forth is very infrequent now.

I know you want me to tell what we did. It kinda worries me for you to be tapin' all this. We're pretty unorthodox. At home we forcibly restrained him from grabbing the phone and banging on furniture, people, glass doors and windows and all of them things. He screeched and strained to do it anyway, and we took everything away from him. I would forcibly hold him down and often pop his bottom with my hand and jar him loose from that kind of behavior. While I held him and he was fussin' and screechin' I would say, 'I love you, Bobby' and he would finally become too exhausted to fight and I would hug him close and love and kiss him all over and tell him he was a dear good boy and that I loved him and all of that.

At first, when he pulled hair we pulled his hair back—a little harder than he would—until he would let go. It took about five times until he discontinued pulling hair. I got to admit that when he kicked me, I kicked him back a couple of times. When we returned that treatment, he gave up.

Now his caseworker was one big help. We came up here twice a week and she worked on his resistance and forcibly held him and worked on his speech in counseling. I've got to say that there is back up help here for anyone needing this type of assistance. Personally, I have worked with disturbed children for over 30 years and I see today children who are far more emotionally and mentally disturbed than children were 30 years ago. I don't know what this means, but one thing for sure is that the need is getting greater and intelligent, qualified workers should be doin' more to reach children while there is still time to change them for the right.

The most eloquent statement concerning the effectiveness of confrontive activation therapy comes from the children themselves. At the time he wrote the following statement, Paul was eleven years old. He wrote this paper as part of a school assignment:

After every session I feel super, just super and I feel like I am a new person. I also feel so good that I could love my enemies. But during the session I actually feel like killing the people that are there. During the session I also feel like the people are actually trying to hurt me. I feel it is a punishment, but I know it is helping me get my head on straight. It has helped a lot.

I myself think that if I had not had the therapy I would probably still be cursing at the teachers, and running away from school and home. I would probably still be smoking and hanging around some of my jockey friends. But now I have new friends and they all like me now that I have changed. Since I have been through the therapy some of the straighter boys are starting to let me play baseball, soccer and football. Now some of the girls are starting to like me because I'm not trying to be a hot shot anymore.

My parents are even feeling great about me, now they are letting me go to the movies by myself. My parents feel that I am more responsible. And best of all, my teacher likes me so much now that I have changed, that he's asked me out to dinner.

Since I had therapy I have been able to learn more faster and understand more of my homework. So I would say that it has helped.

* * * * *

Summary of Differences in Treatment for Character Disordered and Neurotic Children

A character-disordered child has no internalized parent figure and therefore cannot establish good object relationships. We do not immediately try to achieve rapport, positive transference or a therapeutic alliance. The child simply does not have the psychological structures needed to form such bonds.

Therapeutically, attachment to the therapist must be formed by leading the child through, in reverse sequence, the developmental issues of the first two years of life.

The neurotic child has an internalized parent and therefore has object relationships, albeit skewed. Establishment of a working therapeutic alliance and a positive transference is the first goal of therapy. The child is then able to borrow from the therapist's ego-strength and benefit from the therapist's modeling. Even more important, this occurs in an environment where he is "free to be himself." The conflict that has caused his anxiety and symptoms is thereby resolved.

Conceptually, then, there are great differences between the treatment needs of neurotic and character-disturbed children. These differences may be diagrammed as follows:

CHARACTER DISORDER TREATMENT (AGE 10 MONTHS-7 YEARS)	NEUROTIC DISORDER TREATMENT (ANY AGE)
GOAL: DEVELOPMENT OF TRUST AND INTERNALIZED PARENT Child in control.	GOAL: MODIFICATION OF INTERNALIZED PARENT Child in control.
Therapist sets tight limits invariably leading to control battles.	Therapist establishes alliance with positive regard.
Therapist wins control battle.	Therapist sets friendly limits [if necessary] and avoids control battles [if possible].
Therapist gives child positive regard following child's capitualtion.	Therapist gives: a)Interpretation of conflict. b)Behavior modification techniques. c)Family therapy as indicated.
Therapist follows with treatment as if neurotic.	

SUMMARY OF TREATMENT
CHARACTER DISORDER VS. NEUROTIC DISORDER

References

Bible, New American Standard. Copyright The Lockman Foundation, La Habra, CA.

Blos, Peter, *On Adolescence*. New York: The Free Press of Glencoe, Inc. (Collier-MacMillan Canada Ltd., Toronto, Ontario), 1962.

Bowlby, John, *Child Care and the Growth of Love*. Baltimore: Penguin Books (A271), 1953.

Erikson, Eric, *Childhood and Society* (2nd Edition). New York: W. W. Norton and Company, 1963.

Gesell, Arnold, & Ily, Francis, *The Child from 5 to 10 and Youth (The Years from 10 to 16)*. New York: Harper & Row, 1956.

Ginott, Haim, *Between Parent and Child* and *Between Parent and Teenager*. New York: Avon Books, 1969.

Gordon, Thomas, *Parent Effectiveness Training*. New York: Peter H. Wyden, Inc., 1970.

Haley, Jay, *Strategies of Psychotherapy*. New York: Grune and Stratton, 1963.

Harrison, Saul, & McDermott, John F., *Childhood Psychopathology*. New York: International Universities Press, Inc., 1972.

Holmes, Donald J., *The Adolescent in Psychotherapy*. Boston: Little, Brown and Company, 1964.

Kanner, Leo, *Childhood Psychoses: Initial Studies and New Insights*. Washington, D.C.: T. H. Winston and Sons, 1972.

Klaus, Marshall, & Kennell, John H., *Maternal-Infant Bonding*. St. Louis: C. V. Mosby Company, 1976.

Kessler, Jane W., *Psychopathology of Childhood*. Englewood Cliffs, New Jersey: Prentice-Hall, Inc., 1966.

Kleckley, Harvey, *The Mask of Sanity*. St. Louis: C.V. Mosby Company, 1964. (4th Edition).

March, William, *The Bad Seed*. New York: Dell Publishing Company (0385), 1954.

Mussen, Paul Henry, and Conger, John Janeway, *Child Development and Personality*. New York: Harper & Brothers, 1956.

Rabkin, Leslie & Carr, John E., *Source Book in Abnormal Psychology*. Boston: Houghton Mifflin Company, 1967.

Rose, Steven, *The Conscious Brain*. New York: Alfred A. Knopf, 1973.

Sapier, Selma G. & Nitzberg, N. C., *Children with Learning Problems*. New York: Brunner/Mazel, 1973.

Schaefer, Charles E., and Millman, Howard L., *Therapies for Children*. San Francisco: Jossey-Bass, 1977.

Schuster, Lincoln, *A Treasury of the World's Great Letters*. New York: Simon and Schuster, 1940 (3rd Paperback Printing, 1968).

Skolnick, Arlene, & Skolnick, Jerome, *Family in Transition*. Boston: Little, Brown and Company, 1971.

Spitz, Renee, & Cobliner, W. G., *The First Year of Life*. New York: International Universities Press, Inc., 1965.

Stoller, Robert J., *Sex and Gender*. New York: Science House, 1968.

Stone, Joseph L., & Church, Joseph, *Childhood and Adolescence*. New York: Random House, 1957.

Zaslow, Robert W., *The Psychology of the Z Process: Attachment and Activation*. California: San Jose State University, 1975.

12

Disruptions: A Little Understanding Goes a Long Way

Paulette Donahue

As a private family therapist I have sometimes had the sad experience of being involved at the eleventh hour in the disruption of an adoption. As a clinically oriented intervenor one can see many issues at the time of crisis that simply had not been identified during home study and placement.

It is important to identify at the outset that disruptions are difficult, opening the family structure to all types of conflicting emotions. The process of disruption shakes the foundation of the healthy family—the parental bond. Disruption can also call into question the strength of the marital bond itself.

In single parent adoption, the disruption process is equally difficult. In fact the need for individual growth and personal awareness may be even more significant for single parents. The challenge to personal belief in one's role as a parent would be even greater as one would not likely have a "significant other" to help facilitate personal growth and share the burdens.

Patterns

In all cases, I have found certain patterns common to the disruptions. I think of each pattern as part of a shadow structure—a hidden, difficult-to-expose structure. By the time people enter therapy, they are hurting and afraid. Under the pressure of those feelings they are more likely to share these private, hidden aspects of their problems. Since I have had the opportunity of "seeing the unseen" I have come to believe that if more understanding is given, prior to placement, to the usual pattern of elements in the disruptive processes, there will be fewer disruptions.

151

To begin with, the process of locating and placing a special needs child or sibling group typically flows all too quickly. Perhaps, understandably, the combination of parents wanting and children waiting accelerates things; but in the speed of the process, so very much seems to be missed.

Lack of Knowledge

And then there is the problem most commonly stated by the parents: "We just never knew what 'special needs' meant." My experience is, overall, that even the most interested parents, people genuinely desiring to adopt special needs children, have no deep understanding of what they are verbalizing a commitment to. Often they have been victimized by the prevalent myth that "All this child needs is a good loving home." Hopefully, as time moves on, this harmful myth will be eliminated.

Who are then, these special needs children who need so much more than love? They are children from birth to five years of age who have been abused sexually, emotionally, physically, or have been neglected to a harmful degree. They are children six to eighteen years of age who have been sexually, emotionally, and physically abused, and who have been in numerous foster homes. They are also in some cases, children who have, for whatever reasons, already passed through adoptive disruptions, one, two, or three times.

It must be understood that between birth and age five 95 percent of brain growth occurs as well as developmental qualities we so very much value for little ones: for example, security, sense of belonging, ability to explore one's environment, ability to reach autonomy, ability to move beyond the home comfortably. However, when a little child is battered and unloved, much of the development process is closed down, replaced by an emptiness that defies understanding by such a frightened little person. What growing-skills the child develops at this point could be called "the survivor syndrome." When children have been pushed around, they do not *live* life, they only *survive* it. The child's records often read like an ongoing nightmare, compared with what we view as "normal" from such studies as White, Brazelton, Erickson, and others.

Many parents have read a child's records with understanding at the feeling level—"This is sad. This is awful!"—but not on the level of factual reality. By contrast, parents who have a birth child with a severe liver condition would probably not remain purely on a feeling level. Quite to the contrary, such parents would undoubtedly seek every shred of facts regarding the problem—what to do, how to do it, and when to do it.

To me it seems urgent that a child who is available for adoption and who has a traumatic history be placed with parents who have systematically formed the knowledge of what "special needs" means in the case of this particular child. These parents need to know *prior to placement*, what to expect and how to intervene. Parents need to be educated to this unique commitment they desire to make. They will not be expected to act as therapists, but they will definitely be a special type of parent—"mini-therapist" might be one way to put it. They must be given specifics about what to do, how to do it, and when. It could be said that a special needs adoption which does not include positive and comprehensive training for parents about what the child's history means only allows Russian roulette to be played with many lives.

Problems of Parents

Besides the too-rapid placement process and the lack of knowledge and guidance we have just explored, there is another very common factor in disruptions: The parents were themselves abused as children. I have been amazed at how many times the first appointment to discuss a disruption has triggered painful disclosures about the youth of one or both parents. In fact it has been my experience that most disruptions involve some very painful parental roots or blocks. In a 1985 Parent Anonymous study, 22% of the parenting population age 25 to 35 had themselves been sexually abused children. So what we have is the unknown abused child *living within* the parent who seeks to adopt a child.

I have repeatedly seen one or more of the following elements in disruptions:

1. *Sexual Abuse* of one parent in her/his own childhood.
2. *Rape*—often a life crisis that had never before been expressed.
3. *Physical Abuse* in a family of origin where frequent and harsh discipline was part of the upbringing.
4. *Distant or cold emotional relationships* with parents from family of origin.
5. *Marital Stress* that was viewed as solvable through the addition of a child. (Not unlike what can happen between any husband and wife thinking a "new baby" will take care of their marital problems.)
   At this point I would like to state my belief that the cornerstone of any healthy—functioning family is the marital bond. A completely child-centered family cannot adequately grow and develop. Thus the partners must be aware of and focused on their individual growth and development as well as their common goals. The motion and momentum of the family, large or small, rests on this parental base—never more so than when special needs children are part of the family.
6. Parents whose main motivation is that they feel *a social responsibility* to help with displaced children.
7. *Infertility Issues* that may or may not have been adequately researched.

Many childless couples I have seen have received extremely poor medical guidance. In the case of several adoption or disruption referrals I was able to help the couple find better medical care with better techniques of infertility reversal. The end result was pregnancy.

8. *The eleventh hour crisis:* "we simply cannot do this any longer." These cases are particularly sad because several of of them could clearly have been avoided had the parents been more adequately prepared to handle and understand the needs of an emotionally disturbed child. These parents were ideal types to get involved in special needs adoption. They had positive individual and marital strengths, but were not prepared by the system of adoption to know how to deal with a special needs child. Unfortunately, a therapist tends to get such a referral after the spark of commitment has been put out by repeated feelings of failure and frustration.

A Better Approach

Let us explore an alternative approach to special needs adoption and the family unit. I believe two main aspects should be attended to:

A. Provide the children an opportunity to integrate the histories that their young lives have played out, through play therapy and structured dialogues. Weave meaning and balance into the traumas and tragedies, and help the children to retain positive images and moments of joy, as well.

B. Provide the opportunity for parents to clearly understand their child/children. Thoroughly and specifically answer the parents' questions. Provide direct guidance: "Do this; avoid that; try this." Negative behaviors are specifically addressed by specific behavioral direction.

It is impossible to have the parents be good assistants in the therapeutic process if their attention is always on negative behaviors. Thus, a first job is to get the controls in place. Then, with the parents assisting, direction can fully center upon the emotional components that hinder the child's overall development.

In general I work exclusively with the parents. In fact, in some cases I never meet the children in question. The rationale is quite simple. Many of these children have malfunctions which are not permanent or genetic. They have, for example, attention deficit disorders dating from the period of rapid brain growth between birth and age five; or adjustment reaction, oppositionalism, or conduct disorders. All of these are results of traumas and interference with development. However, those children who have a diagnosis i.e., clinical depression, pre-psychosis, personality disorder—are seen in therapy for themselves while the parents are being educated about their needs.

I set up a rigorous and specific schedule to be maintained. Parents are helped to understand all workups completed on their child prior to placement. Every term is defined, every angle reviewed and developed. The parents work with the school and testing centers. They monitor, chart, and coordinate all significant aspects of "turning the child around."

I find that parents respond with full cooperation and excitement. They genuinely feel that they can help: that they can do, with guidance, that extra something that draws the child out, that helps the child explore the past, understand more of the present, and be hopeful about the future.

Marital Bond Strengthened

When a therapist works with the parents all kinds of good things begin to happen. They begin to trust and to ask many things. Doors open and one is free to explore the agendas specific to their marriage—control themes, communication, and a common point of interest, their child. It is exciting to witness this happening, to see that cornerstone marital bond becoming stronger and more helpful to everyone in the family.

In the last eight years I have done pre-placement work with a number of adoptions, emphasizing strong parental involvement. Thankfully, none of these has come close to disruptions. As well as providing parents with facts and guidance, I bring out and discuss any problems in their own lives that they need to ponder. I think "my" parents would be the first to say, "Well, it feels a little like school and a lot like therapy."

While working with a dozen disruptions I was able to facilitate two things: the letting-go of the disrupted family, and the reaching-out of the new family. The children whose disruptions I assisted and who have resettled in new homes are doing well. The process of continuity with the therapist has been a healing element.

Advice for Parents

Overall, it would clearly be advisable for parents early in the process of special needs adoption to:

1. *Commit* themselves to a serious study of special needs children, to know fully the emotional impact of adverse developmental histories upon children.
2. *Realize* that living with children who have painful histories can threaten

parents who may be suppressing their own tragic past traumas and neglect. It is difficult for any parent to give something they never had themselves.
3. Find a family therapist experienced in the area of adoption and seeing her/him as a resource, a guide who can lay out plans and assist in all phases of the growth and development of the entire family.

In conclusion, let me say that well-equipped, well-prepared, and of course well-supported parents are essential for the success of a difficult adoption. Special needs children are indeed special, and special responses of parents are necessary. As more and more parents are adequately prepared, we can grow increasingly optimistic that a good job of parenting will be done and the number of disruptions will be greatly reduced.

References

Cline, Foster, 1982, *Parent Education Test,* Evergreen Consultants in Human Behavior, Evergreen, CO.

Jewett, Claudia, 1978, *Adopting the Older Child,* The Harvard Common Press, Harvard, MA.

Plumez, Jacqueline, 1979, *Successful Adoption: Guide to Finding and Raising a Family,* Crown Publishing Co., New York, NY.

13

Helping Threatened Families

Kathryn S. Donley and Maris H. Blechner

When reviewing the long-term adjustment of adoptive families, we are impressed with the number of parents who see their adoptions as successful and their relationships in tolerable shape as their children pass through the usual crises of adolescence. At the same time we are struck by the small but significant number of families, many with years of successful adoption adjustment behind them, who face particularly frightening experiences during their adopted children's teenage years.

These families are alarmed by exhibitions of self-destructive behavior, especially violence or convincing threats of violence by their adopted children. These are families under enormous stress—"threatened" families who fear the episodic explosions of their own children. Though they are few in number, their alarm and dismay are dramatic. For such families, the crisis can rapidly become overwhelming. For someone seeking to help even one such threatened family, the high levels of stress and anxiety within the family, and the inability of the helper to provide quick relief, can combine to create the perception that *all* adoptive families are in similar danger. Both parents and helpers can lose perspective and respond in panic.

Careful scrutiny of the circumstances of these threatened families may help them and us toward a better course of action. Both parents and helpers of parents must understand *what* is happening and the probable reasons *why* it is happening. Only then can we consider *how* we can best deal with the problems.

What Is Happening?

As children become adults, their families normally experience periods of stress. Some families handle the usual stress well. Others barely manage to survive. Most families fall somewhere between the two extremes. However, the threatened families with whom we are concerned have passed well beyond the threshold of usual stress. They are experiencing extraordinary stress which jeopardizes the equilibrium of the family unit.

There are several hallmarks that usually distinguish these particular situations:

- a long-term adoptive relationship is in place
- there is evidence of repeated self-destructive or violent behavior by the adopted child
- the episodes are intensifying
- numerous efforts at obtaining help have been unsuccessful
- the parents feel that the situation is out of control

When trying to help these threatened families, it is important not to mistake them for chronically troubled families who have never experienced a period of relatively calm adjustment. Nor are they in quite the same position as adoptive families with new additions, who may experience the high stress level associated with the early adjustment phase of adoption. The particular families described here as threatened families are most often veteran families of children adopted early in life. Many have adopted several times and some have seen older children well started into adulthood. It should also be noted that more recent adopters of troubled older children may experience similar patterns of explosive behavior once past the initial adjustment phase.

Because parents in a threatened family are often extremely competent, they may have difficulty in convincing others that the problem is as serious as they know it to be. They may also have difficulty in admitting to the severity of the problem they now face with a particular child. They are often far more skilled than the placement agency staff or mental health practitioners to whom they initially turn for help. In fact, their potential helpers may be intimidated by the parents' experience and skill and feel unable to offer any suggestions. In some instances the parents may be alienated from professionals because of old struggles.

Why Is It Happening?

In our experience, at least four possibilities occur:
1. *Misperceptions:*
   There are two kinds of misperceptions. The first kind is a misinterpretation common among families of adolescents who have experienced early separation trauma. These parents never expected adolescence to be this bad. They are stunned by the reality of the wide range and extraordinary intensity of their adolescent's new and unpleasant behaviors: antisocial and

destructive activities, negative and scornful opinions of family life and values, profane language, and strongly oppositional attitudes.

In the second kind of misperception, the family misreads the outcome of their adolescent's behavior, already convinced that the family equilibrium is permanently destroyed. They have yet to see the "ups" to compensate for all of the "downs." They misperceive and underrate their family's capacity to survive these current experiences.

In both types, sorting out the issues tied to the age group becomes the key to understanding whether the family is indeed threatened. Parents need to ask themselves:

- Is my child behaving differently from other teens?
- Have I asked for help from someone who knows about adolescents and adolescent issues?
- Have I talked to my friends honestly about the scary things that their similar age kids are doing?
- Have I spoken to families who have survived their children's stormy adolescences?
- Have I leveled with other people about how I see my child's behavior?

2. *Family Stresses:*

All families are subject to internal and external pressures. Within a threatened family, a youngster's behavior may be triggered by present family problems. Stress can stem from individual problems, marital instability, or community pressures. Developmental realities can also place children in the storm of adolescence just as parents are dealing with their own mid-life traumas. Family stress often makes it difficult for the parents to discover the true nature of the problem. People rarely have a clear view of themselves and their most personal difficulties. Parents may be reluctant to recognize themselves as part of the problem. When the youngster is easily described as a special needs or troubled child, why look any further for an explanation? Parents need to ask themselves:

- Would I still be having marital or personal problems if this child were doing well?
- Am I aware of any particularly strong pressure from the school, my neighbors, my own family, because of this youngster?
- Am I going through a mid-life crisis of my own?
- Have I been taking good care of myself?
- Have I asked someone I trust for an honest opinion of the source of our difficulties?

3. *Separation/Attachment Problems:*

Adopted children must learn to cope with painful facts. Early in life they were separated from the known and the familiar. They had to meet new families and form new attachments. Children coming from multiple placements are not always able to work through their grief over many losses. Only recently have we acknowledged the need for children adopted as infants to come to terms with separation from their birth families.

At adolescence, adopted children face a double burden. They must, like all teenagers, once again work through identity issues. It is doubly hard for them if during their childhood they have never resolved how they were separated from their family of origin. Parents need to ask themselves:

- Does my child know and understand the details of his/her life up to adoptive placement?
- What have I done to be sure of that?
- How have I helped my child deal with the grief, anger and guilt that are part of the mourning process for past losses?
- Have we talked about these things recently?
- At this particularly sensitive time, am I now truly willing to help my child deal with old issues, missing pieces, and loose ends?

4. *Individual Pathology:*

This may be the most misunderstood possibility. Families under extraordinary stress too often conclude that their child is severely disturbed, in some instances, the adopted child in crisis is indeed a mentally-ill youngster. This is an extremely serious situation and can only be determined by a competent diagnostician and confirmed by a second opinion. Parents need to ask themselves:

- Have I checked out all of the other possibilities for my child's behavior (including misperceptions, family stresses, and separation/attachment problems?)
- Is there any other reasonable explanation for what is happening?
- Have I cross - checked my observations with other people who know my child?
- Has my child been diagnosed by a competent clinician?
- Am I clear about my commitment, or am I looking for a way to justify abandoning this child?

Having considered what is happening and why it is happening, we are ready to move toward the most crucial issue.

How Can We Best Deal with the Problem?

Parents' Options

When working with threatened families, several ideas to explore with parents come to mind:

1. *Do not go through the crisis alone!*

   Remember, it is never too early or too late to reach out. If your instincts tell you that something is worsening in your adoptive family relationships, and your normal approaches are not working, *go for help.* Even if yours is a chronic set of problems, you are entitled to information and assistance and sharing your feelings with others.

   - Contact your placement agency if there was one, to see what resources they presently have to offer. (They also need to know what is going on with families in the years after placement, in order to provide proper services to new families.)
   - One of your best resources for help is another parent who has been through this same type of crisis. Look for local parent self-help groups, school guidance counselors, church counselors, community or hospital mental health resources.
   - You may not be the first adoptive parent to go to your parent group for help. See what networks have been established. If none exist, you may want to establish links with other adoptive families in crisis.
   - Get legal advice if you need it. Be clear about your current and future financial and legal responsibilities.

2. *Sort out the facts!*

   Figure out if the problem is a "kid problem" or an adoption problem. Talk to your friends about the behavior of their adolescents to make a better judgment about the problems in your family. You may be dealing with fairly typical "teenage-itis."

3. *Look for patterns!*

   Take another look at your child's family background and placement history to see how these current problems may have emerged. Problems often follow patterns. It is urgent that adoptive parents have access to the child's complete history before finalization, including early life history. Although many families tend to discard material about their children after the adoption, this critically important information should be saved with other important family papers for use if needed in later crisis counseling. Remember that the sealed records statutes in your state may prevent you from getting another copy after the adoption has been finalized.

4. *Keep a log of major happenings!*

   This can prove useful to protect yourself if your actions are questioned, and to help diagnose problems which may be obscure or hidden.

5. *Avoid over-reacting or under-reacting!*

   Be careful in assessing your child's problems and the threat to your family. You can seriously underestimate or overestimate the danger when the situation gets explosive. You can also become immobilized by guilt.

6. *Do not panic at accusations of abuse or neglect!*

   It is not unknown for older adopted children, previously abused, to reach a crisis point in later years and strike out against their adoptive parents. Consult an attorney, however, for your own protection.

7. *Use effective helpers!*

Use only therapists familiar with placement dynamics. If there aren't appropriate mental health facilities in your area, investigate how other families have organized to solve their own problems (e.g., parent support groups in New York State, Wisconsin, and Pennsylvania, among others, have reached out for funding, and established mental health resources to help local families).

8. *Be open to your child's point of view!*

Are you as a parent both talking and listening? Is there room for your opinion and your child's opinion at your table? Make sure that your child knows where you stand on these important issues: his/her past history, life experiences, current behavior, and, most important, your commitment.

9. *Be the parent!*

Do not relinquish custody as the price of help. Do not conclude that the easy way is necessarily the best way. You and your child have a considerable investment in each other. As your child's legal parent you are in the strongest position to make decisions, find resources, demand assistance, find your way out of difficulties, and help other families in the same circumstances.

Helpers' Options

Finally, we need to examine what the helpers of threatened families should keep in mind. Adoption adjustment is relatively simple for some individuals, incredibly difficult for others. We cannot predict the adjustment with great accuracy. What we can do is:

1. *Provide high quality preparation of the children and their new families!*
2. *Predict periods of potential stress to which every adoptive child is vulnerable!*

These are recognized as birthdays, anniversaries, deaths, holidays, changes in routine (such as a new school or a family move). The originally predicted periods of stress may still account for current episodes.

3. *Review what is known concerning the history and functioning of the child!*

Children who have been in foster homes or group care often take longer to go through the stages of development than nonplaced children. During crisis, it is important to remember that the child who came into adoption with delays in development may still not be caught up. A child's physical body catches up in growth most quickly; emotional/personality growth takes longer. Even a teenager may be struggling with very early developmental issues like basic trust and self-esteem at the same time as he/she is handling normal teenage issues. It is important to review a child's early history and assess where and why there have been developmental lags.

4. *Identify the strengths and capacities already demonstrated by the family!*
   When people are in crisis, it is difficult to remember that things were not always like this. Families need to rebuild their self-confidence. Helpers need to see them as something more than perpetual victims.
5. *Provide an array of post-adoption services which help for threatened families!*
   Both crisis intervention and long-term supportive services are necessary.
6. *Offer balanced advice!*
   Do not panic. There is usually a series of dramatic episodes before one particular event triggers the family's cry for help. Families may not come for assistance until the crisis is seemingly out of control. When they come, they are often desperate and appear hysterical. Because they are so distressed, they are poorly received in schools, mental health settings, and community programs. Their experiences and their reactions are magnified and even distorted.
7. *Be both optimistic and realistic in working with threatened families!*
   Families are really more resilient than they credit themselves with being. All of the work poured into a youngster may not show results for many years. Progress cannot be measured in months.
8. *Reach out toward other helpers and form alliances!*
   This will enable you to have a broader view of the problem and draw on others' experiences. Eventually you will add your wisdom and skill to an expanding resource population.

Conclusion

This material is an effort to reach out to threatened families and their helpers, to begin exploring the possible causes of the explosive behaviors some families report. By no means have we exhausted the topic or resolved the issues raised. Our hope is to open the subject for further scrutiny and effort.

We cannot emphasize strongly enough that most adoptive families will experience a "survivable" adolescent adjustment period. There are no statistics available on how many adoptive families fit into the category of threatened families. We believe that they are relatively few in number. Their pain is impressive, however, and can be demoralizing for them, for their helpers, and for all of us deeply committed to adoption as the best option for children who cannot grow up within their families of origin.

What we cannot afford is the complacent vision that adoption means living happily ever after. It is a lifelong commitment between parent and child. Part of that commitment is facing the struggles when they occur and learning from each adoption in turn.

Suggested Readings

Classics in Child Development And Family Life

Erikson, Erik. "Eight Stages of Man," Chapter Seven in *Childhood and Society,* Second Edition. New York: W.W. Norton & Co., 1963.

Freud, Anna. *Normality and Pathology in Childhood.* New York: International Universities Press, 1965.

Newman, Barbara, and Newman, Philip. *Development Through Life; A Psychological Approach,* revised edition. Illinois: Dorsey Press, 1979.

Rhodes, Sonya. "A Developmental Approach to the Life Cycle of the Family." *Social Casework,* Volume 58, Number 5 (May, 1977), pp. 301–310.

Sheehy, Gail. *Passages: Predictable Crises of Adult Life.* New York: E.P. Dutton, 1976.

Help with Your Teenager

Bayard, Robert & Bayard, Jean. *How to Deal with Your Acting-Up Teenager: Practical Help for Desperate Parents.* New York: M. Evans Co., 1983.

Calladine, Carole, and Calladine, Andrew. *Raising Brothers and Sisters without Raising the Roof.* Minneapolis: Winston Press, 1979.

Cline, Foster. *Parent Education Text.* Evergreen, Colorado: Evergreen Consultants in Human Behavior, 1982.

———*What Shall We Do with This Kid? Understanding and Treating the Difficult Child.* Evergreen, Colorado: Evergreen Consultants in Human Behavior, 1979.

Ginott, Chaim. *Between Parent and Teenager.* New York: Avon Books, 1969.

Glasser, William. *Reality Therapy.* New York: Harper and Row, 1965.

York, Phyllis, York, David, and Wachtel, Ted. *Toughlove.* New York: Bantam Books, 1982.———*Toughlove Solutions.* New York: Bantam Books, 1984.

Understanding Separation, Attachment, and Grief in Adoption:

Bolton, Frank. *When Bonding Fails.* Beverly Hills, California: Stage Publications, 1983.

Bowlby, John. *Child Care and the Growth of Love.* Baltimore, Maryland: Penguin Books, 1953.

———*The Making and Breaking of Affectional Bonds.* London: Tavistock Publications, 1979.

Cline, Foster. *Understanding and Treating the Severely Disturbed Child.* Evergreen, Colorado: Evergreen Consultants in Human Behavior, 1979.

Fahlberg, Vera. *Attachment and Separation*. Michigan: Michigan Dept. of Social Services, 1979.

——*Helping Children When They Must Move*. Michigan: Michigan Dept. of Social Services, 1980.

——*The Child in Placement: Common Behavioral Problems*. Michigan: Michigan Dept. of Social Services, 1981.

Hartman, Ann. *Working with Adoptive Families Beyond Placement*. New York: Child Welfare League of America, 1984.

Jewett, Claudia. *Adopting the Older Child*. Massachusetts: Harvard Common Press, 1982.

——*Helping Children Cope with Separation and Loss*. Massachusetts: Harvard Common Press, 1982.

Kirk, David. *Shared Fate,* revised edition. Port Angeles, Washington: Ben-Simon Publications, 1984.

Kubler-Ross, Elisabeth. *On Death and Dying*. New York: Macmillan, 1969.

Littner, Ner. *Some Traumatic Effects of Separation and Placement*. New York: Child Welfare League of America, 1956.

Rutter, Michael. *Maternal Deprivation Reassessed*. Baltimore, Maryland: Penguin Books, 1973.

Winter, Alice. "Only People Cry." *Woman's Day,* September, 1963.

14

Post-Placement Services Analysis

Kathryn S. Donley

What Is the Post Placement Services Analysis?

The Post Placement Services Analysis is a tool for placement workers to help determine the direction of supportive services before a crisis occurs in the adoptive placement. The analysis is based on careful exploration of specialized adoption techniques and experiences; it is not an infallible means of predicting the survivability of placements.

When Can I Use It?

The Analysis can be used in those instances where adoption is planned and the child is being placed with a new family which was recruited and prepared for the adoptive relationship. It is most effective when used within the first 30 days of a new placement. It is appropriate for most school age children, that is, children of six years and older. The Analysis may not be equally as helpful for severely retarded children.

What Issues Does the Analysis Address?

This Analysis focuses on three issues of particular concern:

1. the child's capacity for attachment;
2. the child's resolution of separation; and
3. family stresses which may affect the placement adjustment.

There are other variables to be considered, but they are beyond the scope of this particular content.

How Do I Use the Analysis?

The Analysis provides a worker with an overview of the relative strengths and weaknesses of a given family by working through:

- evaluation sheets for determining whether or not services are needed;
- specific services for the worker to select and use;
- suggestions for handling resistance;
- an optional worksheet for summarizing your plan; and
- selected references.

Can I Involve the Adoptive Parents in the Analysis?

Workers are encouraged to engage the adoptive parent(s) in completion of the evaluation sheets, particularly those dealing with family stresses. If workers complete the Analysis separately, they should share their assessment with the parent(s). By so doing they can reinforce parent awareness of critical issues, facilitate teamwork in the post placement service plan, and reach a consensus on primary goals.

Who Developed the Post Placement Services Analysis?

The Post Placement Services Analysis was developed by New York Spaulding for Children staff during 1982 through 1985 in conjunction with two consultants: Trudy Festinger, Ph.D., and Arlene Litwack, MSW. New York Spaulding for Children is a special needs adoption and training agency located at 121 West 27 Street, New York, NY 10001; 212/645-7610.

Funding for the Analysis was provided by the Robert Sterling Clark Foundation and The New York Community Trust without whose generous assistance this project would not have been possible.

* * * * *

Several concepts may need clarification as you begin using the Analysis:

Attachment is the most basic emotional bond developed between a child and an adult caretaking figure upon whom the child is dependent. It is a fundamental human ability developed when a positive nurturing atmosphere is present. Kennell, et al define attachment as: "an affectionate bond between two individuals that endures through space and time and serves to join them emotionally'' (1976).

Resolving separation is the overall process whereby the child grieves his loss and becomes free to establish new connections. Elisabeth Kubler-Ross outlines five stages in the separation process: denial and isolation, anger, bargaining, depression, and acceptance (1969). Claudia Jewett describes these five stages: denial, sadness, anger, despair, and finally detachment (1982). A prerequisite for separation is a meaningful human connection.

Kay Donley defines *disengagement* as the process of giving a child permission to make new attachments. This process entails 1) mastering the placement history of the child; 2) identifying the child's main attachment figures; 3) gaining the permission of the significant attachment figure for the child to love and be loved by others; 4) giving the message to the child convincingly; and 5) reinforcing (repeating) the message over time. The aim of this process is to begin integrating the old and new attachment figures in the perception of the child, thus making it easier for the child to forge new family relationships.

Renurturing is a process whereby the parent recognizes the gaps in an older, adoptive child's early life and tries to integrate some of those missing experiences into the child's present life. The process of renurturing involves providing physical and emotional nurture, stability, guidance, and structure at a level appropriate for the emotional age of the child.

Selected References

Bowlby, John. *Attachment and Loss: I. Attachment.* New York: Basic Books, 1969.

Bowlby, John. *Attachment and Loss: II. Separation, Anxiety and Anger.* New York: Basic Books, 1973.

Bolton, Frank G. *When Bonding Fails: Clinical Assessment of High Risk Families.* Beverly Hills: Sage Publications, 1983.

Fahlberg, Vera. *Attachment and Separation.* Michigan Department of Social Services, 1979. (Available from Spaulding for Children, PO Box 337, Chelsea, Michigan 48118.)

Jewett, Claudia. *Helping Children Cope with Separation and Loss.* Harvard, MA: The Harvard Common Press, 1982.

Kennell, J., Voos, D., and Klaus, M., ''Parent-Infant Bonding'' in Helfer, R., and Kempe, C. H. (eds.), *Child Abuse and Neglect.* Cambridge, MA: Ballenger Publishing Co., 1976.

Kubler-Ross, Elisabeth. *On Death and Dying.* New York: Macmillan, 1969.

Rutter, Michael. *Maternal Deprivation Reassessed.* New York: Penguin Books, 1981.

Complete one entire PPS Analysis for each child in adoptive placement and proceed as instructed on each page.

Feel free to duplicate your original PPS Analysis before proceeding so you will have copies for use with other children.

Child: _____

Family: _____

Date of the child's placement with this family: _____

Is this placement in adoptive status? _____

As of what date: _____

Worker: _____

Date this PPS Analysis was completed: _____

Note: Use the worksheet on page 179 to summarize all your findings. This summary can serve as a reminder of your plan for post placement services and a copy can then be filed in the case record.

EVALUATION SHEET # 1
CAPACITY FOR ATTACHMENT

Think about this particular child in responding to the factors below.
Check the response which seems most accurate.

	very or often true	somewhat/ sometimes true	a little or rarely true	not true
1. had multiple care-takers or inconsistent care during first year of life				
2. had extended period of care in hospital or institution during first year of life				
3. was abused or neglected at any time				
4. never had a particular person who really matters to this child				
5. does not form significant relationships with adults				
6. does not form significant relationships with other children				
7. did not have a compensatory nurturing experience after the first year of life				

Circle the number which, in your judgment, best describes this child's
capacity for attachment.

unable to attach   ———————————————————   able to attach
           1   2   3   4   5

If the number is 3 or below, it shows a significant level of inability
to attach. If the number exceeds 3, it means that the child is
relatively capable of attachment. In either case, turn to the next
page and complete Evaluation Sheet #2.

EVALUATION SHEET #2
RESOLUTION OF SEPARATION

Think about this particular child in responding to the factors below.
Check the response which seems the most accurate.

	very or often true	somewhat/ sometimes true	a little or rarely true	not true
1. does not know placement history				
2. has powerful wishes or fantasies about reunion which do not yield to discussion				
3. has not received adequate disengagement signal from significant attachment figures (has not been given permission to move on in giving and receiving of love)				
4. maintains contact with a significant person opposed to adoption				
5. shows inappropriate feelings of sadness or loss				

Circle the number which, in your judgment, best describes this child's
resolution of separation.

separation unresolved	-------------------------------------	separation resolved
	1 2 3 4 5	

If the number is 3 or below, it indicates a significant level of
unresolved separation. Turn to the next page to plan what you propose
to do about the problem. If the number exceeds 3, it indicates that
separation is relatively resolved.

If you believe that the child is capable of attachment and that
separation is resolved, turn to page 8 to evaluate family stresses
affecting placement adjustment.

REMINDER: Use the worksheet on page 12 to summarize all your
findings. You can fill in this summary as you move through the
Analysis or complete it after you have finished the entire
instrument.

SPECIFIC SERVICES
SEPARATION AND ATTACHMENT

Check
services
needed

1. LIFE BOOK WORK
   - reconstruct the child's placement history
   - identify major attachment figures
   - begin talking with child about life history, family members, reasons for separations
   - make a life book with the child summarizing your discussion
   - update life book previously done
   - review/reinforce life book work with child

2. DISENGAGEMENT WORK
   - worker contacts old attachment figure
   - worker gains cooperation of old attachment figure in giving permission for the child to develop new relationships
   - worker reinforces disengagement messages (letters, phone calls, visits, conversations

3. RENURTURING
   (This is the process by which parent(s) integrate missing early experiences into the child's present life. See definition on page 2.)

4. COMMITMENT WORK
   - promoting investment in the family
   - reviewing realities of joining a family (i.e., benefits/responsibilities)

5. PROMOTING ATTACHMENT BEHAVIORS
   - using the words "Mom" and "Dad" (or equivalent)
   - sharing projects or experiences
   - developing physical closeness
   - increasing private time with individual family members
   - caring for a pet
   - participating in special interest groups with strong loyalty ties (e.g., Scouts, Little League team, choir, clubs)

6. REFERRAL
   - identify the type of resource needed
   - evaluate the potential resource
   - facilitate the family involvement with them
   - monitor service given
   - assess impact of service on problem

7. OTHER (specify your choice)
   - _____
   - _____

USEFUL SUGGESTIONS
SEPARATION AND ATTACHMENT

Considering the services you believe are needed, how will you work with this family? Circle the useful suggestions and add others of your own devising.

1. help parent(s) solidify commitment to adoption

2. help parent(s) connect child to extended family, friends, and neighbors

3. stress the futility of preventing contacts with significant others from the child's past

4. create visible evidence of child's place in the family

5. discuss parental concerns about child's commitment

6. explore hobbies, interests, etc., in order to plan joint projects

7. help parent(s) balance risks and gains of the action you you choose

8. explore parental fear of rejection

9. help parent(s) avoid broken promises

10. discuss specific parental questions, doubts, fears

11. help parent(s) better organize their time

12. recall presentation information on child's history and functioning

13. find alternatives to owning a pet

14. help parent(s) reduce expectations about child's attachment

15. urge parent(s) to compensate for early damage (educate parent regarding missed childhood)

16. encourage various family members to express physical affection

17. recall content of family preparation regarding separation and attachment

18. use examples of veteran family experiences (verbal or written)

19. clarify realities (i.e., gaining subsidy approval, achieving legal finalization, etc.)

20. urge parent(s) to be dependable about departures and returns

21. educate the parent(s) to the need for additional services

22. help parents differentiate their own feelings and experiences from those of the child

23. encourage parental mission as helpers

24. other (please specify)

Use the worksheet on page 12 to summarize your findings.

EVALUATION SHEET # 3
FAMILY STRESSES AFFECTING PLACEMENT ADJUSTMENT

All families are affected by stresses, but the addition of an adopted child or children creates additional pressures. The first step in dealing with possible stresses is to identify them. Read the list of factors below which frequently cause stress. In the first column, check if the factor is present. Then decide what degree of stress each factor brings to the family.

	Check if factor is present	Does this factor produce stress on the placement?		
		a little	some	a lot
1. Opposition to the adoption by people connected to:				
a) the adoptive family:				
• spouse				
• biological children				
• immediate family				
• extended family member				
• foster or adopted children				
• other important people (please specify)				
b) the placed child:				
• previous caretaker				
• biological family member				
• other important people (please specify)				
2. Interpersonal difficulties with:				
• previous domestic partner				
• current domestic partner				
• other children in the family				
• other members of the household				
• other important people (please specify)				
3. Existence of:				
• financial pressures				
• job pressures				
• major responsibility for extended family member				
• conflict with school system				
• a living situation not sanctioned by society				
• family member with prison or mental hospital experience				

EVALUATION SHEET # 3 (cont.)
FAMILY STRESSES AFFECTING PLACEMENT ADJUSTMENT

	Cneck if factor is present	Does this factor produce stress on the placement?		
		a little	some	a lot

3. Existence of (cont.):
    ● substance abuse (drugs or alcohol) by any family member
    ● ideas, practices, or beliefs the child may not have previously encountered
    ● recent losses (i.e. ending of a relationship, divorce, separation, death, etc.)
    ● an unexpected crisis
    ● values in conflict with the child's behavior
    ● other (please specify)

    ----

4. Change in:
    ● location
    ● family composition
    ● child care plan
    ● customary routine
    ● other (please specify)

    ----

5. Someone in the home (other than the placed child) with:
    ● physical illness
    ● chronic health problems
    ● physical disabilities
    ● learning problems
    ● mental retardation
    ● emotional problems
    ● other (please specify)

    ----

6. Absence of adequate:
    ● housing
    ● child care arrangements
    ● support system
    ● other (please specify)

Discuss with the family the number on the scale below which best describes the level of stress on this placement.

severe   --------------------------------------   no
stress   1   2   3   4   5   stress

SPECIFIC SERVICES I
FAMILY STRESSES AFFECTING PLACEMENT ADJUSTMENT

If the number from the previous page is 3 or below, it shows a significant level of stress exists which may impede the adoptive adjustment. In that case, you can plan services below. If the number exceeds 3, it means the level of stress does not impose a significant burden on the placement.

In this worksheet, there are three aspects to consider. The first is CLARIFICATION WORK which should be attempted with all families where stress affects the placement. The second aspect is PROBLEM SOLVING designed to reduce the stress on the family. The third aspect is RESOURCE FINDING which may be a particular kind of assistance needed by the family.

Check
services
needed

1. CLARIFICATION WORK is a discussion process by which the worker and family:

    • recognize stress (as on page 8 and 9)
    • predict the potential impact on the placement
    • seek solutions in advance of a crisis

2. PROBLEM SOLVING is often handled directly by the family without worker assistance. When a family needs assistance, it becomes necessary for the worker to help them identify and implement solutions to stress. The worker helps the family:

    • state the problem clearly
    • identify the possible solutions
    • weigh the consequences
    • act on the best choice

3. RESOURCE FINDING is a process by which the worker helps the family:

    • identify who might help
    • specify how they might help
    • ask for the help needed
    • advocate or facilitate on behalf of the family as necessary

SPECIFIC SERVICES (cont)
FAMILY STRESSES AFFECTING PLACEMENT ADJUSTMENT

Below are two categories of resources which you might suggest.   Circle
the helpers and methods you what to promote.

PERSONAL RESOURCES

Informal familial or community
contacts capable of providing
concrete assistance or emotional support to the family
under stress.

OUTSIDE RESOURCES

Formal, organized groups,
agencies, or services designed
to provide concrete assistance,
resource materials, or emo-
ional support to the family
under stress.

4. Who can help?

- family members
- friends
- neighbors
- acquaintances
- other adoptive families
- other (please specify)

----

6. Who/What can help?

- professional services
- organized self help groups
- resource materials
- other (please specify)

----

5. How can they help?

- support (listening, understanding, sharing experiences, giving advice, etc.)

- direct assistance (sharing
  tasks, providing trans-
  portation, loaning money,
  caring for the children,
  introducing people, finding
  a new job, etc.)

7. How can they help?

- tangible assistance
  (tutoring, financial aid,
  medical treatment, recreation,
  child care, etc.)

- information (job or debt
  counseling, housing assistance, parent education, etc.)

- therapeutic intervention
  (individual or group therapy,
  casework services, family
  therapy, parent counseling,
  etc.)

Use the worksheet on page 12 to summarize your findings.

SUMMARY WORKSHEET

Child:

CAPACITY FOR ATTACHMENT
(see page 4):   unable   ------------------------   able
                to attach   1   2   3   4   5   to attach

RESOLUTION OF SEPARATION
(see page 5):   separation ------------------------   separation
                unresolved 1   2   3   4   5   resolved

Summarize services needed in each category. Refer to page 6.

1. Life Book Work:__ _____

2. Disengagement Work:_____

3. Renurturing:_____

4. Commitment Work:_____

5. Developing Attachment Behaviors:_____

6. Make a Referral:_____

7. Other:_____

Summarize Useful Suggestions from page 7 on back of this sheet.

FAMILY STRESSES AFFECTING
PLACEMENT ADJUSTMENT
(see page 9   severe ------------------------ no
                  stress 1   2   3   4   5 stress

Summarize services needed in each category from pages 10 and 11.

1. Clarification Work:_____

2. Problem Solving:_____

3. Resource Finding:_____

4. Which personal contacts can help:_____

5. How can they help:_____

6. Which outside resources can help:_____

7. How can they help:_____

Other Comments:_____ _____

_____

15

A Developmental Approach to Separation/ Loss

Vera I. Fahlberg

Introduction

As the child grows up, he must accomplish varying developmental tasks related to psychological maturation. The child cannot accomplish these tasks on his own, nor can his parents accomplish them for him. The tasks are achieved only in the context of the parent–child relationship. Therefore, we can expect that parent separation or loss will have a major impact on the child's psychological development.

This occurs for four primary reasons: (1) Depending on circumstances, the child has lost either all or a major part of his parent–child relationship; (2) At times of stress, humans regress to earlier levels to regroup their strengths; (3) The child's energies are used to cope with feelings relating to the loss and are not available for coping with more age–appropriate developmental tasks; and (4) Usually after a parent separation or loss, the remaining parent is coping with his/her own psychological stress, and he/she is not as available for helping the child accomplish the developmental tasks at hand.

The steps in the psychological maturation process always follow the same order. Therefore, if we know the age of the child at the time of the parental separation or loss, we can predict the psychological areas in which the child will be particularly vulnerable. If after such loss, the child may be so unfortunate as to live in an environment which does not help him regroup strengths, cope with feelings, and re-establish psychological equilibrium, we can expect serious long-term effects secondary to the parent separation or loss. Indeed, many children who are in today's foster care system or who have been adopted are, to one degree or another, psychologically "stuck" at the age of the initial parental separation.

Effects of Loss on the Tasks of Varying Ages

First Year

The primary tasks to be accomplished within the parent-child relationship during the first year of life are threefold: (1) the meeting of dependency needs; (2) the building up of feelings of trust, security, and attachment: and (3) the first steps in sorting out the significance of various external and internal stimuli. Frequently, children who enter the child welfare system during their first year of life do so because these identified needs are not being met. These children may not show severe effects secondary to separation and loss. Indeed, these children may blossom in their new environment. However, other children whose needs are being met, but who still face parent loss, will show the effects of such loss. There will likely be a regression to earlier levels of dependency and feelings of trust, security, and attachment will surely be undermined. After the loss, remedial measures will have to be taken to address these two areas. That is, the parent must be extremely careful to meet dependency needs and to facilitate attachment.

The third task relates to the child's learning how to learn (Gesell, et al). The first steps in sorting out external and internal perceptions depend on the parent figures, who are mediators between the child and his environment. Even infants pick up the rhythms of a household and begin to develop a primitive sense of cause and effect. The three- or four-month-old child who is hungry starts to calm down when he sees the parent figure who usually provides the physical nourishment (Spitz). This same child who is fed when hungry, but not at other times, starts to connect the internal sensations of hunger with the externally–provided relief supplied by food and starts to recognize hunger as a discrete form of discomfort associated with a particular form of relief. Another example is the seven- to eight-month-old child living in a family whose parent consistently comes home from work at the same time each day. He will probably show anticipatory excitement in response to a car at that time of day. With parent loss or separation, there are usually concomitant changes in the daily routine: thus, cause and effect acquisition is interrupted.

The Toddler Years (1–3)

The primary issue for the toddler switches from dependency to independency with increasing autonomy. Together with the autonomy issues are the identity issues. This is the time of life when the youngster becomes aware of himself as a person separate from his primary caretaker. It is the time when true ego development begins. The child becomes increasingly aware of the implications that various sights, sounds, and smells have, as well as internal body states, such as a full bladder. This is also the time of very rapid language acquisition.

These, then, will be the areas of development most affected by parent loss or separation at this stage. It is quite common for children who experience parent separation at this point in their lives to have difficulty developing an appropriate balance between dependency and autonomy. Some seem to withdraw and become more dependent; they seem to be saying, "It is not safe for me to become independent." Another child, with a different temperament is likely to go to the other extreme, becoming too independent. Such a child is apt to parent himself. He may withhold affection and seem stubborn and resistant in all areas for a prolonged period of time (Fahlberg).

Identity formation at this age seems to relate to several factors including the sex of the child, the child's position in the family, and the child's name. Obviously, the child's sex does not change with parent loss. But his position in the family may radically change, particularly if the loss comes about by the child's moving from one family to another.

Position in the family not only relates to the child's birth order but also to other factors. Clearly, a first male child born into an extended family in which there have been no male children for several generations will have a different position than a female child.

The child's position in the family is, to some degree, determined by the child's temperament. For example, in one family the comment, "This is our active child" may carry a positive connotation; while in another family that trait may be viewed as negative. A child recognizes his name by at least one year of age, and the given name becomes a part of his identity. Changes of first names, especially at this particular stage of development, may cause problems for the child in developing a strong sense of self.

Since young children in a period of rapid language acquisition are usually dependent on a family member to initially be the "interpreter" for others, loss of this person will have a significant impact on language development. Although the actual vocabulary used with children this age may not vary so much from one family to another, the rhythm of speech, the pronunciation, and the way words are connected seems to vary considerably.

Preschool Years (Oedipal State) (3–5 1/2–6)

Continued individuation, increased independence and proficiency in the self-care areas, and continued marked growth in the area of language development are the hallmarks of this age. The biggest problems in resolving separation–loss issues seem to relate to two internal psychological struggles and the particular thinking characteristics of these pre-school children.

Play is the medium used for resolution of two major internal psychological issues: The big-vs-little struggle, and the good-vs-bad struggle. The child this age receives many conflicting parental messages. He hears comments such as ''Big boys don't wet their pants, they use the potty'' combined with messages such as ''No, you are too little to be outside the fence.'' The child of this age has to come to grips with the fact that he is neither big nor little but rather a combination of both. This is when the first real balance between dependency and independency is achieved.

The infant was primarily dependent. The toddler's independency needs are strong in the service of individuation and ego development. The preschooler is truly a combination of both. The child who successfully accepts this psychological position—that it is okay to be both dependent and independent—is well on the way to having a healthy balance between these two factors to fall back on the remainder of his life.

The other internal psychological struggle has some similarities. The child must learn to accept himself as a good person who sometimes does naughty things, not as a person who is *either* good *or* bad. Indeed, these two issues are reflected in the majority of the preschooler's play (Hymes). He is involved in a variety of independent vs. dependent play, such as house, school, doctor. A psychologically healthy preschooler goes back and forth between the dependency and independency roles, enjoying each. The other recurrent theme in play is ''good guys''-vs-''bad guys'' play; again most preschoolers relish both roles.

Children this age have characteristic thinking patterns as well. Egocentricity and magical thinking are especially prominent at this stage. Fear of parental abandonment is the preschooler's greatest fear. These particular characteristics combine to pose some predictable reactions to parental separation or loss. In his attempts to make sense of the events in his world, the child nearly always perceives the events as occurring because he was ''bad'' in some way. It becomes very important, in trying to correct this misperception, to decode the child's particular brand of magical thinking. It is common for children this age, when angry with a parent, to either verbalize or at least think ''I hate you'' or ''I wish I had a different mommy (daddy).'' Then, if a loss occurs, the child may attribute it to his ''bad'' thoughts, thus, reinforcing the perception of himself as the cause.

Another form of magical thinking needs to be closely watched for. This relates to the child thinking that something he does or says can change the loss. Just as he perceives himself as responsible for the loss, he perceives himself as responsible for either regaining or not regaining the parent.

Individuals who in later life, have very high expectations for themselves and who see themselves as really "bad" whenever they make a mistake or are naughty, and who then subsequently "dump" on themselves, frequently have experienced parental separation at this stage of their life.

The child's magical thinking may also relate to big-vs-little issues. This is especially likely to occur if a child leaves a family and other children remain in the family. Then the child's magical thinking may explain the loss in such ways as "The baby stayed. Babies are preferable. It's not safe to grow up."

Because this is also an age of heightened sexual awareness and of the young child's "falling in love" with the parent of the other sex, the child may attribute parent loss, of either parent, to his own thoughts and feelings in this area.

Even though it is very difficult to overcome the child's egocentricity and magical thinking at this age, it is important to understand and decode the child's thinking. This should be done so that, at subsequent ages as the child develops better conceptual skills, he can be helped to give up the old thinking. Unless one knows the particulars of the child's magical thinking, it is very difficult to aid in changing the perceptions even in later years.

Grade School Years (6–12)

The latency-age child is dependent on the security of the family relationships to provide him with the psychological energy to master out-of-family issues. During the earlier years, most of his energy was expended on in-family skills and relationships. Now he must master problems and relationships outside the family unit. Most of the child's energies go into academic learning, improving gross and fine motor skills, and peer relationships, primarily with peers of the same sex. Clearly, repeated moves or separations are likely to have a negative impact on the child's academic and peer socialization skills.

Another major area of psychological growth is conscience development. Conscience development starts prior to this age and continues long after, but it is during this period that the biggest growth occurs. The child moves from fear of displeasing adults to an internalized sense of right-vs-wrong, which is no longer dependent upon an adult's presence.

During these years there are major changes in the child's ability to think and conceptualize. Around age nine, the child makes a major leap in conceptual development. At that point he takes all previously–learned material and re-examines it through new eyes. We know when the child achieves this, as he becomes a "know-it-all." The positive aspects of this growth, however, allow the child to re-examine previous life events and incorporate them into his self-perception in a newer, psychologically healthier manner. Indeed, children who have experienced parent separation or loss at earlier ages frequently can benefit markedly from brief psychotherapeutic intervention at this stage.

Adolescence

Adolescent issues are very similar to the psychological tasks of the toddler–preschool age; and, indeed, egocentric thinking and magical thinking re-emerge in adolescence. This is because both ages are times of marked growth in psychological separation-individuation issues. The young child's task is to separate psychologically from the caretaker(s) and find his place within the family structure. The adolescent's task is to separate psychologically from the family and find his place among peers and in society as a whole. During times of marked growth in individuation, control issues become prominent. The toddler's declaration of independence is contained in the three words, "me," "mine," and "no." The adolescent acts out these same issues. "You can't make me," whether said verbally or behaviorally, is a major issue for adolescents. The goal of the supportive parenting figure during adolescence is not to "make" the child but rather to help the young person explore alternatives, make choices, and take responsibility for the choices.

Teenagers can accomplish the individuation tasks of adolescence easiest if they have a stable parent pair to come up against, push off from, and individuate from. It is very difficult for the adolescent to accomplish the normal tasks of this stage if he is having to cope with physical separation or loss as well as, or in place of, psychological separation or loss. When the teen's primary job is to separate and individuate, it is particularly difficult for him to work on becoming a member of a new family unit at the same time. This is particularly true during early adolescence, when the psychological tasks are most prominent. It does become easier in later adolescence when the physical emancipation, as opposed to the psychological emancipation, is most prominent.

Conclusion

By understanding the varying developmental tasks to be accomplished at varying ages, it becomes easier to understand both the short-term and the long-term effects of parent separation or loss. Since all adopted children have faced parent loss, and many have faced repeated losses, these are particularly important issues for the clinician working with such children. Once we understand which current issues may relate to early loss issues and how they relate to the separations, our task in helping the young person resolve these issues and change his behaviors becomes much easier.

References

Fahlberg, Vera: *Child Development,* British Agencies for Adoption and Fostering, London, England, 1982.

Fraiberg, Selma H.: *The Magic Years,* Charles Scribner's Son, New York, 1959.

Gessell, Arnold, Ph.D., M.D., and Halverson, Ilg, Thompson, Castner, Ames, Amatruda: *The First Five Years of Life: The Preschool Years,* Harper and Row, New York, 1940.

Gesell, Arnold, M.D., and Ilg, Frances, L., M.D.: *The Child from Five to Ten,* Harper and Row, New York, 1946.

Hymes, James L., Jr.: *The Child under Six,* Prentice Hall,, New Jersey, 1969.

Normal Adolescence: Its Dynamics and Impact, Formulated by the Committee on Adolescence Group for Advancement of Psychiatry, New York, 1968, Vol. VI, Report 68, February 1968.

Spitz, Rene: *The First Year of Life,* International Universities Press, New York, 1965.

16

The Mental Health Professional, the Legal Process, and the Child in Out-of-Home Care

M. Jerome Fialkov and Eric Cohen

More than 2 million children were under child welfare supervision in 1980. Of these, over half a million children, almost 14% of all those under 18 years, were, during that period, in out-of-home care under the auspices of the child welfare system; that is, they had been placed in state custody by parental request or as the result of a court order[1]. While some parents voluntarily place their children in the custody of child welfare, most are removed from their homes because of neglect or abuse by their families; some have poor relationships with parents who in desperation seek placement, while others are out of their homes by default because more appropriate alternatives are not available to keep families together. A surprisingly large number of children are in care because of the mental illness of one or both parents or because of their own emotional problems[2].

History

American history indicates that the preference for the family dates to Colonial times. In keeping with English Common Law, children were regarded as chattels—the property of their parents, particularly the father, whose responsibility it was to maintain, educate and protect his offspring. With increasing industrialization and immigration at the beginning of the 19th century, American society began to concentrate in urban areas. Institutions such as orphanages were built to provide mass care until the parentless child could be apprenticed or employed. Since exploitation of children was prevalent, children removed from their parents were placed in private orphan asylums or public almshouses, or went out West to work on farms. However, some families were provided either money or goods to allow their offspring to remain in their homes[3].

When large institutions and orphanages became too expensive to maintain, reformers began to agitate for public protective services, under federal and state legislation, to strengthen the child's own home.

The turn of the century saw the inception of the juvenile court system, which assumed jurisdiction over cases of delinquency and abandonment, dependency, abuse, and neglect. Initially, the legal doctrine of *parens patriae* controlled all judicial proceedings. *Parens patriae* is an ancient legal term which describes the power of the state to act as the ultimate parent on behalf of the child's property interests and their persons. *The best interest of the child* principle emerged somewhat later and refers to the State's responsibility to assure that its actions are not detrimental to the child[4]. The juvenile court evolved as a separate institution from the adult court system intended to humanistically address the child's problems and treat them by directing the care, custody, and control of the child. Although the first White House Conference on Children in 1909, promoted the idea that the child should not be removed from his own home due to poverty alone; children of the poor were in fact found in out-of-home care in increasing numbers often with new families in what today is known as foster care. Many children were placed in institutions where they remained until they were adults.

By the 1950's protracted foster care was perceived as an unsatisfactory solution to the burgeoning social problem because many children remained in "temporary" care for most of their childhood. Even the Courts were operating as extensions of social welfare agencies. The *Kent* decision signalled the restructuring of the juvenile justice system by defining the constitutional rights of a class of citizens, namely minors, who previously were not believed to possess any. In 1969, in a First Amendment case, children were declared "persons" under the Constitution. Since then, major gains have been achieved in the legal rights of children. These gains are attributable primarily to federal action, either by Congress or the Federal Courts.

The Adoption Assistance and Child Welfare Act of 1980 (PL 96-272) is one consequence of these judicial reforms and was implemented to encourage better management of children living apart from their biological parents. It assured special protections, such as the right to separate legal representation, protection against foster-care drift by reunification with the family of origin or establishment of permanency within a new family unit, recognition of the rights of relatives and fosterparents, the right of foster children to protection from abuse and neglect, and the right of handicapped children to services for special needs. In this way the unnecessary removal of children from the original family unit is prevented. Foster children are (under ideal circumstances) returned to their families of origin within a reasonable time after their removal, and permanent homes for foster children are secured when return is unlikely.

This emphasis on permanency for children is based on the belief that children need stability, continuity, and commitment from their caregivers if they are to become emotionally stable and competent adults[5]. A child needs parents who are fully and irrevocably committed to caring for him through most kinds of family crises and who are not likely to abandon him when distressed or dissatisfied with the child's behavior. Belonging to a permanent family is believed to provide a feeling of security, protection of rights, respected social status, and a more secure sense of the future, thereby eliminating the uncertainty and stigma of foster-child status[6]. Children are also thought to be better raised by autonomous families without interference from the state[7].

The Emotional Consequences of Separation Experiences

In the course of psychosocial development, children separate themselves from their parents during toddlerhood and again in adolescence. For children in foster or adoptive care, the natural sequence of this process may be disrupted by temporary or permanent separations from parental figures. The acute reaction to disruption of the parent–child bond is thought to be akin to grief or mourning, with distinct phases of protest, despair, and detachment. Longterm consequences of parent–child separation is dependent upon such factors as the age of the child when separation first occurred, with maximum distress at 6 to 48 months; the quality of the parent–child relationship prior to the separation; the temperament of the child, those showing low adaptability and high reactivity having an increased vulnerability to separation; multiple placements, increasing the likelihood of vulnerability to subsequent separations; the duration of separation; effects of a strange environment, with short- or longer-term ill effects decreased if the child remains in familiar surroundings or in the continued presence of valued others; and the nature of the child's situation after separation.

Such separations are best conceptualized as mourning reactions through which children resolve, by gradual detachment from their primary parent figure, the finality of their loss in order to reattach to a parental substitute. The more distressed the previous parent–child relationship, the more intense the attachment and the greater the difficulty the child has in working through the separation. As a result, the child's distress may interfere with the reattachment process and hinder his acceptance by, and integration in, substitute families.

Over the long term, maladaptive coping behaviors may develop in children who have been involved in numerous separations due to multiple placements. These appear to be due less to separation than to effects of family discord, abuse, or neglect. Children may show a permanent detachment due to unsatisfactory attachment(s) prior to separation, especially following neglect. They reinvest into themselves the energy and love withdrawn from the original parent, interfering with their capacity to relate meaningfully to others. These are the foster children who as they grow older are described as cold, aloof, shallow, superficial, demanding, manipulative, or narcissistic. They tend to use people for what they can provide. Narcissistic investment in themselves may manifest as excessive self-stimulating behaviors such as thumbsucking, rocking, or masturbation. They may be preoccupied by fantasy and withdraw from social interactions. Some children experience persistent, diffuse rage directed at anyone who deprives them of material or emotional gratification. These children also exhibit antisocial behaviors— inability to empathize with others, lack of conscience, and inadequate impulse control. As a result of rejection, they have a very low self-concept, often aggravated by a compulsive need to set themselves up for repeated rejection, thereby confirming their lack of loveability. Such children may be chronically depressed, apathetic and dependent. Their exaggerated demands for nurture and support persist into adulthood, and they produce offspring who are similarly physically and emotionally deprived, thereby perpetuating the intergenerational cycle of abuse and deprivation while remaining socially, emotionally, and economically dependent. These individuals form the majority of the clientele in public child welfare agencies.

The Mental Health Professional's Role

Although psychiatric conditions and disordered conduct in both parents and children comprise a substantial proportion of the caseload of child welfare agencies[2], little attention has been focused on the topic in the mental health literature. Some reports have addressed the psychiatric evaluation of parent and child[8,9], consultation with child welfare agencies[10,11], expert testimony[12], ethical issues, and role conflicts[13]. However, mental health professionals can play a more extensive role, incorporating advocacy, consultation, assessment, education, expert testimony, treatment, and research.

Advocacy is the *sine qua non* for any mental health professional involved in this field. Indeed, the other functions should be subsumed under that role. Under optimal conditions, most parents are able to assure their children's nurturance and security and, when distressed, are able to negotiate with other child-caring systems to obtain help and support. However, with a dysfunctional family unit, the child often requires persons other than his parents to intercede on his behalf to assure that his developmental needs are met and his rights protected[14,15]. Often it is the mental health professional upon whose shoulders this responsibility falls. The mental health professional however, must avoid an adversarial position *vis a vis* the parents or agency but rather adopt an impartial stance, with the child's best interest uppermost.

The traditional role of the consultant is that of a specialist who offers an expert opinion on the child's developmental needs, emotional and behavioral status, or relationship with the family. The mental health professional may be so fortunate as to become involved with the child and his family during the crisis that precipitated the referral to the child welfare agency. Whenever possible, the integrity of the family should be maintained without removal of the child from the home. However, placement out of the home often occurs by default because alternative housing and other supportive services are lacking[16]. Sometimes, in order to assure appropriate educational or social services for physically or emotionally handicapped children, parents are told they must place their children in out-of-home care. Children have also been separated from their families because of unacceptable life style or childrearing practices. In the final analysis, removal of the child must be the least detrimental alternative. The time to consider removal and placement, ideally is *before* the child is placed, as part of an adequately formulated and comprehensive plan of longterm management [17].

Situations likely to deteriorate enough to warrant removal should be identified promptly. Thorough, comprehensive assessment by a psychiatrist, psychological and developmental testing by a psychologist, and knowledge of the child's behavior in the school, at home, and in the community can quite accurately predict the likelihood of the child being maintained in his family or requiring out-of-home placement. Regardless of outcome, such an evaluation can provide the caseworker and the court with valuable recommendations for disposition, thereby minimizing the risk of multiple placements[18].

The Adoption Assistance and Child Welfare Act of 1980 requires that once children are removed from their own homes, reasonable efforts be made to reunify the family, a written case plan developed to facilitate reunification, and review by court or agency every 6 months to assure that the plan is fully implemented.

In such cases the mental health professional, in conjunction with agency personnel, may be asked to advise whether the child should return to his own parents or an alternative placement sought. All that may be required is review of the case plan, a written service agreement, which gives direction to the transactions that must occur between clients and caseworkers[19]. These service plans contain specific tasks that the client must complete in order to reach predetermined goals, described in observable and measurable terms, within a specific period. One of the major pitfalls of case planning in the past was the vague and nonspecific nature of treatment objectives, which frequently resulted in misunderstandings between client and caseworker. Clearly-formulated case plans provide a yardstick against which change can be measured. Poorly formulated case plans in the past proved a major obstacle to permanency planning for children in out-of-home care[20].

Termination-of-parental-rights actions are brought to secure permanent homes for children who are unable to return home, freeing the child for adoption by removing the parent's right to withhold consent to an adoption [21]. With termination of parental rights, the parents do not have the legal right to visit or communicate with the child or to receive information about the child. In most states, it also abrogates the duty to support the child. Generally, termination proceedings are separate hearings resulting from special petition or motion.[22] When contested, termination actions should be fully adversary hearings[23]. The burden of proof in a termination-of-parental-rights case has recently been held by the Supreme Court in *Santosky v Kramer*[23] as that of "clear and convincing evidence," a higher standard than the less strict "preponderance of the evidence" which is used in most dependency or neglect cases. (The highest standard of proof required in United States courts is "beyond a reasonable doubt," applied in criminal and delinquency proceedings that could result in incarceration[24]. This higher standard of proof is required because of the serious consequences of termination proceedings—the complete, legal destruction of the parent–child relationship.

State statutes for termination proceedings were until recently quite vague and nonspecific. The legal process requires the court to determine whether the child can or should be returned to the parent within a reasonable time. Common indicators that the child cannot safely return home are: extreme lack of parental interest; failure of a parent to remedy the conditions which caused the separation; extreme or repeated neglect or abuse; parental incapacity to care for the child; and extreme deterioration of the parent–child relationship[8,20,25]. The court also has to determine whether termination is in the child's best interest and will, indeed, lead to a more secure and appropriate home.

Expert Testimony

The mental health professional can play a valuable role in court as an expert witness and should be impartially appointed by the court rather than by one or the other litigating party. The expert may address himself to the child's needs by: presenting information of which the court is unaware (the *discovery* function); presenting the emotions of the parties who may have difficulty expressing themselves (the *articulating* function); bringing to the court's attention factors that might otherwise be accorded too little weight in the decision-making process (the *highlighting* function); and analyzing psychological concepts to help the court reach a conclusion based on that knowledge (the *analyzing* function).

Mental health professionals are viewed by most lawyers with skepticism and cynicism but they do have much of value to offer the court, particularly if they are well prepared by their sponsoring lawyers as to the nature and purpose of their testimony[12]. Two of the major obstacles that a mental health professional has to overcome are his own ignorance of the judicial process and his reluctance to participate in the unfamiliar arena of the court. This can be remedied by a sensitive lawyer who acts as a guide to the mental health professional. Where possible, this should occur through a multidisciplinary process in which the sponsoring lawyer is educated as to what he can expect from the other disciplines interfacing with the legal profession. The lawyer in turn must make the other participants familiar with the workings and expectations of the law and of the court.

As a result of inadequate preparation, the mental health professional may fail to understand the expectations of the legal process, inadequately meet the needs of the court by talking in jargon, present conclusions without an underlying rationale, and ultimately fail to answer the questions needed to assist the court's determination of the case.

The expert need not necessarily be a child psychiatrist, but should possess a sufficiently high level of expertise in his field to assist the court in arriving at the right decision. Although an expert may be called by either of the parties, it is probably best that the court itself appoint an expert witness. Such a witness still has to be found qualified but is not associated with either party to the litigation and can be cross-examined by both parties.

Prior to testifying, the expert should have acquired a familiarity with the facts of the case; by his presence in the courtroom when evidence was presented, by first hand knowledge through examination of the child and pertinent family members, and/or by reading the relevant records and files.

The expert should be extremely cautious about offering an opinion based solely on information first heard in the court room. It is advisable to have first hand knowledge of the child and the parents and to have reviewed all records from ancillary sources such as the child's school, pediatrician, mental health clinic, and children's protective services. The child should also be examined individually as well as in the presence of his/her biological parents and foster parents. The examiner should focus on the child's developmental, physical, emotional, and mental status; the child's relationship with his natural parents; and the relationship with the foster parents, particularly if the latter are considering adoption. The child's parental preference should be determined, together with the child's perception of his parents' abuse, neglect or unavailability. The child's interactions with the parents in both structured and unstructured settings also need to be assessed.

The parents' attitude towards the child, their knowledge of parenting skills, and their own experiences during their own development are further crucial elements of the evaluation. Finally, all parties need to have psychiatric (mental status) examinations to assess for psychopathology.

Based on the findings of the expert's evaluation, an opinion can be offered as to possible psychiatric grounds for termination of parental rights. If insufficient grounds exist for such a conclusion, the mental health professional can make recommendations for further management in out-of-home care or for return of the child to the natural parents with the necessary supports and interventions.

If parental mental or physical disability is severe, it is essential to have an expert's diagnosis to establish the parent's incapacity to care for the child. The expert is required to demonstrate the existence of the disability, the parent's inability to provide proper care and the likelihood of the condition persisting over time, regardless of treatment or services. Principal causes of parental incapacity are; mental illness in general or specific diagnostic entities such as schizophrenia or affective disorder; mental retardation; drug or alcohol addiction; personality disorders; or extreme physical disabilities.

(a) Mental Illness: The offspring of mentally ill parents are more at risk for developing psychopathology than are the children of well parents [26,27]. They are also at increased risk for later problems in adulthood. The child is at increased risk for such childhood difficulties as developmental disabilities, mental retardation, learning problems, emotional and psycho-physiological disorders, attention deficit and conduct disorders, physical growth problems (obesity, failure to thrive), abuse and neglect, and psychosis[28].

Aspects of development that may be affected include affect and cognition, attention, feelings of competence and mastery, peer relationships, and adaptability to new developmental tasks. While these consequences are relatively nonspecific, the risk for the child increases critically when the parents have a personality disorder, a chronic or recurrent depression, or emotional (neurotic) disorder. The effect on the children is due less to the parents' mental illness than their level of functioning, affective responsivity, and the degree to which the condition involves the child. Such parental variables affect the family environment by causing marital discord, conflict over child rearing practices, and disruption within the family[29].

While the type of mental illness is significant, the parents' level of functioning as a result of the illness appears critical. Thus, children of depressed parents are most adversely affected, with children of schizophrenic parents being less affected and manic-depressive parents having the least effect of all[30-32]. The chronicity of parental impairment has been found to be more pathogenic than acute episodes, and when associated with an impaired level of functioning with a narrow range of affective responsivity to have the most adverse influence on the child [33]. The sex of the ill parent is also relevant with worse family difficulties when the mother is the patient rather than the father[34]. Relatively less ill mothers (diagnosed schizoid or borderline rather than hebephrenic or catatonic) but symbiotically overinvolved with the child also are thought to have a negative impact on the child[35]. Children under two years, still in the phase of separation–individuation, are especially sensitive to the disturbing influence of the chronically ill mother. Growing up in the home with a psychotic mother is likely to affect the child's development, particularly if the parent is isolated, without social supports, and unable to fulfill parental roles[36].

(b) Mental Retardation: Severity of retardation is usually confirmed by standardized, individually-administered intelligence tests. When the level of intellectual functioning is found to be below 50, the parents are generally unable to care for their children. They are unlikely to function at more than a second grade level, although they are able to contribute to their own support by performing unskilled or semiskilled work under close supervision in sheltered workshops. These parents do not have the capacity to understand the need for early infant stimulation, or they may go to the opposite extreme by overstimulating their offspring in inappropriate ways.

Intellectual functioning in the mild range (IQ Level 50–70) is roughly equivalent to the educational category of "educable." Such parents are likely to be functioning at about a sixth grade level and are usually able to acquire social and vocational skills adequate for self support, although under unusual social and economic stress they may need guidance and assistance. Their ability to parent effectively may be largely dependent on such resources as extended family or community support. Marginally retarded parents (those in the mild and borderline range, i.e., IQ levels from 50–70 and 70–85) are often able to care for young children but have trouble with child rearing as the children grow older and enter adolescence. The older child or adolescent may require more sophisticated parenting skills than the intellectually limited parent is capable of. In their early years, children of retarded parents may appear considerably less intelligent than they actually are, because of understimulation in a relatively impoverished environment.

Intelligence tests should not be used in isolation to assess an individual's functional ability, but rather in conjunction with the individual's adaptive behavior (the effectiveness with which an individual meets the standards of personal independence and social responsibility for his age and cultural group). Many people in the population who on psychometric tests fall in the retarded range actually do function adequately. Indeed, a diagnosis of mental retardation is not given when individuals adequately meet the demands of their environment[37].

(c) Drug and Alcohol Addiction: Chronic alcoholism or drug dependence also may be a basis for termination of parental rights. Children of addicted parents have a much greater risk of neglect or abuse than do children of nonaddicted parents[38,39,40]. Such parents are not only unavailable during the day while at work but may be involved in other activities to obtain drugs or alcohol. They are also unavailable while intoxicated or ''high,'' and when sober are frequently irritable or withdrawn. Once the effect of the drug has worn off, they tend to assuage their guilt for neglecting or abusing the child by being overindulgent. This inconsistency and unpredictability can play havoc with a child's life.

Evidence of a substance abuse problem is insufficient to terminate parental rights. The parent must be shown to have abused alcohol or other drugs to the detriment of the child, either by mistreatment or by failure to provide the ordinary care required for all children. It will be necessary for the expert to indicate that the dependence is likely to continue, and that assistance was offered to the parent which either failed or was rejected [22].

In the case where there is a non- substance- abusing spouse who acquiesced to abuse by the other parent, the expert may conclude that the child's problems were caused by the parent's act of omission, i.e., his or her failure to protect the child.

Children who are in care may be able to return home if the parent is willing to participate in treatment. Also, the presence of another adequately-functioning adult in the home who can intervene constructively when the ill parent is drinking is an alleviating factor.

(d) Personality Disorders: Personality disorders in the parents have been linked to conduct disturbance in sons[41], particularly if the parents show marked irritability, aggression, and hostility. While no single personality type has been identified as being unsuitable to parent a child, the parent who is impulsive, with poor control of his or her aggression, is highly likely to place a child at risk for physical and emotional harm [42]. Many of these individuals were themselves brought up in seriously unhappy or disrupted homes which may have been associated with institutional care, markedly poor parent–child relationships, violence, or abuse. Individuals who suffered from childhood adversity tend to lack planning or coping skills, have diminished sensitivity to their childrens' cues and needs, and show increased irritability[29]. Many parents who engage in criminal activities, have police records, or have been incarcerated suffer from personality disorder. The characteristics are strongly related to delinquency in their offspring[43], the association being strongest when both parents are criminal, recidivist, and the criminal records extend into the period of child-rearing[44]. If a pattern of antisocial behavior in the parent can be demonstrated from adolescence into adulthood with recidivism, a reasonable prediction can be made that the individual's behavior is likely to persist and to affect the parent–child relationship adversely.

(e) Extreme Deterioration of the Parent–child Relationship: Another ground for termination is the serious erosion or nonexistence of the emotional bond between natural parent and child. Since separation from the natural parent, the child may have developed a relationship or emotional attachment to his fosterparent or preadoptive parent. The interruption of this relationship by removal from an important caregiver with whom the child has resided for a significant part of his life usually results in, at least, acute distress as well as, indirectly, longterm consequences[5]. For these reasons, it is essential to take great care to insure adequate contact between parent and child during the period of separation. In general, the younger the child, the more vulnerable, and the more necessary are frequent visits to maintain the attachment and decrease the stress of separation.

In those instances where the child is unable to preserve emotional ties to his primary caregiver because of prolonged absence, the chances are great that a relationship will develop with his new caretaker, who will become his new "psychological parent."[7] The determination of who a child's psychological parents are and the existence of emotional ties to them is crucial if the child is to be placed in the appropriate caretaking environment. There is no infallible test for attachments and observations of the child's responses to attempted reunions often must be relied upon. The child caught up in this stressful process may experience sleep disturbances, including nightmares; clinging to significant adults; loss of recently-acquired developmental milestones, such as bowel or bladder control; increased aggression; shortened attention span; and deterioration in academic performance and classroom behavior.

If reunification proves too disturbing for the child or if little likelihood exists for returning the child home, then it may be best for the child to remain with the "psychological" parent to whom an emotional tie does exist. Since adoption by another caretaker is no guarantee that the placement will succeed[43]. Failure of the placement and disruption of the parent-child relationship can result in multiple placements and psychiatric disturbance.

If adoption is not contemplated, termination is only appropriate if there is a need to decisively and permanently end all parent-child contacts. The child may be better off remaining with his present caretaker, despite an unwillingness or inability to adopt the child, since the risk of substantial emotional harm may be greater if removed from the placement. The older child or adolescent may retain ties to his biological parents because of residual affection or affiliation, causing an understandable reluctance to interrupt the relationship. In some cases, termination of parental rights may be undesirable from a financial standpoint because it may result in possible loss of Social

Security benefits, child support, inheritance, or foster care payments[21]. Alternatives for children in out-of-home care when adoption is not possible include formal longterm foster care, or foster guardianship.

Special Needs Children

Another consideration in permanency planning is related to children with special needs (also known as "hard-to-place" children). They are children difficult to place because of age; physical, mental or emotional handicaps; or membership in a minority or sibling group. In these cases parents may be able to provide minimally sufficient standards of physical and emotional care to the "average" child but may not be able to take adequate care of a special needs child. In assessing the suitability of natural parents to raise a "special needs" child, it is crucial that the parents have an understanding of the child's needs and a demonstrated ability to assure that the child's needs are fulfilled in practice.

Although child mental health is an inexact science and is limited by insufficient knowledge about many aspects of child-rearing and parenting, enough factual information on diagnosis and treatment exists to allow us to make fairly accurate predictions about parents' capacity to care for their children. Further study is required to delineate the mental health professional's role in the management of the child in out-of-home care and to communicate both benefits and limitations to the courts.

Notes

1. Shyne AA and Schroeder AG *National Study of Social Services to Children and Their Families,* Washington DC: US Department of Health, Education and Welfare, 1978.
2. Knitzer J *Unclaimed Children* Washington DC: Children's Defense Fund, 1982.
3. Bremmer R Care of Dependent Children in *Children and Youth in America* pp. 262–263 American Public Health Association: Baltimore, 1970.
4. Horowitz RM and Davidson HA *Legal Rights of Children* Colorado Springs: Shepard's/McGraw-Hill, 1984.
5. Rutter M *Maternal Deprivation Reassessed* Second Edition New York: Penguin Books, 1981.
6. Emlen AC *The Value of Caseload Screening and Periodic Case Review.* Portland, Oregon: Regional Research Institute for Human Services, Portland State University, 1977.
7. Goldstein J, Freud A, Solnit AJ *Before the Best Interests of the Child* New York: The Free Press, 1979.
8. Schetky DH, Angell R, Morrison CV, Sack WH *1979* Parents Who Fail—a study of 51 cases of termination of parental rights *Journal of American Academy of Child Psychiatry* 18:366–383.
9. Rosenberg LA The Techniques of Psychological Assessment as Applied to

Children in Fostercare and Their Families in *Foster Children in the Courts* (Edited by M. Hardin) Butterworth Legal Publishers: Boston, 1983.

10. Glasser MG The Role of the Mental Health Consultant in Fostercare Planning in *Protecting Children through the Legal System* Washington, DC: American Bar Association, 1981.

11. Glasser ME Mental Health Consultation in Longterm Planning for Foster Children in *Foster Children in the Courts* (Edited by M Hardin) Butterworth Legal Publishers: Boston, 1983.

12. Duquette DN Collaboration Between Lawyers and Mental Health Professionals: Making it Work in *Foster Children in the Courts* (Edited by M Hardin) Butterworth Legal Publishers: Boston, 1983.

13. Schoettle, UC Termination of Parental Rights—Ethical Issues and Role Conflicts *Journal of the American Academy of Child Psychiatry* 23:629–632, 1984.

14. Bolman WM, McDermott JF, Jr., Arensdorf AM A New Concept in Social Psychiatry:Child Advocacy. *Social Psychiatry* 8:26–31, 1973.

15. Westman JC *Child Advocacy* New York: The Free Press, 1979.

16. Knitzer J and Allen ML *Children Without Homes* Washington: Children's Defense Fund, 1978.

17. Steinhauer PD Issues of Attachment and Separation: Fostercare and Adoption in *Psychological Problems of the Child in the Family* Second Edition Eds. PD Steinhauer and Q Rae-Grant) New York: Basic Books, 1983.

18. Steinhauer PD The Management of Children Admitted to Child Welfare Services in Ontario: A Review and Discussion of Current Problems and Practices *Canadian Journal of Psychiatry 29,* 473–483, 1984.

19. Stein TJ and Rzepnicki TL *Decision Making at Child Welfare Intake* New York: Child Welfare League of America, 1983.

20. Pike VA, Downs SW, Emlen AC, Downs G *Permanent Planning for Children in Fostercare: A Handbook for Social Workers* Washington, DC: Government Printing Office, 1977.

21. Hardin MA and Shalleck A Children Living Apart from their Parents in *Legal Rights of Children* (Eds. RM Horowitz and HA Davidson) pp. 353–421 Colorado Springs: Shepard's/McGraw Hill, 1984.

22. Mlyniec WJ Prosecuting a Termination of Parental Rights Case in *Foster Children in the Courts* (Ed. M Hardin) pp. 193–228 Boston: Butterworth Legal Publishers, 1983.

23. Santosky v Kramer, 455 US 745 (1982).

24. Caulfield BA *The Legal Aspects of Protective Services for Abused and Neglected Children* US Department of Health, Education and Welfare: Washington, DC, 1978.

25. Hardin MA and Tazzara P *Termination of Parental Rights: A Summary and Comparison of Grounds for Nine Model Acts* Washington, DC: American Bar Association, 1981.

26. Rutter M *Children of Sick Parents: An Environmental and Psychiatric Study* Institute of Psychiatry, Mandsley Monograph No. 16 Oxford University Press, London, 1966.

27. Garmezy N Children at Risk: The search for the antecedents to schizophrenia Part 1 conceptual models and research methods *Schizophrenia Bulletin* 8:14–90, 1974.

28. Swain DB, Hawkins RC, Walker LD, Penticuff JH (Eds): Preface, in *Exceptional Infant* Vol. 4 New York: Brunner/Mazel, 1980.

29. Rutter M and Cox A Other Family Influences in *Child and Adolescent Psychiatry:*

Modern Approaches Second Edition (Ed. M Rutter and L Hersov) p 58–81 Oxford: Blackwell Scientific Publications, 1985.

30. Rolf JE, Crowther J, Teri L, Bond L: Contrasting developmental risks in preschool children of psychiatrically hospitalized parents, in *Children at Risk for Schizophrenia: A Longitudinal Perspective* Edited by Watt NF, Anthony EJ, Wynne LC, Rolf JE New York, Cambridge University Press, 1984.

31. Cole RE, Al–Khayyal M, Baldwin AL, Baldwin CP, Fisher L, Wynne LC A cross setting assessment of family interaction and the prediction of school competence in children at risk in *Children at Risk for Schizophrenia: A Longitudinal Perspective* (Ed. Watt WF, Anthony EJ, Wynne LC, Rolf JE) New York, Cambridge University Press, 1984.

32. Grunebaum H, Cohler BJ, Kauffman C, Gallant D Children of depressed and schizophrenic mothers *Child Psychiatry Hum. Dev.* 8:219–229, 1978.

33. Fisher L, Kokes RF, Harder DW, Jones JE Child competence and psychiatric risk: VI Summary and integration of findings *J. Nerv. Ment. Dis.* 168:353–355, 1980.

34. Kokes RF, Harder DW, Fisher L, Strauss JS Child competence and psychiatric risk: V Sex of patients and dimensions of psychopathology *J. Nerv. Ment. Dis.* 168:348–352, 1980.

35. Anthony EJ A Clinical Evaluation of Children with Psychotic Parents *American Journal of Psychiatry 126:* 2 pp. 177–184, 1969.

36. Grunebaum H Parenting and children at risk in *Psychiatry Update:* Volume III (Ed. L Grinspoon) pp. 129–144 Washington DC: American Psychiatric Association, 1984.

37. Sattler JM *Assessment of Children's Intelligence and Special Abilities* 2nd Edition Boston: Allyn and Bacon Inc., 1982.

38. Black R and Mayer J *Parents with special problems: Alcoholism and Opiate Addiction in the Battered Child* 3rd Edition (Edited by CH Kempe and RE Helfer) Chicago: University of Chicago Press, 1980.

39. El–Gruebaly N and Offord DR The Offspring of Alcoholics: A Critical Review *American Journal of Psychiatry* (4), 357–364, 1977.

40. El–Gruebaly N and Offord DR On Being the Offspring of an Alcoholic: An Update *Alcoholism: Clinical and Experimental Research* 3 (2, 148–157), 1979.

41. Stewart MA, Deblois LS, Cummings C Psychiatric disorder in the parents of hyperactive boys and those with conduct disorder *J. Child Psychol. Psychiat.* 21, 283–292, 1980.

42. Spinetta J and Rigler D The child abusing parent: a psychological review *Psychol. Bull.* 77, 296–304, 1972.

43. Sack WH and Dale DD Abuse and Deprivation in Failing Adoptions *Child Abuse and Neglect* 6 443–451, 1982.

17

Multisystems Therapy: Helping Families Help Themselves

Families adopting "special needs" children—those that are older, handicapped, or come in sibling groups—often find they need help from professionals. Many such families turn to the field of mental health to find that help, with varying degrees of success. For the wellbeing of the children and their new families it is crucial that psychotherapists understand the particular needs of adoptive families. Parents and the institution of the family, need to be respected and also, it is important to realize the traumatic effect earlier separations can have on the life of a child.

Multisystems Therapy History

Since the mid-60's, agencies such as Spaulding for Children and the Council on Adoptable Children have spearheaded the national movement to place waiting parentless children into permanent homes. Increasingly they have also made a commitment to support these new families after finalization of the adoptions. This step marks a radical change in the adoption process.

In the early years of special needs adoption it was believed that if adoptive parents were treated with consideration and had the support of other seasoned parents in a parents' group, successful placement would be certain. Many parents had faith that love would cure all. Over the years, however, there has been an increasing understanding of the emotional damage suffered by children who have been repeatedly separated from caretakers early in life. Often well intentioned, even well-trained parents began to return youngsters to the child welfare system; the parents had "burned out."

More and more parents have been referred to psychotherapists for help in holding their families together. Basic family therapy proved effective with many of these clients. For some cases, however, it never seemed enough; primarily, these cases involved children who had suffered many early moves. I participated in research done at the University of Michigan Psychiatric Hospital which found that children placed between 18 and 36 months were especially traumatized by separation and later presented severe behavioral disturbances.

These children proved to be particularly challenging to parents. Separation anxiety in the children produced a long list of symptoms in the child leaving parents feeling helpless, inadequate, and guilty. Although the children in this study had been in psychotherapy for several years, few if any improvements had been noted. The older the children grew, the more troublesome they became as their destructive behavior began to impact on the larger community.

My experience as the adoptive mother of a difficult child and as a psychotherapist led me to develop an approach to working with troubled families that has become known as Multisystems Therapy. Focusing on both the emotional and physical health of a family, this holistic model addresses the underlying problem, not merely surface issues. It is based on the work of psychiatrist Murray Bowen.

Frustrated parents have too long looked to professionals for solutions, while professionals have seldom asked parents what they feel would be of most help. But each has something to offer towards a solution. A therapy model which respects parents and builds on their strengths rather than their weaknesses offers the greatest hope. One that enhances parents' therapeutic skills is of primary importance, for parents are with the child night and day to offer emotional support, and are available throughout the remainder of their lives. Adoptive families are like biofamilies in this regard: the therapy model which strengthens adoptive families insures emotional connectedness in all families.

Multisystems Therapy has drawn increasing attention from professionals who serve a cross-section of clientele. A three-day videotaped training was done for the staffs of the Oregon Department of Human Services, the Boys and Girls Aid Society of Oregon, and the Episcopalian Counseling Service. Family court judges have also requested training in the Multisystems model, seeing it as an answer to the increasing incidence of family dismemberment resulting from placing children outside the home. More and more adoptive parents in both the United States and Great Britain are finding it effective when other therapies have failed. Results from a two-year English research project on cases I began treating and turned over to therapists I trained show extremely favorable outcomes.[1]

Theoretical Concepts

In describing various aspects of Multisystems Therapy and how they may be useful to therapists, parents, and children, it is important to first review the various concepts of Murray Bowen's systems theory which have provided the base for the development of the newer holistic therapeutic model.[2]

- A misbehaving child must not be allowed to interfere with the marital relationship. A concern of many of those working with parents who have adopted emotionally disturbed children is their high divorce rate, for a troubled child often brings to the surface potential problems in a marital relationship which otherwise might have remained dormant. Differences in the parenting styles are to be expected. However, if one parent criticizes the other's parenting, their child is able to drive a wedge between them. A remedy for this is a one-to-one relationship between the child and each parent. This prevents the youngster from gaining too much power in the family. The child loses his ability to manipulate his parents, as he deals with two separate authority figures, without the other parent's assistance. He must obey the stricter parent in each instance or face the consequences.
- Conflict between any two family members is likely to attract others who move in emotionally to try to help. The "help" generally makes matters worse by increasing anxiety. What began as a difference between two people may soon involve every member of the family, as well as outsiders. Even well-intentioned psychotherapists are apt to become enmeshed in the family system, thereby reducing the effectiveness of the professional. The ability of the original twosome to work out their differences is reduced when others "triangle," protecting one person from another. Respect for the individual and intimacy in relationships are possible only when personal relationships are permitted.
- Healthy family functioning necessitates giving up cause-and-effect thinking with its high degree of blaming. It prevents a family member's taking responsibility for him- or herself. The therapist who researches with one or both parents the process at work in the family has an improved chance of effecting positive change in that emotional system.
- Systems theory respects each family member, but stresses the importance of working primarily with its leaders to bring about lasting change. It must be noted that anxiety tends to settle not on those in charge but on the most vulnerable in the family. This is likely to be the adopted child, who tends to be the "weakest link in the emotional chain" and the one who presents the greatest number of symptoms. If one person can be helped to rise to a higher level of functioning, and if that individual

wields power in the system, then the anxiety in the system as a whole will decrease, and with it the symptomatology.

- One or both parents must work toward "differentiation." Emotional maturity depends on one's ability to differentiate the rational from the emotional part of the brain. When a person is differentiated, he or she becomes fairly independent of emotionality in the surroundings and is able to remain calm and solve problems rather than react automatically to crisis. Such an individual assumes responsibility for himself and is not likely to blame others for any unhappiness he experiences.

- Anxiety in an emotional system leads to fusion of family members. Such an uncomfortable state, in turn, propels individuals to distance reactively from each other. When a person has not learned how to remain comfortable with his or her own parents, he is more likely to want to get away from them, blaming them for his discomfort. Divorce becomes an answer to marital problems, and placement of children may be seen as a way to resolve conflicts with a child. People who blame others and choose distancing as a solution often brag about how unimportant their parents are to them, and how independent they themselves are.

- The methods used by individuals to deal with problems are generally the ones used by their parents. If parents choose divorce or placement, the next generation is likely to do the same. When people realize such driving forces are behind their actions, they become better able to choose functional behavior rather than automatically do what their ancestors did.

- Under normal circumstances, children can be expected to emerge at the same level of emotional maturity as their parents, for parents serve as role models. Bowen's research yielded evidence of a transmission of family patterns over generations, making it possible to predict the future from the past. Because anxiety in a family generally settles on the most vulnerable family member, that person can be expected to emerge less mature than his or her siblings. People generally marry others at about their same level of maturity, therefore the person at the lower level marries another who is at the same low level. Some of their children will predictably turn out even less mature. The process continues over the generations.

- Sibling position affects personality. Two eldest children who marry are likely to compete, with the result that their marriage is likely to be heavily stressed. Understanding the effects of birth position on one's personality helps one to maintain flexibility and comfort in relationships.

- Bowen's final theoretical concept is related to the regression of society over time. Just as prolonged anxiety results in a single family's slipping to lower levels of functioning, sustained anxiety over time can affect larger groupings. Society as a whole loses its ability to make long-range plans to solve problems, resorting to automatic stopgap solutions designed to ease the discomfort of the moment.

As Bowen developed his family theory at Georgetown University Medical School, he shifted from placing his students in traditional psychoanalysis which is customary. Instead he began to send them into their families of origin to work on differentiating themselves. Relationship skills learned in their extended families were automatically put to use in nuclear family relationships. As a result, the psychiatry students became much more effective in their work with clients than any of the preceding classes. Bowen continues to use this training program rather than the traditional one of other medical schools.

Therapeutic Holding

Since I specialized in work with adoptive families, particularly those who had adopted older children, agencies referred families who were already at the point of wanting to return a child. Verbal therapy alone was not enough to reduce anxiety when a difficult child was spurring it on. A holistic systems approach was necessary if the placements were to be saved. Multisystems Therapy incorporates two important components in addition to traditional verbal therapy: the nonverbal techniques of therapeutic holding, and nutritional therapy.

Several theoretical concepts support the use of holding therapy. John Bowlby has reported that fear of separation produces many symptoms. Those working with or parenting youngsters who have suffered the trauma of repeated moves well know the variety of symptoms: lying, stealing, enuresis, aggressive behavior, low self-esteem, hyperactivity, lack of respect for authority, basic distrust, learning problems. The child may cling too much to its new parents, or may do the opposite—not permit touch. Bowlby wrote,

> When I began my studies of the effects on young children of their being placed away from mother in a strange place with strange people, my theoretical framework was that of psychoanalysis. Finding its metapsychological superstructure unsatisfactory, however, I have been developing a paradigm that, whilst incorporating much psychoanalytic thinking, differs from the traditional one in adopting a number of principles that derive from the relatively new disciplines of ethology and control theory.[3]

I find that holding can both break down the negative child's resistance to touch and reassure the child who hangs on to his parent. It enables parents of a child who has usurped control to resume leadership. This is an essential step so that parents can again feel tenderness toward the youngster. Talking is not always the most effective way of accomplishing resumption of power. Therapeutic holding offers a means by which parents can make a physical statement when words remain unheeded.

Nobel laureate ethologist, Niko Tinbergen, views therapeutic holding as the best therapy possible for children who have become emotionally "derailed." He reports that he wrote the book, *"Autistic Children": New Hope for a Cure,* in order to encourage psychotherapists to use the technique. Tinbergen adds that verbal therapy which is supportive of the family, together with nutritional therapy, can help by further speeding the recovery of emotionally traumatized children.[4]

In therapeutic holding, as in Bowen's systems approach, the child benefits through the work done with his parents rather than the therapist's direct work with the youngster. This is especially helpful in adoptive families in which the parents desperately need to claim their child and to consider themselves effective mothers and fathers.

Troubled youngsters from the child welfare system have not been able to develop a sense of their own competence in relationships with others. In the course of normal development a child learns that he has some ability to make his mother friendly to him or cause her to be unhappy with him. He learns to enchant her after he has misbehaved and suffered her discipline. Youngsters who have not had appropriate parenting emerge with the belief that a mother is all good if she is handing out compliments or rewards and all evil if she is critical. They feel totally helpless in the relationship. Also these youngsters are likely to see their therapist as a "good parent" and their own parents who must provide limits, as "bad." Parents often become jealous that their child relates positively to the therapist but not to them. Parents also are apt to fear that the child's stories about how mean the parents are will be believed by professionals. They often feel a lack of respect from therapists who advise them on how to be better parents.

Therapeutic holding enables the parents to be effective with their own child, supported by the therapist, who puts the mother and father in the position of nurturing and control. A typical holding session has the mother "cocoon" the youngster in her arms. The father helps the mother hold firmly. The child usually giggles at first, thinking it is a new game. Then the child squirms and protests, trying to regain its physical freedom and control. Becoming angry, when the parent will not let go, the youngster screams and threatens, trying to push the parents away. Eventually out of sheer exhaustion there is submission by the child to the caretakers. During the holding there is no need for the parents to say anything. It is an opportunity for their child to express him- or herself and the parents' time to listen.

Parents who have difficulty liking their child, and would probably stop going to a therapist who even subtly suggested that the child needed to be hugged, generally jump at the chance to take their youngster through a holding. They view it as showing their child that they have sufficient strength to parent him. At the end of the holding they finally find their child likable. The child's armor which had kept others at a distance is broken through by the parents, and the youngster is available to receive nurturing and to respond at last.

It is fairly easy to hold a young child; but when a child becomes an adolescent, parents often become fearful and may need extra help. There is an unspoken taboo against touching older children in our society. [Adolescents may turn to sexual promiscuity to get physical attention lacking from their parents.] Nevertheless, parents have often naturally turned to holding when one of their teenagers has been bent on self-destruction. A juvenile court judge at one training session described his automatic response when his eighth child reached his teens and had become a problem even beyond the home. The judge had talked extensively with the son and, feeling desperate, finally threw his arms around the boy in a silent, extended, forced bear hug. Soon they were both sobbing. The son's behavior improved dramatically.

Children cry out to be stopped from self-destruction. They seem to be asking, "Do you really care enough?" Punishment is often interpreted by the child as proof of lack of parental love. Holding appears to be effective because the child, rather than being deprived or hurt, is simply held close while being prevented from hurting himself or others. Because of the control parents feel in this position, they are able to permit, even encourage, the child's verbal self expression—negative feelings as well as positive.

Therapeutic holding, like verbal systems therapy, restructures the family emotional system, establishing the parents as caring leaders. Holding is simple: Parents are to remain silent. It is inexpensive and widely applicable, and it is easily taught. Usually scheduled weekly, holdings are continued until the child feels sufficiently secure that symptoms fade. Sometimes a single session can bring the change parents have been seeking.

Nutrition Therapy

In its holistic approach, Multisystems Therapy addresses the needs of the physical body, for the body has an effect on emotions. With many older adopted children who have had to be taken from bioparents, physical wellbeing has been erratic at best. It is important to consider the health history of a child in planning a treatment program. For example, a child whose biomother suffered from diabetes may be overly sensitive to processed foods, especially sugar, sweetened liquids, and alcohol.

Very little attention has been focused by American medical practitioners on the widespread malnutrition resulting from the overprocessing of foods, the conditioning of people from infancy to desire sweets, and the great dependence of our society on artificial colors and additives. While many people can eat processed food and not have easily-identifiable problems, children who have suffered the trauma of being moved from one mother-figure to another may be unable to handle the added stress of unnutritious food assault.

Stress has been known to deplete certain essential minerals required by the body to metabolize food. Processed foods further deplete the body of these minerals. Chromium, for example, is present in sugar cane but is removed in the making of white sugar. Metabolization of sugar in the body requires chromium; therefore, when sugar is consumed, not only does it fail to add chromium to the body, but it also depletes existing body stores of the element.

Depletion of essential minerals and vitamins may make it impossible to maintain adequate supplies of glucose for the brain and the nervous system. Glucose, the only fuel for the brain, cannot be stored in the brain. It needs to be delivered by the blood in a steady slow seepage, possible only when proper levels are supplied through ingestion of nutritious foods.

Also related to nutrition is the fact that emotional bonding occurs automatically in families in which the anxiety level is relatively low. When anxiety is elevated, comfortable relationships become difficult to maintain. Anxiety is generally related to fear of separation; however, it can be a consequence of too much sugar in the diet. An hour or so after consuming sweets, many people suffer from reactive low blood sugar, which causes such symptoms as rapid heart-beat and the feeling of unrest.

The incorporation of nutritional therapy into the Multisystems model made success possible when other therapy had been ineffective. In certain cases, more than simply a change to less-processed food was required. Vitamin and mineral levels of family members were evaluated and necessary imbalances corrected. Wholesome snacks were added between meals in order to prevent glucose levels from falling too low and triggering anxiety and problem behavior.

Allergies are sometimes found to be provoking problems in family members. Allergies are often responsible for learning problems, misbehavior, and hyperactivity, as well as the more commonly expected skin eruptions. Americans are used to eating a few foods with great frequency: beef, wheat, tomatoes, milk, corn. The body was designed to consume a wide variety of foods. Often, the food that a person likes best is the very food to which he is allergic. When the problematic food is eaten the person experiences a temporary "high" due to the physical excitement of reactivity. Vitamin supplements such as B_5, B_6, E and ascorbic acid ("vitamin C") can successfully reduce allergic reactions along with avoidance of the known provocative foods. Rotating the diet over a 5-day period is another way to provide relief. In fact, it can be helpful for everyone to eat this way, for there is evidence to show that people can develop allergies late in life from consuming the same foods too frequently.[5]

Nutritional therapy has been suspect because of a scarcity of controlled studies clearly documenting its value, however, one need only try improved nutrition to understand the tremendous benefits possible. In one relevant study, a professional on the staff of the Tidewater Residential Treatment Facility in Virginia was curious about the role of sugar in the behavior of boys in that facility. He devised a study of a limited number of residents. The staff and residents were told that due to funding cutbacks the usual desserts were being replaced by fruit. With concentrated sweets thus removed, the number of reported behavior problems requiring disciplinary measures declined by about half. Wanting to check these remarkable findings, the researcher extended the study to include a greater number of boys. Again, the favorable results occurred.[6]

Foods in treatment facilities meet traditional nutritional standards; however, they do not meet the actual nutritional needs of many people who are sensitive to overly-processed foods such as white flour, polished rice, and fruit juices. The consumption of whole grains, vegetables, whole fruit rather than fruit juices provides the vitamins and minerals nature intended in a form which the body can use to its physical and emotional benefit, with the result that longer and more symptom-free life may be possible.

Food served in the cafeterias of public schools has been a concern of increasing numbers of parents and professionals. It is difficult for students to walk through the cafeteria line without succumbing to the temptation of cookies, cupcakes, ice cream, and chocolate milk. Rarely is whole grain used. School lunches can produce headaches, fatigue, heart palpitations, lack of concentration, or aggressive and over active behavior in the afternoon. Unfortunately a major reason for schools to continue supplying low nutrition, high sugar foods has been a financial one: while healthy foods cost no more for the school to provide, revenue from the astronomical markups in junk foods are lost. The school purse is richer when children buy Twinkies rather than meat and vegetables. A concerted effort to meet nutritional needs can help everyone handle stress in everyday life, both in the family and at school.

Systems Beyond the Family

Multisystems Therapy incorporates dimensions outside of the family, for the family exists in the larger community. A child with a learning disability needs to be evaluated and provided with an appropriate educational program. Too often the youngster or his family are viewed as the problem and the child's underlying needs are ignored. Parents and therapist working together in the framework provided by federal legislation on education for the handicapped can be powerful advocates for the child. Parents alone are often viewed with suspicion by a school system, but the knowledgeable therapist can influence special services staff in the school system and help the student receive what his condition actually calls for. When educational needs are more fully met, the child's adoption often becomes much smoother. Parents can be caretakers with less friction when the school responsibly assumes its role as educator.

A therapist can also be more helpful to families who have adopted older children when that professional becomes well acquainted with the child welfare and court systems. Previously traumatized children have been and may well again be involved with these institutions. Too often the family faces these systems in an adversarial role. Heightened anxiety leads to triangling and mutual blaming, with the result that the best interests of the child are lost in the process. The objective therapist who knows the strengths and weaknessess of the family and the outside systems can have an important calming effect which reduces anxiety and enhances clear thinking and planning.

A Therapist's Differentiation

In order for a therapist to effect positive changes in families, he or she needs to function at a relatively high level of emotional maturity. One's level of professional maturity is dependent on how well differentiated one is in one's own family emotional system. With good differentiation and with systems concepts as a theoretical base, anything the therapist says or does has an automatically positive effect on the family. The therapy, even with extremely chaotic families, becomes fairly effortless. Sidetaking, judgmentalism, blaming and the need to control are replaced by a respectful research stance in which the therapist earnestly studies the emotional process operating in the family.

In the course of therapy, the family leaders are able to get their own heads thinking about how things can be different. While their feelings are heard, the focus is on helping each parent to take responsibility for his or her part in altering dysfunctional patterns. With systems theory as a guide parents are finally able to get some control over themselves and are able to be emotionally responsive rather than simply reactive to others whom they blame for their discomfort.

Summary

Many who have worked in postplacement services for families who have adopted older emotionally disturbed children claim a systems approach is not useful for the adoptive family: Their position is that the adoptive family did not produce the symptoms the child brought with him into the family. Such a stance generally results in placing the focus of therapy on the child, who is the family member least motivated for change.

Attachment theory has emphasized that the environment plays a crucial role in whether a youngster becomes comfortably related to those around him. The adopted older child enters the new family with an extremely high level of inner anxiety. The success of the adoption depends on reducing that anxiety as quickly as possible so that bonding can take place. The child is unusually sensitive to anxiety in his environment, picking up discomfort and unrest in others which he adds to his own. Anxiety is contagious in a family emotional system; thus the child's elevated level, in turn, raises symptom-producing anxiety in each family member with whom he lives. To reverse the dangerous spiral, a holistic systems perspective seems the most promising.

Parents are motivated to improve conditions in the home. However, they usually come into therapy saying three things: "Change the child;" "It's his fault, not mine;" and "Leave me as I am." The gentle, respectful systems approach provides the emotional support the parents need. The system principles begin to make sense to the parents. As they are helped to see the emotional process at work in the family and their potential for altering what has not been effective, they become leaders of significant change which benefits the entire family. The cycle of increasing anxiety is finally reversed. The emotionally derailed child has a new opportunity to move in a healthy direction. Parents can take credit for their youngster's gains because the therapy works through them.

The family emotional system is the environment in which the child lives. Successful efforts to enhance the health of that setting have a positive effect on everyone who comes into contact with it. Since behavior patterns are passed from one generation to the next, the benefits to be reaped are multiplied manyfold. An adopted child challenges his new family to climb to higher levels of functioning. The family can actually gain strength by the spotlighting of its weaknesses. The work is never easy, but systems theory provides a guide.

Once the theoretical concepts are incorporated into one's behavior patterns, there is no turning back. Unusual stress may bring some temporary slippage backwards to previous lower levels of maturity. But as the crisis passes, family members resume their gains in differentiation with the result that new, more useful behavior is passed on to succeeding generations.

Notes

1. "A Pilot Project in Holding Therapy," Parent to Parent Information on Adoption. 36 Regent Park Road, London, NW1. June 1986.

2. Bowen, Murray, M.D. *Family Therapy in Clinical Practice*. Jason Aronson Press, 1978.
3. Bowlby, John, M.D. *Attachment and Loss: Sadness and Depression*. Vol III. New York: Basic Books, NY. 1980. p.38.
4. Tinbergen, Niko & Tinbergen, Elizabeth. *"Autistic Children:" New Hope for a Cure*. George Allen & Unwin, 1983. p. 158.
5. Mandell, Marshall, M.D. & Scanlon, Lynn W. *Doctor Mandells Five-Day Allergy Relief System*. Thomas Y. Crowell, Publisher, 1976. p. 34.
6. Schoenthaler, S. J. "The Effects of Citrus on the Treatment and Control of Antisocial Behavior: A Double-blind Crossover Study of an Incarcerated Juvenile Population." *International Journal of Biosocial Research*. 5 (2): 107–117, 1983. p. 108.

References

"A Pilot Project in Holding Therapy," Parent to Parent Information on Adoption Services. 36 Regents Park Road, London, NW1. June 1986.

Atkins, Robert C., M.D. *Dr. Atkin's Nutrition Breakthrough: How to Treat Your Medical Condition without Drugs*. Bantam Books, 1981.

Atkins, Robert C., M.D. *Dr. Atkin's Super-Energy Diet*. Bantam Books, 1981.

Bowen, Murray, M.D. *Family Therapy in Clinical Practice*. Jason Aronson Press, 1978.

Bowlby, John, M.D. *Attachment and Loss: Sadness and Depression*. Vol. III. Basic Books, Inc., 1980.

Mandell, Marshall, M.D. *Mandell's 5-Day Allergy Relief System*. Thomas Y. Crowell, Publisher, 1976.

Pfeiffer, Carl C., M.D., PhD. *Mental and Elemental Nutrients*. Keats Publishing, Inc., 1975.

Ross, Harvey M., M.D. and Saunders, Jeraldine. *A New Revolutionary Regimen to Control and Combat Hypoglycemia: The Disease Your Doctor Won't Treat*. Pinnacle Books, 1980.

Tinbergen, Niko and Tinbergen, Elizabeth. *"Autistic Children:" New Hope for a Cure*. Allen and Unwin, 1983.

Toman, Walter. *Family Constellation: Its Effects on Personality and Social Behavior*. Springer Publishing Company, 1976.

18

Mental Health Issues of Native American Transracial Adoptions

Charlotte Goodluck

Introduction

The following is a discussion of the relative merits of transracial, intertribal, and intra-tribal adoption, as well as extended-family guardianship, of American Indian children, with emphasis on mental health issues. The topic is complex and controversial, with many dimensions and varied opinions. As part of an introduction it is necessary to discuss other relevant topics in order to put the paper into a wider perspective.

Background

The U.S. census reports that there are 1.4 million Native Americans, 0.6% of the total population. Approximately half reside on reservations. Children under the age of eighteen make up 45% of the American Indian population. There are over 300 federally recognized tribes in 27 states.

The American Indian is at greater risk of poverty, alcoholism, low education, high dropout rate, unemployment, homicide, suicide, and mental health problems such as depression than the rest of Americans. The list of potential mental health problems is lengthy. Many of these problems result from a long history of conflict between cultures, and federal policies[1] of eradicating Indian cultures and assimilating the Indian people into the mainstream. However, these policies have not always been successful. Many tribal people have serious difficulty responding to these policies and coping with today's life. However, there are strengths in tribal communities, such as the extended family, clan relationships, tribal identity, spiritual life, and tribal sovereignty. Too, there are positive role models and leaders for youth to identify with and emulate, but often these leaders are not in the public view.

Indian Child Welfare

During the mid-1970's there were national efforts by Indian leaders to let Congress know about the widespread systematic breakup of Indian families by state foster-care systems and private agencies. The documented foster-care placement rates were alarming.[2] As a result of these efforts legislation was drafted to protect Indian tribes, families, and children. The public law was called the "Indian Child Welfare Act of 1978 (ICWA) (P.L. 95-608)"; it was signed into law by President Carter in November of 1978. This public law has made monumental changes in the decision-making procedures of state social services and court systems.[3]

The law brought three major changes: 1) tribes must be notified of any state foster care and/or adoption proceeding involving Indian children, 2) tribes can intervene at any time during a proceeding when Indian children are involved, and 3) Indian parents and Indian custodians must be given due process in the action. Another significant aspect is that tribes can request a transfer of jurisdiction from state court to tribal court. These major legal changes have returned major decision-making roles to tribal authorities in order to promote and protect the Indian family and child and the tribal culture.

ICWA has been implemented for over seven years and case law[4] has developed from different court decisions [5,6] involving both state and tribal viewpoints. Many Indian children are returning from various state foster and adoptive placements to many different tribes. These tribes often have had to provide mental health and reunification services[7] to the children in question and their families.

Mental health services are delivered in three major ways on reservations. The first major source of mental health services for a family is the support and caring from an intact functioning extended family and nuclear family system. Children, siblings, cousins and other relatives are looked after by the informal helping network including advice seeking from spiritual leaders within a tribal environment.

When this structure is not available for various reasons then external, formal structures are sought. With the inclusion of Indian Health Services, a public health hospital system on reservations during the early 40's they became the major source of health care provision for Indian families. The second source of mental health services comes via the Indian Health Service, either directly within the particular hospital setting or by contract with social workers, psychologists, or psychiatrist. Each IHS service area has its own mental health budget and its own mental health priorities so attention to different needs is seen in each geographic area. Services may include: prevention, education, counseling, assessment, evaluation and follow-up depending on the need of the particular case. Placement into foster care, group home and other institutional settings may be required depending on the severity of the mental health problem. Placement into state hospitals is a complex jurisdictional matter involving state and tribal issues and beyond the scope of this paper.

The third major source of services is available off reservation. Eligible Indian clients have access to Indian health services (if geographically available, like in a major city) similar to on reservation clients plus access to the state, private, and county resources regarding mental health services. Also, employed Indian clients have access to third party providers through employee fringe benefit policies but this is dependent on the employer's health insurance program. Services for mental health are dependent on various eligibility criteria, access to services, funding sources, and severity of problem.

There are various research studies on ICWA such as the one by the American Indian Law Center entitled "Indian Child Welfare Impact and Improvements under P.L. 95-608 and P.L. 96-272." Comprehensive questionnaires were sent to all tribes and states to assess the impact of the Indian Child Welfare Act of 1978 and the Adoption Assistance and Child Welfare Act of 1980 on their child welfare systems. The answers point to problems with the implementation of ICWA, such as inadequate federal funding to tribes for preventive and rehabilitative programs, the high turnover of tribal staff, and inadequate training, all of which are detrimental to the maintenance of programs at the tribal level. Ultimately children suffer.

Adoption Issues

With regard to child-care practices, tribes for centuries have parented and cared for their children in both nuclear-family and extended-family structures. Native Americans differ from Anglos in that out-of-home placements are open: that is, children are generally not placed with strangers outside the tribal kinship network and thus remain known to the birth family. One important value in tribal ethics is that a child who loses a parent is accepted and cared for by other relatives in the tribal system. There was no concept of legal termination of parental rights before the Americanization of the tribal court systems which followed the Wheeler–Howard Reorganization Act of 1934. In fact, the words "adoption" and "termination" are not found in many native languages except where they are borrowed from English words.

However, due to numerous factors such as the impact of relocation, removal to "government and mission boarding schools," and the decrease of the indigenous tribal teaching systems, many Indian children were being raised away from their own families and tribes. In the 1950's, numerous tribal children were being raised in cities in the east and midwest after being placed for adoption[8] by state, Bureau of Indian Affairs, and private agencies. The history of these transracial placements (Indian children with Anglo parents) is discussed by Fanshel,[9] and the mental health risks of the children (emotional problems, identity confusion, depression) are analyzed by Berlin.[10]

Adoption of an Indian child into a family system from another culture and race will promote a double identity problem; first a loss and separation from the tribal parent (biological parent) and second, a loss from the tribal culture. In addition a child must contend with the issues of adoption itself and searching for tribal identity as a young adult and reunification with tribe. These various attachments and separations are multiple and will promote identity confusion (self and culture) and serious mental health problems. Then add to this the dynamics of foster care placements and adoption disruptions are to be expected. The effects of disruption (principally Indian children running away) are painful for the child, the adoptive parents, and siblings. Grief reactions from the separation and loss are frequently seen in the total family system.

Federal policy has been affected by changes in popular attitudes toward the concept and practice of transracial adoption, with the result that Indian children have been made victims of the cycle of changing policy.[11] During the 1960's advocacy movements, such as Black social workers denouncing transracial placements, forced agencies to make changes in recruitment practices, home study policies, and agency hiring practices. This approach began to affect American Indian child welfare, when in the early 1970's a private agency in Arizona started a program[12] to place Indian children with Indian adoptive families. Within seven years over 100 children were placed into Indian adoptive families. Children were returned to their tribes after spending many years in non-Indian state foster care. This program included infants as well as older and special-needs children. Tribal resources were contacted and made available to children and their parents once again. There are many current programs in the nation focusing on recruiting Indian families for Indian children. Issues related to who may adopt Indian children and how state and tribal social services can work together to continue to implement the Indian Child Welfare Act are discussed in Louise Zokan de los Reyes' "Adoption and the American Indian Child." Effective recruitment of Indian families and development of appropriate tribal child-care standards are a critical part of minimizing mental health problems.

There are Indian children who were placed in adoptive homes outside their own culture and race. The psychological literature demonstrates a child's need for a nurturing and stable environment to enhance a stable identity.[13] The impact of transracial adoption on a child creates a developmental crisis and one has to come to terms with it during the process of growing up. This crisis impacts one's sense of self-esteem and identity, and culture attachment and acceptance. Adoption itself is a crisis and implies a lifelong developmental process of accepting one's history and different familial relationships. The dynamics of adoption[14,15] are complex and impact emotional and psychological well-being throughout life.

The adoption field has made many systematic changes[16] since the early 1970's. Current adoption policy should be a life-long commitment by all the parties serving the biological parents, adoptee, and adoptive parents. Post-adoption services[17,18] such as mental health services for the entire triad are appropriate and necessary particularly in cases when Indian children have been raised in homes outside their own culture.

Due to the preceding factors earlier, mental health professionals across the country have come into contact with children living in various familial situations including transracial adoption. They need to understand the complex issues facing the Native American child and incorporate approaches that address these issues.

Informal Survey

The next section of this paper is in "question and answer" format. The questions were posed to child welfare professionals[19] with experience in foster care, adoption, and Indian affairs. The theme was adoption practice as it relates to American Indian children and culture.

1. What does the term "transracial placement" and "transracial adoption" mean in your work with American Indian children and families?

- A child is placed outside the community; a child loses his tribal identity.
- Placement (adoption or foster care) of an American Indian child with non-Indian parents. Caucasian parents who already have Indian children are counted as "middle ground." Placement of an Indian child with such a family is still a transracial placement, but not quite as transracial as it would be if a child were the only Indian family member.
- Placing Indian children in families where the lifestyle is different from their own culture. The child may look Indian but be acculturated internally to the family's culture. Such placement may set up confusion and nonacceptance by the Indian culture as well as rejection by the adoptive family's culture in the long run; in other words, the child runs the risk of being rejected by both worlds.

- Placement of an Indian child in a non-Indian family. Usually it is assumed that both of the parents are non-Indian; however, these terms would also apply in cases where one parent is an Indian and the other parent is not. This is especially pertinent when the Indian parent is not of the same tribe as the child.

2. What are the positive aspects of a transracial placement?

- Gives a family a special child; it can provide a family for a child who otherwise might not have one.
- There may be positive aspects for the adoptive parent (they can raise a child), but from a child's point of view there can be too many negative aspects.
- Professionally and morally, children should be members of families who are of their own racial, ethnic, and cultural background, unless there are circumstances that do not permit it. Dealing with the issues of placement and adoption for children and families is difficult enough without the additional burden created by transracial placement or adoption.
- I fail to see any positive aspects and would support such placements only when it has been determined that no tribal or Indian resources exist for this child.

3. What are the negative aspects of transracial placements?

- The native language is not learned, nor are cultural skills such as weaving, silver smithing, herding sheep. An Indian child traditionally learns the importance of the land, learns the ethos of moral and spiritual lessons from elders, participates in a complex tribal religious system, and learns the significance of living in a relative/clan family system from a tribal point of view. A transracially-adopted child loses this source of a feeling of identity.
- Loss of tribal community and erosion of the tribal community system.
- The child runs a high risk of making a bad bargain: trading his culture and heritage for a new family.
- Poor identity foundation of adoptees; loss of support networks and extended family; drain of human resources for target groups; fulfilling the needs of adoptive parents, not the children.
- Places the child at higher risk of serious mental health problems during adolescence, such as difficulties with dating and selection of mate, and with having children themselves ("Who am I and where do I belong?")

4. How does the Indian Child Welfare Act affect your decision-making regarding children in foster care and adoption? Have you had any children

who were placed for adoption in non-Indian families and then had to be replaced with an Indian family? Discuss what happened.

- From a tribal standpoint, all efforts are made to keep children within the family or at least within the community. If that is not possible, then an outside resource is sought. In that situation it is essential that the non-tribal guardians or adoptive parents become involved in the child's tribal community, in order to sensitize them to the environment from which the child comes and keep some form of meaningful relationship with the specific tribe.

- We are careful to follow the letter (not always the intent of the ICWA. There was a case where a child was placed with a non-Indian family without having the tribe participate in planning. The agency said the tribe didn't respond, but the tribe moved to overturn the adoption, saying they weren't given an opportunity to respond. After lengthy court maneuvering they won the right to move the child. The tribe decided to let the adoption stand, because their goal was to make the point about the importance of including the tribe in planning, not to disrupt a placement that was working well.

- ICWA is a federal law and it does affect decision-making regarding Indian children in state foster and adoptive placements. There are times however, when the workers are finding loop-holes in the law such as allowing "voluntary placements" and not contacting the tribes, varies considerably. Because private adoptions are legal in some states, Indian parents voluntarily[20] place children outside the tribe without notifying the tribe when these adoptions are finalized.

- Our philosophy and approach to placement of Indian children with Indian families preceeded ICWA, so that ICWA in that aspect did not affect our decision-making process in placement. Problems with ICWA have more to do with having Indian "parents' rights" and "confidentiality." Several adolescents who have been placed with non-Indian families in infancy have come to our attention because of problems related to transracial placement superimposed on adoption issues of adolescence.

- When workers follow the spirit and intent of ICWA it works best. When workers, lawyers, and judges are ignorant of or opposed to the concept, children suffer. In one case, a child adopted by a non-Indian family had to be returned after the tribe learned that ICWA regulations had not been followed. The decision was the right one, but the child suffered needlessly because of the lawyer's mistake. One case involved a young Apache teenager who had been adopted by non-Indian parents in the early 60's in the East. She became pregnant by an Indian youth and she placed the baby with a private agency for voluntary foster care. Her parents wanted her to relinquish her rights and since she did not want to the state became involved. They filed a Petition to terminate her rights as her parents claimed neglect, emotional instability and abuse. The state had to notify the tribe and the tribe intervened and requested transfer to tribal court. The tribal social services department has given services to the mother and are helping mother and child remain together with close supervision of the child.

5. Under what circumstances would you decide to place an Indian child in a family not of his own culture? Why?

- Only when all community and related family resources have been exhausted; generally this service is for a child with severe emotional and/or physical problems. A written agreement with the tribe would be necessary.
- If we had made repeated (more than required) attempts to include the tribe in planning and received no response, and if these attempts were well documented.
- Only under the rarest of circumstances. The issue is preserving the culture. Tribes are serious about not losing their children. It's not worth the risk to make a placement that has such a high probability of being overturned.
- If reasonable efforts within a reasonable time span do not develop an appropriate Indian home. May be related to special problems of the child, special problems of the natural family that make it necessary for the child to be removed from the area of the parent's residence, or a special restriction within the tribe (i.e., reluctance to accept child of another tribe).
- An Indian child should be placed with a non-Indian family only when we can document that the resources required by the placement preference provision of ICWA are not available. This requires the provision of remedial efforts on behalf of the child and the family if they are indicated. Unfortunately, efforts in remediation are not only scarce but not well developed.
- In an emergency when no resource within the culture is available. In reality there is no excuse for not developing the resources necessary to respond to even the most urgent need. The question is: How?

6. There were many American Indian children placed into non-Indian adoptive families years ago. Have you worked with these children as adults or teenagers? What problems or positive reactions did they express about their experiences? How have the tribes integrated these adults into their community?

- I have worked with two cases, one positive and one negative. In the first, the non-Indian family was stable and sensitive to the boy's cultural background, giving positive support, accepting the need to search for biological parents, encouraging his development of a positive self-esteem and image. They eventually helped their son locate his Indian parents. He now moves freely between the two families and two worlds.

In the other case, the adoptive family was dysfunctional and the young girl exhibited low and negative self-esteem, self-destructive behavior such as drug/alcohol abuse, and eating disorders. She had poor personal interaction skill, was often depressed and disliked any association with Indian culture and held a low opinion of her own Indian identity. She tended to over-identify with the non-Indian culture. The young girl was eventually placed in a residential treatment center. Contact has since been made with her birth father and a reunion was completed. It seems vital to this young lady (age 19) to have someone from her tribal birth family to show some interest in her development and growth.

- One adolescent placed with non-Indian adoptive parents wants to contact her tribe because of tribal benefits. The tribe is willing to help with her college support, but no contact is planned with birth parents.
- Unfortunately, the bonds of affectional ties and sense of permanency that this project (BIA/CWLA) sought to develop did not bear fruit. Instead the children who were the subjects of this project have experienced lives of severe identity confusion. Many of these people are now in their thirties and forties and experience severe problems of abuse of alcohol and other drugs. Some of the families have financial resources to afford private psychiatric resources for their children but find that, even with the best of help these adult children remain severely troubled.

In the book *Far from the Reservation,* Fanshel reviewed 97 families of Indian children raised in non-Indian families. This number is low because it deals with only one research project. Another report cited at the Indian Senate Select Committee hearings estimates at least 1/4 of Indian children placed were placed into non-Indian homes. The total number of Indian children affected by some sort of non-Indian place-ment is high. A significant number of these Indian children have subsequently been seen in mental health settings across the country.

- I have had numerous calls from non-Indian adoptive parents wanting to know how to provide their Indian children with a sense of Indian identity and culture. External means such as attending pow-wows and visiting museums don't give a child a whole sense of ''being Indian'' or ''having a tribal identity.'' In fact they may leave him with a sense of confusion, since Indian children represent numerous tribal backgrounds, different histories, and different values and beliefs. Being exposed to a sterotyped ''pan-Indian'' cannot provide a person with positive self-esteem and positive tribal group identity nor the unique tribal survival skills (e.g. coping with racism, learning about inter-tribal differences, understand-ing tribal-cultural-spiritual ways) related to belonging to a particular tribal group and community.

Mental health services need to be available during the entire life of the children who were adopted in this project to help them with their sense of alienation, rejection, and separation from traditional tribal identity. Daily contact with positive Indian role models in the community will help deal with the acceptance and identity issues. Universities, colleges, and urban Indian centers have Indian clubs and activities to help encourage connections with other members of the tribal community.

One helpful Indian-oriented mental health approach is the "Talking Circle",[21] where Indian elders, parents, and children can come together in a 'circle' and help heal one another by talking about their issues and accepting one another. The "Talking Circle" is a form of group therapy within a cultural framework. The circle has special meaning to Indian people as a symbol and function. The techniques included are listening, sensitivity to the group, spiritual focus, sharing strengths and problems, and the use of informal helping networks. (For more information, contact the Native American Rehabilitation Association, an Indian alcohol program in Portalnd, Oregon. It has been in operation since 1981.)

- We have had some Indian clients who as children were placed in non-Indian adoptive families and are now young adults who have come back to the agency. A number of them were pregnant young women wanting to place their expected babies for adoption. These young women express a positive adoptive experience, and are rejecting their Indian background, wanting their children to be placed in a non-Indian family. This may be a "double whammy" for the child in dealing with adoption issues later on: "Why didn't my parents want me, and what is so bad about my Indian heritage?"
- The cases I have heard about have had major identity problems in adolescence. The placements fall apart during these critical years of development as the Indian youths start searching and yearning for their Indian birth parents and tribal identity. The tribes are contacted, and positive or negative reunions may occur; but still there is a sense of emptiness, loss of relatives and ties to a tribal community, and lowered self-esteem. Higher incidence of alcoholism and attempted suicide are seen in this population of Indian adults. Professional counseling in tandem with Indian healers may provide the necessary bridge between the two worlds.

7. What is the most critical issue you want others in human services to know about American Indian adoption and the special issue of transracial adoption?

- Transracial adoption should only be considered after all tribal resources are exhausted. It should be a very rare option for tribal children. The development of urban, non-reservation resources is a critical issue because many of the Indian parents are living in fractured families already. The crisis nursery concept[22] can prevent the breakup of young Indian families by providing preventive child protective services to both the young Indian mother and father and the high risk newborn or young child.

- If one ignores ICWA it will be at considerable risk to the child's stability.
- Children who consider themselves to be "Indian" should be treated that way, even if they don't fit the letter of ICWA eligibility. If they aren't eligible for enrollment, or had been voluntarily relinquished, they should still be placed with Indian families. We do that with Black children when no law requires it—why not with Indian children?
- Indian children can be placed into Indian foster and adoptive homes when tribal and state policies and practices concerning staff hiring, recruitment, and home studies are changed to advocate same-race and-culture families for Indian children. There are existing programs which can be models for other social service programs. ICWA is a federal law on which other countries are now modeling their own child welfare laws and policies to achieve tribal independence and sovereignty. The mental health problems of transracial adoption can be prevented by not placing Indian children in transracial adoptive families and by not continuing previous transracial placements. Then Indian tribal communities and families can be developed at the local level as a resource for special needs children needing placement.
- It must be clearly understood that each of us has the requirement of ensuring the integrity of the family. Continued separation of Indian children from their families and tribes ensures the destruction of Indians as a people. The underlying racism involved in these practices must be reckoned with. There are many ways to assist Indian families and their children. Removal of these children is a most destructive practices.

8. ICWA promotes tribal decision making regarding tribal children. Given the fact that there are Indian children awaiting families, how would you plan to achieve permanency within the tribal system?

- Our tribe has a tribal termination statute, but it has never been used by our judge. Relatives are also hesitant to participate in any parental termination, for social and emotional reasons. Long-term guardianship is frequently the option used.
- Termination of parental rights has no place in tribal society. It is an impossibility in view of the relational systems of Indian people. It is an Anglo notion that parental rights can be terminated. Indian children have been reared and cared for by other members in their communities, relatives and non-relatives, since the beginning of time. Why is it necessary to change essential life-ways of the people?

- Termination of parental rights is not the plan of choice for most Indian children. Extended family care is a tradition; therefore a good permanent option is usually achieved by guardianship. Permanency for Indian children has as much to do with extended family and tribe as it does with biological parents.
- Tribes can define their own meaning of "permanency" in light of community standards and practices. It may mean long-term guardianship with a relative or another family chosen by the tribal human services. The goal is to provide the child with a loving and protective family; tribal definitions of this seem appropriate. In the urban area, tribal life takes on different characteristics; then it is up to the tribal elders and leaders in the given community to help with the planning and decision making, with a bridge to the tribe always available. Indian permanency planning teams[23] are functioning in some states to assist states and tribes with these important decisions and plans.

9. Do you think other ethnic groups should have federal laws similar to ICWA to help to protect their children, families, and culture?

- I don't know that federal laws are necessary, as current social work practice seems to follow cultural, racial guidelines. The added element in the Indian case is not only the needs of the child, but the survival of the tribal community. Removal of children from the community deprives the tribal community of the strong numerical base needed to maintain tribal strength and power.
- No other racial group in the U.S. has a structure like the American Indian tribes, so there could not be the same implementation. Conscientious professionals should, however, give racial factors serious considerations and place children within their own racial group whenever possible.
- I think it's a shame that there even had to be ICWA. Adoption workers should try to keep a child in his culture because it is best for him, not because it is the law. I prefer unrelenting pressure from the tribes, National Association of Black Social Workers, and National Association of Indian Social Workers instead of laws. There always seem to be loopholes in the laws.
- This is an interesting issue which I certainly have to give more thought to. Perhaps there should be legislation or strict guidelines so that the rights of children and parents of these ethnic groups are not abused.
- Currently there are a few states (Minnesota, New Mexico, and New York) which have incorporated special statutes into their own state laws to protect and ensure that every child retains the right and opportunity to grow up in the world of his/her identity. Indian tribes have a unique governmental relationship with the U.S. government and this difference must be taken into consideration.

Summary

The Indian Child Welfare Act of 1978, now the law of the land, mandates that Indian children needing families be placed within their own tribal community if at all possible, and that transracial adoptions are to be avoided. The placement preference section of the ICWA considers only immediate family members and then other tribal members as a source for the child; placement with another culture is only a last alternative. Recent casework experience with the results of transracial adoptions of Indian children and with the implementation of ICWA demonstrate the wisdom of the principles on which ICWA was based. Transracial adoptions tend to result in more mental health problems than same-culture or same-race adoptions, although it must also be said that some transracial adoptions have been successful from the viewpoint of the child and the adoptive parents, if not from the viewpoint of a tribe which has lost a member. However, much remains to be done before it can be said that ICWA has been fully implemented. In many areas there is an urgent need to develop a pool of Indian foster and adoptive parents in order to achieve more fully the goal of same-culture placement, and to develop reservation and urban-Indian resources such as guardianship programs that will minimize the mental health consequences.

In conclusion, Indian children who are placed in non-Indian adoptive homes need sensitive caring adoptive parents who will advocate and address the child's need for a tribal-cultural identity as well as address the special issues of adoption itself. Adoptive parents can provide for positive Indian role models to be present in their child's life and to allow for a spiritual based healer to give a ceremony for acknowledgement of Indian heritage and identity. Providing an Indian hero from music, recreation, sports, literature and the arts allows for a positive Indian image and self-esteem to grow and develop. When an Indian child and his family request mental health services, a number of options have been demonstrated to be effective. Individual, peer and group counseling are particularly helpful with older children. For younger children, the use of play therapy using Indian dolls and objects for Indian and non-Indian culture (hogan-house, horses, dancing, drums, eagle) enable the child to begin to understand his own connections to an Indian heritage. The use of these symbols can foster the ability to balance and integrate the best from both worlds. The child has a better chance to achieve acceptance of one's own self and background when both cultures are presented in a positive, constructive manner. The Indian child needs help to acknowledge the reality from both cultures and how not to become self–destructive, hateful, bitter or stuck in loss and rage. He or she must learn to move past these negative emotions and on to acceptance and integration of his Indian origins.

The following are resources which a mental health professional might want to contact for specific help in addressing Native American children and issues.

- Tribal governments and social services
- B.I.A. Social Services
- Fos-Adopt Program with the Urban Indian Child Resource Center
- Northwest Indian Child Welfare Institute in Portland, Oregon
- National Indian Social Worker's Association
- Native American Adoption Resource with Council of Three Rivers

Notes

1. Johnson, Barbara Brooks. 1982. "American Indian Jurisdiction as a Policy Issue," *Social Work Journal*, Vol. 27, No. 1, 31–37.
2. Byler, William. 1976. "Statistical Survey of Out of Home Placement of Indian Children," Association on American Indian Affairs, 5.
3. Blanchard, Evelyn Lance and Barsh, R. 1980. "What is best for tribal children?," *Social Work Journal*, September, 350–357.
4. Grossman, Toby. 1985. "Indian Child Welfare Case Synopses," American Indian Law Center, Albuquerque, New Mexico.
5. Donovan, Bill. "Culture Shock: Half-Navajo Boy is Ordered to Reservation Despite His Fears," *Arizona Republic*, 2/20/86, Section B 1, B4.
6. Rigg, Melissa. "Helpful Law doubles grief for Papago Couple," *Arizona Daily Star*, 11/28/82, Section K, p.2.
7. Navajo Nation, Division of Social Welfare, Indian Child Welfare Program, Window Rock, Arizona.
8. Green, Henry J. 1983. "Risk and Attitudes Associated with Extra-Cultural Placement of American Indian Children: A Critical Review," *American Academy of Child Psychiatry*, 63–67.
9. Fanshel, David. 1972. *Far From the Reservation: The Transracial Adoption of American Indian Children*. New York: Scarecrow Press.
10. Berlin, Irving N. 1978. "Anglo Adoptions of Native Americans: Reprecussions in Adolescence," *American Academy of Child Psychiatry*, 387–388.
11. Benet, Mary Kathleen. 1976. *The Politics of Adoption*. New York: Free Press.
12. Goodluck, Charlotte and Short, Deirdre. 1980. "Working with American Indian Parents: A Cultural Approach," *Social Casework Journal*, October, 472–475.
13. Dixon, Samuel L. and Sands, Roberta. 1983. "Identity and the Experience of Crises," Social Casework Journal, Vol. 64, No. 4.
14. Hartman, Ann. 1985. "Practice in Adoption," *A Handbook of Child Welfare*, Larid and Hartman, Editors, New York: Free Press, 667–691.
15. Jewett, Claudia L. 1982. *Helping Children Cope with Separation and Loss*. Harvard: Harvard Common Press.
16. Cole, Elizabeth. 1985. "Adoption—History, Policy, and Program," *A Handbook of Child Welfare*, New York: Free Press.
17. Jewett, Claudia L. 1978. *Adopting the Older Child*. Harvard: Harvard Common Press.
18. Fales, Mary Jane. 1985. *Post-Legal Adoption Services Today*. New York: Child Welfare League of America.

19. A questionnaire was sent to professionals in the field of Indian child welfare on their thoughts on transracial adoption among American Indian children. The results were given at the North American Council on Adoptable Children National Conference in August, 1985. The professionals were from the following agencies: Gila River Indian Community, Arizona; Northwest Adoption Exchange, Seattle, Washington; Jewish Family and Children's Service of Phoenix, Arizona; Area Indian Health Service, Portland, Oregon; Northwest Indian Child Welfare Institute, Portland, Oregon; and, American Indian Law Center, Albuquerque, New Mexico. Their opinions are given in the second part of the paper. Credit and appreciation is extended to them for their effort and experience and willingness to share their ideas with other professionals interested in the welfare of Indian children.
20. Anderson, Annette. 1984. "Suggested Checklist for Voluntary Adoptions and Foster Care—American Indian Children," Depelchin Children's Center, Houston, Texas.
21. "Talking Circle," a preventive mental health concept operating at the Phoenix Indian Center, Phoenix, Arizona.
22. Denver Family Crisis Center, Denver Department of Social Services, Denver County, Denver Indian Health Board, Denver, Colorado, and the local Indian Child Welfare (ICWA) programs across the country (contact B.I.A. Area offices for their names and addresses).
23. Indian Permanency Planning and Indian Task Forces existing in states such as Washington and Oregon. Contact state department of social services for model programs and contact tribe for locally operating child protection teams.

References

Berlin, Irving N. 1978. "Anglo Adoptions of Native Americans: Repercussions in Adolescence." *American Academy of Child Psychiatry,* 387–388.

Blanchard, Evelyn Lance and Barsh, R. 1980. "What is Best for Tribal Children"? (September) 350–357.

Byler, William. 1976. "Statistical Survey of Out of Home Placement of Indian Children." Association of American Indian Affairs, 5.

Cole, Elizabeth. 1985. "Adoption—History, Policy, and Program" in *A Handbook of Child Welfare.* New York: Free Press.

Cross, Terry. 1986. "Drawing Cultural Traditions In Indian Child Welfare Practice." *Social Casework,* Vol. 67, No. 5, May-1986, p. 283–289.

Dixon, Samuel L. and Sands, Roberta. 1983. "Identity and the Experience of Crises." *Social Casework,* Vol. 64, No. 4.

Donovan, Bill. "Culture Shock: Half-Navajo Boy is Ordered to Reservation Despite His Fears." *Arizona Republic,* 2/20/86, Section B1 and B4.

Fanshel, David. 1972. *Far From the Reservation: The Transracial Adoption of American Indian Children.* New York: Scarecrow Press.

Fischler, Ronald. 1980. "Protecting American Indian Children." *Social Work Journal,* Vol. 25, No. 5, September, 341–357.

Goodluck, Charlotte and Eskstein, F. 1978. "American Indian Adoption Program: An Ethnic Approach to Child Welfare." *White Cloud Journal,* Vol.1, Spring, 3–6.

Goodluck, Charlotte and Brown, M. 1980. "Decision Making Regarding American Indian Children in Foster Care." Jewish Family and Children's Service of Phoenix, Spring.

Goodluck, Charlotte and Short, Deirdre. 1980. "Working with American Indian Parents: A Cultural Approach." *Social Casework Journal,* October, 472–475.

Green, Henry J. 1983. "Risk and Attitudes Associated with Extra-Cultural Placement of American Indian Children: A Critical Review." *American Academy of Child Psychiatry,* 63–67.

Grossman, Toby. 1985. "Indian Child Welfare Case Synopses." American Indian Law Center, Albuquerque, New Mexico.

Hartman, Ann. 1985. "Practice in Adoption." *A Handbook of Child Welfare,* Laird and Hartman, editors, New York: Free Press, 667–691.

Heritage and Helping. A Model Curriculm for Indian Child Welfare Practice, Northwest Indian Child Welfare Institute, Portland, Oregon.

Ishisaka, Hideki. 1978. "American Indian and Foster Care: Cultural Factors and Separation." *Child Welfare,* Vol LVII, No. 5, May, 299–308.

Jewett, Claudia L. 1978. *Adopting the Older Child.* Harvard: The Harvard Common Press.

Jewett, Claudia L. 1982. *Helping Children Cope with Separation and Loss.* Harvard: Harvard Common Press.

Johnson, Barbara Brooks. 1982. "American Indian Jurisdiction as a Policy Issue." *Social Work Journal,* Vol. 27, No. 1, 31–37.

Jones, Charles E. and Else, John. 1979. "Racial and Cultural Issues in Adoption." *Child Welfare Journal,* Vol LVIII, No. 6, June, 373–382.

Long, Kathleen Ann. 1983. "The Experience of Repeated and Traumatic Loss Among Crow Indian Children: Response Patterns and Intervention Strategies." *American Journal of Orthopsychiatry* 53(1), January.

McRoy, Ruth and et al. 1982. "Self Esteem and Racial Identity in Transracial and Inracial Adoptees." *Social Work Journal,* November, 522–526.

Reyes, Louise Zokan de los. 1985. *Adoption and the American Indian Child.* National American Indian Court Judges Association, Washington,D.C.

Rigg, Melissa. "Helpful Law Doubles Grief for Papago Couple." *Arizona Daily Star,* 11/28/82, Section K, p. 2.

Stack, Carol. 1984. "Cultural Perspectives on Child Welfare." *Review of Law and Social Change,* Vol XII:539–547.

"Transracial Adoption: Black Children and Native American Children." Research Capsule/18, Northwest Resource Center, University of Washington, School of Social Work.

19

The Mental Health Professional, the Black Child, and the Adoption Process: Increasing the Chances of Successful Intervention

Willie T. Hamlin

Embodied in the question of how the mental health professional can effectively intervene in providing therapeutic assistance to Black children and their adoptive families are three subquestions: (1) What are the unique implications for Black children, and the Black community as a whole, of the developmental traumas generally associated with children who have been removed from the care of their biological parents? (2) What are the expectations of the Black adopting family, and their ability combined with willingness to cope with their special needs child? (3) How well does the therapist understand the cultural differences that distinguish him or her from the patient, and what role do these differences play in treatment?

Effects of Developmental Traumas

There are few who would disagree with the assertion that an appropriate, nurturing, and stable home environment during the early years of life has significant influence on the attitudes a child formulates in later life. A child who experiences repeated disruptions in that stability is more likely to become an adolescent or adult who is not able to form a positive attachment to others; who has a diminished sense of self-esteem and self-worth and a poorer self-image; and who is more likely to engage in activities that serve as a means to act out their feelings of rejection, abandonment, and neglect.

While Black people as a whole comprise a mere 12% of the nation's total population, with Black males accounting for 5% of that, 55% of our prison population is comprised of men from this racial group. The unemployment rates for Black youth in our major cities are in excess of 50%, and by the year 2000 it is projected that 70% of all Black men will be under- or unemployed.

The topic of teen pregnancy in the Black community has been the subject of intense national focus in the last few years and will not be re-examined here except for the following point: Children who have not been effectively parented themselves are not likely to effectively parent their own children. Children who have not been given the opportunity to develop positive attitudes about themselves and others can be expected to exact a negative toll on themselves, the community in which they live, and society as a whole. The implications here are monumental.

I believe that the mental health community has not only an ethical but a moral duty to utilize its individual and collective energies to develop the needed expertise to assist this historically traumatized populace in maintaining adoptive placements that will serve as the first line of defense against perpetuating the cycle that put the children up for adoption in the first place.

The Child

It is a commonly accepted premise that the degree to which a child is able to accept and adapt to his or her adoptive placement is influenced by the "length of placement and the number of broken attachments" prior to that placement.[1] This would suggest that the younger the child is at the time of placement, the better the chances are that the placement will last through the legalization process and result in a positive experience for both the child and family.

Many of the children being placed for adoption today, however, are not young. It is the child who has gone through a number of temporary placements, losses of primary caretakers, and repeated school disruptions who poses the greatest challenge to the mental health professional and the adoptive parent.

A social history that notes repeated placements can tell us a great deal about the child and the developmental traumas he or she has experienced. At the very least, we can assume that the child's ability to bond to his adoptive parents may be severely impaired. The youngster has learned to anticipate loss and rejection and thus provokes it. Repeated narcissistic injury results in a diminished sense of self-worth, self-esteem, and self-image. Multiple changes in residence result in multiple school placements and disruptions in the educational process. Strategies for the remediation of any learning difficulties may never be implemented.

The older the child becomes before a permanent placement is found, the greater are the chances that learning delays, whether cognitively or emotionally based, will become a source of frustration and acting-out behavior. Kagan observed that "… the greater the number of placements, the less likely a youth was to attend a non-institutional school…."[2]

Growth and developmental traumas associated with repeated disruptions in residence may be compounded for the Black child as a result of historical and institutionalized racism. The Afro-American child growing up in an intact family in our society receives a variety of subtle and sometimes blatant messages that there is something inherently wrong with him. Standards of beauty as projected in media advertising, television programming, movies, etc. tell the Black child that his physical features fall outside of the desired norm. Beauty in America has been associated with blonde hair, blue eyes, white skin, pointed noses, and thin lips. Much attention has been focused on assisting the Black child (and adult) in changing those things about him that society finds physically unappealing. Most of the advertising that specifically addresses the grooming of Black people deals with the chemical denaturization of their natural hair to make it straight or more loosely curled.

There are few who disagree with the assertion that television has had an increasing influence on the attitudes of all children. Research tells us that by the time the average American child graduates from high school, he or she has spent more time watching television than in the classroom. A study conducted by the University of Michigan in 1950 revealed that the five major factors that influence children's self-image, in order of their ranking, were: home, school, church, peers, and television. Thirty years later, the same study was repeated and found that television had risen from position five to position three (ahead of school and church).[3] In 1985 it is commonly asserted that television now ranks as the number two influence in every child's life. For the time being, home barely maintains its number-one ranking.

The impact of the media on the growth and development of all children is a matter of great concern. This is particularly true with children who have experienced multiple placements, resulting in attachment difficulties with people, for they tend to turn to television for a sense of companionship.

Unfortunately, Black characters on television have usually perpetuated negative stereotypical myths. In recent years, two of the most popular television series have had as their central theme Black children being adopted by White parents. The real-life message there is that Black adults are incapable of taking care of, providing for, and nurturing a Black child. Such a perception may closely parallel that child's own personal experience and further complicate his ability to trust the capabilities of Black adoptive parents.

A Black child with no adult he trusts, and no one willing to combat the negative inferences on television and advertising is more susceptible to the negative and/or inappropriate indoctrinations of the media. Over a period of time, Black children may come to believe that society expects nothing more of them than to be good dancers or to communicate their feelings through monosyllabic grunts and brute force. An emotionally damaged child may endeavor to act that out.

To sum up: any child who has experienced the trauma of multiple residences and caretakers has an increased tendency toward inability to form positive attachments with subsequent caretakers. Frequent changes in the educational setting increase the likelihood of undiagnosed learning difficulties and missed opportunities for remediation. Added to those difficulties, for the Black child, are the negative programming that leads them to believe there is something wrong with their physical appearance, that society does not have the same expectations of them that it has for their non-Black peers, and that Black parents are ineffectual. Addressing these issues with the goal of resolving the problems presents a major challenge to the clinician as well as the parent.

Black Adoptive Parents

Black adoptive parents share at least one bond of commonality with the children they have adopted—they have been raised in a society that views their racial heritage as a pathology. The degree to which they are sensitized to this, and the internal coping mechanisms that have been developed, will have a significant influence on their ability to handle problems that arise with an adopted child.

Noshpitz, et al describe the adoptive parent as being middle class with above average intelligence.[4] More often than not, for a person of Afro-American heritage to have achieved "middle class" status in our society, he has to overcome a host of real and/or perceived obstacles. The desire to achieve and the fear of failing spur them on. The notion that they have to be twice as good as their nonwhite peers and/or colleagues in order to gain acceptance on a social, academic, or professional level is commonly accepted. Such individuals attribute at least a portion of their success to their ability to put more pressure on themselves to accomplish a goal than anyone else would put on them. The approach to overcoming obstacles in the past might well have been to put their internal resources in overdrive and to forge ahead with increased determination and will power. Unfortunately, more often than not, this strategy proves unsuccessful in dealing with their adopted child.

Many adopted parents view the agency that facilitated the placement with fear and resentment. It has the power to give and to withhold a child. Such feelings may inhibit families from returning to the agency when problems initially arise. Attempting to handle these difficulties on their own without the benefit of professional help may contribute to increased feelings of frustration and anger. All too often, by the time the family does seek out the agency it is to tell them that they have decided to terminate before legalization.

Transcultural Issues and Parents

Transference and countertransference are terms that most of us become familiar with in the earlier stages of professional training. Their impact on the therapist-patient relationship is perhaps most evident in the formation of a therapeutic alliance between a Black patient and a non-Black therapist. Elementary though they may be in terms of our early exposure to the terms, these have become central ideas of focus as we attempt to gain a greater understanding of the dynamics involved in cross-racial therapy relationships. In this situation, the onus of understanding the phenomena of transference and countertransference is placed squarely on the shoulders of the clinician rendering the service.

Inherent in the "getting-to- know-you" phase of all therapy situations are expectations that the patient has of the clinician. Some may want to cast the therapist in the role of a mother or father figure. In the case of a Black patient, the process of transference can take on far more dramatic and painful proportions. For many, the White therapist represents anything but a loving, caring, or all-knowing figure. To this individual, the therapist may take the form of the embodiment of 250 years of oppression, degradation, de-humanization, and suffering. Instead of viewing the clinician as an entity unto him- or herself, the individual may identify this therapist only in the context of the deeds of his ancestors from generations past who enslaved and destroyed a culture or, their present-day mirror images who create the public policies that have systematically destroyed the fabric of the Black family, thereby placing so many of its children in the adoptive system to begin with.

For patients grappling with these feelings the very thought of seeking assistance from an individual seen as part of the system, in order to regain one of "their own" children, may seem ludicrous. More often than not, these feelings are unstated and/or unacknowledged in the treatment session. They may, however, surface in a general attitude of hostility, a sense that the therapist is simply incompetent or an "I-just-don't-like-you" sentiment.

The severity of manifestation varies from one individual to the next. The parent may maneuver interviews so that the discussion is always focused on "safe" subjects—ones that do not afford the therapist an opportunity to introduce exploration of more substantive (perhaps painful) areas. Or, in an attempt to win the acceptance of the therapist, parents may restrict their responses to questions or their comments in general to only those they perceive as pleasing to the therapist. In doing so, so much time may be spent in trying to prove their lack of stereotypical pathology that the issues that caused them to seek therapy in the first place are shelved.

In yet another scenario, the parent(s) may be so resentful of (what they perceive to be) the therapist's inability to view them as complete and capable human beings that they will not even feign the motions of establishing the therapeutic alliance. Their energies may become fixated at all the reasons why they do not need or cannot afford the time and/or resources to be in treatment.

In the latter instance, termination of treatment is generally more abrupt, with fewer sessions attended. In the case of the former examples, there may be more sessions involved but lack of focus on substantive matters makes the end result the same. The needed assistance is not received and the problems within the family escalate. A therapist who is not sensitized to these issues may well contribute to the manifestation of these obstacles and never have the opportunity to provide meaningful service to those clients who sought his or her help.

Transcultural Issues and Therapists

The issue of non-minority mental health professionals providing appropriate treatment to minority families involved in the adoption process is as complex as the economic and psychosocial relations between the races in our country as a whole—in fact, it is merely a reflection of our society. To fully understand the barriers to effective communication in a therapeutic situation, we must be willing to step outside the context of the professional area and acknowledge the 250-plus years during which there has been negative treatment (apartheid/slavery) of, and indoctrinations about, our citizens of African heritage. We, as mental health professionals, must take into account the subtle and blatant messages that we have absorbed about a specific race of people—messages that have led to the perpetuation of negative myths and stereotypes. Having spent so much of our professional lives honing the ability to delve deeply into the personalities of others, learning to assess even the most minute of details. We must now turn the inquiring eye onto ourselves.

Like patients, therapists bring their own set of baggage into the treatment session. Many clinicians that I have worked with, representing a cross-section of disciplines, candidly admit that they have had little or no prior exposure to Black people in a professional, social, or academic setting. They go into an initial therapy session armed only with the negative stereotypical views ingrained since childhood—views that gained "validity" during the years of professional training (with multiple racist theories) when fellow trainees or supervisors from racial minorities were conspicuously absent.

A significant number of this country's training programs for health-care professionals do not address transcultural issues as variables in the service delivery system. If at all, they are dealt with as nuances that one gains proficiency in with the passage of time. Coming to a treatment session with such attitudes may result in the therapist's viewing the patient as inferior in intelligence, parental skills, compassion, ability, and motivation. The clinician may feel it necessary to adopt a position of imposing his or her will, with the attitude that the patient should be grateful for it. Of course this pathologic arrogance is not voiced, but it does come across to the recipients of care. When the patient reacts to that, the insensitive therapist will attribute it to the "patient's unsuitability for treatment." The end result may well be that the therapist never puts himself in a position to learn about the dynamic of the family, and the possible result is a negative report to the agency facilitating the adoption.

The area of transcultural "literacy" is a unique, fascinating, and complex one. As with any subject that presents a threat to our own self-esteem, self-image, and self-concept, there is a tendency to want a "quick-fix" remedy for dealing with it; a cook-book approach, if you will. Inasmuch as transference and countertransference issues, reflecting our personal background and history, did not develop in a simple fashion, it is unrealistic to expect that they can be resolved in a simple manner. Nor can we expect that a human being can be completely objective about him- or herself consciously and/or unconsciously.

It does require an earnest desire on the part of the therapist to engage in ongoing introspection into his own psyche. He must continually seek assistance in assessing his own feelings about being cast in such an emotionally charged and occasionally negativistic role while being willing to admit, where warranted, that he encourages and/or colludes with it. We must develop our own "emotions checklist": "Do I feel that this person is inadequate? Do I think of myself as somehow better? Do I feel that I want to give the very best that I have to offer as a clinician and a human being, or am I simply going through the motions?

It is only by confronting these issues head on through careful introspection that any real growth can take place. The failure to do so gives credence and support to the theory that the clinician will do more harm than good. Facing up to these personality problems, situational stresses, and group dynamics in oneself and between human beings opens the door to being able to deal with them and move forward in a therapeutic relationship.

Increasing Effectiveness

Spiegel summed up the situation well in the statement, "It will be a long time, if ever, before there exists an adequate supply of minority professionals to take care of the needs [of minority patients]... In the meantime, non-minority, nonethnic mental health professionals, poorly trained, if at all, in dealing with cultural diversity, are providing services to minorities and ethnic groups in ways that are often not helpful and sometimes harmful."[5] Training in sociocultural issues during the course of medical school is absent from almost 40% of the program curricula throughout this country.[6] In light of this, the observation can be made that a fair number of clinicians practicing today may never have had a formalized teaching experience in transcultural issues that influence the delivery of care and the patient-therapist relationship.

In response to this obvious void in the total educational process, the Department of Behavioral Sciences at the University of California, Los Angeles School of Medicine designed a cultural medicine workshop as a component of the introductory human behavior course in 1983.[7] Wells, Benson and Hoff describe the program as "providing an overview of stress response, illness behavior, psychological defenses, interviewing skills, the physician–patient relationship, stages of normal human development and related topics."[8] The six-month required course involved carefully formulated preparatory reading lists and large group panel presentation by faculty members followed by two-hour small-group discussion. At the conclusion of the workshop, students were asked to evaluate the program. Overwhelmingly, students found the experience had been beneficial to them and felt better prepared to serve a multi-ethnic, multi-racial patient population.

Lefley observed that, "Social and cognitive distance between patients and therapists from different cultures continues to be an issue for mental health professionals who serve ethnic minorities."[9] The Cross-Cultural Training Institute developed at the University of Miami–Jackson Memorial Community Mental Health Center was an educational experience that focused on the already practicing clinician. At the end of the three-year program, an evaluation concluded that participants had an increased effectiveness in their interactions with minority patients.

Therapy drop-out rates were decreased and the involvement of minorities in the use of mental health services was increased.

The foregoing would appear then to support the assumptions that the formal addressing of cultural issues during the education process gives the clinician a sense of competency in dealing with patients from a diverse background and that proficiency in this area is not just "picked up" along the way during professional practice, as evidenced by the fact that the minority drop-out rate for experienced professionals decreased after participation in this specialized program.

Before therapists can avail themselves of the opportunity to fill the cultural-understanding void created by a lack of training, they must first be willing to admit that one exists. The lack of attention paid to the scholarly study of cultural differences between the caregiver and the recipient of that care suggests a certain arrogance on the part of the medical community as a whole and the mental health community particularly. Acosts's research in the area of minority drop-out rates in therapy supports the hypothesis that minority patients drop out primarily because of negative attitudes toward the therapist or because therapy is perceived as nonbeneficial.[10]

A return to school or involvement in an intensive training program may not be a viable option for many. An alternative as described by Griffith, would be the "cultural broker."[11] This individual plays a consultative role in the treatment process by helping the therapist to understand the influence his other cultural perspective may have on the development and maintenance of a therapeutic relationship with minority patients.

Conclusion

How much have we been influenced by an apartheid-like system that was designed to destroy the fabric of self-esteem and self-image of a segment of the population in this country? We must ask ourselves how it is that a people who come from a heritage, an ancestry that served as a model for civilization throughout the world, came to be viewed as anything but civilized human beings. In examining the broader picture, we must also be cognizant of the role public policies have had and continue to have in the disintegration of the Black family that causes so many of its children to be available for adoption in the first place. There must be a willingness to give credence to the fact that after nearly three centuries, American society still maintains a certain arrogance and pathology toward its citizens of African heritage, reminiscent of the traders who forced them from their homeland. Whatever pathology exists, is *not* genetic in nature; it is an unfortunate sequel of multigenerational abuse. Once the therapist is willing to acknowledge that and is able to focus on the urgency of the job at hand, the seeds for the formation of a productive alliance have been planted.

In the same manner that observing a surgeon at work does not qualify one to perform surgery, accepting the fact that one may have cultural biases does not necessarily mean that one has overcome them to the point of being able to render effective treatment. The therapist must be willing to admit to himself (and to his patients) gaps in understanding, and allow himself to be taught by his patients. When it is perceived that the therapist is sincere in wanting to be enlightened about cultural practices, it has been found that patients are quite willing to explain. As was mentioned previously, the therapist might need to seek formal and/or informal consultation from a Black colleague. Whatever route is chosen, the important thing is to admit that there is a deficit and take active measures to correct/compensate for it.

It is critical that a statement be made regarding the urgency with which individual practitioners in general and the mental health profession as a whole need to make a concerted effort to increase its knowledge of and sensitivity toward the needs of the Black patient. This is particularly true in the instance where their clinical expertise may make the difference between a successful and permanent placement for a child or a traumatizing series of foster/group home placements or other forms of institutionalized care.

Given the stakes involved, the price is entirely too high for us not to make a concerted effort to improve the quality of service available to these deserving children and their families.

Notes

1. Spiegel, JP: "Hispanic training for non-Hispanic mental health professionals." *World Journal of Psychosynthesis,* 13:25–30, 1981
2. Wyatt, GE, Bass, BA and Powell, GJ: "A survey of ethnic and sociocultural issues in medical school education." *J. Med. Educ.* 53: 627–632, 1978
3. Wells, KB, Benson, MC and Hoff, P: "Teaching cultural aspects of medicine." *J. Med. Educ.* 60:493–495, 1985
4. Ibid
5. Lefley, HP: "Cross-cultural training for mental health professionals: Effects on the delivery of services." *Hospital and Community Psychiatry.* 35(12):1227–1229, 1984
6. Griffith, EEH: "The impact of culture and religion on psychiatric care." *J. Nat'l. Med. Assoc.* 74(12) 1175–1177, 1982
7. Acosta, R: "Self-described reasons for premature termination of psychotherapy by Mexican-American, Black–American and Anglo–American patients." *Psychological Reports.* 47:435–443, 1980
8. Kagan, RM, Reid, WJ: "Critical factors in the adoption of emotionally disturbed youths." *Child Welfare League of America.* LXV(1) 63–72, 1986
9. Ibid
10. Kunjufu, J: "Developing positive self-images and discipline in Black children." *African-American Images.*
11. Noshpitz, JD(ed): *The adopted child. Basic Handbook of Child Psychiatry.* Basic Books. 1:342–347, 1979

Supplemental Reading

1. Brown, C: *Manchild in the promised land.* Macmillan, 1965
2. Calnek, M: *"Racial factors in countertransference."* Amer. J. Orthopsy. 40:30–46, 1970
3. Curtis, LA: *Violence race and culture.* Lexington Books, 1975
4. Ehrlich, PR, Feldman, SS: *The race bomb.* New York Times Book Company
5. Fibush, E: "The white worker and the Negro client." *Soc. Casework.* 46:271–277, 1965
6. Hamlin, WT: The chains of psychological slavery. Publication pending. 1979
7. Hill, R: *The strengths of Black families.* Emerson Hall, 1972
8. Hunt, RG: "Occupational status and the disposition of cases in a child guidance clinic." *Int. J. Soc. Psy.* 8:199–210, 1972

9. Jackson, A, Berkowitz, H and Farley, G: "Race as a variable affecting the treatment involvement of children." *J. Ch. Psy.* 13(1): 20–31, 1974
10. Thomas, A, Sillen, S: *Racism in psychiatry.* Citadel Press, 1974
11. Rosenberg, LA, Trader, HP: "Treatment of the deprived child in a community mental health clinic." *Amer. J. Orthopsy.* 37:87–92
12. Rubin, RH: "Adult male absence and the self-attitudes of Black children." *Child Study Journal.* 4(1):33–46, 1974
13. Turner, WH: *Myths and stereotypes: The African man in America. The Black male in America,* 1977
14. Waite, RR: "The Negro patient and clinical theory." *J. Consult. Psy.* 32:427–433, 1968
15. Wilson, AN: The developmental psychology of the Black child. Africana Research Publication
16. Yamanoto, J, James, QC, Paley, N: "Cultural problems in psychiatric therapy." *Arch. Gen. Psy.* 19:45–49, 1968
17. Yette, SF: *The Choice: The issue in Black survival in America.* Cottage Books.

20

The Adoptee's Dilemma: Obstacles in Identity Formation

Mary D. Howard

I bring to this task both a professional and a personal interest. As a sociologist I have specialized in family life. I have spent the past 10 years studying the members of the adoption triangle (adoptees, birthparents, adoptive parents). As an adoptee I have experienced some of what I have found in others.

Having written (Howard 1975, 1980) and lectured on the topic, I have had contact with hundreds of members of the adoption triangle. Turning some of these contacts into research opportunities, I have focused on search and reunion experiences.

The Research Question

This article examines issues of identity, with particular attention to adoptees. Identity, self-identity, self, self-concept, as it has been variously called in the social and psychological literature, has both personal and social components. Its personal dimension is the subjective sense of connectedness and continuity of one's self. The social dimension concerns the integration of social roles one plays and one's sense of interconnectedness with other role players.

Erikson, a psychoanalyst, who has written extensively on identity, speaks of three components: (a) a conscious sense of individual uniqueness; (b) an unconscious striving for a continuity of experience; and (c) a solidarity with a group's ideals (role expectations and values) (1968, p. 208).

C. Wright Mills (1959), writing from a sociological perspective, spoke of

243

the intersecting of history and biography and its consequences for identity. "Neither the life of an individual nor the history of a society can be understood without understanding both" (p.3). The history of the society, its institutions and value configuration, is the context within which the individual's biography takes on meaning. Who one is, according to Mills, is a relative question; it is a matter of mapping one's peculiar history (biography) against the backdrop of a society at a given stage of its history in which certain characteristics, traits, and experiences are more valued and rewarded than others. The same biography would take on different meaning, (i.e., values and expectations would be different) in another society, in a different time period in the same society, and at different locations within society.

Lurking within each adoptee is the suspicion that he or she could have been a very different person but for accidents of birth and placement. To understand who he or she has become, there must be knowledge about what could have been.

Social psychologists point to the importance of communication and interaction for the development of the self (Mead 1934; Cooley 1902). From birth on, the individual is dependent upon interactions with others to acquire a sense of self. By school age, the child has the cognitive capacity to imagine him/herself as others might see him or her; and to feel a sense of pride or mortification in that appearance (Cooley 1902; 184). This reflexivity of self accounts for the individual's ability to anticipate others' reactions, as well as to internalize others' evaluations and use them as a measure of his/her own behavior. Others' evaluations, positive or negative, are integrated into the definition of self.

The social and psychological sciences offer theories of identity which are not contradictory indeed at several points reinforce each other, while dealing with phenomena at different levels of abstraction. Taken together, these theories provide an integrated perspective which points to three problematic areas in adoptees' identity formation.

First, the fact that adoptees do not know of their pasts makes it impossible to integrate this with their present roles. Their continuity of self is affected.

Second, adoptees interact with adoptive parents who have come by their parental roles in unusual ways. Their preparation is different: parenthood occurs abruptly without the physical, social and psychological preparation of pregnancy and birth; they are subject to oversight by an outside agency; they are allowed to have the child for some time before they are granted final approval to keep the child. They are seen as "different" by others. Adoptive parents see their adoptive children as "different" (wanted, chosen, rescued) and share this information with them. Yet, in closed adoptions, the tragedy that made possible the union of child and adoptive parents is shrouded in mystery. Adoptive parents who do not want to discuss it, and encourage the child not to think about it, compound the problem. What for the child is an essential fact of his or her biography, something which he/she had no control over and is powerless to change, is treated by the adoptive parents as a threat (Pannor and Nerlove, 1977).

For those from whom information is withheld, the secret is a badge of inferiority. When the secret is about who one is, its dehumanizing effect reaches maximum force.

Third, men and women play different roles in society, and when adopted, seem to respond differently to (and probably experience differently) the identity dilemma. Women are more intimately connected to the care and nurturance of children. It is women who report the most distress at not having children (Kirk, 1964) and who show more affiliative behavior (Parsons and Bales, 1955); and, not surprisingly, it is female adoptees who are most prone to search for their biological relatives (Farber, 1977; McWhinnie, 1969; Stein and Hoopes, 1985).

In summary,

1. The theoretical literature—psychological, social psychological, and sociological—points to: (a) the importance of a knowledge of the past for a sense of the continuity of self; and (b) the stigma of being different, especially when this status is negatively evaluated and one is captive in this position by forces beyond one's control.
2. While identity is a process grounded in an inner psychological dynamic, it is responsive to environmental conditions.
3. In a receptive environment, the identity problems can be minimized, although not entirely eliminated.
4. Adoption social workers, because of their contact with each member of the triangle, as well as other mental health professionals working with triangle members, are in a key position to effect change and improve the outcomes for each triangle member; first, by being sensitive to the special circumstances that affect their identities; then, by working to eliminate some of the obstacles to a healthy identity which the traditional adoption process involves; finally undertaking research to evaluate the varieties of "open: adoption that are being experimented with today.

The Limits of Research

The question "Are adoptees normal?" does not permit of an answer. If it were possible to identify all adoptees (sealed court and agency records preclude this), then we could draw an appropriate sample, along with a comparison group of non-adoptees, and the resulting psychological profiles could be compared and the results generalized to the respective populations.

In the absence of these data, we can turn to a rich research literature of over

150 studies done during the past 50 years by researchers in different disciplines: psychologists, psychiatrists, psychoanalysts, and sociologists, using clinical and non-clinical populations; some using comparison groups, case studies, interviews, surveys, a few longitudinal studies, and cross-sectional surveys.

No one of these studies is generalizable beyond the subjects studied. Yet the findings of these many studies follow the predictions of the social and psychological identity theories: adoptees have some additional hurdles to surmount in the process of identity formation obstacles which are not present for non-adoptees. Specifically the studies show that the problems vary in intensity among adoptees, from curiosity and prolonged fantasizing through disruptive behavior and problems in school to extreme pathological reactions termed ''adoptive child syndrome,'' which figured in the DeGelleke murder case (Lifton, 1986). Studies showing that adoptees from non-clinical populations compare favorably with similar non-adoptees still acknowledge, as in the recent Stein and Hoopes (1985: 66) study, that '' ... adoptive status complicates the lives of all adolescents....''

The adoptive child syndrome, which includes such aspects as pathological lying, running away from home, learning difficulties, lack of impulse control, and conflict with authority, is found in a tiny minority of adoptees. But the lesser disturbances which bring some adoptees into therapy are present in mild form in many adoptees, even those who never seek therapeutic intervention.

Identity theories predict, and research studies demonstrate, that the adoptive status makes for problematic identity formation. The question should no longer be ''Are adoptees different?'' but ''How can the adoptee's environment (family and peer relationships) be managed so as to facilitate identity formation?''

Below, the research on identity and development is reviewed, with specific reference to how it relates to adoptees.

Identity and Life Cycle

Eric Erikson's (1968) discussion of identity as it emerges over the life cycle is well-suited for organizing the research findings on the special difficulties which adoptees encounter. Each developmental stage, while identifiable, is nonetheless dependent on the previous stage. Impairment in development at an earlier stage will complicate the development at a later time. Furthermore, the sociological and social psychological findings fit nicely into Erikson's schema.

Erikson's stages speak to the inner dynamic of identity development and nest it in the environmental context; so while he speaks of the infant's development of a sense of object-permanence and the importance of this for a sense of trust in others and one's self, Erikson is also speaking of the role of caretakers (environment) in stimulating this development.

While Erikson begins his discussion of identity with birth, it is obvious that prenatal care dramatically affects the reactivity of the infant to its world. Many out-of-wedlock adoptees were born to very young mothers who were poor, knew little about the importance of nutrition and prenatal care, and did not have regular medical attention (Sugar, 1976; Pasamanick and Knoblich, 1972). The risk of neurological problems is increased, and with this, subsequent developmental aberrations. Some prenatal deficits can be alleviated by adequate postnatal care, but others are more lasting.

Infancy to Age Two: Trust

The foundation for identity is laid in the first year of life and comes to maturity in adolescence. The infant experiences the world through its senses and these must be stimulated routinely and sufficiently for trust to develop. The infant's dealings with its caretakers are critical for the development of a sense of awareness of the world as a place in which it can count on its needs being satisfied.

In addition to consistency, there must be a regular and limited cast of caretakers with which the infant can pattern its responses (Bowlby, 1969). Reciprocal patterns of interaction develop in early infancy and provide the foundation for later cognitive functioning. Frequent interruptions in early reciprocal relationships (changing foster homes, for example) and emotional withholding of the adoptive parent while waiting for the adoption to be finalized make the achievement of reciprocity more difficult for adoptees (Brinich, 1980).

Adoptees who have lived in institutions during infancy (Spitz, 1945; Tizard and Rees, 1975) or have been moved among foster homes (Brinich, 1980; Goldstein et al, 1973) are likely to have impairment in this stage of development. Spitz (1945) found that this deprivation resulted in retarded speech and motor development, lowered I.Q., and the stunting of emotional development. In addition, Erikson has found these children to exhibit a basic mistrust in others and in themselves, as well as an inability to give credence to the expressions of trust others would place in them.

It is not uncommon to find adoptees reporting a sense of mistrust toward the world and other people. In general, the severity of emotional problems has been found to correlate with the age at placement and the extent of early maternal deprivation (Humphrey and Ounsted, 1964; McWhinnie, 1967; Offord et al, 1969; Whitmer et al, 1963). These problems may not surface until adolescence or adulthood, when the adoptee has problems forming intimate relationships. Adult adoptees have reported to the author that mistrust gets in the way of establishing long-term relationships with others. They engage and disengage, often with the same person over time.

Age Two to Four: Autonomy

During the third year of life the child strives to experience autonomy and self-control. Weaning, bowel control, and walking all are activities in which adults play a major role in their channeling of the child's efforts. Parental supportiveness or lack thereof foster a sense of autonomy or of doubt and shame in the child.

Adoptive parents can be insecure in their parental role (Bourgeois 1975). This anxiety which can lead to overprotectiveness (Schecter 1960), is unsettling for the child and may be compounded by the revelation of the child's adoptive status (which often occurs around age 3).

Later the child may come to feel habitually ashamed, apologetic, and afraid to be seen. Some overcompensate by becoming defiant, joining a gang. As adults, doubt translates into paranoia, fears that others are out to do them harm.

Preschool: Initiative

By age 3 the child has mastered the skill of walking, running, and general locomotion. A great deal of exploring is done, and here the parent can either encourage the development of initiative by encouraging this behavior or stifle it by over-concern with safety, neatness, and the like. Most children at this stage will exhibit a tireless capacity for repetition. When mastery is achieved, repetition ceases, if the caretakers encourage exploration.

It is during this stage that the Oedipus complex is resolved. Boys begin to transfer their loyalties from their mothers to their fathers; and girls, after an initial fascination with the father and much approval-seeking, begin to identify with the mother.

Much has been written of the adoptees' difficulties in this stage (Colon 1978; Feder 1974; Easson 1973; Kornitzer 1971; Sants 1965; Schecter et al. 1964). Schwartz (1970) and Clothier (1939) advise waiting to inform the child of its adoptive status until after this stage is complete, in order to avoid problems in the resolution of the Oedipus complex.

For many years the social work profession counseled secrecy, even to the point of not admitting to the child the fact of its adoption. Efforts were made to match the child as carefully as possible in terms of coloring, ethnicity, and parental backgrounds, with the adoptive parents. In this way, it was thought, the secret could be kept. Recent research has found that matching has had no impact on the outcome of the adoption (Hardy-Brown et al. 1980; Scarr et al.

1980). In the early 1940's this practice was superseded by that of encouraging the adoptive parents to reveal the fact of adoption to the child at an early age.

This, of course, led to questions about the birthparents. Adoptive parents solicited help from the agency, and social workers assisted in devising "acceptable" stories. The "chosen baby" story came out of these collaborations, along with the "car crash" to account for the demise of the birthparents. No child was told he/she was born out-of-wedlock. This and other discrediting information about the birthparents was withheld by the agency in the belief that adoptive parents and children would adjust better without it (Eppith and Jenkins 1948).

The revelation of adoption, paired with the "chosen baby" story presented many a child with mixed and confusing messages to incorporate into its developing sense of self. An older child will wonder why all the emphasis on being "chosen," "Why couldn't I just have been had like everyone else?" And still later, the child realizes that in order to be chosen, the birthmother had to have given him/her up. Then doubts can turn to fears because of "rejection" by the birthmother. (Adoptees rarely concern themselves about the behavior of the birthfather. He is a shadowy figure whose possible identity and motivations take on importance, if at all, after the birthmother has been found.)

Like adoption, rejection by the birthmother is something over which the child has no control. These events "happen"; or, in sociological argot, this status is ascribed to the child. Knowing that others view it as different, problematic, discrediting, adoptees learn first at home (and it may be reinforced among peers later) that they have a blemished character, a stigma. The fact that the adoptee does not "earn" but has the stigma "bestowed" means there is nothing that can be done to undo the events; there is no way to change this fact. In the absence of any ameliorative options, many adoptees acquiesce in seeing themselves as deviant. Ascriptive stigma often leads to negative self-concept (Mankoff 1971). They label themselves in ways consistent with the public definition of their situation. Guilt and shame can become regular accompaniments of their emotional lives. A poor self-concept has been found in some adolescent adoptees (Blos 1962; Frisk 1964). It is worth speculating whether there might be male/female differences in the assimilation of a negative self-concept. The tendency of even very young males toward independence and separation in contrast to the female's proclivity for intimacy suggests that there may well be a difference (Gilligan 1982, 1979).

School Age: Industry

Upon entering school, the child becomes more fully a member of society. Large portions of each day are spent in the company of teachers and fellow students, and through them the child becomes acquainted with their prejudices, and learns new roles. Adoptees learn at school from other children that being adopted is odd, strange, different, and sometimes even negatively evaluated. Feelings of isolation, uncertainty, anxiety and difficulty in making friends (Schwartz 1967; Blos 1962) are in sharp contrast to the spontaneity and emotional vitality of nonadopted youngsters studied by Schwartz (1967). Hostility (Eiduson and Livermore 1963; Menlove 1965; Schecter 1960), tenseness, dependency and fearfulness (Nemovicher 1960) have also been found in adoptees during this period.

Freud (1909) at the turn of the century, and others since then (Sants 1965), have found that most children, irrespective of adoptive status, are curious, usually around 11 years of age, as to whether they are biologically related to their parents. The so-called family romance becomes genealogical bewilderment (Sants 1965) in adoptees.

The evidence of this is clearest in the studies of transracial adoptions. It is a foregone conclusion that transracial adoptees, usually Black children raised in white homes, have special concerns about who they are. The studies have confirmed these concerns (Zastrow 1977; Ladner 1977; Simon and Alstein 1977; Grow and Shapiro 1974). In a recent study (McRoy et al. 1984), transracial adoptees were found to have more concerns when they were reared in an entirely white setting and when racial differences were not discussed. The more openly and positively race was discussed and the more racially integrated the setting, the better adjusted were the black adoptees. Stein and Hoopes (1985) attribute some measure of their adoptees' favorable adjustment to the quality of family relationships, including the adoptees' perception of the openness of family communication about adoption issues.

In summary, most persons entertain some curiosity about their biological origins, suggesting that this is an important matter. The lack of biological connection has been shown to affect one's identity, one's sense of self. This has been frequently demonstrated in transracial adoptees; it is present in intraracial adoptions as well. But its disruptive potential can be blunted by adoptive parents who pay special attention to these problems (Marquis and Detweiler 1985; Stein and Hoopes 1985; McWhinnie 1967).

Adolescence: Identity

In adolescence the capacities achieved during the earlier stages of development come to fruition, and the young person can be said to have a sense of identity. The sense of connectedness to the past through preceding generations is complete. Anticipatory socialization into occupational roles begins. However, as Erikson indicates, where there remains confusion over background characteristics such as ethnicity or sexual identity, then identity confusion results. To Erikson's list we need to add confusion about the past and how it relates to the present.

Identity confusion'' is a term Erikson uses to refer to a sense of not fitting in—where the roles (occupational roles, sex roles) one is expected to play do not seem appropriate. These expected roles may seem inappropriate because the person lacks a sense of connectedness to the past, cannot move into these roles easily and therefore cannot anticipate the future. Delinquency, truancy, and mood swings (Lindholm and Touliatos 1980) found in adoptees can be signs of resistance to roles which the adolescent adoptee sees as forced on him or her and into which he/she feels he/she does not fit.

Adoptees often experience difficulty in this stage. Feelings of inferiority (Frisk 1964; Sorosky et al. 1978), abnormality (Triseliotis 1973), insecurity (Frisk 1964; Lifshitz et al. 1975; Schwartz 1967) and fearfulness (Blos 1962; Lifshitz et al. 1975; Nemovicher 1960; Schwartz 1967) have been noted. Some of the identity confusion which these traits signify is of course related to difficulties experienced in earlier stages of identity formation. It is a mistake to assume that adolescent adoptees are only beginning to experience difficulty. For most, the problems can be traced to earlier stages in which their awareness of being adopted made for feelings of differentness. In treating the adolescent adoptee, it is often necessary, then, to explore these earlier developmental stages for evidence of difficulties. Still, this adolescent stage offers its own peculiar hurdles for the adoptee.

A follow-up of 500 independent adoptions in Florida (Witmer et al. 1963) (aged 16 or younger) found adoptees and their controls to be performing adequately in school, although the controls were doing better. The adoptees were less popular among classmates than were the controls (statistically significant). On measures of personal, social, and total adjustment, adoptees scored less than nonadopted controls (statistically significant). Teachers' ratings (the teachers probably were not aware of the adoptive status) scored adoptees significantly lower on leadership and significantly higher on aggressive maladjustment.

The identity confusion of many adoptees helps to account for their tendency to do poorly in school, to feel at loose ends, to associate with others of lower social status than themselves, to approach parenthood with more insecurity, to put off having children, and to marry later (Am. Acad. of Pediatrics 1971; Barinbaum 1974).

It was not uncommon among those interviewed by the author to find middle class adoptive youngsters associating with working and lower class companions, eschewing their class equals. Adoptees explain that they don't feel as if they belong to their adoptive parents' status level (usually true, if to belong means to be born into it). They gravitate toward others of lower social status because they are "safe" companions, so the adoptees don't have to prove themselves. This tendency to associate with companions of lower social status may have to do also with the feeling of having been rejected by the birthmother. This rejection is related to a feeling of lack of self-worth. Lacking self-worth, one finds it difficult to make demands on others, demands to be treated as an equal. When a person does not feel like a worthy person, he/she is unable to trust others to treat him/herself as worthwhile.

Young Adults: Intimacy

Following adolescence, the adult who has experienced a normal identity evolution matures into psychological, emotional, and sexual intimacy with others. They can share themselves and enter into confidences with others. Many adoptees, however, report feelings of isolation, the opposite of intimacy. They have a sense of estrangement from others, a sense of a void instead of an identity. They have an incapacity to feel really "themselves" (Lifshitz et al. 1975; Sorosky et al. 1978; Triseliotis 1973; Schwartz 1967).

This sense of isolation probably accounts for the heightened sense of joy many female adoptees report when they bear children. For many, the child is the first person they are in contact with to whom they are biologically connected. In the adoptees-cum-mothers encountered by the author, many report a persistent sense of precariousness about the future and a particular fear of losing the child through an accident or other unforeseen circumstance.

Searchers V. Non-Searchers

Any discussion of adult adoptees must distinguish between those who search and those who do not.

Those who search have the more obvious identity concerns. In fact, it is the very question "Who am I?" which motivates the search. Interestingly, the search often does not commence until the adoptive parents are no longer on the scene (they are no longer living with the adoptee or they have died).

In a recent study of nonclinical adolescent adoptees, Stein and Hoopes (1985) found that a third of them were seriously interested in searching. A survey of 400+ mail inquiries received by the author over the past ten years indicates that, on average, searchers are in their thirties, although the trend is toward younger searchers.

Those who deny an interest in searching seem no less interested in identity; they have a different strategy for dealing with it. They are often closely identified with their adoptive parents, taking on their ethnicity, character traits, ideology, and mannerisms. Some will go so far as to use their adoptive parents' histories on medical forms when asked about hereditary disorders. They collude with the adoptive parents, who play down the significance of adoption. When this denial takes on the aspects of moral servitude to the parents, the result is self-alienation (Goffman 1961: 386).

Nonsearchers can be hostile toward adoptees who search, characterizing them as ungrateful, from unhappy homes, irresponsible, malcontented. They sometimes see the biological parents as irresponsible, rejecting of the child, unworthy of parenting the child.

The open records movement (a political, social, educational drive by adoption triangle members to gain access to the original birth certificate, adoption agency files, and hospital records) has for the first time presented adoptees (and other triangle members) with an alternative to silently suffering their curiosity or pioneering the search. There are over 300 organizations throughout the nation which they can join for psychological support and sophisticated assistance in the search. It is easier to be different when there are kindred spirits providing a positive image of one's behavior.

Policy Considerations

Adoption is not likely to disappear in the foreseeable future, although the professionals in charge will less often be social workers and more often attorneys. It is the responsibility of mental health professionals to improve the adoption procedures as research reveals what works and what does not. Secrecy is one factor which erects barriers to a healthy identity.

Basically, a secrecy policy encourages all of the performers in the adoption drama to build their lives on the premise that an event central to the lives of all parties never occurred. A sealed-records policy, implicitly, asks for an extreme form of denial.

It is a fundamental and elementary tenet of every school of psychotherapy that sound mental health rests on acknowledging and incorporating into one's sense of self all important elements of personal experience. There is no school of psychotherapy which regards denial as a positive strategy in forming a sense of self and dealing with day-to-day realities. Yet a sealed-records policy encourages precisely that kind of denial.

While secrecy is known to be an obstacle to identity formation, there is almost nothing known about the best time to reveal to the child the fact of his/ her adoption (see Wieder 1978, 1977 and Stein and Hoopes 1986 for contradictory conclusions). Nor do we know how to optimize identity formation by regulating the kind, the amount, and the timing of information to the adoptee concerning his/her background.

Research is clearly needed.

Adoptive parents need to be more extensively counseled about their own grief at infertility. They need help in understanding that their parenthood is different and that adoption will affect their sense of self, since the continuity of their past with the future is based on an adoptive rather than biological connection.

Adoptive parents should be advised that their adoptive children may want more information on their backgrounds than is available. This may lead to a search for the biological relatives. This should not be viewed with alarm. Some of the most psychologically-successful searches reported to the author were ones in which the adoptive parents actively assisted.

Birthparents, who have been so long overlooked, have their own loss and grief with which to contend. Counseling which is sensitive to their plight can facilitate their adjustment.

It is ironic that just as adoption agencies are learning what the consequences of adoption are for the triangle members, and revising their policies accordingly, there are fewer and fewer infants available.

More would-be adoptive parents are turning to private adoptions, which often lack adequate psychological counseling and followup. As problems arise in these adoptions, families will turn more to mental health professionals for advice and counseling. As a rule, these professionals have less experience in adoption matters than do adoption social workers. Some adoption agencies are in turn finding themselves trying to place older and special needs children, a population with which they have little experience.

An Argentinian film, "The Official Story" (1985), makes several of these points with stunning clarity. The film opens with an adoptive mother, a high school history teacher, telling her students that "history is a people's memory. Without memories there cannot be a people."

Against the backdrop of a repressive political regime that rewrites textbooks to tailor history to its preferred version, this mother works at remaining a political innocent, discounting rumors of such official license. From a lifelong friend and political dissident, she learns of infants being taken from their mothers and sold to wealthy couples who ask no questions. Until then she had allowed herself to believe that her child's biological mother had not wanted her. Thus she begins the quest for information about her daughter's background, realizing that at some point this will become necessary for the child's sense of who she is. The adoptive mother's sense of herself is also tied up with knowing the truth about her role in acquiring this child and thus more fully understanding her part in Argentinian history.

This film might be required viewing by all prospective adoptive parents.

Conclusions

This article has covered the theoretical literature and research studies on identity formation and spelled out the implications for adoptees who because of their fractured pasts and the secrecy with which these pasts are shrouded, cannot pursue a normal pattern of identity development.

The resolution of the adoptee's dilemma rests with the mental health professionals. First, professionals can provide more realistic preparation for adoptive parents in how to confront openly and positively the fact of the adoptee's separate origins. Second, by being sensitive to the adoptee's unique status, they can be of more assistance to those who show up in treatment. Third, they can work to change state laws and agency policies which keep records sealed. Finally, they can undertake research needed to answer questions about the optimal dissemination of information to adoptees so as to enhance the identity formation process.

References

American Academy of Pediatrics (1971). Committee on Adoption, "Identity Development in Adopted Children," 47:948–949.

Barinbaum, Lea (1974). "Identity Crisis in Adolescence: The Problem of an Adopted Girl," *Adolescence*, 9(36):547–554.

Blos, Peter (1962). *On Adolescence*. New York: Free Press.

Bourgeois, M. (1975). "Psychiatric Aspects of Adoption," *Annales Medico-Psychologiques*, 2(1):73–103.

Bowlby, J. (1969). *Attachment and Loss* Vol. 1: *Attachment*. New York: Basic Books.

Brinich, Paul M. (1980). "Some Potential Effects of Adoption on Self and Object Relations," *Psychoanalytic Study of the Child*, 35:107–133.

Clothier, F. (1939). "Some Aspects of the Problem of Adoption," *American Journal of Orthopsychiatry*, 9:598–615.

Colon, Fernando (1978). "Family Ties and Child Placement," *Family Process*, 17(3):289–312.

Cooley, Charles Horton (1902). *Human Nature and the Social Order*. New York: Charles Scribner's Sons.

Easson, W. M. (1973). "Special Sexual Problems of the Adopted Adolescent," *Medical Aspects of Human Sexuality*, July:92–105.

Eiduson, B. T. and Livermore, J. B. (1963). "Complications in Therapy with Adopted Children," *American Journal of Orthopsychiatry*, 23:795–802.

Eppith, Ethel D. and Jenkins, Alma C. (1948). "Telling Adopted Children," in Gladys Meyer (ed.) *Studies in Children*. New York: King's Crown Press, pp. 98–129.

Erikson, Erik H. (1968). *Identity: Youth and Crisis*. New York: W.W. Norton.

Farber, Susan (1977). "Sex Differences in the Expression of Adoption Ideas: Observation of Adoptees from Birth through Latency," *American Journal of Orthopsychiatry*, 47(4):639–650.

Feder Luis (1974). "Adoption Trauma: Oedipus Myth/Clinical Reality," *International Journal of Psychoanalysis*, 55(4):491–493.

Freud, S. (1909). "Family Romances," reprinted in J. Strachey (ed.) *Collected Papers*, Vol. 5. London: Hogarth Press, 1950, pp. 74–78.

Frisk, M. (1964). "Identity Problems and Confused Conceptions of the

Genetic Ego in Adopted Children During Adolescence," *Acta Paedo Psychiatrica,* 31:6–12.

Gilligan, C. (1982). *In a Different Voice: Psychological Theory and Women's Development.* Cambridge, Ma.: Harvard University Press.

Gilligan, C. (1979). "Women's Place in Man's Life Cycle," *Harvard Educational Review,* 49:431–446.

Goffman, Erving (1961). *Asylums.* Garden City: Doubleday.

Goldstein, J. et. al. (1973). *Beyond the Best Interests of the Child.* New York: Free Press.

Grow, Lucille J. and Shapiro, Deborah (1974). *Black Children, White Parents.* New York: Child Welfare League of America.

Hardy-Brown, Karen et. al. (1980). "Selective Placement of Adopted Children: Prevalence and Effects," *Journal of Child Psychology and Psychiatry and Allied Disciplines,* 21(2):143–152.

Howard, Mary D. (1980). "The Case for Opening Adoption Records," *New York Times,* February 24.

Howard, Mary D. (1975). "I take after somebody...," *Psychology Today,* December, pp. 33–37.

Humphrey, Michael and Ounsted, Christopher (1964). "Adoptive Families Referred for Psychiatric Advice: II. The Parents," *British Journal of Psychiatry,* 11:549–555.

Kirk, H. David (1964). *Shared Fate: A Theory of Adoption and Mental Health.* New York: The Free Press.

Kornitzer, Margaret (1971). "The Adopted Adolescent and the Sense of Identity," *Child Adoption,* 66:43–48.

Ladner, Joyce A. (1977). *Mixed Families.* New York: Anchor Press.

Lifshitz, M., Baum, R., Balgur, I., and Cohen, C. (1975). "The Impact of the Social Milieu Upon the Nature of Adoptees' Emotional Difficulties," *Journal of Marriage and the Family,* 37:221–228.

Lifton, Betty Jean (1986). "How the Adoption System Ignites a Fire," *New York Times,* March 1, 1986, p. 27. Lifton is quoting Dr. David Kirschner, a child psychologist.

Lindholm, Bryon W. and Touliatos, John (1980). "Psychological Adjustments of Adopted and Non-Adopted Children," *Psychological Reports,* 46(1):307–310.

Mankoff, Milton (1971). "Societal Reaction and Career Deviance: A Critical Analysis," *The Sociological Quarterly,* 12:204–218.

Marquis, Kathlyn S. and Detweiler, Richard A. (1985). "Does Adopted Mean Different? An Attributional Analysis," *Journal of Personality and Social Psychiatry,* 48(4):1054–1066.

McRoy, Ruth G. *et. al.* (1984). "The Identity of Transracial Adoptees," *Social Casework,* 65(1):34–39.

McWhinnie, A. M. (1969). "The Adopted Child in Adolescence," in G. Caplan and S. Lebovici (eds.) *Adolescence—Psychosocial Perspectives.* New York: Basic Books, pp. 133–142.

McWhinnie, A. M. (1967). *Adopted Children and How They Grow Up.* New York: Humanities Press.

Mead, George Herbert (1934). *Mind, Self, And Society*. Chicago: University of Chicago Press.

Menlove, F. L. (1965). "Aggressive Symptoms in Emotionally Disturbed Children," *Child Development*, 36:519–532.

Mills, C. Wright (1959). *The Sociological Imagination*. New York: Oxford University Press.

Nemovicher, J. (1960). "A Comparative Study of Adopted Boys and Non–Adopted Boys in Respect to Specific Personality Characteristic," *Dissertation Abstracts International*, 20, p. 4722.

Offord, D. R. et. al. (1969). "Presenting Symptomatology of Adopted Children," *Archives of General Psychiatry*, 20(1):110–116.

Pannor, Reuben and Evelyn A. Nerlove (1977). "Fostering Understanding between Adolescents and Adoptive Parents through Group Experiences," *Child Welfare* (Sept-Oct) Vol. 56(8):537–545.

Parsons, Talcott and Bales, Robert F. (1955). *Family Socialization and Interaction Process*. New York: Free Press of Glencoe.

Pasamanick, B. and Knoblich, H. (1972). "Epidemiologic Studies on the Complication of Pregnancy and the Birth Process," in S. I. Harrison (ed.) *Childhood Psychopathology*. New York: International Universities Press, pp. 825–837.

Sants, H. J. (1965). "Genealogical Bewilderment in Children with Substitute Parents," *Child Adoption*, 47:32–42.

Scarr, Sandra *et. al.* (1980). "Perceived and Actual Similarities in Biological and Adoptive Families: Does Perceived Similarities Bias Genetic Inferences?" *Behavior Genetics*, 10(5):445–458.

Schecter, Marshall D. *et. al.* (1964). "Emotional Problems in the Adoptee," *Archives of General Psychiatry*, 10:109–118.

Schecter, Marshall D. (1960). "Observations on Adopted Children," *Archives of General Psychiatry*, 3:45–56.

Schwartz, E. M. (1970). "The Family Romance Fantasy in Children Adopted in Infancy," *Child Welfare*, 49:386–391.

Schwartz, E. M. (1967). "A Comparative Study of Some Personality Characteristics of Adopted and Non–Adopted Boys," *Dissertation Abstracts International*. 27:2518–B.

Simon, Rita James and Alstein, Howard (1977). *Transracial Adoption*. New York: John Wiley.

Sorosky, A. D., Baran, A., and Pannor, R. (1978). *The Adoption Triangle*. Garden City, New York: Doubleday.

Spitz, Rene, A. (1945). "Hospitalism: An Inquiry into the Genesis of Psychiatric Conditions in Early Childhood," in Anna Freud (ed.) *The Psychoanalytic Study of the Child*, New York: International Universities Press.

Stein, Leslie M. and Hoopes, Janet L. (1985). *Identity Formation in the Adopted Adolescent*. New York: Child Welfare League of America.

Sugar, M. (1976). "At Risk Factors for the Adolescent Mother and her Infant," *Journal of Youth and Adolescence*, 5:251–270.

Tizard, Barbara and Rees, Judith (1975). "The Effects of Early Institutional

Rearing on the Behavioral Problems and Affectional Relationships of Four-Year-Old Children,'' *Journal of Child Psychology and Psychiatry and Allied Disciplines,* 16(1):61–73.

Triseliotis, J. (1973). *In Search of Origins: The Experience of Adopted People.* London: Routledge and Kegan Paul.

Wieder, Herbert (1978). ''On When and Whether to Disclose about Adoption,'' *Journal of the American Psycholanalytic Association,* 26(4):793–811.

Wieder, Herbert (1977). ''On Being Told of Adoption,'' *Psychoanalytic Quarterly,* 46(2):185–200.

Witmer, Helen L. et. al. (1963). *Independent Adoptions: A Follow-Up Study.* New York: Russell Sage Foundation.

Zastrow, Charles (1977). *Outcome of Black Children/White Parents Transracial Adoptions.* San Francisco: R and E Research Assoc.

21

The Special Needs of Sexually Abused Children

Missy Behrents Iski

In recent years the problem of child sexual abuse has received growing publicity. Through the efforts of researchers, clinicians, related professionals, and the media, the growing dimensions of child sexual abuse, once considered an unusual phenomenon, have been brought to public and professional awareness.

Surveys regarding the prevalence of child sexual abuse have proliferated in the past decade. The number of cases reported to the American Humane Association have increased from 1,975 in 1976 to 22,918 in 1982.[1] David Finkelhor's 1979 survey of 796 college students found 19% of the females and 9% of the males had experienced sexual victimization.[2] Finkelhor estimates that 210,000 new cases of child sexual abuse will occur every year.[3] The sexual abuse of children occurs most often with an adult known and trusted by the child. In one study 80% of all abused children were victimized by a known, trusted adult; approximately 60% of the time the abuse occurred in the child's own home.[4] Even with recent surveys, the scope of the problem appears to be much larger than current statistics indicate.

Avoiding the Problem

It is remarkable, in light of this heightened awareness of the problem, that many children continue to circulate through a maze of social services, foster homes, and treatment facilities with little genuine therapeutic effort made to address the problems resulting from sexual abuse. The following examples are offered as illustration.

259

Becky, age 16, had been hospitalized three times for significant suicide attempts and severe depression. The fact that she had been molested by her older brother for four years had been shared upon her first admission. Following 12 months of inpatient treatment in two separate hospitals, she was transferred to an inpatient residential program that provided her the opportunity to deal directly with the sexual abuse which had strongly contributed to her self-destructive impulses.

Bobby was removed from his natural mother when he was three because of severe neglect. He was sexually abused in his first foster placement by his foster father for a period of three years. He was removed from this home and placed in two other foster placements unsuccessfully because of behaviors which included destruction of property, lying, poor hygiene, and running away. He was then placed with his natural father, who referred him for hospitalization. At 15 years of age, Bobby's presenting problems included extreme isolation, compulsive eating, hygiene problems, and sexually propositioning neighborhood boys. He disclosed the sexual abuse following his admission to the hospital unit. In reviewing the case history, it became apparent that the presenting problems began to surface following the sexual abuse at age three.

By the time Shawna was hospitalized at 15, she had been in and out of five foster homes. She was removed from her mother's home at age six because of neglect, and placed with an uncle. She was molested by her uncle for two years, and removed following her disclosure. In her foster home placement she was molested by her foster father, and removed because she kept running away. Her next four foster placements were unsuccessful because of behaviors which included stealing, authority conflicts, sexual promiscuity, and repeatedly running away. She would often trade sex for transportation out of state. She was hospitalized for impulsivity, self-inflicted cigarette burns, rage reactions, and sexual acting-out.

Multiply-placed children seem to be more vulnerable to sexual abuse. Their difficulties developing trust, their feelings of powerlessness, and their tendency towards passivity increase the potential for victimization. The absence of familial or developmental ties with adoptive or foster parents may loosen sexual boundaries thereby increasing the possibility of abuse.

Children removed from home due to familial sexual abuse are much more likely to be re-victimized. Incest victims learn to normalize the offender's behavior, have difficulties differentiating nurturance from sex, view sexual contact as a form of love, and have learned to behave in a seductive manner. Professionals working with multiply-placed children should routinely ask if sexual victimization has occurred and should always investigate for the possibility of abuse.

There are several factors which inhibit helping professionals from coming to grips with the reality of the sexually abused child. First, most children do not verbally acknowledge their abuse. Instead they present behavioral indicators which warrant additional investigation. Therefore, it is incumbent upon all helping professionals to familiarize themselves with the behavioral symptoms suggesting child sexual abuse. Even so, a professional may choose to ignore the presence of strong behavioral cues because of his/her own personal discomfort in dealing with sexual issues. And some professionals may avoid the issue because they feel ill-equipped to help.

Once a child admits sexual abuse, planned therapeutic intervention is required. Unfortunately, there continue to be cases of known child sexual abuse with little remediation offered. Two of the strongest fears that inhibit children from disclosing the secret—the fear of not being believed and the fear that nothing will be done—are reinforced when a helping professional discounts the child's problem through ignoring the cues or providing ineffective direction towards therapeutic intervention.

We began developing a sexual abuse treatment program for adolescent females several years ago at our facility, a freestanding adolescent psychiatric hospital, after reviewing the difficulties we were having with our sexuality groups. The adolescent incest victims, most of whom had not disclosed the abuse, proved to be understandably resistant, disruptive, and anxious in the groups. Further investigation with group members revealed the prevalence of sexual abuse victims. This knowledge proved to be the catalyst for receiving training and devising our survivors group for victims of incest.

Prior to the development of this approach, we knew of few cases of sexual abuse. Clearly, in retrospect, we neglected to reach and treat many un-acknowledged victims. Once we provided a group, the number of adolescents who revealed their victimization increased dramatically. The group and its members encouraged disclosures and referrals. The experience, and the richness of the survivors group, provided the framework for this article.

Behavioral Indicators

The professional should look for a constellation of behaviors when considering the behavioral "red flags" suggesting the presence of sexual abuse. Behaviors in younger children could include: advanced sexual knowledge for the child's age; sexualized play, storytelling or drawing; pseudo-mature or regressed behavior; seductive behavior, sleep problems; inconsistent school performance; a sudden drop in school performance; difficulty concentrating; withdrawal; poor peer relationships; fear of a person previously trusted; moodiness; over-compliance; acting-out. Pre-adolescents and adolescents may present these behaviors as well as self-mutilation, drug and alcohol abuse, suicidal ideations and gestures, depression, promiscuity, teenage pregnancy, prostitution, and low self-esteem. Girls may function in a "parental" role at home, assuming major household and child-care responsibilities. In adolescent male victims, behaviors may also include: rebellion, lying, stealing, sexual behavior directed toward younger children or animals, physical aggression towards persons and property.[5] The presence of several indicators warrants the need to explore the child's situation.

Impact of Sexual Abuse on the Child

"Child sexual abuse is a sexual act imposed on a child who lacks emotional, maturational, and cognitive development."[6] Sexual abuse is exploitive. Participation is coerced, directly or indirectly, and most often occurs within the family or with a trusted, known adult. Children are impacted in a variety of ways.

Love = Pain. A common result of incest identified by members of the survivors group is the equation "love = pain." Incest victims learned to accept the offender's behavior as a form of parental love. Many girls, feeling limited warmth and support from their mothers, received from the father figure a majority of their nurturance in addition to the sexual contact. For some the relationship included a romantic component, with the offender writing love letters and giving gifts, money, and special attention to the victim. At the same time these girls felt forced to live in a world of secrecy and exploitation, with a growing sense of the inappropriateness of the relationship. For them the concept of love involves inequality, coercion, and betrayal.

Such girls may commonly become involved with abusive boyfriends, avoid relationships, or maintain superficial relationships, due to their fear of emotional closeness.

Distrust. All child sexual abuse victims have significant difficulty developing trust. This lack of trust creates an impediment in engaging the child in treatment and in effecting successful placement. Children learn to trust from their parents; but "incest represents the ultimate betrayal of trust."[7] These children are often "on guard," limiting their interactions with adults and shutting down quickly when emotional issues are raised. Many present a tendency to test members of the staff prior to establishing even minimal interactions.

A majority of child sexual abuse offenders are male. Male and female victims have difficulty establishing trust with male authority figures, but developing trust with women is also affected. Many victims viewed their mothers as powerless figures, unable or unwilling to protect their own children. The experiences and projections of these children must be taken into account in directing a successful placement experience.

Feeling Issues. Victims struggle with a variety of emotions following disclosure. Guilt, depression, anger, and fear are among common feeling responses.

According to Suzanne Sgori, M.D., "intense guilt feelings following disclosure of sexual abuse are practically a universal victim response."[8] She indicates that victims experience guilt at three levels: responsibility for the sexual behavior and their participation, responsibility for the disclosure, and responsibility for the disruption in the family.[9] Adolescent victims commonly verbalize regret over their disclosure. The fact that most adolescents are removed from their homes following disclosure tends to reinforce feelings of regret and guilt. Subsequently, the removal leaves many victims feeling punished for having told.

Depression appears to be present in nearly all child sexual abuse victims. Depression may be evidenced by withdrawal and sad, subdued affect, or may be hidden behind psychosomatic complaints. Members of our survivors group commonly acknowledge suicidal ideations, with many victims entering inpatient treatment following a suicide attempt. Adolescents may harm themselves via self-mutilative behaviors, such as self-inflicted burns, lacerations, and tattoos.

Victims experience anger towards the offender for abusing them and towards other family members who failed to protect them. Anger may be repressed or overtly expressed. In our experience, female adolescents are more likely to repress and turn anger in on themselves; male adolescent victims tend to act out their anger through physical aggression or property destruction.

Fear and anxiety are seen in interactions with others, particularly adults; in difficulty concentrating; and, commonly, in sleep disturbances. Victims complain of difficulty falling asleep and of severe nightmares. Adolescent females commonly express the presence of flashback experiences in which the victim "sees" scenes of her own victimization. Fear of reprisal or of contact with the offender is frequent even in children who are permanently removed from the home. Since boys tend to be sexually abused by men, boys are likely to "fear becoming homosexual" because of a belief that the "homosexual molestation can cause homosexuality."[10]

Low Self-esteem. Child victims of sexual abuse often see themselves as "ugly" or "unclean." Many feel that people can recognize on sight that they were abused. They reveal limited ability to identify positive traits in themselves or receive praise from others. They tend to be highly self-critical. Many may exhibit poor personal hygiene and may overeat or develop anorexic tendencies in an effort to make themselves unattractive targets for further sexual abuse. They reveal little capacity for self-nurturance.

Powerlessness. Child victims robbed of control over their own bodies are left with significant feelings of powerlessness. When needs are neglected and rights violated, the child learns to be passive and feels little sense of control. The passive stance creates reluctance to articulate needs or to participate in treatment planning or placement considerations.

The Issues of Touch. Physical touch becomes a toxic issue for sexually abused children. Touch is often associated with the abusive experience. "Being touched affectionately by an adult is therefore unlikely to be pleasurable; rather it is threatening or terrifying."[11] At the same time, children who have been taught to behave in a seductive fashion may encourage sexual contact rather than the nurturing affection all children need. "Sexual acts are often accompanied by nurturing gestures. As a result, the daughter grows up not knowing how to separate the two or even knowing that sex and nurturing are different."[12]

Accommodation Process. Children who live in a sexually abusive situation adjust by normalizing the behavior. As the abuser is most often a parental figure that the child looks to for love, direction, and survival, the fact that this person is committing wrongful, inappropriate acts is incomprehensible. In an effort to cope, the child tends to see herself as "bad" and deserving of the abuse rather than risk viewing the adult as acting inappropriately. Consequently, adolescent victims may engage in exploitive, abusive male-female relationships—relationships they accept as normal because of their experiences. A female incest victim described her desire to be listened to and supported in her male-female relationships as "fantasyland."

Self-victimization. Adolescent victims are adept at self-victimization. They arrange this through negative self-statements, by becoming "scapegoated" by peers, by engaging in abusive male-female relationships, by drug and alcohol abuse, by running away, by attempting suicide, and by self-mutilation. Their tendencies toward self-criticism and passivity reinforce the victim stance.

Treatment Options. "(All) child victims of sexual abuse need some level of therapeutic intervention, regardless of the identity of the perpetrator."[13] The most common form of child sexual abuse, incest, is best treated when the entire family is involved. In many cases, family involvement does not occur. We concur with Dr. Sgroi that "much can be achieved by working with the child alone, either individually or in a group therapy milieu."[14] The following discussion of treatment efforts will focus on multiply-placed children who are not able to return home.

Individual Therapy

The first and foremost issue with multiply-placed adolescent victims is engaging the child in a trusting, therapeutic relationship. The formation of a trusting relationship is not a swift process, and the child may test the commitment of the therapist with manipulation, passive-aggressive behaviors, excessive demands, oppositionality, and an unwillingness to communicate. The professional must employ joining, affirming techniques with clear, reasonable limits. Initially, the child should be given permission to pace the length of encounters, content of sessions, and depth of interchange as the relationship develops. Efforts should be made to allow the child as many choices as possible to begin encouraging self-direction. At all times the therapist must convey the message that the child was not responsible for the abuse. Assigning the case to a professional who has experience with sexually abused children and acknowledges this experience to the child encourages the child to feel less inhibited and alone in discussing her experiences and feelings.

From the context of this relationship a variety of feelings can be explored and processed, utilizing techniques such as role-playing, problem-solving, and having the child write and discuss a personal journal. The therapist can help the child identify problem areas stemming from the sexual abuse and can engage the child in devising strategies and establishing achievable goals. Short-term contracts can be developed to enhance the child's control over impulsive, self-destructive behaviors such as suicidal gestures and running away. The child's fears can be sorted out with attention paid to valid and unrealistic concerns. The child's tendency towards self-blame and assuming responsibility for the problems of her family can be supportively confronted. The therapist directs the child to release feelings of anger and guilt while providing safety through reassurance and acceptance.

Group Treatment

The efficacy of group therapy with survivors of incest is well-documented in articles and books pertaining to the treatment of child sexual abuse victims. A group approach helps reduce a child's sense of isolation and differentness and encourages participants to verbalize thoughts and feelings with peers who share a common bond. Members provide and receive emotional support, identify and work on personal goals, and confront each other on self-victimizing behaviors and denial, while encouraging trust and developing peer relationships.

Since we began our survivors group we have experimented with group format and membership. Currently we provide an ongoing, process-oriented treatment group for female adolescent incest victims. We feel it is developmentally appropriate to separate latency-age children from the adolescents, as group issues and the ability to process are dissimilar.

Prospective members are referred by their therapists and interviewed by the group leaders to determine appropriateness, and readiness for group work. Girls who are unable to verbally process, are highly distractable, psychotic, or unable to maintain confidentiality are referred back for continued individual intervention. We limit the group size to 10 participants, and close the group for a period of four to six weeks to encourage cohesion prior to admitting new members. In this manner we are able to maintain a core group of more seasoned members as well as provide the girls with the opportunity to work with peers who are at various stages of treatment.

Primary goals for the survivors group include: enhancing self-esteem; decreasing self-blame and guilt, encouraging the release of blocked emotions; reducing self-victimization; increasing assertive behaviors; and providing education regarding the cycle of abuse, sexuality, and treatment issues. Each girl is encouraged to participate. However, a girl's right to participate at her own level should be respected at all times. We have limited our members to survivors of incest because of the educational format and the uniqueness of this particular experience. Girls are encouraged to develop group goals and suggest topics. The group is structured to promote goal attainment and provide educational experiences that follow-through with suggestions. In this way, girls are able to experience a sense of control and assume more "ownership" of the group's functioning.

Group techniques are varied, depending upon the group's composition, goals, and needs. One of our group leaders, a clinical art therapist, provides invaluable input via the use of art therapy techniques designed to enhance awareness and provide for emotional expression in a metaphorical manner. For nonverbal adolescents, the use of artwork provides the first step towards self-expression.

A potent technique for directing emotional awareness and release is having the girls write an unsent letter to the offender. The following is part of an unsent letter written to her father by a 15 year old female victim of incest:

Dad,
Hi! How are ya? I'm doin' great! I realize now that what you wanted to do was destroy me, my brother, and my mother. You never loved us. I know that and accepted it a long, long time ago. The first and last time you ever told me that you loved me I couldn't believe you. If you really meant it then I'm sorry, but it came too late. We have all agreed, that we no longer claim you as family. You are my biological father, the man who made me, not my actual father, the man who will protect and love me like a real father should. I am in an institute learning to control my hate, anger and violence that you've taught me to have. I'm almost through with my treatment. I'm expected out by August. I'm a better person now. I'm no longer the little child that you tortured. I can't say that I love you or even like you. I hate you with all my heart, but I also pity you because you'll never experience the happiness that I'm now able to feel. All you can feel is hate, violence, selfishness,

conceit, and sneakiness. In other words you're a lieing bastard. It hurts me and makes me feel ashamed to know that I'm related to you. I once loved you many, many years ago, but you killed it when you rejected it.

The letters are shared in the group, with members encouraged to let go of feelings in the process. Many girls choose to mail the letters to the offender as a vehicle for confrontation.

Other techniques include utilizing sentence completion exercises to identify common feelings, role playing, bringing in an adult victim of child sexual abuse to speak with the girls, and the use of films such as "Something About Amelia." Efforts are made to educate the girls regarding the cycle of abuse and to disseminate accurate information regarding sexuality.

We would encourage professionals contemplating the development of a group approach to devise a program that fits the needs of the victims and the facility. Flexibility and periodic re-evaluation have proven to be necessary tools in program development.

Milieu Intervention

The ingredients necessary for successful milieu treatment of victims are, perhaps, similar to those necessary in foster or group home placements. A successful milieu will reinforce the aims of individual and group therapy while providing a safe arena for the development and practice of productive social skills. Three areas need to be considered with a milieu approach: 1) the issue of touch, including seductive behaviors or sexual acting out; 2) the sexual climate; 3) dealing with inappropriate attention seeking behaviors.

Some girls have a strong aversion to touch. Many others exhibit seductive behaviors, particularly with male staff members. The adolescent should be encouraged to set her own boundaries regarding nurturing physical touch. The staff member should check out the child's boundaries prior to initiating physical contact. The staff member can and should model this process by verbalizing his/her own physical boundaries and limits to the child. Clear, appropriate limits regarding physical contact with adults and peers need to be established with the child and maintained by the staff. Seductive behaviors require supportive confrontation with verbal reassurances given that the child is cared for. Through confrontation and role modeling, a child's seductive behavior can be shaped into healthier behavioral patterns.

Heterosexual or homosexual acting-out with peers must be dealt with immediately and in a noncritical manner. Such behaviors may result in the need for a physical examination and must be communicated to other members of the treatment team for follow-up.

The sexual climates of incest families characterized in *The Broken Taboo* may be permissive or repressive.[15] Permissive family climates allow for the frequent use of sexually explicit language, and public disrobing, with little personal or bodily privacy. In the repressive family climate, the subject of sex is taboo. A therapeutic environment will allow for privacy, will permit children to discuss sexual matters in an age-appropriate manner, and will provide accurate information regarding human sexuality.

Many survivors have learned to become manipulative. As their attentional needs were often ignored, they tend to seek attention in inappropriate ways. Common behaviors include excessive demands, acting-out for negative attention, and psychosomatic complaints. Confrontation, a nurturing environment, and giving attention to assertive statements are utilized to decrease manipulative efforts. Adolescents may use their abuse as an excuse for irresponsible behavior.

Victims of sexual abuse do require a specialized treatment approach but should not be treated differently than other peers within the structured program, limits, and expectations of the milieu. Giving special allowances or buying into excuses for irresponsible behavior only serves to again set these children apart and reinforces the victim-stance.

We are able to employ additional treatment strategies with our adolescents, including: assertiveness training, drug and alcohol treatment when appropriate, occupational therapy, and the selective use of group or individual dance/movement therapy and individual art therapy.

Suggestions for Helpers

Working with sexually abused children is a challenging task. Not all professionals who work with children are suited for this particular area.

"It is essential that therapists feel comfortable with all aspects of human sexuality so that they can facilitate discussions of sexually abusive experiences and their client's feelings about those experiences."[16] Two components for successful intervention include observing the child's right to self-determination and respecting the child's point of view: "Above all, the personal values of the victim must be recognized, in light of her individual circumstances, separately from the therapist's personal values."[17]

A victim's passivity, guardedness, and powerlessness may trigger nonproductive responses in the helping professional. Many professionals display the tendency to "rescue" the victim via over involvement and sympathy. When the rescue attempts are unsuccessful or progress is minimal because of difficulties in developing trust and the tendency towards self-victimization, the helper may then assume a pushing, critical position. A rescuing or critical position reinforces the victim's passive, powerless position.

Patience, the ability to establish realistic short- and long-term goals with the child's participation, and respect for the range of feelings expressed by the child are necessary qualities in the helping professional.

Summary

The problem of child sexual abuse has received growing attention in recent years. In spite of heightened awareness, many child victims continue to migrate through a network of helping services unrecognized or inadequately treated. Most children are reluctant to disclose their abuse but tend to provide behavioral clues. Professionals who work with children need to familiarize themselves with symptomatic behaviors which warrant further investigation.

Sexual abuse impacts a child on many levels emotionally, inhibits the child's ability to trust, lowers self-esteem, and limits healthy interpersonal interactions. All child victims require therapeutic intervention.

In each survivor there is a core of strength and potential. The task of assisting a child to discover her own source of strength and beauty is both difficult and inspiring. Effectively addressing the treatment needs of the child may best be accomplished by utilizing a blending of individual and group therapy with a therapeutic environment. Professionals involved need to feel comfortable with all aspects of sexuality and should avoid rescuing or critical responses. Successful intervention demonstrates respect for the child's values and his/her right to self-determination.

Notes

1. David Finkelhor, *Child Sexual Abuse* (New York, 1984), p. 1.
2. Ibid., p. 2.
3. Ibid.
4. J. Peters, "Children Who Are Victims of Sexual Assault and the Psychology of Offenders," *American Journal of Psychotherapy 30*, (1976) pp. 398–421.
5. Alexander G. Zaphiris, "The Sexually Abused Boy," *Preventing Sexual Abuse,* Vol. 1, No. 1 (Spring 1986), p. 2.
6. Suzanne M. Sgroi, M.D., *Handbook of Clinical Intervention in Child Sexual Abuse* (Lexington, Mass., 1982), p. 9.
7. Adele Mayer, *Sexual Abuse* (Holmes Beach, Floriday, 1985), p. 54.
8. Sgroi, p. 115.
9. Ibid., pp. 115–116.
10. Beverly Janes and Maria Nasjleti, *Treating Sexually Abused Children and Their Families* (Palo Alto, California, 1983), p. 9.
11. Ibid., p. 6.
12. Blair Justice and Rita Justice, *The Broken Taboo* (New York, 1979), p. 185.
13. Sgroi, p. 111.
14. Ibid., p. 110.
15. *The Broken Taboo*, p. 146.

16. James and Nasjleti, p. 49.
17. Adele Mayer, Incest: *A treatment Manual for Therapy with Victims, Spouses, and Offenders* (Holmes Beach, Florida, 1983), p. 65.

Bibliography

Finkelhor, David. *Child Sexual Abuse*. New York, 1984.

James, Beverly and Maria Nasjleti. *Treating Sexually Abused Children and Their Families*. Palo Alto, California, 1983.

Justice, Blair and Rita Justice. *The Broken Taboo*. New York, 1979.

Mayer, Adele. *Incest: A Treatment Manual for Therapy with Victims, Spouses, and Offenders*. Holmes Beach, Florida, 1983.

Mayer, Adele. *Sexual Abuse*. Holmes Beach, Florida, 1985.

Peters, J. 1976 "Children Who Are Victims of Sexual Assault and the Psychology of Offenders." *American Journal of Psychotherapy,* 30, 398–421.

Sgroi, Suzanne M. *Handbook of Clinical Intervention in Child Sexual Abuse*. Lexington, Mass., 1982.

Zaphiris, Alexander G. "The Sexually Abused Boy, *Preventing Sexual Abuse."* Vol.1 No.1 (Spring 1986), 1–4.

22

Attachment Enhancing for Adopted Children

Ann M. Jernberg

Whether adopted at birth or at a later stage, adopted children have certain experiences in common. These shared experiences include the following:

1. All adopted children have experienced a discontinuity between the physiological and emotional style of their original mother and the physiological and emotional style of their later one.
2. All adopted children have had to make an adaptation that very few children are called upon to make. Adopted children must adapt not only to two separate women's physiologies and psychologies but often are expected to do so with the least possible show of stress.
3. All adopted children know loss, rage, and the feeling of grief.
4. All adopted children have experienced a serious threat to their self-esteem.

Given the profound hurt that can result from any of these experiences, separately or in combination, it is no surprise that inadequate bonding and poor attachment may result. Inadequately bonded and poorly attached children will have in common low self-confidence and too-little trust in the world around them. Feeling unworthy and not fully trusting, adopted children often behave in some or all of the following inappropriate or troublesome ways.

1. They may withdraw emotionally and/or physically. They may look away, run away, and, if adopted as infants, sometimes arch their backs when held and pull away. The uncommunicativeness of these children, their aloofness and poor eye contact, give one message: "I don't need Nobody! NEVER!"

2. They may engulf. They may fail to show a respect for individual boundaries, making an appearance, for example, when not invited. Adoptive mothers of engulfing children report, "I can always tell when he's shadowed me somewhere. I don't even have to check. I know he's standing there behind me at the kitchen sink boring holes right through me with his eyes. It makes me feel creepy." Workers familiar with this phenomenon term it "frozen watchfulness."

3. They may turn to what appear to be delinquent behaviors, lying about their homework or stealing money from their mothers' purses. Their behavior is delinquent, however in appearance only. In fact, a clumsy, pathetic, and pleading quality underlies their deeds, and their "delinquency" often clears up, given the appropriate treatment to be discussed later.

The adopted child who exhibits any or all of the above behaviors causes great consternation, if not outright pain, to his new family. The preparation and intervention steps to be described are designed to avoid or ameliorate that pain.

Preplacement Preparation

In the preplacement period, workers listen to prospective parents' expectations and caution them about potential pitfalls. The preparation phase is accomplished through the following means:

1. *Discussion.* Discussions will help the adoptive parents begin to understand that what may look like a breeze of an undertaking may turn into a nightmare if they do not expect surprises. The primary surprise may be that rather than a lovable, sweet, cooperative child, they have taken a tyrant into their house. It is during this phase that parents come to see how the adopted child's need to "save face" at any cost may result in tyrannical behavior. Discussions with the worker may include the asking of hypothetical questions: "Yes, but suppose Jimmy refuses to join you for the family picnic?"

2. *Videotapes.* Prepared tapes of "typical tyrants" are presented to prospective adoptive parents. As they watch tyrants having temper tantrums in response to their frustrated efforts to "take charge," parents are asked two questions: 1) "What do you think makes him behave that way?" and 2) "What would you do with him at this point if you were his parent?"

3. *Role playing.* The steps of *Preplacement Preparation* then become more concrete. As the prospective parents involve themselves more in the role playing, the situations come to seem real and ever more likely to happen. With the introduction of the role playing phase adoptive-parents-to-be have the opportunity to experience not only being the parent but also being the child. Prospective parents are asked to describe their most-dreaded scenarios, perhaps bedtime, grocery shopping or turning their child over to

a baby sitter. One parent is asked to play the role of adult, the other the role of child, as they explore what works and what doesn't work. All along they are encouraged to be very sensitive to what the child might be saying to himself and what might be his secret, unspoken wishes.

4. *Presentations by "Old Timers."* Experienced adoptive parents are usually more than happy to discuss their adopting experiences either with a group of prospective adopters or with one individual couple. At this session prospective adoptive parents hear all about the seasoned parents' early expectations, their frustrations, and their successful solutions.

Postplacement Assessment

The Marschak Interaction Method (MIM) (13) (14) is a valuable tool not only for initial "match-making" but also for helping adoptive parents adjust to their new child once he is placed with them. The MIM is available for assessing the parent-child relationship at a number of different age levels, including Prenatal (6), Infant (7), Toddler (1), Pre-schooler (8), School age child (9), and Adolescent (10). A Marital MIM has been developed (2) and is sometimes useful for assessing how the strengths and weaknesses of the marriage and the relationship between the two parents has an impact on their adopted child. The MIM provides clues about a number of different interactional dimensions, including capacity to guide purposeful behavior, capacity to reduce child's distress, and both the adult's capacity to enhance attachment and the child's capacity to attach. The MIM consists of instruction cards directing parent and child to perform a number of playful tasks together, such as "feeding dolly" and "playing peek-a-boo." Parent and child sit side by side at a table or place themselves on a floormat, depending upon the developmental level of the child. If possible the sessions are videotaped. If this is not possible the worker learns to make quick observational notes of both verbal and nonverbal interactions.

Feedback

The Feedback session serves two purposes. It apprises the parents of the child's Emotional Developmental Level (EDL) and it allows the parents to view their characteristic patterns in interaction with their child.

It is important that, through the processes of viewing and discussing, the parents come to understand that the chronological level their child has attained and his level of physical and intellectual competence may have nothing at all to do with his emotional developmental level. The latter very likely represents the age at which he had his loss experience. It is in this session that the worker begins to help the parents understand that these children need to be related to in terms of their Emotional Developmental Level (EDL) not in terms of their chronological, physical, cognitive, or visual motor attainments. At this time they are also prepared for how difficult this particular focus (EDL) may prove to be for them. They are warned that such treatment may engender resistance, not only on the part of the child himself (who is fearful of finding himself back in a situation which proved to be so traumatic), but also on the part of his neighbors and schoolteachers.

It is equally important that the new adoptive parents come to understand the realities of their interactions with their child. Thus it is important, for example, that the adoptive mother hear the worker say, "Look how you offer her a lovely, joyful relationship. And notice, what does she do with it? She turns away from you with a look of contempt on her face. It must feel horrible when she does that to you." For many adoptive mothers this is the first time they have heard compassion for the hurt they have been feeling for a long time. Adoptive mothers require empathy, not condemnation, for their efforts to avoid further rejection by a child they have been treating with warmth and kindness. The worker must urge the adoptive father to provide this empathy for his wife. It should be noted here that we cannot be sure exactly why it is generally the adoptive mother rather than the adoptive father to whom the child's attacks are directed. We can only speculate that her wish to hurt her new mother is a direct function of the hurt she suffered from the abandonment by her old one.

In the best of all worlds the feedback session even if it demonstrates appropriate attachment would be followed by yet another three or four sessions. These would be Theraplay sessions arranged not to overcome bonding defects but to help solidify healthy bonding. These sessions would 1) help the parents and child learn additional ways of playful interaction by engaging in activities like family-share-a-pretzel, for example (Rule: Each feeds the others. Nobody feeds him or herself), 2) help the child become part of the cohesive family unit (by coming to see which parent's toes are long— or curved or knuckly—for example, like his. Or the ways his whistle is just like theirs.)

The "ideal situation," of course, is not always possible. Unfortunately limited funding and staff constraints make us more attentive to "fixing" than "preventing." Thus Theraplay is most often done for purposes of intervening into an adoption which is disruptive—a situation that is threatening to go from bad to worse. Koller (APA article) (12) suggests that the point of undertaking or referring the family of an adopted child for Theraplay most often involves cases where either 1) the family has reached such a point of desperation that they make inquiries regarding "returning" the child to the agency or 2) the parents are so divided regarding their perception of, and their behavior toward, the child that the marriage begins to show stress and disharmony. Generally, marital disharmony takes the following form: husband fails to perceive the child's relentless "testing" of his wife. Wife responds by feeling hurt by, if not acting overtly abusive toward, the child and by pulling away from, showing oversensitivity with, or becoming provocative toward her husband.

Clearly, intervention is indicated.

Intervention

1. *Theraplay* (4). Theraplay is a method for providing the child a therapeutic experience with an adult—an experience modeled on the wholesome interaction between parent and infant. The approach works as follows: For the first four sessions the parents observe their child through a one-way vision mirror playing with his therapist. On the other side of this mirror the Interpreting Therapist, who sits with them, explains what is happening to their child and why.

The Interpreting Therapist may explain, for example, "Do you notice how his therapist cuddles him when she holds him? That's because he's still such a little baby inside" or "Do you see his efforts to escape her? When he can't physically run away he avoids eye contact. Is that something you find him doing with you at home? Remember how we discussed in our early visits together that some of these kids have such an inordinate need to call the shots and run the show? Well there it is; you can see it happening with Johnny right in front of your eyes. And you can see how his therapist keeps focusing his attention on her in spite of it. At home I want you to begin relating to him just the way she does in that regard."

And, perhaps explaining later, "And now look, she's counting his freckles with his toes. If you look closely you'll see he just loves it because it's so funny and he's having such fun. But he'll never let *her* know that. I want you to recognize that mostly everything they do together is playful. She makes no demands on him to be big or to perform. She just keeps letting him know that he's a dear, lovable little boy just the way he is." After four sessions in the observation room the parents spend a part of each of the following four sessions, with close guidance and support from the therapist, joining in the fun in the Theraplay room.

2. *Grief work.* Throughout the adoption period and for years thereafter, many adopted children continue to experience both profound grief over their abandonment and overwhelming rage toward a world that hurt them. Although not always necessary, it is helpful for adoptive parents, (again generally it is the mothers) to learn how to help the child deal with these unresolved issues. Should the rage continue past the Theraplay period, the worker may instruct the mother to hold her child tightly, as recommended by Braden (3) sometimes perhaps for hours, while he rages at her, at his past, and

at those others who live around him. Or perhaps he may express a rage that has no articulated content.

Should the grief continue beyond the Theraplay period, the worker will show the mother how to deal with this as well. She will instruct her to allow him to express his despair and his sadness for the mother he no longer has—obviously no easy job for a woman who is trying so hard to be the mother of his desires and who wants so much for him to be happy with her in the present, not sad over a loss in the past.

In addition there may come a time when the adopted child indicates by one means or another that he is ready to attempt bonding to his new mother. He may show this need for a primitive closeness when he is making the move into nursery school, for example, or at the point where she takes a new job. A mother who is comfortable doing so may be encouraged to wrap herself and her adopted child tightly inside a blanket or beach towel. In that position a mother should begin quietly singing or humming to her ''baby,'' or softly talking to him about ''when you were a little baby.'' Some children find it meaningful just to lie side by side in silence.

3. *Couple counseling.* Couple counseling should be made available to adoptive parents not only during the adoption period but also as a part of the follow-up. It is common in these sessions that wives indicate neediness and husbands a bewilderment at their wives' ''uncaring'' attitudes with respect to the adopted child. As before, the husband will have to be helped to be empathic with his wife for the hurt she suffers at the hands of the rejecting child.

4. *Support groups.* Parents should be helped to locate, or generate, a group of other parents of adopted children. The group sessions will not only provide support and reassurance but will become a good source of new ideas for coping with the many unique problems that come with having an adopted child in the family.

5. *School.* Teachers should be informed of the child's Emotional Developmental Level, of what they can therefore realistically expect of him, what he requires (e.g. extra attention and physical contact) and how they can cope when his behavior becomes difficult (5) (11). Teachers must know that it is legitimate to regard the adopted child in a different—younger—way and to handle his apparently delinquent behavior as only the fallout behavior it is, fallout from his grief, mistrust, low self-esteem, and anger. Should it become necessary to correct or discipline the adopted child, she should disregard his chronological age and set limits as she would with a much younger child.

Follow-Up

Follow-up Theraplay sessions are scheduled with families of adopted children every quarter during the first year and annually thereafter. The sessions provide continuity and allow the child and his parents to keep track of how he has grown, how many new teeth he has and, for example, how strong his muscles have become, how curly his eyelashes, and how many new ways he's learned to leg wrestle.

Finally, parents of late-adopted children should always know that if worst comes to worst—that is, if none of the methods suggested above is effective—they do have other options. It would be a violation of all principles of sound mental health were we to allow any child to destroy what had been a happy and well-functioning family. Alternate placement may sometimes be the only possible decision.

Case Study

Mr. and Mrs. Bayley came to the Child and Family Agency having made the decision that, in the absence of an available infant, they would be willing to adopt a slightly older child. Following an intake interview designed to gain insight into their family history, their marital relationship, the reasons for their decision, etc. a series of Pre-placement Preparation sessions were scheduled.

In discussion with their adoption worker, Mr. and Mrs. B. came to understand that they might need to modify their rosy expectations of what life as a family would be like if this family were now to include an older adopted child. The videotapes they next viewed showed adopted "tyrants" attempting to "run the show," whining to get what they want when they want it, and wailing when their parents refused to give in.

In the next scheduled session Mr. and Mrs. B. and their worker carefully designed the kinds of scenarios that best illustrate what life with a tyrannical child could be like. They set up bedtime scenes, room cleaning scenes, and scenes at the grocery store. Then they went about acting out each one. Sometimes Mrs. B. was the child and her husband the parent, sometimes they reversed the roles. They practiced the scenes over and over until they felt quite at ease dealing with a tyrant under even the most trying of circumstances.

In an effort to help her clients understand some of the dynamics that accompany interactions like these, their worker often raised the questions, "How do you suppose he is feeling right now?" and "How are you yourself feeling right now?" Occasionally their worker stepped in to demonstrate an alternate solution. Having had a go at it themselves, Mr. and Mrs. Bayley arrived at their next session to find Mr. and Mrs. Johnson, seasoned "pro's" at rearing an older adopted child. Mr. and Mrs. J. had a repertoire of anecdotes, including not only frustrating experiences but also the methods they had found useful for conflict resolution.

Mr. and Mrs. B. subsequently received their child in placement. They were not as apprehensive as they might have been. Their preplacement experience had prepared them to some extent though they knew the bulk of their "training" had yet to come.

They arrived for their Postplacement Assessment phase and made the decision that Mr. B. would be the first MIM participant. Sitting side by side at a table he and his new son, Sammy, performed a variety of playful tasks together. They tried hats on each other, talked about when Sammy would be a grownup, fed each other apple slices, and so on. The following week it was Mrs. B.'s turn. Some of the tasks she and Sammy did were repeats of Mr. B.'s, some were slightly different. Instead of trying hats on each other, for example, they combed one another's hair, and they fed each other animal crackers instead of apple slices. At the feedback session the following week their worker encouraged them to examine closely the nuances of their interactions with Sammy.

At the same time the worker supported Mrs. B. in her discomfort and encouraged Mr. B. to do the same. The worker continued this pattern of pointing out Sammy's typical behaviors during his Theraplay sessions over the next eight weeks. But now both parents first sat behind a one-way-vision window observing Sammy and his therapist and then, for the last four sessions they too joined in the fun. Three months after the termination party Sammy and his family came back for the first of their quarterly checkup visits. In the years that followed they always returned for their annual checkups. They reported looking forward to these sessions. They loved bringing the agency up to date on their development as a family and Sammy enjoyed the chance to show off his new height and his strong muscles.

Work with Sammy continued even after the termination party. His mother had been taught to help him deal with both his grief and his rage. Occasionally, moreover, she and Sammy wrapped themselves up tightly in a beachtowel for a session of togetherness. In this intimate posture Mrs. B. sang songs to him or just hummed or was silent. His teachers were kept apprised of his progress, particularly of what would be necessary for them to do if they were to help it along. A group of other adoptive parents provided Mr. and Mrs. B. ongoing support.

When last heard from Sammy and his family were doing quite nicely. His parents reported that they had gotten an entirely new view of Sammy two or three years after the completion of the program, when Sammy unexpectedly announced that he wanted them to know about his past. Since that time he has shared with them all kinds of skeletons in the closet of his early life. They respond with quiet empathy.

Bibliography

1. Allert, A. & Jernberg, A. (In process) *MIM Manual: Adult-Toddler*. Chicago, IL. The Theraplay Institute.
2. Booth, P. & Jernberg, A. (in process). *A New Method for Assessing Adult Couple Interactions*. Chicago, IL. The Theraplay Institute.
3. Braden, Josephine. *Attachment Therapy: Parent as Therapist*. Presented at DePaul University, Chicago, March 19, 1985.
4. Jernberg, A. (1979). *THERAPLAY*. San Francisco, CA. Jossey-Bass.
5. Jernberg, A. (1984). *Guidelines for Teachers of Older Adopted Children: 1.* Chicago, IL. The Theraplay Institute.
6. Jernberg, A., Wickersham, M. & Thomas, E. (1985) *Mothers' Behaviors and Attitudes Toward Their Unborn Infants* Chicago, IL. The Theraplay Institute.
7. Jernberg, A., Allert, A., Koller, T. & Booth, P. (1983) *Reciprocity in Parent-Infant Relationships*. Chicago,IL. The Theraplay Institute.
8. Jernberg, A., Allert, A., Koller, T. & Booth, P. (1982) *MIM Manual: Adult-Pre-Schooler*. Chicago, IL. The Theraplay Institute.

9. Jernberg, A., Allert, A., Koller, T. & Booth, P. (1982) *MIM Manual: Adult-School Age Child.* Chicago, IL. The Theraplay Institute.

10. Jernberg, A. & Koller, T. (in process). *MIM Manual: Adult-Adolescent.* Chicago, IL. The Theraplay Institute.

11. Koller, T. K. (1984). *Guidelines for Teachers of Older Adopted Children: II.* Chicago, IL. The Theraplay Institute.

12. Koller, T. K. "Older Child Adoptions: A New Developmental Intervention Program." Presented at the Annual Meeting of The American Psychological Association. Los Angeles, August 1981.

13. Marschak, M. (1960) "A Method for Evaluating Parent-Child Interaction Under Controlled Conditions." *Journal of Genetic Psychology.* 97, 3–22.

14. Marschak, M. (1980). *Parent-child Interaction and Youth Rebellion.* New York: Gardner Press, Inc.

23

The Adoption Process of Special Needs Children: A Family Therapy Perspective

Patrick J. Koehne

Family therapy, family systems thinking and adoptions work have all changed and developed greatly in the last thirty years. Anyone familiar with the adoptive fields can attest to the changing views on who needs to be adopted and who wants to do the adopting. Adoption has become a complicated process, with the simplicity of infant adoptions definitely in the minority and the adoption of special needs children clearly in the majority. Special needs children can mean many things, ranging from noninfant children to children with physical, emotional, and learning disabilities. Placement of these children is by far the most demanding for adoptive workers, and, increasingly, for mental health practitioners who are providing services to these children and their adopting families.

The services and the theory base that clinicians bring with them when working with adopting families have also undergone a dramatic transformation. This transformation from an emphasis on intrapsychic work with individuals to a multiperson, interpersonal orientation developed slowly through the 1940's and 1950's. Early family-system thinkers and family therapists worked mostly behind closed doors. They were venturing into territory that the mainstream of psychotherapy did not view as appropriate. Several of these early pioneers are worth mentioning.

Pioneers

Murray Bowen, M.D., is regarded as one of the major contributors to the field of family-system theory. He has worked over the last 35 years in developing and refining his concepts. Dr. Bowen, in his work with schizo-phrenics, became interested in the connection between the schizophrenic patient and the patient's family. To observe the interaction more clearly, Dr. Bowen would hospitalize not only the patient but the entire family as well. From this unique vantage point, Dr. Bowen was able to observe the family's dysfunctional pattern of interaction and just who seemed to be most pathologically involved with the patient.

Dr. Bowen developed several family-systems concepts which are very useful when working with adopting families. The first is the concept of triangles. Dr. Bowen observed that a two-person system is basically unstable and will seek to draw in a third person, thus creating a triangle. In any triangle there are two people who remain relatively close during times of low stress, with a third being less close. Typically, when the stress increases between the two for whatever reasons, one of the two makes a move to bring the third person closer to resolve or reduce the tension. Families can be made up of a series of triangles, with the most prominent one being the mother-father-child triangle. Two of the major purposes of triangles are to lower tension between individuals and to diffuse too much closeness or intensity.

A second concept is that of fusion or emotional closeness. Here a person has a difficult time separating out his/her emotional and intellectual function-ing from a significant other. In the extreme, a person would feel that he doesn't exist or would not be able to function without the other person. Another way of describing this concept would be "over-dependency." The amount of fusion between two individuals in a family can vary, depending on the stress level. Typically, the more fusion there is, the greater the potential for dysfunctional behavior.

Another early innovator was Milton H. Erickson, M.D., who was a pioneer in clinical hypnosis as well as strategic family therapy. Dr. Erickson viewed the client as part of a family system which played a significant role in the ongoing health and development of the client. Early on he recognized the stages of the family life cycle. He made the connections between an individual's problematic behavior and the family's having difficulty in moving to the next stage. He viewed a family that presented itself for treatment as needing help with the transition to the next stage, with moving on to new goals. Later innovators based many of their ideas on Milton Erickson's work.

Salvador Minuchin, M.D., approached troubled families from a different angle. He paid close attention to the power structure within the family— specifically, how the hierarchy of the family was set up. His technique was to establish the mother and father in charge of the family, with both fulfilling their role as parents. His concept of "enmeshment," where a parent would draw in a child and form an alliance with that child for a specific purpose, was often seen in dysfunctioning families. Minuchin's concept of "parental child"—a specific child is singled out to perform parental behaviors not being performed by a parent—is very significant in the family therapy field. Children placed in this role find themselves between generations—they are neither full parent nor full child. This can lead to problems for that child and the family.

Lastly I will mention Virginia Satir, recognized as one of the founders of family therapy: specifically, the study of communication within families. She paid strict attention to the types of communication in families and the resulting feelings. Her many books on family and marriage therapy, especially *People Making*[1] have had a profound impact in the field of family therapy.

The list could go on and on. These four are but a few of the many professionals who have had great impact in this field. They are significant to me because they and their teachings have influenced me most in my practice as a family therapist. Their ideas have forced me to develop my own belief system concerning families and the way I put that belief system into action; namely, what I do and how I act as a family therapist.

Assessment as Intervention

By definition, a family therapist approaches a problem or a client from a particular perspective. Family therapy views the whole family system, not just an individual, as being part of a problem, and views it as providing the ingredients for a solution.

Adopting families presenting themselves to mental health practitioners for assistance bring a particular set of challenges. First, there are at least two distinct family systems involved: the adopting family's and the child/adolescent's biological family. Second, the adopted child brings his/her own unique level of functioning, which is both a function of the child's fit with the current adopting family and the previous experiences with the biological family. This situation is often complicated by the number of nonbiological families the child has lived with (both foster families and previous adopting families). A mental health professional approaching a family of this configuration is presented with a here-and-now family situation plus the influence of the previous ghost-shadow families. As a proponent of treatment/interaction following diagnosis/assessment, I have developed my own set of assessment criteria. My assessment "check list" is by no means unique or my own creation, since I borrow heavily from the teachers and writers that I have studied. What may be unique is the blend that I use and the way I apply these tools and approaches. I am particularly indebted to Stephen Lankton, ACSW, for his six parameters in assessing a client and his/her system. Mr. Lankton trained and studied extensively with Milton Erickson in the mid and late 1970's and is co-author of the book, *The Answer Within: A Clinical Framework of Ericksonian Hypnotherapy.*[2]

Check List

I choose to start with the here-and-now adopting family, for this gives me a current reference point. This look at the existing family will include the adopting child as he/she fits with the present family, but without a detailed assessment of the particular child at this point.

1. The genogram is particularly useful for obtaining a lot of information quickly and efficiently. I start with the genogram of the adopting family, with a brief sketch of the adopted child's family. The emphasis here is on what the family system of the adopting family looks like, with its unique development and characteristics. A good article describing the use of the genogram is "A Guide to the Genogram Family Systems Training" by Eileen Pendagast and Charles O. Sherman.[3] The genogram offers the family an opportunity to share their family history and think about it in a more objective way.

My experience over the last six years has been that families are tremendously interested in doing their family genogram. It is fun to watch a family's eyes literally light up as a particular piece of family understanding almost hops out at them. Also, the kids seem to enjoy seeing the family laid out in circles and squares as much as or more than the adults. The genogram is a cognitive way to get the family thinking on a family systems level and assessing how this is relevant to their family functioning today. Doing a genogram with families is also an excellent way to learn about family theory.

2. The eco-map is an equally useful tool in assessing adopting families. The focus here is on the external environment of the family and what connections the family has outside of itself. It is a good way to assess support systems and the natural network the family has. An eco-map is a very insightful look at how much energy a family has and in what directions. Who they are involved with and what they are getting out of this involvement can be indicative of how well the family functions at this time. An excellent book on eco-mapping and its usefulness in adoptions work is *Finding Families: An Ecological Approach to Family Assessment in Adoption.*[4]

3. Closely connected to the eco-map is what I call a person's Life Pie. This is a concept I picked up in training with Dr. Robert Dick, a clinical psychologist, who integrates transactional analysis, gestalt therapy, and hypnosis. It is a simple and efficient way to help clients assess where they are focusing their energy and from where they are getting their "warm fuzzies." Since a picture is worth a thousand words, I will show the Life Pie just as I do with clients.

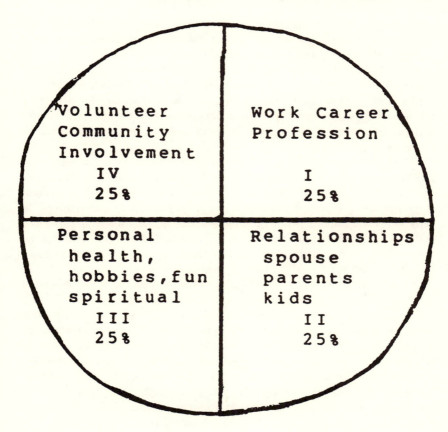

My assumption is that if the sections of our life are reasonably balanced, and each section has close to 25% of our energies, we have a well balanced life. Of course our emphasis will change as we grow through the life cycle, but I find the Life Pie useful in pointing out where there are glaring deficiencies or surpluses.

4. The next two assessment tools are closely connected. The first is our knowledge of the family life cycle and the specific stages of development of the family. There are predictable crises associated with each of these stages, especially when a family is in transition to the next stage. Also, a family must successfully deal with the developmental tasks that are associated with each stage. The six stages of family development are: (1) Between families—the unattached adult; (2) Starting a family—the couple; (3) Family with young children; (4) Family with teenagers; (5) Family launching young adults; (6) Couples in maturity. Clearly, viewing the adoptive family from this perspec-

tive is helpful, and knowing what the developmental tasks and challenges are will be useful. What impact adopting a child or teenager will have on a particular developmental stage will remain to be seen.

5. A closely-allied assessment tool is our knowledge of the stages that individual adults go through. *Seasons of a Man's Life*[6] is an excellent book as well as a longitudinal study which breaks ground on adult development. As I begin working with a family I am mentally checking off the ages of the adults and plugging their ages into the developmental stages as developed by Levinson et al.

The stages are: a) Early adult transition, 17–22 years; b) Early adulthood, 22–40 years; c) Mid life transition, 40–45; d)Middle adulthood, 45–60; e) Late adult transition, 60–65; f) Late adulthood, 65 and up. Within the second stage there are two crucial areas that I pay close attention to with families. In early adulthood comes a period described as the "age-30 transition." This is a period where some big decisions are usually addressed and answered and the stage set for the rest of the thirties. In the thirties there is the "settling down period," 31–35 years, and the "becoming one's own person period," 35–39 years. The authors feel that adulthood is reached at this phase, and real adult productivity can be generated.

From here I begin to direct questions aimed at assessing two things: a) Is the adult roughly in the stage of development that his/her chronological age would indicate? b) How successful is the adult in this particular stage? I usually ask questions about goals that an adult has, and has had, and ask how he is doing in pursuit of these. Using this framework is not a surefire way of determining a person's satisfaction and health level, but offers ways of approaching this subject. I am basically looking to elicit the adults' holistic view of themselves and how they measure their success.

This whole data-gathering process is used to develop as clear an understanding as possible of the family now dealing with a special-needs-child adoption. It is critical to the working relationship in therapy that the therapist know on what levels and what fronts he/she can join with the adopting family to offer support and guidance.

The first three assessment steps lay the groundwork for the final three, and from there the more active intervention strategies and techniques begin. Let me stress the importance of this assessment period: It is the initial part of the treatment process; it is the foundation for the working relationship between the family and the therapist.

6. The next assessment step is checking out the availability of resources, both direct and indirect. On one level this refers to the physical resources that are available in the family's network, i.e., extended family, close friends, church organizations, and the like: what resources are available to assist the adopting family with the energy it often takes for a special needs child. On a

more formal level, we need to ascertain: what resources are available from government agencies responsible for assisting with special needs children; what subsidies are available for child care, therapeutic intervention, summer camps, etc.; what advocacy groups for special needs adoption this family is tied into; what support groups. There can be even more resources.

It is equally important to check out the indirect resources available. By this I mean psychological resources lying dormant in the family as a whole and in individuals in particular. Most people who present themselves to a therapist are aware at some level that they have more to develop in their personality. They now have energy to tap into and create with. Participating with them in this process is for me the real worth and the fun of doing therapy on a regular basis.

Adopting families are no different in this area. When a person begins to search for hidden potential and discovers untapped resources, the excitement and hope level of the family is raised. This is bound to ripple over into the adopting situations. Most SNA's (special needs adoptions) need time and more time; a recently discovered hope helps the family to live in a difficult situation.

Also, developing indirect resources directly related to the adoption situation need to be explored. Who has been contributing too little to the situation? Why? This can often be a crucial element in an SNA's being successful or disintegrating. A well-known phenomenon in organizational theory is that in order for a group to function optimally, all members must contribute, and there must be an atmosphere which supports and encourages "brain storming." When this doesn't happen, and one or two members of the group do most of the contributing, productivity is markedly reduced. I have observed this over and over again in families, and have seen the dramatic results when all members start to contribute their talents and resources. In family work, I look for individuals who look as if they have something to offer but are sitting on it. Oftentimes, the most powerful resources are the resources that are just below the surface, waiting to be tapped. Like drilling for oil, however, one may have to drill deeper and through tougher rock to reach good oil. Again, SNA's need time.

7. Now we can assess the *flexibility* and *sensitivity* of each member toward the others: who is sensitive to whom, and why. Assessing these two variables often takes much time. Completion indicates that a therapist can start with his real work with the family. Part of the art of doing therapy is figuring out ways to take what is offered you—flexibility and sensitivity—and use these to facilitate change in the system without losing members who have less of these attributes. How this is done varies from family to family and is based on the data which has been previously collected.

8. The last step in the assessment process is taking a look at the motivation

to adopt an SNC (special needs child) at this time: "What's in it for whom, and why?" I save this question for last, after much of the other data have been collected, because so often it really gets the work started. Rarely do both parents (assuming this is a two-parent intact family, and that may be a big assumption today) have the same investment in adopting an SNC. I look at the motivation of both folks, and how their degrees of motivation blend and complement each other.

Many times an adoption is an attempt on the part of the adopting family to solve some problem in their family, such as inability to conceive or loss of a child through death. However, as we seek to alleviate a problem in one way, the solution becomes a different kind of problem/challenge in another way. Sometimes couples/families are aware of this motivation and understand its full meaning. Other families are less aware, and this lack of understanding may be part of the problem. The task of the therapist will be to assist in this understanding if he/she feels it will alleviate some of the stress. However, understanding just for understanding's sake is not what I am advocating.

Having begun my career as a helping person in a residential child care setting, Hoffman Home for Youth, Gettysburg, Pennsylvania, I have worked with some very difficult and challenging kids. I can appreciate the tremendous amount of energy and commitment it takes to parent them. I try to assess the experiences and exposure level the adopting parents have had with these kinds of kids. It can be a real shocker to an adopting family, all ready to provide love and understanding, to get snorted and spit at. Education about these kids and their issues and personality styles is definitely needed when adults/ families haven't been exposed to them. Sometimes offering this education is enough to help families be more understanding and patient; other times it sends them on their way.

These are the basic assessment tools that I use in working with families, adoptive and nonadoptive. I run through them in an order that seems to make most sense for a particular family. They really aren't much different for adoptive families, since the basic components of family functioning and dysfunctioning are quite similar. What then makes SNA therapy different is the special attention that needs to be paid to the SN child or teenager. Here we leave the mainstream, and the less familiar terrain of SNA therapy begins.

The Special Needs Child

I assess the child in a four-part process. First is what I term the comprehensive understanding of the child. A full scale diagnostic assessment is worked up, using information already available. It is important to assess the strengths and weaknesses of the child's functioning. Psychological and educational testing and scores are helpful.

Blending this information about the child with the actual child is then the second task. Using whatever means necessary—play therapy, one-on-one discussions—I want to grasp two complex wholes; First, how does this child see and interact with the outside world, and what are the repercussions of these connections? Second, what internal constructs of experiences, emotions, hurts, and defenses has the child built to make sense out of the world? How a child orders his/her world within his head determines what avenues are open for the therapist and significant others to approach the child and possibly offer some options which may be more productive.

In this same view I allow my inner thought process to conjure up what thoughts and feelings this child is stimulating in me. I develop and use this information to formulate a fantasy image of the child which assist me in the treatment process. Assessing the child's stage of emotional development compared to the chronological age level is equally important. It is not unusual to see a 10-year-old child be closer to a three year old in his/her emotional development. Knowing this will be very useful in the treatment process.

The third step is to assess the number and intensity of previous attachments and rejections. Who the child was attached to, for how long, what caused termination to be initiated, and how well the termination was handled are vital questions. How the child understands and has dealt with these previous connections is important when thinking in terms of family systems theory. A sketch of an SNC's genogram is graphic proof of the complexity and forces that the child has had to deal with. A further complication is that some of the past relationships and hurts are on a conscious level and can be dealt with there, but others have become unconscious and can only be addressed on that level.

My formula for the amount of therapeutic intervention needed is a direct correlation to the number of previous attachments and rejections. Here's how it looks on a graph.

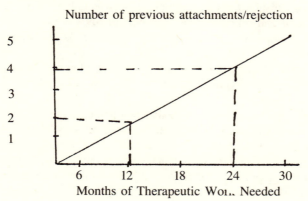

Number of previous attachments/rejection

Months of Therapeutic Work Needed

I believe this pattern is repeated consistently for SNC's. Recognizing this, will be an advantage in treating the SNC and the adopting family.

All the assessment of the child leads to an "attachment potential assessment." This is really what it is all about when working with SNC's. Can the child re-attach in a healthy way to a group of individuals who do not come from their past, but want to go into the future with them? This is the $64,000 question. It cannot be accurately predicted at this stage, since many forces will determine the ultimate success or failure of the venture. However, I have found it helpful to give the adopting family a realistic assessment so that they can prepare themselves for the task at hand. When the child is driving the adopting parents bonkers, they may summon up the therapist's assessment that says, "This is to be expected." An attachment-potential assessment is not to be construed as a self-fulfilling prophecy but rather a realistic assessment of the hard work needed to be done by all.

Therapy in Action

The ideal therapy situation is to be involved preplacement with both the adopting family and the SNC. An old axiom in sports is that if you get the techniques right the first time—i.e., have lessons from a pro—you'll be practicing the right stuff and not reinforcing bad habits. I believe this analogy has something to tell those of us who work with adopting families and those who adopt as well. It makes sense to seek out a therapist early on who has an interest in SNA work, has pursued some specific training as well, and will use an attachment-potential assessment process.

I am familiar with two types of problems that have arisen with therapy referrals. The first occurs when a family has been referred after the situation is beyond the point of no return. The second occurs when a family has been referred to a therapist who is *individually* oriented. This is likely to produce less than optimum results for the adoption. I believe individually oriented therapies are useful and relevant. I do, but not for SNA work. Combining some individual therapy with a family systems approach is the most viable choice, I believe.

Let's have a look at some family therapy with SN adopting families. I'd like to combine a few theoretical concepts with some examples from my practice.

More often than not, the adopting parents when first seen are frustrated and confused. This wonderful undertaking which started off so well is falling to pieces. The first step is to help settle down the situation. I let the parents know they have a support person and find out where the trouble is most pressing.

Typically we find a great deal of anger and hurt feelings. Assessing these, finding out who's not talking to whom and why, helps too. Usually, the addition of an angry or acting-out child will create tensions in a marriage dyad, bringing to the surface some old issues or causing new ones. Addressing these early helps. Are the problems more pressing to one parent than the other? Do both parents want the adoption? Do both want treatment? Who will assist the therapist at this time? Who won't? These are all questions and thoughts that I take with me into the initial stage.

With one family I saw, the mother was in a state of panic. She was at home most of the time with a sibling group of several children adopted all at one time. The father was a very good dad and husband, yet had a lot of responsibility outside of the home. He felt there was no need for a therapist to be involved. It took the wife's reaching the point of saying, "Either the kids go or I go" before the husband agreed to contact a therapist. It took several sessions to get the husband involved beyond a superficial level, since he had come reluctantly to pacify his wife. "Who wants to work and why?" "Who's got the problem and how come it hurts?" are two sides of the same coin.

When working with a family situation I work on the assumption that relationships in a family should be reasonably balanced to obtain the most for its members: so I begin exploring any overattachments and cutoffs that exist. In the above case, the mother was remaining physically involved, but emotionally she was distancing herself for her own survival. The father was emotionally very involved but less so physically. Some redistributing of these two involvements by the parents resulted in a more workable situation. The mother's emotional distancing was saying, "Help, I'm drowning!" The messages behind the distancing and overattachments are important to explore.

A practical consideration that I pay attention to is what I call the "comfort level" of a family. On a scale of 1 to 10, with the 1 being low comfort level and 10 being lots of comfort, I ask this family to rate their comfort level. Establishing where a family is on this scale, I explore with them the contributors to and detractors from a high comfort level. Encouraging a family to make a list of the contributors and a plan to implement some of them can get their level into a higher zone.

With one family who had adopted a sibling group of three, January and February were difficult. The children had a poor foundation in school, so the academic area was always a hassle for everyone. When asked what would raise their comfort level, everyone responded, "A TRIP!" But during school, how unthinkable! But they finally decided that a four-day trip in February was what they needed to give the comfort level a real shot. The parents took the kids out of school for two days, coinciding with a business trip the mother had to take, and left the structure and discipline of the books at home. The trip worked so well that this family decided to plan a week at the beach as soon as school let out as something to look forward to, something to raise the comfort level. This family learned the importance of balancing work/school with pleasure/fun. It got them through another school year. If it works, use it; if it doesn't, figure out a different option. In adoption work, it helps to be a pragmatist.

Sometimes the way the family feels toward the child is readily apparent, but often there are feelings that are out of conscious awareness or are not acceptable for the adults to express. Helping the family members to formulate and to express their feelings is most helpful. (See the little book *There Is No Such Thing as a Dragon*)[7] Problems/feelings remain big as long as they are hidden. If we look at them in the light of day, half of the solution has already been achieved.

I have found that the use of fantasy can be a very effective tool. The use of fantasy has long been accepted in the world of child therapy, and for most young children is the most useful approach. I find that even with adults, using fantasy is a way to bypass the conscious mind, which often restricts what the person is willing to discuss. We go right to the unconscious mind, which typically has a vast storehouse of useful material. I will ask a family member to pick out a fantasy, fairy tale, or any story that seems relevant, and then to build on and embellish it. Adults can be uncomfortable with this and not see the use of it; but if it's presented in a non-threatening, fun-oriented way, they usually will respond—with results.

Along with fantasizing is the use of imagery to develop and heighten the fantasized feeling. Guided imagery is a relatively new concept in the field of psychotherapy and is being used for many different purposes with some very good results. It involves constructing images within the mind and elaborating on them internally.

One of my clients was an adopting father trying to adjust to the newest family member, a 10-year-old son. He seemed frustrated yet committed to the boy. The son was a classic SNC who had experienced several major attachment upheavals and had the knack of keeping people emotionally distanced. The father was seeking a way to get over his understandably angry feelings toward the boy.

I asked the father if he would be comfortable with fantasizing a situation to see what his mind would bring up. The father said he'd try anything. He sat very still and relaxed while I talked about different situations and the mind's power to create useful plans. After five minutes or so he had a slight smile, and then he broke into a huge grin and was just beaming. I asked him what was happening, and he said, "I got it! I got it!" I suggested he leave my office and savor his new understanding—really let it sink in. He was to call me when he wanted to and let me in on his discovery.

He called several weeks later to say that while he was sitting in my office an image floated through his mind which had a powerful effect on him. He saw a little fawn all curled up, sleeping in the woods. He said it reminded him of his son, who seemed to be as vulnerable and in need of protection as that fawn. He felt then that he could and would provide protection for his newest son. That adoptive father made very good use of his ability to fantasize and create with his unconscious thought process.

A somewhat similar technique is what I call "future projecting." I like to ask folks to let their minds wander and play with some ideas and situations that they would like to see happen in the future. As they do this, I suggest that they concentrate on certain aspects of the experience, especially what they want to come to pass in the future.

Several years ago, I was part of a training group studying clinical hypnosis, and had a powerful personal experience using this technique. Using future projection, our trainer asked us to visualize two situations that would make us very happy and content in the future, and then to sketch pictures of the two images for ourselves. First I imagined myself sitting in a very nice, comfortable office seeing a family as a family therapist in private practice. Second, I was playing with several children and my wife on a grassy knoll. Both images were very clear and powerful for me. For a long time I kept my two sketches hanging in my office. Each of my projections has come to fruition. Because I believe this technique helped me attain my goals, I use it confidently with my clients.

Another benefit is that it puts us into the future, out of our own "here and now" setbacks and hassles. For the adoptive family it offers a mechanism for transcending their present frustrations and pain, and constructing a future environment that offers satisfaction to all. If it raises the comfort zone indicator a notch, it is useful. It also gives a family a situation to shoot for, and with that, hope.

Bonding

The last point I wish to address in the therapy process is the issue of bonding. Assessing the bonding/attachment potential was addressed earlier. The flip side is *promoting* the process of bonding. This becomes the acid test for adoptive therapy work. Facilitating a strong bonding, guiding it in the positive direction, becomes the significant work for the therapist.

I believe that three things promote bonding: commitment, understanding, and a reciprocal relationship.

Commitment is self-explanatory. Although rarely is the adopting family's motive totally altruistic, there is always a desire to contribute to the bettering of society through helping an individual child.

With time, however, commitment can wane. This is when understanding is needed—understanding of what is happening in the here and now, especially an older adopted child's present behavior as a manifestation of past experiences. This work tends to be on an intellectual level, though it is intended to trigger an affective response from the depths where bonding takes place.

The initial attachment to a child is usually intellectual, mingled with individual images of what the adoption will be like for each person. As the reality of the adoption manifests itself, there is a gap between the initial images/hopes of the adopting person and what is actually going on. This tension is a catalyst, a vehicle for the person to use in exploring his or her original wishes and at an affective level come to grips with the child as he or she actually is.

Another way of saying this is that the adopting person experiences the highs and lows of the relationship, finally arriving at a more realistic understanding of what is and what can be. It is at this point that a more realistic bonding can start to take place, with the adoptive parent's inner images more closely aligned to the outer realities. If the adopting person cannot attain this understanding, seldom will the bonding process be successful.

The last bonding-promoter is a reciprocal relationship, a two-way street between the adopting parent and the child. I have seen situations where only the parent was willing to try to improve a relationship. When this is the case, a lot of wheel-spinning occurs.

I believe it's critical for a therapist to help the adopted older child give something back to the adopting parent. The child may be reluctant to give feedback to adults because of experiences in the past, so he stays shut up. In my experience this is the worst possible scenario for bonding, because the parent gets nothing to take in and think over and respond to. The therapist must promote and arrange situations that will foster feedback and reciprocal relationships between the adopting family and the adopted older child, for this is critical to the bonding process. A key element here is that bonding is a process, continuing through time. Like a snowball rolling downhill, it gains in size and momentum as it continues.

Since bonding between people takes place at a psychological level, it is obviously difficult to define and observe. My yardstick is a relaxed, trusting, atmosphere between two people. As the trust level increases and the relaxation/comfort level improves, I figure that psychological bonding is going on below the surface. In the therapy sessions I deal with the issues that appear to be blocking trust and comfort. As "homework" I encourage activities that will increase relaxation and trust. They usually involve playfulness and fun.

I have learned that much of the bonding process in older child adoptions comes through conflict-and tension-resolution, allowing family and child to move to a more intimate relationship. The therapist can provide a supportive atmosphere and system while this process is developing, and can see that it doesn't go down any blind alleys.

Case Example

The bonding process can be like a Mexican hat dance—two or more people with an illusionary boundary between them, constantly in motion and gauging their distances to one another. The hat represents the issues between the participants, whose relationships turn on how they interact over the hat.

This is how I saw a mother and her youngest adopted son relating to each other. The boy was a classic SNC—lots of serious hurts, lots of reluctance to enter into a loving relationship. The mother in this case had burned out. She had given and given, with little positive return. The bonding process was at a standstill, with copious amounts of anger everywhere.

For both, the point had been reached where a decision had to be made. The son had to decide either to start investing in the relationship, i.e., respecting the mother as a person: or to walk away from the hat dance. The mother had to decide either to accept her helplessness in this situation, care for her own needs, and witness her son's struggle: or to throw the towel in and walk away.

Just walking away was not acceptable to her; she began working gradually on the former option. This was not easy. She needed lots of assistance and strokes from the therapist as well as the other family members.

The son was aching to run away, while at the same time he had begun to believe that maybe, just maybe, here was a relationship he could finally hang in with. This struggle was played out in the therapy sessions. Here difficult issues were addressed and the son forced to deal with them. If he refused, we would either wait him out or give lots of strokes to the other family members until he could stand it no more and would chime in. In the process he came to grips with who he was and what he could contribute.

Early in therapy the son would leave the hat dance on the slightest provocation. As we progressed he was forced to verbalize his anger and to recognize that the anger he had toward his adopted mom went back to his early mothering experiences and the disruptions/rejections he had experienced. As he got in touch with this anger and struggled to understand who he was, he began to have greater commitment to his adopting mom and to being adopted. Verbalizing his anger went hand and hand with allowing himself to be more vulnerable to the family, i.e., to state that he did indeed want to be a contributing/receiving member of the family.

I believe that this outer manifestation represented an inner psychological process: bonding. The boy started out confused and angry, but the reason for the anger was unconscious. His anger brought his and his mother's bonding forces to a standstill. Bonding couldn't proceed till a past hurt was identified and the grieving process stimulated. It took patience and persistence to force the issue and allow the child to deal with it when he was ready.

Summary

For me, family therapy with adopting families involves a grasp of family systems theory, the ability to do assessment and diagnosis, a feel for special needs adopted kids, and the ability to integrate all of the above to facilitate the bonding process in the family. It also requires a respect for the work required from the family outside of the therapy office. *The Other Twenty Three Hours* an excellent book by Trieshman, Whittaker, and Brendtro on residential treatment of emotionally troubled youth, highlights the importance of the therapeutic milieu during the twenty-three hours the kids aren't in the therapist's office.[8] The energy and commitment it takes for the adopting family to provide a nurturing milieu for the SNC deserves much attention and support.

For these adoptions to be successful, a team approach is needed, where all sides are working together. Mental health practitioners dealing with SNA families can be a great help to the adoption process when they appreciate the family's challenge and their own role as a vital support. In the end, everyone can benefit and enjoy the satisfaction of a truly worth while effort.

References

1. Satir, Virginia. *Peoplemaking*. Science and Behavior Books, Inc.
2. Lankton, Stephen R. and Carol H. *The Answer Within: A Clinical Framework of Ericksonian Hypnotherapy*. Bruner/Mazel, Inc., 1983.
3. Pendagast, Eileen and Sherman, Charles D. "*A Guide to Genogram Family Systems.*" *The Family*. Vol 5, No. 2.
4. Hartman, Ann. *Finding Families, An Ecological Approach to Family Assessment in Adoption*. Sage Publications, 1979.
5. Elizabeth A. Carter and Monica McGoldrick, Editors. *The Family Life Cycle, A Framework for Family Therapy*. Gardner Press, 1980.
6. Levinson, Daniel J. et al. *Seasons of a Man's Life*. Ballantine Books, 1978.
7. Kent, Jack. *There's No Such Thing as a Dragon*. Children's Press, 1985.
8. Trieshman, Albert E., Whittaker, James K. and Brendtro, Larry K., *The Other Twenty Three Hours*. Aldine Publishing Co., 1969.

24

Adoption and Divorce: The Double Life Crisis

Dorothy W. Le Pere and Carolyne B. Rodriguez

Adoption and divorce both initiate life crises for children. Often they interfere with or disrupt the child's development. Even children who are adopted during infancy, or whose parents divorce while they are infants, suffer from a sense of loss and experience grief (Brodzinsky). Claudia Jewett relates all losses to the child's primitive terror of abandonment, the child's fundamental anxiety about "Who will keep me safe." (Jewett, page 14)

Because loss is part of each act of adoption or divorce, it is logical to assume that adopted children whose parents later divorce experience a heightened sense of loss. In order to explore the issues in treatment of these children several areas must be examined:

1. How does divorce affect children?
2. How does adoption affect children?
3. What are the developmental issues in both types of losses?
4. What treatment strategies are most effective, considering the variables described in numbers 1–3?

The Meaning of Adoption

The philosophy and practice of adoption is a fast changing field. For centuries, adoptions were practiced without legal sanction. During the ninteenth and twentieth centuries, adoption became formalized. Procedures developed for keeping "secret" the identity of the birth and adoptive parents. Along with this secrecy came a profound loss of information about the birth parents, their history and heritage. During the 1970's, therapists treating adopted children began to question the benefit of this secrecy as they saw adopted children struggle with "Who Am I?" in the absence of information about their birth parents. (Berman and Bufferd, page 3)

In the late 1970's and continuing into the 1980's, some adoption agencies began to practice more open adoptions, where the adoptive and birth parents might exchange letters and pictures, sometimes meet, and in a few cases actually maintain an ongoing relationship. This move toward openness is seen as a response to the adopted child's need for knowledge about his biological heritage.

Noted developmental psychologist David Brodzinsky has also questioned the assumptions about how the child's loss of one set of parents is handled through adoption telling. (Brodzinsky, page 871) Common practice has been to tell children they were adopted when they were old enough to speak and understand the words (sometime between 2 and 4 years old). Dr. Brodzinsky's studies demonstrate that while children can repeat back the word "adoption" and tell the story at this age, children do not understand the abstract concept of the loss until they are developmentally old enough to understand that to be adopted means someone gave you up. Children are intellectually prepared to do this between the ages of 8 and 11. (Brodzinsky, page 876)

Berman and Bufferd have recognized that adopted children, when they realize the loss they have experienced, are hindered by the lack of adequate means to mourn the loss of the birth parents. (Berman and Bufferd, page 5) They are often hesitant to discuss their sense of loss with their adoptive parents because they are afraid that their adoptive parents will feel they don't love them. Along with grief for the loss of the birth parents, the child feels anxiety: if one set of parents can reject him, it is likely that his adoptive parents will do so also.

For children who were adopted after infancy and have experienced a series of foster home placements, adoption may be experienced not as a positive step forward but as another rejection. Many such children develop a sense of responsibility for the moves. Thus each move, even into adoption, reinforces the child's sense of guilt and reaffirms that he is bad. (Jewett, "Adopting the Older Child," page 74)

Because of the guilt and the fear of seeming disloyal to the adoptive parents, many adopted children do not talk about their feelings of loss and grief. If the adoptive parents have conflicting emotions about their infertility and/or about the birth parents, it may not be possible for them to establish a climate where the child feels free to discuss his feelings. (Berman, page 5) This inability to communicate feelings can lead to depression, behavior disorders, and parent child conflict in the adoptive family.

The Meaning of Divorce

As with adoption, our society's philosophy and practice of divorce is changing rapidly. Beginning in the late 1960's and continuing into the 1970's and 80's, our divorce rate has increased dramatically. Even more dramatic has been the increase in divorces of parents with children. Between 1972 and 1979 over one million children each year experienced the divorce of their parents. For many years the philosophy was ''stay together for the children's sake.'' However, for the last three decades, the prevailing philosophy is that children are more damaged by a bad marriage than a divorce. (Wallerstein and Kelly, page 5)

Wallerstein and Kelly's study of the impact of divorce on children indicates that the period of the parents' separation and subsequent divorce were the most stressful time of these children's lives. (Wallerstein, page 35) Again the central theme seems to be, ''Who is going to protect and take care of me?'' In addition, the parents are dealing with their own feelings about the divorce and are often not able to provide the child with the reassurance he needs.

The Wallerstein & Kelly study of children whose parents had been divorced five or more years demonstrated that certain factors indicate how the child will handle the divorce. These factors, stated briefly, are:

1. The parents' ability to put their conflicts aside
2. The parenting provided by the custodial parent
3. The child's feeling of acceptance or rejection by the noncustodial parent
4. The child's personal resources and adjustment prior to the divorce
5. The child's support system
6. The presence or absence of continuing anger and depression in the child
7. The sex and age of the child (Wallerstein and Kelly, page 209)

One special concern would be that adopted children whose parents divorce are likely to experience more difficulties. The child may have experienced adjustment problems related to the adoption, and when confronted with their grief about the divorce, adopted children face anger and depression from both experiences.

Developmental Issues

The developmental stage at which the divorce experience occurs will dictate certain behavioral and emotional reactions. Children will show in treatment developmentally specific disturbances needing the clinical response of the therapist.

Infants. The psychological tasks in the first year of the child's life are to increase recognition and awareness, to differentiate primary care takers from strangers, and to increase reciprocity and mutuality in terms of interpersonal relationships. Infants are particularly sensitive to developing attachment behaviors during the first six months of life. Primary among the infant's tasks is the development of a sense of trust. (Fahlberg, page 13) When a child enters adoptive placement during the first year of life, there has not yet been the opportunity to learn to trust parental figures. The major task of learning to trust can be severely impaired if disruption through divorce occurs at this time.

For infants, the impact of divorce is indirect. What they feel is not their own distress but that of their parent. (Francke, page 48) If the parent responds to the infant with tense and distracted attention, the behavioral reaction may be one of becoming dull and unresponsive, or irritable and over-active. (Paul Henry Mussen, et al., page 176) Infants' play activities, for example the response to tickling or peek-a-boo games, can be negatively affected if the custodial parent is responding, as the result of the divorce, in either an angry or anxious way. Often the behaviors presented are compounded by not only the loss through divorce of one parent but also the need for the remaining parent to leave the infant in an alternate care situation in order to enter the job market. (Francke, page 49)

Divorce poses certain dangers for the adopted infant. Generally the infant "recognizes" his mother and father by the age of six months and responds to them individually. Disappearance of one of the newly-recognized parents from the infant's early life can constitute a serious first loss. Even though the infant continues to receive attention from the remaining parent, it should be reiterated that distraction, anger, and anxiety will produce a diminished sense of trust. (Francke, page 49)

Toddlers. The overriding task at ages 1 through 3 years is psychological separation from the mother and beginning development of self-confidence and self-esteem; the urge for autonomy becomes most visible between ages 12 and 30 months. Separations at this stage tend to have a strong impact on the development of the child's autonomy. Children who experience divorce at this age may have problems in developing appropriate balances between dependency and autonomy. The behavioral implications may include becoming very dependent and demonstrating clinging behavior, since these children do not trust that adults will be there when needed. The child insists on keeping adults constantly in sight and may become demanding or clinging. In reverse, some will become too autonomous and react by withholding affection or by being stubborn and resistant. Both kinds of reactions demonstrate a lack of trust; and, if not recognized, can persist for years. It is not uncommon to see 9- to 11-year-old children who are still constantly clinging or demonstrating extreme effects of autonomy in both school years and adolescence. (Vera Fahlberg, pages 27–28)

When separation from the person to whom he is most deeply attached occurs at the point when the child can think for himself, the impact of divorce is direct. It can usually be predicted that if the noncustodial parent "drops out of a child's life completely," the child will almost always look for him or her during adolescence. Children aged 18 to 24 months find the divorce experience particularly painful, especially boys. Old enough to feel vulnerable and beginning to identify with the father, a young boy affected by divorce is apt to feel unprotected. Boys of all ages suffer deeper reactions to divorce than girls, in part because 90% of the time it is the father who leaves the home situation, but also because of both inherent and learned behavior. (Francke, page 49) Francke notes that in comparison with girls, boys have been found to be more controlling, more mischievous, and more demanding, and will frequently experience more collisions with authority. Boys' noncompliance escalates with age and is intensified by the divorce experience. (E. Mavis Haetherington, page 41)

Preschoolers. The preschool years mark the birth of the child's conscience. Developmentally, the child's third through fifth years contain many elements that will reappear during adolescence. It is at this stage that both boys and girls are establishing the beginning of their sex role identitites, and new sexual identification includes a powerful love for the parent of the opposite sex. Divorce can have serious implications in five major presenting ways. These include regression, heightened aggression, pervasive neediness, low self-esteem, and the overuse of denial as a defense mechanism. A child's reaction to divorce at this stage will mirror the way that the adoptive parents are handling it. (Francke, pages 54–76)

Frequently, by observing children's verbalization during play, a parent or therapist can discover clues as to a child's misconceptions of the loss experience. Children who lose a parent through divorce will often tend to blame themselves for this event; this is because of their egocentricity and the magical thinking prominent at this developmental stage. (Fahlberg, pages 34–38)

For preschoolers, particularly boys, a constant and continued involvement with the father can do much to reassure him about his own budding masculinity and assuage his self-assumed guilt and fear of revenge for causing the father to leave. Although the pain of divorce may be felt more deeply at this stage than any other, the recovery time tends to be shorter. It will be helpful for parents to re-establish a sense of continuity and caring in the separate households that are created as a result of the divorce situation.

School-Age Children. Mixed feelings about divorce-created loss are common. Children can be helped by being told that such mixed feelings are normal. There is a capacity for the child to identify "the part of me that feels sad and the part of me that feels mad.'' (Fahlberg, p. 63) Because of the emphasis on fairness at this developmental stage, the child will spend considerable energy on ''why me'' or ''it's not fair;'' this may well impair the child's ability to resolve the loss. Without question, honesty with the child about the divorce circumstances is crucial at this time.

Coping with the divorce during the school ages can interfere with accomplishment of primary developmental tasks, including school performance and development of friendships with children of the same sex. (Fahlberg, p. 64) There can be temporary regressions to earlier developmental stages; the child may demonstrate less mature behavior, and there can also be interruption of normal progression of conscience development. Divorce during early latency can be cruel, for children may feel the pain as acutely as do younger children. Anger, fear, and betrayal in the post-divorce household, as well as a deep sense of deprivation, are characteristic responses for the school-age child. These reactions may well call for treatment, even though the developmental dangers are not usually as critical as with a child who experiences divorce at the preschool age level. Though school-age children are not as burdened as preschoolers by guilt for causing the divorce of the adoptive parents, they are apt to take the departure personally, feeling that the parent has actively left them. To handle such personal feelings, children will often invent elaborate stories to enable them to frequently see the departed parent. Clearly, parents' hostility towards each other will make school-age children's recovery from the divorce experience more problematic. (Francke, p. 79–82)

Reasons for the divorce need to be spelled out clearly for the school-age child so that blame of one or the other parent will be less likely. This is important since latency age children often relegate one or the other parent to the role of ''bad parent.'' Since this is often expressed in anger, therapy will need to address the anger and recognize it as a defense against feelings of shock and depression. (Francke, p. 104–110) According to Richard Gardner, a noted psychiatrist, it is important to give the child specific, concrete reasons for the divorce as opposed to less tangible ones. As noted in Kelly's and Wallerstein's study of children of these ages, none of them was found to feel happy about the divorce even in cases of chronic, violent conflict; children studied, without exception, wanted their parents to reunite.

Children in this age group who are victims of divorce often present for treatment with problems relative to inappropriate handling of anger. Therapists note that anger is often channeled into every aspect of these children's lives. All in all, both boys and girls at this age group do not take divorce ''sitting down.'' This is largely due to their higher energy and action levels at this age. For 9- to 12- year-olds, particularly girls, sexuality begins to complicate the problems of divorce. Usually, sexual issues relative to the divorce experience will need intervention in treatment.

Wallerstein and Kelly (p. 105) note that preoccupation with sexual issues on the part of the divorced adults can spill into the parent-child relationship. The boundaries between psychological repercussions experienced by the parent and the inappropriate involvement of the children frequently lose clarity at the time of divorce. Sexual worries, consequently, reach a new prominence at this time, generally reflecting the parental preoccupations of the same. Mothers will often present for therapy with fears that their daughters' sexuality will surface after sexual encounters they (the mothers) have had which have left them with feelings of anxiety.

Most latency-age children's extreme reactions to divorce will abate after about a year's time, except for the sexual tension. (Wallerstein & Kelly) Given the normal focus on morality at this developmental stage, and being on the fringes of adolescence, this group of children find clashes with their strict moral code and their single parent's new laissez-faire attitude toward sex. (Francke, p. 136) They cling to "sex is reserved for marriage" as a strong part of their belief system; they welcome this as an excuse to postpone their own sexuality. With the parent's sexual activity belying this belief, they are often threatened, emotionally. The conflict that will often need to be addressed in treatment with the "divorced child," then, is the reconciliation of balance between the normal significance of things being either good or bad/right or wrong, and their parent's earning of "wrong" behavioral labels.

Summarily, it is important to the treatment process for there to be a clear awareness of children's perceptions of their single parent's relationships. As Francke notes, the parent's flaunting of sexuality, the perhaps rapid turnover of partners and the parent's preoccupations with sex both in conversation and attitudinally may either encourage a child's premature, precocious sexuality or leave the child in disgust. (Francke, p. 137)

Reactions of latency-age children may manifest in ways such as:

- Intense jealousy of the parent's sexual behavior;
- Preoccupations with sexual thoughts and fantasies;
- Seductive dressing and flirtatious behavior toward significantly older males;
- Conflicts seated in the parent's solicitation (from the child) of advice regarding their relationships;
- Eagerness to grow up and become sexually active;
- Little impulse control coupled with vulnerability for hurt; or,
- Disdain for the parent's behavior, and a strong desire to delay normal movement toward development of own sexuality.

The child's presenting reactions will serve to guide the therapist's clinical interventions in the treatment process.

Adopted school-age children need support and reassurance to understand that their place in the new family structure remains even after divorce.

Without a sense of this security entering into adolescence will usually be either delayed or dangerously premature. (Francke, p. 139)

Adolescents. The developmental tasks of adolescence are both exaggerated and blurred by divorce. Adolescents' feelings of anger, sadness, embarrassment, betrayal, and shame may deepen as a result of divorce. Severe reactions can lead adolescents into very adult kinds of trouble, including alcohol and drug abuse, promiscuity, and over-aggressive behavior. (Francke, p 141–142) The divorce experience is apt to make adolescence more turbulent and stressful. Normal for this age group are heightened sexual tensions, significant emphasis on emotion, and vulnerability to dangers of the adult world. There may be exaggerated responses in these areas by the adolescent who experiences divorce while in adoption.

If the child has experienced a fairly stable time prior to entering adolescence, divorce will be upsetting but should not seriously disturb this less-developmental stage of childhood. Divorce can actually be a positive experience for many single parents and their adolescent children. The single-parent-adolescent relationship can be positive if criticism of the absent parent is avoided. (Francke, pp 167–168.)

Not surprisingly, teenage children of divorced parents often approach their own heterosexual relationships with trepidation. At this time they drastically need encouragement from the remaining parent to risk such commitments (Wallerstein and Kelly, p. 86.) Since major issues for adolescents normally revolve around separation, individuation, control, sexual issues, and relationships with family, parents can anticipate intensified reactions in these areas.

Adolescents' resiliency in overcoming the divorce experience should be a focal point in therapy. Focusing on the strengths that have been evident in the adoption situation prior to divorce will be critical to the child's recovery.

Treatment Strategies

In treating the child of adoption and divorce, and his family, treatment strategies should focus on the double loss the child has experienced. The adoption experience should not be overlooked in treating the more recent divorce loss. In addition, treatment should focus on helping the family stabilize those factors in the child's life which they can control, such as how the divorced parents communicate and cooperate, the parenting provided by the custodial parent, with the non-custodial parent, and the child's support system. All treatment must be focused at the child's age and developmental level.

The treatment modalities recommended here are a synthesis of successful interventions with adopted and divorced families. As in any therapeutic situation, some strategies will work with some families, while others are more successful in other family systems. It is our intent to offer a variety from which the therapist may select the most appropriate.

The treatment of choice with adopted families is family therapy. (Berman and Bufferd, p. 6) Family therapy focuses on the adoptive family as a unit. Many adoptive families, especially those who have adopted older children, do not yet identify themselves as a family unit. Family treatment can solidify this relationship. In addition, family sessions give the therapist important information about how the family has handled losses and how they communicate the acceptance of feelings about losses.

In family therapy, powerful messages are conveyed to the family in that events in the family's life are seen as complex interactions rather than events fraught with blame. The therapist models an interaction style which encourages sensitivity, support and insight rather than conflict, blame and guilt. (Hartman and Laird, p. 307)

Family therapy with divorcing families is much more difficult because the overriding issue may be the couple's communication and their ability to handle the continuing relationship in the intimacy of therapy. Several noted family therapists, including Carl Whitaker, often treat families where the divorce was finalized years before. Therefore, he often requires that stepmothers, stepfathers, and siblings be included in treatment. (Whitaker)

Richard Gardner also treats the entire family when possible. He too recognizes the difficulty of treating couples who are still very angry and unable to focus on the child's needs. He recommends that joint sessions with the parents, without the child, may be more successful until the parents can learn to communicate with less hostility. (Gardner, pp 3–11)

Gardner also believes that while family sessions are often needed, individual sessions with the child may be indicated. Gardner's example is a child with an extremely dependent relationship with his mother. Gardner's plan is to see the child individually and in regular joint sessions. In treating children under 12, Gardner often sees them with the custodial parent in the room as an observer. (Gardner, pp 47–55)

In our experience we have used a combination of these techniques. Whenever possible, family therapy with both parents is indicated. Several sessions with the parents alone are planned if there are problems in communication between the two parents. Once family sessions are initiated, they may be accomplished in several different ways.

It should be noted that families with more than one child, and all families with children over 12, are seen by a team of two therapists. We have found the team method to be effective in handling the myriad of issues the adoptive, divorced family faces. The team approach enables sessions to be split: each therapist sees part of the family, as well as the entire family and both therapists meet together as well. This method is helpful when several sessions have been held with the parents prior to the initiation of family therapy. In this way the child and the second therapist join the sessions at the same time and so are on equal footing.

Adopted adolescents are especially amenable to treatment using the team/split session approach. In this way the adolescent, in the split session, may be able to express his/her feelings of loss in regard to the birth parent and the divorce. The adolescent is then encouraged to discuss these topics in the family session.

Treatment of younger children may involve the use of life story books, with the therapist assisting the child in dealing with the double loss through a story process. The therapist gathers information from the parents about the child's adoption, his birth parents, the adoptive parents' history, and the story of their divorce as it has been presented to the child. The therapist then uses the split sessions with the child to assist him in writing the book if he is old enough or to write the book for him in his words if he cannot write. This life story will be different from the one developed for older children by their child welfare workers, for it will focus on the themes of loss and grief and utilize pictures the child draws describing the events.

Gardner uses a similar technique for younger children, called "mutual story telling," in which stories are elicited from the child to assist him in recognizing and dealing with his feelings. Gardner uses a tape recorder and asks the child to tell his story into the tape recorder. Then Gardner uses the basics from the child's story to create a story of his own in which there is a healthier or more mature resolution. (Gardner, pp 57–62)

Berman and Bufferd describe several techniques in family therapy which are appropriate for divorced, adoptive families. One of the most valuable is "reframing;" the redefinition of a problem so that it is seen as a positive. Basically there are two types of reframing: the first type is that the therapist takes a linear causal relationship and assists the family in gaining a more global understanding. An example given by Hartman is the husband with a sick wife. A linear causal view of this relationship is that the wife gets taken care of because she is ill. A more systematic view is that the husband needs someone to care for and the wife is ill, so they meet each others needs.

A second type of reframing is where a problem is seen as a solution to another problem; as a way to maintain a family or as a family tradition. (Hartman and Laird, pp 307–308).

This type of reframing can be examined with a case example of a family in the process of divorcing who are having difficulties with their 8-year-old. Sarah was adopted at eighteen months after a series of five foster homes. It is likely that she was abused in one of these homes. Nine months after Sarah joined the family, Tim was born into this family. The children are very different in their development, and temperments. Sarah is an aggressive, take charge child, who while bright, does have some learning difficulties. Tim, on the other hand, is an easy going, very affectionate little boy. While not as bright as Sarah, he doesn't have her learning problems, and has been more successful in school.

Jan and Joe, their parents have always found Sarah a challenge, but have been able to manage her and advocate for appropriate school programs for her. Recently, Jan and Joe separated, stating that Jan has fallen in love with someone else. Their plan is to divorce. Sarah has been very distressed by the separation. She is staying with her mother, but states that she wants to be with her father. She has become very verbally aggressive with Tim and is failing in school.

Family treatment was begun at Joe's insistence, because he feels that Jan is not handling Sarah appropriately. He states emphatically, that while he was not the one originally wanting the divorce, he wants it now and wants custody of the children because he can do a better job. He believes Jan is too tied up in her love affair to have time and emotional energy for the children.

In terms of Sarah's development, the separation has come at a very difficult time. She is dealing with her rejection by her birth parents, her difficulties with peers and her feeling that Tim is her parents' "real child." In order to boost her self esteem, to retreat from the blameful interactions around the separation and to assist the family in handling Sarah's behavior, reframing can be used.

It is good to point out that Sarah is a survivor, she survived 5 foster homes. In addition she lets people know when she is in trouble. These are similarities that she has to Jan who is also a take charge person. By taking problems and assisting the family to see them in a more positive light, Sarah and Jan can both be partially relieved of the blame and guilt they feel. In addition, the family can begin to look at other positive interactions. Thus, reframing is especially helpful with families where children are experiencing behavior problems.

Another useful technique, especially with adolescents or very resistant families, is "paradox." Paradox exists for the family when problematic behaviors are often essential for the family to function. In therapeutic paradox the therapist must assume that a problem in the family's functioning is necessary to the maintenance of the family. Next a reason for the problem is developed which includes the participation (actively or passively) of all family members. This theory is stated to the family and the family is cautioned not to change since change could bring about specific detrimental outcomes. Through this process, the therapist joins the family rather than attempting to confront their resistance to change.

An example of paradox in a divorcing family could be that the therapist cautions divorcing spouses from trying to cooperate with one another because this behavior (the hostility) gives them continued contact and if they were cooperating they might have to spend less time together fighting. In addition the children may contribute to keeping the hostility going because they want their parents to have contact with each other.

The last technique which Berman and Bufferd describe, which we have found very effective, is "circular questioning." Asking questions is the primary tool. Through questioning, rather than direct confrontation, the therapist can challenge current behavior and introduce new themes. This is especially helpful in dealing with the losses of adoption and divorce. Many families are very resistant to dealing with the feelings associated with their losses. Circular questioning can elicit information about how the losses have been handled while pointing out that the losses remain unresolved. (Berman, p. 8)

Finally, families need education about the effects of adoption and divorce on the family system and all of its members. While there are many excellent books on divorce, with Francke's, Wallerstein's and Kelly's being foremost, there exists little information about the effects of divorce on the adopted child. Because of this lack of information, the therapist plays a crucial role in presenting the issues related to adoption and divorce.

Summary

While adopted children whose parents divorce often experience more difficulties than nonadopted children, these difficulties can be overcome with treatment and with the cooperation of all adults involved in the child's life. For the therapist involved with these families, the central issue to recall is the loss the child experiences and the heightened sense of abandonment when the parents divorce. Therapy focusing on these issues, no matter which modality is chosen, can be effective in helping resolve these crises for the adopted child and his family.

References

Berman, Lauren C. and Bufferd, Rhea K. "Family Treatment to Address Loss in Adoptive Families." *Social Casework*, 67,1 (January, 1986), pp. 3–11.

Brodzinsky, David M., Singer, Leslie M. and Braff, Anne M. "Children's Understanding of Adoption." *Child Development*, 55 (1984), pp. 869–878.

Fahlberg, Vera. *Child Development*. Michigan Department of Social Services, 1982; London: British Agencies for Adoption and Fostering, May, 1982.

Francke, Linda Bird. *Growing Up Divorced.* New York: Fawcett Crest, 1983.

Gardner, Richard A. *Pyschotherapy with Children of Divorce.* New York: Jason Aronson, 1976.

Haetherington, E. Mavis. "Children and Divorce." in *Parent Child Interaction: Theory, Research and Prospects.* New York: Academic Press, 1981.

Hartman, Ann, and Laird, Joan. Family-Centered Social Work Practice. New York: The Free Press, 1983.

Jewett, Claudia L. *Helping Children Cope with Separation and Loss.* Harvard: The Harvard Common Press, 1982.

Jewett, Claudia L. *Adopting the Older Child.* Harvard: The Harvard Common Press, 1978.

Mussen, Paul Henry, Conger, J. J. and Kangan, J. *Child Development and Personality.* New York: Harper and Rowe, 1979.

Wallerstein, Judith S., and Kelly, Joan B. *Surviving the Breakup: How Children and Parents Cope with Divorce.* New York: Basic Books, 1980.

Wallerstein, Judith S., and Kelly, Joan B. "The Effects of Parental Divorce: Experiences of the Child in Later Latency," *American Journal of Orthopsychiatry,* 46 (No.2), April, 1976, pp. 256–69.

Whitaker, Carl. Presentation to the San Antonio Group Psychotherapy Society. Trinity University, San Antonio, Texas, January, 1986.

25

Fostering Understanding between Adolescents and Adoptive Parents through Group Experiences

Reuben Pannor, and Evelyn A. Nerlove

Requests for services for adolescent adopted children had come to Vista Del Mar Child-Care Service from adoptive parents, other adoption agencies, private therapists, and adopted adolescents who had asked if there were groups where they could meet and talk without their adoptive parents being present.

A review of the literature supported the need for such groups. An increasing number of articles have pointed out that some adopted children are particularly vulnerable to the stresses of adolescence [1; 2; 4; 5; 6]. Problems frequently seen include acting-out behavior and disorders, intense identity crises, and conflicts with the adoptive parents.[7]

Adoptive parents seem to be more anxious than natural parents and less capable of dealing with these stresses. Any unresolved conflicts they may have add to the child's sense of turmoil. Confronted with a reawakening of their infertility distress, the adoptive parents may have great difficulty accepting their child's emerging independence.

Adoptive parents need a better understanding of themselves in order to empathize with their child's position. The problem is compounded by the fact that adoptive parents tend to be 7 to 8 years older than the biological parents. They need support in recognizing their own role as the psychological parents. This role does not change just because of the adopted child's curiosity about his birth parents. The child's curiosity is healthy. Unfortunately, it is often construed by adoptive parents as an indication that they have failed in their role as parents, or as a sign of their child's lack of love for them.

Adoptive parents also need help in dealing with the birth parents, the forgotten or "hidden" parents around whom the adoptee and the adoptive parents weave fantasies.

For the adopted adolescents the problems may range from genealogical bewilderment to compulsive pregnancy, to the "roaming phenomenon" in which the adoptee is aimlessly seeking the fantasied "good 'real' parents," and finally to a need to make a physical contact with the biological relatives.[8]

Objectives of the Group

The need for the adolescents to meet without the presence of their parents was recognized. They could more easily express their curiosity about the birth parents, which in many cases they had suppressed because they sensed that it was threatening to the adoptive parents. They could talk about what being adopted meant to them. Meeting with other adopted children would mitigate the feeling of being different.

For the adoptive parents, the agency goal was to help them develop insights and self-awareness that would improve their way of relating to the children. Given the chance to ventilate and clarify their feelings, to see themselves as not unique, and to be supported by each other's understanding, they might gain relief from their anxiety. The agency hoped to help them understand the normal problems of identity formation that occur during adolescence, and to differentiate those problems attributable to adoption and those attributable to the teenager's normal efforts to separate himself from the parents and achieve ego identity. The parents' concerns about the possible opening of sealed records, the child's wish to search for the birth parents, and the effect on their relationship with their children could be discussed.

We hoped to improve communication between parents and adoptees, and to dispel the mystery that has built up around adoption.

The Makeup of the Group

The group was limited to eight families—those of five married couples and three single female parents. The husbands ranged in age from 45 to 53; the mothers from 40 to 52. There were 23 children, of whom 14 were adopted and nonrelated, one was adopted and related, and eight were born to the mothers. The adopted children who came to the group ranged in age from 12 to 19.

Some families said they came to the group to learn the special problems of the teen-age adopted child, especially those inherent in the sense of dual identity due to having two sets of parents. Others wanted help in handling problems of sibling rivalry, especially between natural and adopted children. All wanted to know more about the search for the natural parents and the effects of adoptees' reunions with natural parents.

Sessions with the Parents

Male and female therapists met weekly with the parents for the first 4 weeks. The female therapist met with the parents the next 4 weeks, while the male therapist met with the children. After a joint sesssion with parents and children, a summing-up session of the parents was held at their request.

The cotherapists agreed that one would act as a facilitator, smoothing the way for discussion, encouraging participation while making it the parents' responsibility to bring up problems. The facilitator was to create an atmosphere of warmth, honesty, and a probing for insights and self-awareness. The other therapist would at times act as a resource person, providing research data and relating his experience with reunions of birth parents, adoptees, and adoptive parents.

The tone set enabled the group to engage immediately in lively discussion. At some meetings the focus was on a particular couple and their concerns, all members presented opinions, suggestions and often astute insights. General topics such as discipline and the effect on childrearing of today's society were related to the parents' own problems. Specific problems related to adoption were discussed at every session.

From the outset the parents were intelligent, articulate, earnest and anxious about their situations. The women's need to be "perfect" mothers was clear. Two of the women had not borne a living child; they seemed the most distressed, and had the greatest need to be "perfect."

All the parents appeared aware that the adopted children were subject to pressures and emotions that already complicated their lives, and could bring even greater problems in the future.

One woman who had not been able to give birth to a child had a history of psychiatric problems. In previous groups with one of the therapists she had been nonparticipating. In these sessions, however, she was alert and responsive. Another mother was deeply disappointed in herself, and at the first meeting referred to herself as "barren." The word set up a wave of shock, resentment, dismay and sympathy for her. Several in the group rebuked her for using the word. The supportiveness of the group and its "mothering" function were important to both these women.

Discussion was about evenly divided between problems of adoption and everyday problems of rearing children and handling problems of adolescence. There was intense interest in the experiences of adoptees, birth parents and adoptive parents in reunions, and in the possible effects upon themselves and their children of opening the sealed adoption records.

One mother expressed concern that her adopted son would find his birth mother and prefer her over his adoptive mother. This was a fear of many of the mothers. A description by one therapist of the results of numerous reunions proved reassuring to the group. The therapist told them: "Adoptees are not looking for mothers or fathers. They already have them in their adoptive parents. They are the only real parents they have known. They are looking for more knowledge about themselves and their origins."

Helping adoptive parents to detach themselves emotionally from their child's interest in his origins enables them to be more accepting of the adoptee as a person with his own needs.

As the groups continued to meet, changes in attitudes about adoption took place. Laqueur writes about this process:

"We found that when several families are brought together in a group with a therapist, (they) learn from each other indirectly, through analogy, indirect interpretation, mimicking, and identification. They observe what happens to others and apply part of that knowledge painlessly to their own case, or at least with less stress than direct interpretation would entail. They see themselves as in a mirror in an atmosphere that is more permissive than is the case when only one family is the center of attention at all times."[3]

The following remarks were made by one of the adoptive fathers after some parents said they felt threatened by the possibility that their child might try to search for the birth parents and prefer the birth parents to themselves:

> I am almost hearing that children are chattel, and they are not. My relationship with the kids has been established by the fact that I have been with my adopted daughter for 13 years. I don't know that her relationship to her friends or anybody else particularly affects her relationship with me. This is well established. I am not afraid. Eventually she is going to get out and live her own life. But she does have another set of parents. That is a fact, and it concerns her. Since it does, I want her to find out as much as she can about it and I'll help her do it.

The quieting effect upon the group of these remarks was almost palpable. Heads nodding in agreement, the group became aware of a new way of looking at a situation that disturbed them.

Sessions with the Adolescent Adopted Children

Thirteen adolescent adopted children—four girls and nine boys—met weekly for four sessions.

Topics discussed included teen problems, parent-child problems, how to prevent pregnancy, and problems related to adoption. The therapist attempted to bring out troubled feelings about adoption that the children had not been able to express within their families or other natural groups.

The concerns expressed revealed areas not dealt with satisfactorily at home. In some instances, communication had been blocked. The children had sensed that raising certain questions threatened or embarrassed the parents either because they aroused feelings the parents were unable to handle, or because the parents simply were not prepared to deal with the questions. Some adoption agencies themselves have failed to recognize these issues and to prepare parents to deal with them.

In other instances the children had not been able to talk about issues that were too painful for them. When they realized that they were not unique in this, they burst out of their reticence. They shared their pain, revealing their anger, their uncertainty, their sorrow.

Chief among the questions asked repeatedly by nearly all of the children was:

Why was I given up for adoption?

A 17-year-old said, "Since they gave me away, they probably wouldn't want to see me again. I don't think they are really interested in me." Another had seen the television program "A Stranger That Looks Like Me," and said, "I think that's just what would happen. In this TV movie, this girl was adopted and she found out where they lived. She went to her parents' house and her mother said, 'Hey, get lost; we don't want you; we don't need you.' I wouldn't want that to happen to me." Another youngster said, "I was placed for adoption because they didn't want me to start with. They had other children. The father had children from another marriage-so did the mother. They had a business that went down the drain. They didn't have enough money to support me, so they put me up for adoption." Another youngster said, "We were adopted by parents who wanted us and there is no reason to bother them (the birth parents) because they didn't want us in the first place."

It became clear that this issue had had not been dealt with satisfactorily and that a strong feeling of rejection by their birth parents remained.

What were they like? What did they look like? What happened to them?

These questions were also raised by every member of the group. When asked, "What would you like to know about your birth parents?" one adoptee said: "Are they still alive? If something happened to them, would I be told? I would also like to know if they started a new family." Another youngster said, "I would like to know what my birth parents looked like, their ages, and whether they have any diseases that are inherited, like cancer."

One group member said she had pictures of her birth parents. The entire group responded with envy, and said they wished they, too could see what their birth parents looked like. All members of the group wanted to know more about their birth parents.

Why do people give children up for adoption?

One girl in the group answered this by saying she knew a 14-year-old who had had a baby and that the baby was "taken away from her." She then told of another situation where a girl was taken to "a home" and "wasn't permitted" to see the baby. Another group member told of a girl who was going to have a baby, but who would keep it.

The group leader asked the girls how they thought a 14-year-old could keep a baby. Most of the group offered suggestions. "Her family could help." "The father could help." "She could get help from welfare." The idea of "giving the baby away" was not favored. The group agreed, though, that at age 14 it would be difficult to keep a baby.

It became clear that the group was not sympathetic to mothers who gave up babies for adoption. This revealed their own feelings about having been given up for adoption.

How is Pregnancy Prevented?

One teenager mentioned a 14-year-old girl who, trying to rear her baby, neglected the child and gave it beer. All agreed she should not have had the baby. This led to a discussion of how to prevent pregnancy. There was some uneasiness in this discussion, although the group was receptive to suggestions from the leader, and some group members proved knowledgeable about contraception, abortion and venereal disease. All agreed that knowledge about contraception was desirable, and that more honest and accurate information should be available to them at home and in school.

Were they satisfied with the information about their adoption given to them by their parents?

To this question, one youngster responded: "What is the point of asking them anything when they won't tell you? They think we are too immature."

Two members of the group said they were satisfied with what their parents had told them; the others said they were not. Asked if they could question their parents further, one said, "My mother told me that my biological mother loved me very much and wanted a family for me, and therefore gave me up for adoption." The others said much the same story was told to them.

It was obvious that the adolescents sensed that to ask about their background was threatening, and therefore, they did not pursue the matter with their adoptive parents. It was also clear that they were curious, and in need of more information about their biological parents.

Are you interested in finding your biological parents?

Several indicated concern about whether the birth parents would want to see them. They related this to the feelings of rejection involved in adoption.

One said, "If they did not want me then, why would they want to see me now?"

One youngster said he would like to meet his biological parents, to find out what they looked like and whether they had other children. When asked if he thought this would change his feelings toward his adoptive parents, he said: "I wouldn't feel any differently. My parents are my parents. I love them. I'm not going to leave them for my 'real' parents. To me, the people who raised me are my real parents." The leader suggested that he might want to share this feeling with his adoptive parents.

One youngster said that it might be too late for him to look for his parents because they could be dead and it would be a waste of time to be searching. When one youngster suggested that the birth mother who gave him up might want to block this from her mind, a girl responded: "How could she block it out of her mind? She will always remember it on your birthday."

At the end of the fourth session, the children and adoptive parents joined in a multifamily meeting. To the surprise of the parents, the children were able to raise serious questions with them about adoptions, and to make statements that were forthright and supportive. It was obvious that an atmosphere for more open and honest communication had been created.

Conclusions

In the summing-up session with the parents, they expressed enthusiasm about the program. Typical comments were: "The meetings lifted a big load off our backs;" "A lot has changed;" "We feel freer about adoption;" "We can talk about it now;" "Our children have changed and we have changed toward each other...our relationship is better...we have a different attitude toward them."

The parents were surprised at things the children were able to talk about. "There was a veil between us-now it is gone. Maybe getting together in a group by themselves they could talk about things that they couldn't talk about before." One mother whose child had been obsessed by his wish to find the birth parents said, "Steve is calmer now; finding them doesn't seem as important to him any more."

Some parents reported that as a result of the meetings their children had shared with them some of their fantasies about birth parents. The parents were more comfortable now about telling the adopted children about their backgrounds. The parents said they felt less threatened by the birth parents.

This short-term, educative group experience, focused on the specific problem of the vulnerability of adoptive families during the adolescence of adoptees, proved helpful to both the adoptive parents and the youngsters.

References

1. Kirk, David. *Shared Fate*. New York: Free Press, 1964.
2. Kirk, David, Jonasson, K., and Fish, A. D. "Are Adopted Children Especially Vulnerable to Stress?," *Archives of General Psychiatry*, XIV (September 1966).
3. Laqueur, H. P. "Mechanisms of Change in Multiple Family Therapy," in *Progress in Group and Family Therapy*, edited by C. Sager and H. Kaplan. New York: Brunner/Mazel, 1972.
4. Lewis, Dora, et al. "The Treatment of Adopted Versus Neglected Delinquent Children in the Court: A Problem of Reciprocal Attachment?," *American Journal of Psychiatry*, CXXXII (November 1975).
5. Schecter, Marshall. "Observations on Adopted Children," *Archives of General Psychiatry*, III (1960).
6. Smith, Evelyn, editor. *Readings in Adoption*. New York: Philosophical Library, 1963.
7. Sorosky, Arthur, Baran, Annette, and Pannor, Reuben. "The Effects of the Sealed Record in Adoptions," *American Journal of Psychiatry*, CXXXIII (August 1976).
8. .... "The Reunion of Adoptees and Birth Relatives," *Journal of Youth and Adolescence*, III (March 1974).

26

Identity Crisis among Adolescent Adoptees: Narcissus Revisited

Alvin L. Sallee, and Elaine S. LeVine

Adolescence is commonly viewed as a particularly trying time for adoptees and their parents. Surprisingly, however, there is little research to support this contention, and there are some practitioners who feel that there is really no difference between adoptees and biological children during adolescence. Goldstein, Freud and Solnit in 1979 wrote, ''Blood lines carry no weight with children who are emotionally unaware of the events leading to their birth'' (p. 12–13). Kadushin, on the other hand (1980, p. 487), writes, ''The adopted child faces all the general problems of development encountered by his nonadopted peers. In this sense, he is a child among other children. But, in addition, like the adopted parent, he faces some special problems that are related to the fact that he is an adopted child.''

Our experience with adoptive families and a review of the literature lead us to believe that adoptive parents and adoptive children do have a more difficult adjustment during adolescence than do biological children. This difficulty is centered primarily around resolving the identity-versus-role-confusion conflict with which most adolescents contend. This paper attempts to develop a theoretical model for viewing adopted adolescents by: 1) analyzing the research on adolescent adjustment among adoptees and adolescents in general; 2) identifying the sources of pressure that are unique to adopted adolescents, through a new application of ego analytic theory; and 3) positing some strategies to minimize stress created by the identity crisis among adoptees.

Before presenting our model, however, we wish to present our assumptions about the critical issue of the relative impact of biology and environment upon a developing child. Many times, adoptees and their parents raise the issue of genetically-caused versus socially-determined aspects of growth and development. Recent research conducted in Great Britain, concerning obesity, compared the weight gain of adopted children as opposed to biological children. The preliminary research indicates that genetics may play a relatively large role in the development of obesity. Of course, it is premature to generalize these initial findings to social and psychological development. Yet there is a dearth of literature which attempts to determine whether adoptees' overall psychosocial development is primarily determined by genetics or parenting. Therefore, based upon preliminary empirical research, theoretical writings, and our clinical work, we assume the position that behavior is multidetermined and that the interweaving of genetics and socialization determines the adoptees' development.

The theoretical argument presented in this paper concerning this basis of the adolescent crisis among adoptees is based upon the assumption that the behavior of these adolescents is determined by the interaction of their genetic predispostion, developmental needs and urges, and early life experiences. First, we present a review of the literature which attempts to define the nature of the adolescent crisis among adoptees. Then our model, based upon a biological/social view of etiology, is examined.

Adoptees' Adjustment

Although the feelings of adopted children towards their adoptions have not been systematically investigated, a number of studies have compared the overt adjustment of adopted and nonadopted children. Historically, such studies were ill-designed, often lacking controls, and replete with the writers' biases. Thus, in reviewing the studies of the adjustment patterns of adopted children, Lawton and Gross (1964) reported such inconsistency in methodology between studies that conclusions about adjustment among adopted children could not be reached.

More recently, some well designed studies do indicate special adjustment concerns among the adopted. Some of these studies evaluate the success of adoptive placements and define outcomes ranging from "capable and satisfactory" to "removed and experiencing adjustment problems." Kadushin (1980) cites 20 major agency and nonagency adoption outcome studies from 1924 through 1980. Based upon the referral of adoptive children to mental health services, 72% of the placements were successful, 16% of the children were labeled as having intermediate success, and 12% had very poor adjustments and were unsuccessful. These studies address family characteristics which create stress if the adoptive parents are older, if the marital interaction is characterized by strife, and if the adoptive child is an only child. The acceptance of adoption also impacts upon the effectiveness of the placement.

What is clear from the literature is that adoptees face some unique social pressures by virtue of their adopted status. First, the process of parent-and-child bonding is unique for the adopted. For many adopted adolescents, significant time elapsed between their birth and placement in an adoptive home. This elapsed time can disrupt the natural sequence of bonding and the development of basic trust and security. With the increasing number of placements of older children, the issue of bonding and later adjustment of the adolescent is becoming one of increased concern.

Adopted children are always faced with the possibility of a disruption (removal of the adopted child from the home) of their new family. Based upon his analysis of nine major studies related to failed adoptive placement, Kadushin (1980) concludes that for all adoptions, the disruption rate is 3.1%. These studies were conducted between 1955 and 1970, a period when most placements were made for infants and not for special needs children. With the signing of Public Law, 96–272, the Child Welfare and Adoption Assistance Act of 1980, states and agencies are placing more older and handicapped children in adoptive homes. These children are more likely to encounter a disruption.

Spaulding for Children, a highly publicized placement agency of special needs children, completed between 1968 and 1976 a study of 199 older, handicapped children. The disruption rate was 10.6% (Unger, Dwarshuis, Johnson, 1977). Many agencies expect disruption rates for special needs children to run approximately 12%. A United States and Canadian study of placement success of 735 developmentally disabled children found a disruption rate of only 8.7%. If the child was adopted by foster parents the disruption rate was only 4.4%, while the new-family adoption rate was 10%. Age was found to be an important variable for disruption rates as well. Developmentally-disabled children under the age of 7 had a low (3.3%) disruption rate; however, children 8 years and over showed a high disruption rate of 17.7% (Coyne & Brown, 1985).

It is estimated that only about 1% of all children in the United States are nonrelative adoptees; however, research indicates that 4.6% of the children in psychiatric facilities are adoptees (Kadushin, 1980). These data are particularly interesting in light of Schechter's (1964) study which examined the tendency of adoptive parents to use pediatric clinics. Schechter (1964) concluded that adoptive parents did not frequent pediatric clinics more than biological parents. Therefore, if adoptive parents use agencies at the same level as biological parents, the 4.6% use of psychiatric facilities may reflect a high frequency of adjustment problems among adoptive children.

Several well designed studies point to greater maladjustment of adopted than nonadopted children. Bohman (1972) systematically sampled 168 adopted children in Stockholm, Sweden. He studied the children's school records, interviewed all parents, and talked with all but five of the teachers.

No difference was reported in academic performance between the adopted and nonadopted boys and girls. However, 22% of the adopted boys versus 12% of the nonadopted boys were reported to display significant behavioral problems. A similar, nonsignificant statistical trend was noted between the adopted and nonadopted girls.

A study by Weiss (1984) compared the parent/child relationship of adoptive and nonadoptive adolescents receiving treatment in a Philadelphia psychiatric hospital. Data were collected through review of the medical records of 140 youth between the years of 1970 and 1979. The adoptive parents were more restricted in their visits with their adopted children than were parents of natural children. Furthermore, the adopted teenagers were more likely to be hospitalized for serious psychopathology than the teenagers of natural parents who were typically diagnosed with less serious disturbance.

A parent may be secretive about the child's adoption. The child may then feel he or she is an embarrassment to the family. A classic study shows that telling the child as early as he or she is developmentally capable of understanding about the adoption minimizes this risk (Mech, 1973). Yet some theorists believe the move to open adoptions may be detrimental to the child because the biological parent may then have an impact on the child's environment (Kraft, Palombo, Mitchell, Woods, Schmidt, & Tucker, 1985).

Parents may overestimate the child's ability to understand the adoption process and confuse the child with early discussions of adoption (Brodzinsky, Pappas, Singer, & Braff, 1981; Brodzinsky, Singer, & Braff, 1984). Brodzinsky employed open-ended interviews with adoptive and nonadoptive children in grades 1,3,5,7,9, and 11. The children were interviewed about their knowledge of adoption. Responses were organized into "levels" of understanding the complex adoption process. Children in the first grade could usually differentiate between birth and adoption but had only a vague awareness of a third party serving as an intermediary in the process. Not until children reached the upper elementary years did a majority recognize the role an agency played in the adoption process to assure the mutual rights, needs, and welfare of children and their parents (Brodzinsky, Singer, & Braff, 1981). Therefore, early telling may be important to diminish anxiety and mystique concerning adoption, but the discussion must be tailored to the child's cognitive development.

The research demonstrates the complexity of adoption and the difficulty of assessing the impact the adoption process has on a given child. For example, adopted boys and special needs children are subject to more adjustment problems than adoptive girls or their nonadoptive peers. But the research is inconclusive on the impact of other variables such as age of parent, socioeconomic status, income, etc. Yet the important question from our perspective is "success of adoption," at what emotional and developmental cost to the child. Besides the fact that adopted children have a much higher representation as clients in mental health services, we have little research to guide treatment.

In summary, the adopted adolescent faces some unique strains by virtue of his or her adopted status. There are unique pressures in bonding to parents with whom one does not share biological traits. Bonding and related issues seem to lead to unique adjustment difficulties among some adoptive adolescents, including disruption of the adoption and increased academic and emotional difficulties.

Normal Development Issues

In order to understand the unique adjustment problems of adopted adolescents, it is important to consider the typical stresses of adolescents. The emotional state of many adolescents is well exemplified by the Greek myth concerning Narcissus. Narcissus was a youth of incredible beauty who fell in love with his own image reflected in a pool of water. Because he could never grasp this image, he eventually pined away. The gods, feeling sorry for him, named a fragile flower "narcissus" in his honor, to remind all of his futile search for ultimate beauty. Narcissus was misguided in his efforts because he had not recognized that energy invested totally in oneself does not lead to more enduring meanings. The story of Narcissus, in a symbolic sense, parallels many of the struggles of the typical adolescent. During adolescence, dramatic physical, social, and psychological changes lead to enhanced power which the teenager must harness for his or her own good and for others' betterment. As outlined below, changes in any developmental dimension may lead to excessive, nonproductive self-preoccupation. This may be a major challenge for the teenager and his or her parents to resolve.

Rapid changes in physical growth can cause stress for many adolescents. Their coordination may be awkward as their extremities grow in rapid spurts, and they may become self-conscious regarding this awkwardness. Too, adolescence is a time of rapid development of secondary sexual characteristics. Most teenagers are enthralled by their new beards, low voices, and shapely figures; but, for some, these changes occur so rapidly that difficulty is experienced in integrating them with their concepts of their "ideal" physical selves. Some teenagers are intimidated by the foreboding of responsibilities that their new mature looks imply. Their emerging sexual awareness is exciting, but many teenagers are awed by the powerful forces within them which they feel they cannot control. As a consequence, some teenagers appear totally absorbed by the other sex, while others seem totally concerned with avoiding sexual encounters. In sum, most teenagers are preoccupied with their physical selves. They spend many hours preening in front of mirrors, and the majority are extremely self-conscious about their appearances.

Teenagers also must address new changes in regard to the social dimensions of their lives. Adolescence is a time in which society begins to demand of young people that they assess their roles in society and begin to consider what careers they will choose. Yet, in our technological society, there are limited employment opportunities and few avenues for expression of their competencies. Many adolescents feel that they cannot contribute meaningfully to society. Although it appears they are always busy, they complain of being bored, for they feel that their many activities lack meaning. Like Narcissus, they become preoccupied with themselves as a way of seeking redress for their frustrations.

Compounding these difficulties on the physical and social level, adolescents encounter tremendous psychological changes. The development of their cognitive abilities begins to stabilize their identities, deepen their interests, expand their caring, and humanize their values. However, these cognitive feats are not accomplished without effort. Their emotions soar to elation with each new awareness and mastery, but their feelings are as likely to sink to despair if they do not achieve their goals. They can talk endlessly about their thoughts and ideas as if they were rediscovering the meaning of the world without any reference to the masters of the centuries. On the other hand, sometimes they may not discuss issues with their parents and others whom they view as authority figures because they are so sensitive to criticism. Teenagers may speak on the phone for hours on matters that seem trivial to adults; but, in fact, these discussions are a critical way of their identifying their personal meanings in life. For the adolescent who is undertaking this personal search, other responsibilities, such as school work, doing chores, feeding pets, and taking care of younger siblings pale in comparison.

In sum, the identity crisis of the typical teenager is a time of intense sensitivity, emerging power and awareness, and much narcissism. Again, by narcissism we mean gratification for, contemplation of, and preoccupation with the self. To some degree we can view narcissism as a reenactment on a sophisticated level of the narcissistic behavior of the newborn, as will be explained in a later section of this paper.

Development of Adopted Adolescent

All adoptees who reach adolescence encounter the struggles we have just outlined. However, for many of them, there is a special fervor in their search for identity, a magnification of the typical adolescent narcissism.

According to the Diagnostic and Statistical Manual III (American Psychiatric Association, 1980), the narcissistic personality can be identified by five primary traits. First of all, narcissistic adolescents focus on their own self-importance, at times to grandiose proportions. They exaggerate their talents and their achievements as well as their needs and problems. Secondly, they may be characterized by a constant need for attention, preferring positive attention but settling for negative attention rather than none at all. The need for approval or admiration cannot seem to be quelled. Thirdly, their emotions swing to extreme proportions so that they often seem isolated and difficult to reach. At one moment they may express a cold indifference: at the next moment a feeling of rage, inferiority, shame, humiliation, or emptiness. These swings may be prompted by relatively minor events, since even a minor correction may be perceived as an attack. Fourthly, they may express feelings of entitlement—that is, the expectation of special favors without assuming reciprocal responsibility. Surprise and anger may follow when people do not do what they want or expect. Finally, interpersonal exploitation may become pronounced, so that they seem to be concerned with others only to meet their own advantage. They may try to indulge their desires by rejecting empathy and expressing an unwillingness or inability to recognize what others feel. Other people, especially parents, tend to be seen in absolute terms that alternate between over-idealization and devaluation.

Masterson (1981), a national expert on narcissistic disorders, adds that among the overly narcissistic youth we often see the expectation of "perfect mirroring." Narcissistic adolescents assume that the parents will understand exactly how they feel at all times. They expect their parents never to hurt their feelings. The study by Brodzinsky (1981) cited earlier stressed that many adopted adolescents become preoccupied with fantasies of finding their biological parents. What they may be seeking in their search for the natural parents is the "perfect mirror," the feeling of being perfectly understood by a person who will never hurt their feelings.

All of these characteristics may bring the families of adoptive teenagers to seek special clinical assistance. It is not that the parents view their teenagers' behavior as bizarre, but that the parents find it most difficult to communicate and relate to their teenagers.

Etiology of Adoptees' Narcissism

While narcissistic behaviors may be seen in all teenagers, the additional stresses which accompany adoption may lead the adoptee to more difficulties than nonadoptees. We propose that the etiology is twofold: 1) a disruption in the normal bonding process and 2) a disruption of a healthy identity formation.

Disruption of Normal Bonding.

The ego analytic literature (Mahler, 1968) espouses the concept that children are born in an almost totally narcissistic state. Their existence centers on meeting their needs for comfort, for control, and for physical nutrients. When the newborn child's needs for nutrients are met, he or she begins to bond to the individual meeting these needs. Newborns quickly learn to reciprocate what is shared with them by offering their caretakers their most prized gifts—their smiles, coos and cuddles. In other words, they offer themselves. In time, the narcissistic and egocentric newborn is a social being who revels in mutuality with the caretaker. When this symbiosis of giving and receiving satisfies both the baby and caretaker, the baby gradually develops a sense of security. By age two, the child is an autonomous individual with a healthy sense of investment in self (narcissism) and in others. If the process of bonding and attachment followed by gradual separation is disrupted, the movement from total narcissism to healthy narcissism combined with mutuality is impeded.

A number of factors make the probability of disrupted bonding more likely among the adopted than the nonadopted child. As mentioned earlier, most adopted children are not available for adoption immediately after birth. There may be a few weeks to many years of interim caretaking before the child is adopted. Moreover, there is an emerging body of literature suggesting that attachment may occur even before the birth of the child. For example, it has been noted that the newborn may track the mother's and father's voices more than those of other adults. (Fagan, 1971; Thomas & Chess, 1980). According to the tenets of ego analytic theory, a disruption after a few weeks of life can be enough to block or impede the normal attachment processes.

Secondly, in examining why there may be greater propensity for bonding disruption among adopted than nonadopted children, there is emerging research which suggests that an essential part of bonding is congruence between the primary caretaker's temperament and the child's temperament. Thomas and Chess (1980) state that if there is an incongruence of temperament between biological parents and child, the potential for bonding difficulties increases. For example, a hyperactive child and an anxious mother are likely to experience problems in relating to each other; while an anxious mother and a calm child, or a calm mother and a hyperactive child, have less potential for bonding conflict. It seems possible that the potential for bonding conflict due to temperament clashes may be exacerbated when children are placed with adoptive families because in adopted homes there is less genetic material in common and therefore a greater possibility of genetic/temperament incompatibility.

The theoretical material concerning bonding provides a background for understanding the critical issue at hand—the narcissistic problem of the adopted adolescent. We suggest that the developmental issues of adolescence prompt a return among all teenagers to an earlier narcissistic state. Once again, but in more sophisticated fashion, the teenager must learn to make meaningful commitment to self and others. If there were early conflicts in bonding and concomitant difficulty in managing narcissistic energy, adolescence prompts an exaggeration of the narcissistic state and an inability to transform the narcissism into more profound relationships.

Disruption of Identity Formation.

The disruption in identity formation is a second factor that may spur adjustment difficulties among adopted adolescents. Their adjustment difficulties may reflect their desire for an identity in the world. In part, teenagers' identities are formulated by identification with parents and by juxtaposing themselves to their roots. Young adolescents see themselves as links in their biological families' genealogical chains. However, most adopted adolescents know little or nothing about their biological parents or about their roots. Frisk (1964) stated that the adoptee's "genetic ego" is replaced by a "hereditary ghost." In the case of transcultural adoptions, a "cultural ghost" may also complicate healthy identity development. This frustration in forming their identities leads to "interference" that can escalate to major behavioral problems such as acting out against teachers, parents, and other adult authorities.

The identity crisis of adolescence can stimulate specific concerns regarding the biological family. Healthy children learn to accept their parents as both loving and rejecting; however, adopted children have two sets of parents. The adopted adolescent, with renewed interest about his or her biological family, may discriminate these sets of parents along the lines of "loving" and "rejecting." The adolescent may envision that one set of parents assumes all the negative parental attributes while the other set assumes all the positive ones. Adoptees often idealize the unknown biological parent. Yet, at some level, the adoptee knows that these are the parents who gave the child up for adoption. The fragmentation in perception of the biological and adoptive parents can be a large impediment to developing a sense of identity built upon acceptance and association with both one's biological and one's adoptive roots.

Strategies to Minimize Stress

What can we as professionals and parents do to minimize these problems? First, some social strategies will be addressed and then some psychological strategies will be presented.

Social Strategies.

A major issue is how parents and others should present and discuss the teenager's adopted status. McWhinnie (1967) interviewed adoptive adults concerning their feelings as teenagers. These adoptive adults agreed that they did not want their adoptive status shrouded in secrecy. However, they did not want constant reference made to it. They wanted an ambiance in which their adopted status was acknowledged without embarrassment and then somewhat "forgotten" so that they were treated exactly as if they were biological sons and daughters. They were emphatic that they did not want to be introduced as adopted children. They wanted to belong to a family in which they were fully accepted as sons or daughters.

Beginning with Mech's work in 1967 (Mech, 1973), theorists have urged parents to tell children at a young age about their adoption. As discussed previously, this early telling must be tempered by an understanding of what a child can comprehend (Brodzinsky, et al.,1981).

Emerging literature suggests that during early adulthood, records should be completely opened to the adoptee. Adopted adults' painful stories recount their search and, usually, their successful reunion with the biological parents. These stories help document that healthy identity formulation is best served by open records.

These open records may be a critical key to establishing roots beyond the adoptive family. The more adopted children know of their past, the more that past is demystified. Demystifying the past helps prevent the children from creating false fantasies regarding their biological parents, such as seeing the biological parents as all good and all knowing and the adoptive parents as "negative." Open records can help counter the child's feeling of being different or of "bad blood." Of course, adoptive parents must always be prepared to deal with the child's feelings of rejection by the biological parents. A positive yet realistic knowledge about the biological parents can help obviate feelings that the biological parents actively rejected the child.

Another social strategy for minimizing stress among adopted adolescents centers around the parents' interaction with teachers, social workers, friends, etc. The parents of an adoptee can help other adults to become sensitive to the adoptee's feelings regarding his or her struggle for identity. Significant others in the adoptee's life should be made aware of the tremendous personal struggles that the adopted adolescent may experience. Of course, care must be taken not to create a self-fulfilling prophesy by leading others to expect and inadvertently stimulate problems among adopted adolescents.

One method of alleviating or at least reducing adoptees' feelings of being different and isolated is the use of peer-group sessions led by professionals knowledgeable about concerns of the adopted. In these groups, issues of identity formation, the lack of biological roots, and the labeling of adoptive children by other children can be explored. At the same time, adopted children can gain emotional support by discovering that their feelings are shared with approximately half a million other people in the United States. In an informal manner, adoptive family organizations and social functions also communicate the message that adoption is not unusual and that having special concerns about being adopted is to be expected.

Strategies must be developed for changing social policies, laws, and regulations regarding the adoption process. In particular, dealing with adoptive families, public and private agencies must come to grips with a crucial issue: Who is the client? Is the client the adult who cannot have children? Is the client the abusive parent who cannot provide a safe environment for the child? Is the client the social worker, the doctor, the attorney? Is the client the unmarried girl who cannot raise her baby? Or is it the child who seeks a new permanent legal home where he or she can grow to full potential. If the client is indeed the adoptive child, then, based upon the premises proposed in this paper, the policy question of whether records should be opened is clearly answered.

Psychological Strategies.

The strategies for dealing with the psychological problems of the adopted adolescent are based upon two premises. First, the adopted adolescent may have special concerns by virtue of his or her being adopted. Second, adopted children often need help to work through earlier unmet needs and to channel their narcissistic energy properly.

In accord with these assumptions, it is important to maintain firmness and control. Often, the families we have worked with have found it helpful to maintain a routine with structured tasks for their troubled adopted adolescents. Achieving this goal is a delicate operation for parents and social service personnel, because most adolescents resent and resist firmness and control, particularly if they are highly self-preoccupied. However, this approach is necessary to move the distressed, adopted adolescents from extreme self-absorption. Significant others need to encourage and shape empathic, giving behaviors. Discipline is a way of saying to the adopted adolescent that he or she is expected to cooperate and help others. Firmness and control combined with cooperative behavior can bring an adoptive adolescent out of his or her self-centeredness. After some time, he or she will begin to feel reinforcement from being more cooperative with others. Of course, the firmness must be provided without being critical of the teenager. Adolescents who are overly preoccupied with themselves and overcome with self-doubts find any criticism deeply attacking. They are then likely to reject others' messages completely.

It is also important to help adopted adolescents talk about themselves.

Parents and other significant adults must monitor their lecturing and assure that the teenagers have the opportunity to present their viewpoints, particularly concerning their adoption. In fact, any self-expression should be encouraged. As the adolescent expresses himself or herself, the isolation and self-preoccupation is diminished.

Finally, individual and/or family counseling can be helpful in assisting the troubled adopted adolescent to understand the sources of his or her distress. The adolescent can better handle the felt distress when the special strains he or she has encountered are made clear.

Summary

In summary, the task of forging an identity presents critical challenges to most adolescents and their families. In one way or another, every adolescent asks the questions, "Will I make it in the world as a worthwhile, individual?" and "Will my life have some meaning?" Adopted adolescents' resolution of these questions is rendered more difficult if they have experienced bonding disruption and/or if they have not reconciled feelings about their adoption and connections with their biological and adopted parents. It is a major challenge to transform the energy of the identity crisis of troubled adopted adolescent into constructive, prosocial behavior. The unique struggles of the adopted adolescent are captured well by the words of Herman Melville (1851, p.64) in Moby Dick (see Bartlett, 1980): "And still deeper the meaning of that story of Narcissus, who because he could not grasp the tormenting, mild image he saw in the fountain, plunged into it and was drowned. But that same image, we ourselves see in all rivers and oceans. It is the image of the ungraspable phantom of life; and this is the key to it all."

References

American Psychiatric Association (1980). *Diagnostic and statistical manual of disorders*. Washington, D.C. Author.

Bartlett, J. *Bartlett's familiar quotations*, (1980), Boston: Little Brown.

Bohman, M. (1972). *Adopted children and their families—a follow-up study of adopted children, their background environment and adjustment*. Stockholm: Proprius.

Brodzinsky, D., Pappas, C., Singer, L., & Braff, A. (1981). "Childrens' conception of adoption: A preliminary investigation." *Journal of Pediatric Psychology, 6*, 177–189.

Brodzinsky, D., Singer, L., & Braff, A. (1981). "Childrens' understanding of adoption: A comparison of adopted and nonadopted children." Unpublished manuscript. (SRCD, Boston, 1981).

Brodzinsky, D., Singer, L., & Braff, A. (1984). "Childrens' understanding of adoption." *Child Development, 55*, 869–878.

Coyne, A., & Brown, M. E. (1985). "Developmentally disabled children can be adopted." *Child Welfare, 64,* 607–616.

Erickson, M. T., (1978). *Child Psychopathology: Assessment, etiology, and treatment.* Englewood Cliffs, NJ: Prentice Hall.

Fagan, J. F. III. (1971). "Infants' recognition memory for a series of visual stimuli." *Journal of Experimental Child Psychology, 2,* 244–250.

Frisk, M., (1964). "Identity problems and confused conceptions of the genetic ego in adopted children during adolescence." *Acta Paedo Psychiatrics, 31,* 6–12.

Goldstein, J., Freud, A., & Solnit, A. (1979). *Beyond the best interests of the child.* London: The Free Press.

Kadushin, A. (1980). *Child welfare services* (93rd Ed.). New York: Macmillan.

Kraft, A. D., Palombo, J., Mitchell, D. L., Woods, P. K., Schmidt, A. W., & Tucker, A. G. (1985). "Some theoretical considerations on confidential adoptions." Part III: The adopted child. *Child and Adolescent Social Work, 2* (3), 1939.

Lawton, J. J., & Gross, S. F. (1964). "Review of psychiatric literature on adopted children." *Archives of General Psychiatry, 11,* 635–644.

Mahler, M. (1968). *On human symbiosis and the vicissitudes of individuation; Infantile psychosis.* New York: International Universities Press.

Masterson, J., (1981). *The narcissistic and borderline disorders: An integrated developmental approach.* New York, Brunner L. Mazel.

McWhinnie, A. M. (1967). *Adopted children-how they grow up.* London: Kegan, Paul.

Mech, E.V. (1973). "Adoption: A policy perspective." In B. Caldwell & H. Riccuitti (Eds.), *Review of Child development research* (Vol.3, pp.467–508). Chicago: University of Chicago Press.

Schecter, M. (1964). "Emotional problems of the adoptee." *General Archives of Psychiatry, 10.*

Thomas, A., & Chess, S. (1980). *The dynamics of psychological development.* New York: Brunner/Mazel.

Unger, C., Dwarshuis, G., & Johnson, E. (1977). *Chaos, madness and unpredictability.* Chelsea, MI: Spaulding for Children.

Weiss, A. (1984). "Parent-child relationships of adopted adolescents in a psychiatric hospital." *Adolescence 19,* 77–88.

27

Prevention As an Integral Part of Mental Health Therapy in Adoption

Barbara T. Tremitiere

Does every adoptive family need to be actively involved in therapy from the onset of the placement of a "special needs" child in their home?

Although many would answer this question with an unqualified "yes," it has been our agency's (Tressler Lutheran Service Associates, York, PA) experience that the use of a realistic educational process for adoptive parents prior to actual placement can, and does, for the majority of our adoptive families, equip them with parenting skills and therapeutic tools that enable them to successfully parent very difficult children—most times without the need to be involved in formal therapy sessions. This type of realistic educational process takes into account an awareness and understanding of issues unique to adoption and foster care as well as preparation for the resulting behavior patterns that can usually be anticipated.

Formal therapy, which would be defined with the context of this paper as therapy provided by a qualified therapist who is knowledgeable in adoption issues, could then be minimized and integrated into the family experience as often as requested to deal with the more pressing and compelling problems that arise. It is interesting to note that, with this approach used in over 1,800 placements, only about 75 families have needed to make use of the long term formal therapy that is readily available to them.

"Shared Memories"

To zero in on an awareness and understanding of issues unique to adoption and foster care, I will be dealing with a concept of "shared memories." This concept, so crucial in adoption, is often negated or ignored when preparing potential adoptive parents for placement. Adoption, oftentimes, is seen as "ownership" of a child—as somehow cutting him off from his entire past as though only life after his adoption has relevance and impact upon him. Only in recent years has there been emphasis on "shared parenthood," a realistic approach which says to the adoptive family that they are but a part of their child's life. They share parenthood with those who gave him birth and with all others whom that child has seen and experienced in a parenting role. His memories of the past and his fantasies about the future are not the adoptive parents' to negate. They are uniquely his: he is a product of the impact of all these forces upon his life. He does not, at the point of placement, share the adoptive family's memories of their past experiences any more than they share his. Hopefully, present placement experiences will become future "shared memories" for both family and child, but, at the time of placement, we are dealing with memories he already has. I call them "the ghost of placements past."

"Ghosts"

This "ghost of placements past" has a profound effect on the present placement success potential. Therefore it is crucial that the adoptive parents understand how and why this is true. Otherwise they could easily find themselves, as many parents have, with a very negative response to a child that could eventually lead to such things as excessive physical discipline.

Because, in my experience, most adoptive parents come from backgrounds where they were parented with a positive reinforcement approach (stars on papers, money for good report cards, rewards for doing well), they are familiar with this approach to parenting and automatically try to use it with their adopted children. The problem is, that many times the children have not had that type of "shared memory" experience in the past. Instead of getting positive reinforcement and attention, many of them were parented with negative reinforcement and attention. They see this as a normal way of life. They have become experts at *soliciting* that negative attention, also, just as the parents became expert at getting their share of positive attention. The worst experience for all of us is not to be noticed and to be totally ignored.

The conflict comes when the well meaning parents try to use positive reinforcement with a child who does not hold that as a "shared memory." Then such comments are heard as, "Every time I do something nice for him he acts awful" or "Nothing seems to work with him, I don't understand why he feels he needs to be so nasty."

I experienced this frustration personally when we adopted a six year old child who had been severely abused. My only desire and inclination was to love and cuddle him—to overcome his past. I had to learn that I could not *overcome* his past—that I had to *understand* it and help him *work through* it. He taught this to me in a vivid way. He harrassed me from the first day of placement. He did everything wrong, hated the family, the house, the other children—everything. He disrupted the household constantly and never stopped complaining, it seemed. My resolve to be positive with this child and treat him just like our other children crumbled after two solid weeks of trying to deal with his extremely exasperating behavior. Finally I found myself so frustrated at trying to deal with this behavior and lack of a positive response to any of us that one day I actually found myself hitting him in order to get him to "shut up."

I was devastated. I have never felt so utterly defeated in my life. I was in tears—questioning all my parenting skills and abilities. I looked at my child—he was laughing. He said, and I'll never forget his words, "I got you—I knew I would. It just took you longer than the rest!"

At this point, when the parent's lack of ability to cope becomes so blatantly obvious and real, many disruptions tend to occur. To prevent this, the ability of the parents to understand what is actually happening is essential. To learn further how to realistically *deal with it* is crucial.

Getting a child like this to begin to understand and see value in working for positive reinforcement necessitates *not* reinforcing his quest for negative reinforcement. For example, parents need to actually leave the room when the child triggers them to the point of verbally or physically responding to him negatively. This frustrates the child, as the expected response is missing. Filling in the gap by telling the child anything and everything he is doing well or right can begin to create a need and desire for positive reinforcement.

It is a slow, painful process, often taking years to accomplish. The child, who needs so badly to be noticed in some way, gradually starts to work for this positive reinforcement and to believe in his own ability to get it. To experience one child working through this change is to see the accomplishment of a miracle that the parent has had an active part in bringing about. The struggle to get to that point, then, becomes a "shared memory," both painful and positive, for the adoptive parent and their child. This I call "the stark harshness of present reality" which eventually leads to "the realistic promise for the future."

Often, supportive help from other adoptive parents is needed during this behavior modification struggle. Therapy at some point, usually to help the parents in carrying through on this approach, is also sometimes requested.

Conscience Building

Another "shared memory" of the past that belongs to the child but must be understood by the adopting parents is the significance of multiple placements and the problems such multiple placements present in the development of conscience in the child. We often hear parents say that their child "has no adequate concept of right and wrong as you would expect from a child his age."

Why would you expect it? Most children his age were taught right and wrong, good and bad from a very young age by people they saw as stable figures in their lives. If they were lucky enough to grow up with the parents who gave them birth, and those parents gave them adequate moral guidance, such concepts were easily absorbed and acted on as values. The adopted child, however, often coming from a multitude of placements, may have experienced every one of them, whether he realized it or not, as a conflict of value systems and a regression of his ability to adequately develop conscience. *Every* replacement, including the removal from birth parents, became a disruption to him and to the working through of his developmental tasks.

Oftentimes, children experience extreme value conflicts that they may or may not be equipped to cope with well—such as being Pentecostal, Catholic, and Agnostic in one year because "those were the only available foster homes at the time."

Many times, the child has never been made to take any realistic consequences for his negative actions. He has learned how to "home hop" when the pressures to conform to family standards become too great for him to handle in his present placement. Often this is done by accusing the adoptive parents of abusing him. The parents, frustrated, ask, "Don't you care what you are doing?" The child, verbally or with actions, often answers, "No."

"The stark harshness of the present reality" forces parents to begin the task to build conscience into the frustrating child. He *must* take the consequences for *all* of his actions, from breakage to delinquent acts to stealing from his family. He *must* also learn to make choices by being given alternatives that build in penalties for the wrong choice (logical and natural consequences). A simple example of this would be "either change the TV to a decent program or I will turn it off." He doesn't change channels—the parent turns it off. By making enough "wrong choices" and paying the penalty for doing so, the child gradually learns to make better choices and to build into himself a basic value system. This, again, can be another "realistic promise for the future."

Sexual Experience

Recognizing that another "ghost of placements past" could well include sexual experience is another area of preventive information which needs to be thought out by and discussed with the adopting parents. Nothing can cause parents to "come unglued" faster than to find their newly adopted child in bed with one of their birth children. Knowing this could happen and why, as well as knowing how to prevent and handle the situation prior to placement, is *vitally* important.

Many of the children our agency places have had sexual experience. Although the world may well call this "abuse," often the child does not. Perhaps it was experienced by him as pleasure or as a special form of closeness. It may well have been enjoyed. The situation, then, needs to be seen from the child's perspective. Otherwise he can end up feeling bad about himself, because he enjoyed it too but only the other person is being punished.

"The stark harshness of present reality" is that once a child is introduced to sexual activity it is very hard, if not impossible, to make him stop it totally. What *can* be done—and this might well require help from other adoptive parents who have experienced similar situations, and/or a therapist—is to work with the child toward more acceptable sexual alternatives than using other people. This usually ends up being masturbation in the privacy of his own room or the bathroom. The most important ingredient in working towards a "realistic promise for the future" in *this* area of concern is to make the adoptive parents aware of the potential problem so they can build in preventive measures (like no bed sharing) and know the correct responses to be made, instead of panic, if the problem does indeed become an overt one for them.

Anger

Anger, for these children, is an almost universal emotion. This anger is usually in response to the situation they are in and the people who put them there (usually birth parents and social workers). It is important for adoptive parents to recognize the existence of this anger and to be able to realize that, although they often bear the brunt of it, it usually is not really directed at them but at the past "shared memories." It is important that the children are provided with an outlet for their anger that is acceptable to the family. This may be verbal or action-oriented, and, in extreme situations, may well need a therapist's help.

Summary

In summary, adoption is not just a process of placing. If it is, in fact, to be successful, ways must be found to *keep* the children in placement—to keep disruptions from occurring.

It is crucial for these children and their futures that adoptive parents with lifelong commitments provide them with realistic stability. "The ghosts of placements past" must be understood and dealt with; "the stark harshness of present reality" must be coped with day by day, with an understanding of techniques that work and the support of other families and/or therapy. With these ingredients acknowledged and in place, a child's "shared memories" of the past can well blend into a "realistic promise for the future," in which the families *and* children can get beyond the majority of the struggles and begin to build "shared memories" together.

Bibliography

Tremitiere, Barbara and William. *Team Training Manual*. North American Council on Adoptable Children, 1981 (Rev. 1986)

28

Discipline and the Difficult Child

John E. Valusek

Adopted children have special needs that often set them apart from other children. Although every child, adopted or not, is unique, the adopted child *does* have a special history which often requires extra efforts in order to meet the special needs created by that history. Nevertheless, in my opinion, when it comes to discipline, the approaches and requirements are really very similar for both adopted and nonadopted children.

In what follows, I'll be sharing some of my personal beliefs, observations, and some ways of thinking which I have found helpful in my work with parents and children in conflict.

Two Faces of Discipline

Discipline usually refers to the imposition of external limits or controls in order to achieve a desired and orderly response from a child. Discipline does not require a set of rigid rules but rather a set of flexible guidelines. The eventual goal is to help the child learn self-control or self-discipline. If discipline is thought of as a teaching process rather than a punishment process, the way becomes clear for improved human relationships at home, at school, and throughout society.

Unfortunately, many of us as parents lean toward the punitive view of discipline. In fact, for many parents and teachers, to discipline a child has come to mean to punish him or her. Because the actual definition of discipline and its traditional use embraces both a teaching and a punishment aspect, one of the first hurdles that needs to be overcome in working with parents is to help them move from a punishment modality toward a teaching modality which keeps punishment at a minimum. This is no easy task because in many respects our whole society operates on a blame-oriented and punitive basis. And both of these notions are especially non-helpful when attempting to deal with the difficult child who is adopted or in foster care.

Characteristics of the Difficult Child

If we think of a difficult child in a generic sense, then the difficult child is any child brought to you because he or she is hard to live with. According to parents, the difficult child is one who is not cooperating and is a constant source of family conflict, turmoil, and dissension. The child misbehaves, causes trouble, or is out of control.

What parents refer to as misbehavior which creates difficulties in family relationships might be the result of a variety of contributing causes. If the child was hyperactive at birth, the stage will have been set very early for potential management problems. The child may be difficult because of organic factors or because he was physically or sexually abused or neglected. Of course, the impact of these and other causative elements must be given due consideration. But as far as an approach to discipline is concerned, the diagnosis and personal history might not be as important as one might expect.

From a therapeutic viewpoint, we can assume that the difficult child was either born that way or learned to be that way through a variety of life experiences. If born that way, we still have the problem of how to deal with him. Therefore, the teaching-learning modality is still appropriate. We need to help the parents learn to relate differently with the difficult child regardless of the origin of individual characteristics. And the difficult child needs to unlearn and relearn a variety of responses in order to modify the perceived maladaptive behavior.

Comments about Therapy

Each of us has our own orientation to guide us in our approach to working with our patients/clients. But, in spite of different life experiences and professional training and the varied contexts in which we work, we are all engaged in a teaching process. I believe this is so even though many of us might not have thought of our work in those terms before.

We actually start teaching from the moment we first meet our clients. We teach by our expectations, by what we do and what we avoid doing, by how we speak, what we say, by how we listen, where we look, by if and how we touch and by every other move we make. All that we are now, at this moment, is always a part of all that we do in relation with others. Most of the time we need not be directly aware of this axiom. But we must never forget its validity. And, most important, if this is true for us, then it is even more critically true of the parents we work with. Everything they do, moment to moment, always teaches, informs and models behavior for their children. Everything—whether they want it to or not.

As teachers, we become translators of certain kinds of information for our clients. We also seek to assist them to define their concerns in such a way that more effective methods of dealing with those concerns can come into being. We translate certain information we believe we possess about human behavior and emotional functioning so that they, our clients, can choose to act or react differently and, we hope, more effectively. We also, I believe, must spend thoughtful time trying to help parents and children reduce the often huge legacy of guilt which our society and their personal past experiences might have dumped on them. Some small measures of guilt can serve useful functions for any of us by making us aware that something about our activities might require examination and possible change. However, high guilt levels can be debilitating and must be reduced or eliminated.

By the way, although our theoretical views might be quite different, most of the ideas presented here can be incorporated with any therapeutic approach. However, one major difficulty will arise if you strongly favor physical punishment as an effective means of discipline. It is very difficult to teach others not to spank if you yourself believe in the merits of spanking.

A final point: After you have determined the general nature of the parents' concerns or complaints, it is helpful to follow up by having them write out a list of specific concerns that *both* parents agree are problem areas. In doing so, try to have them focus on actual observable behaviors rather than the children's motives, moods, or attitudes. Also try to determine what rules are most important in the family, what purpose they are intended to serve, and whether or not they seem to be working.

Useful Premises for Parents

1. If it's true that beauty is in the eye of the beholder, where do you suppose misbehavior must be? Misbehavior is also in the eye of the beholder. This is my way of restating the old adage: Nothing is either good or bad but thinking makes it so. It is important for us to help parents understand that their own beliefs and attitudes are extremely important in helping to create or sustain behavioral problems in their children.

2. It is better to view our children's "misbehavior" as mistakes or errors in judgment. Once you start thinking in terms of mistakes, you will soon realize that mistakes are not sins or crimes. Most mistakes do not merit punishment. Instead, they require guidance, more information, or new directions.

3. Each of us does the best we can at any given moment in time. Therefore,

to blame yourself for your current or past errors in judgment or action is not helpful to you or your children. To blame your children for their past action is also not helpful. Blame is a relatively useless emotion or attitude.

4. If we learn to be the way we are, we do so with the most marvelous organ in the universe: the human brain. Because the human animal is truly the choice-making animal, we can call upon our brains to help us relearn or unlearn almost anything that we now know.

5. Theory X and Theory Y are two contrasting views of human behavior. Theory X represents a traditional viewpoint which tends to see people in a negative way, as essentially bad. It assumes that the average person can't be trusted, is lazy and irresponsible. It implies that people always need close supervision and control and must be motivated by external rewards (money, medals, titles, etc.) in a carefully controlled fashion.

Theory Y, on the other hand, adopts a much more positive view of human beings. It assumes people are essentially good, creative, strong, capable of seeking and accepting responsibility. Theory Y assumes that people are motivated internally and do want to make a difference in their relations with others. They are willing to cooperate and are desirous of doing what's right because it's right. Our discipline approaches will be quite different depending on which theory we prefer.

6. The emotionally disturbed child or the difficult child in great conflict usually feels unloved, unwanted, unaccepted and has come to believe that he or she can't trust any other human being. Although these descriptions are accurate, the child will not necessarily be aware of these feelings. Nevertheless, his behavior will be a reflection of their underlying impact.

7. A useful approach in talking about self-esteem and its effects on behavior is to view the self as a bucket. Start with the premise that every human being, adult or child, has within him an invisible bucket and carries with him an invisible dipper. If your child feels good about himself, that means that his bucket is fairly full. If he doesn't feel good about himself, that means his bucket is low or approaching empty. Anytime you criticize, attack, demean, run down, scold, or otherwise imply that he is bad, no good or a rotten human being, you are dipping out of his bucket.

Bucket levels are important because, to a large extent, they determine how we feel and act at any given time. Low bucket levels lead to angry, hostile, sullen, whining, rebellious or noncooperative responses. High bucket levels lead to warm, positive, loving, helping and cooperative responses. Consequently, when you provide positive reinforcement, when you approve of or encourage him, when you help the child succeed and feel good about himself, you are putting drops in his bucket. On the other hand, everytime you signify disapproval, by any means, you are dipping out of his bucket. Our task as concerned parents is to provide more approval than disapproval in order to help fill buckets rather than empty them.

8. Understanding is forgiveness. If I could truly understand what motivates you—why you do what you do—I believe I could forgive almost anything you do. I might still disapprove or feel I have to act in some way or hold you responsible for your behavior, but I would not have to condemn you as a person for being the way you are. Each of us must be the way we are until we learn to be different. Therefore, understanding is forgiveness.

9. When in doubt, try honesty. By this I mean: We sometimes get caught up in trying to figure out the "right or wrong" ways to discipline; we get caught up in our gimmicks or methods. Instead, we would do better to try to say what we mean and mean what we say. When in doubt, simply be honest.

10. Assume the older adopted child has experienced the worst type of discipline history. If so, the child might be expected to gripe, whine, be angry, be sullen, or withdraw. The child will test your patience, try to provoke you to yell, threaten, condemn or strike out. These behaviors indicate internal distress, hurt, and confusion. This child is in need of enlightened guidance. It does not need further condemnation, pain, or punishment.

Guidelines For Discipline

Some of the questions we need to help parents to ask of themselves are: What kind of children and adults do we want in our family and in our society? What are we trying to do in our relationships with our children? What do we intend to teach? Am I treating my child with respect? What's the goal of any of my efforts to develop discipline?

The following guidelines are a sampling of some of the ideas I focus on in my work with parents. You will, of course, add your own interpretations and expand or modify as desired.

1. Stop spanking, hitting, and hurting your children as soon as you can convince yourself to do so. But, if you do spank, limit yourself to *one* slap on the buttocks or thigh with an open hand.

2. Avoid threats but, if you make a threat, be sure to carry it through or rescind the threat and apologize.

3. Try to focus on the *behaviors* of your child, not the child's motivations.

4. Select one problem area at a time to work on. Instead of attempting to modify six or seven areas of concern, focus on one for a period of time until progress has been made in that area.

5. Catch them while they're doing good. If you pay more attention to the behaviors you desire and approve of and less attention to behaviors that are not as pleasing, the former will be increased and the latter will diminish.

6. Teach rather than punish. The goal in all of your activities and relationships with children who are in conflict is to have them learn another way of behaving that's more acceptable. Therefore, even though you may have chosen to use punishment as a means to try to teach something, or to

modify their behavior by influencing their motivation, you really need to work more on teaching and less upon punishment.

7. Examine your rules. For a good rule to serve a useful purpose at home or elsewhere, it must be clearly stated and serve some reasonable purpose. Expected consequences or penalties should be known and explained ahead of time. Also, it should be recognized that the fewer rules you have to enforce, the greater the likelihood that you will not have to spend much time enforcing them.

8. If you decide to punish, don't overreact. Too often parental punishment is overdone and overextended. Keep it simple.

9. Don't talk too much when a rule has been violated. In this instance, less is more. The less you say, the more effective your actions. Tell the child: You know the rule, you've broken it and this is the penalty or punishment.

10. Be very firm when you feel called upon to correct, assess a penalty, or arrange for a consequence to occur. Avoid getting into an argument or attempting to justify your actions.

11. If you are going to use pain as a negative reinforcer, *you must use it while the event to be punished is occurring.* The value of eliciting pain as a form of punishment after the fact is almost always useless in the long run and highly dubious in the short term as well.

12. Good manners need to be consciously employed when you are trying to redirect a child's behavior. Parents ought to use good manners with one another as a form of modeling as well as use good manners directly with the children. What this means is simply making greater use of "please" and "thank you" and "may I" and "excuse me" as well as "I'm sorry."

13. For older adopted children, including teenagers, the main discipline emphasis should be to focus on communicating more effectively, cooperative sharing, and leveling (when in doubt, try honesty). In addition, it is extremely important to solicit the teen's input on rules and expected consequences. Family conferences are helpful here.

14. Much effective discipline can occur simply as the result of the appropriate use of approval, withholding of approval, and ignoring certain behaviors. Direct disapproval of the child and threats of disapproval should be used rarely, if at all.

15. Human touch is an important nonverbal means for demonstrating acceptance and approval of others. In addition to regular hugs, kisses, etc., five minutes worth of gentle backrubs (preferably around bedtime) often helps to create improved relations within a relatively short period of time.

16. The use of tokens, stars, points, etc., can be helpful with some children. However, be cautious about becoming so enamored of the system that you fail to change it if it isn't producing the desired results.

17. Anger expressed as frustration need not be harmful to a relationship with a child. However, if the anger lasts more than a few minutes and leads to

yelling, screaming, or name calling, it is probably detrimental to both the adult and the child.

18. If you find yourself filled with great anger or rage because of a child's actions, know that it is your own thoughts, expectations and wishes that are the probable source of your anger and not the child's actions. No person can anger or demean you without your consent.

19. Developing useful alternatives for physical punishment usually requires: time and patience, effort and planning, anticipation and goal setting, rational thinking and problem solving, mutual respect and a cooperative relationship. Spanking or hitting for punishment purposes can be done in an instant, with little or no thought, and without concern for the long range effect. As a three year old girl told her irate father when he was about to spank her, "Daddy, it doesn't take a brain to cause pain, you know." And she was right: anybody can cause pain.

20. It is helpful for the therapist to provide parents with short outlines or summaries of disciplinary procedures to serve as reminders after they have been explained and understood. The therapist should also recommend only those books or other materials with which he or she is highly conversant so that clarifying the content and simplification procedures can be conveyed to the parents.

Case Study #1

Client: Billy, five year old male, adopted in infancy.

Chief Complaint: Conduct problems at preschool and at home.

Background Overview: Billy's parents work during the day. They have been married ten years. Two years after adopting Billy's, mother gave birth to a daughter. Mother describes Billy as aggressive, sassy, resentful of authority, hyperactive, and hostile toward his sister. He argues, talks back, and refuses to obey at home and at school. Although he has "always been a problem," his behavior has become much worse during the past two years. Now the preschool teacher is threatening to expel him unless he gets help soon.

Mother describes herself as a tense, nervous person who tends to defer to her husband's wishes. She is lenient with the children, doesn't spank them, but does yell and nag excessively. Her husband is very strict, rigid, and aggressive. He is an ex-"biker" who uses harsh language, spanks frequently and sometimes excessively, and won't take any nonsense from the children. He has a short temper, is quick to criticize, and tends to overreact. Both parents want therapy and regret waiting so long to seek help.

During my interaction with Billy, I find him to be a bright, alert and quick learning child. He is also restless, speaks rapidly, has a short attention span, and expresses strong anger toward his sister. Although he is cooperative with me, he makes frequent use of many negative comments, such as: "I'll kick her butt out of the house. Nobody gives me any lip. No way, Jose," etc.

Most of the behaviors observed by me and reported by his parents appear to be related to erratic and inconsistent approaches by the various adults with whom he interacts. The impact of sibling rivalry plus parental attitudes and behaviors appear to have taught him to defy others and throw his weight around. Because I noticed that Billy had an excess amount of hair on his arms and back, I was also led to wonder about possible sexual precocity as a contributing element to his maladaptive behavior.

Procedures and Initial Recommendations: After having the parents sign Release of Information forms, I called Billy's pediatrician to request a physical exam and any recommended blood work to assess possible early sexual development, testosterone levels, or other indicators of possible glandular overactivity. (The exam and blood work found no evidence of early sexual development or glandular contributors to explain his hyperactivity.)

To begin the change process at home, mother agreed to try to reduce her yelling, to consciously practice using good manners and to *request* Billy's cooperation rather than order it. Billy's father would begin to modify his spanking procedures. He would limit the number of reasons which merit spanking. He would also think before he spanks, spank only one time with the bare hand and will not curse while doing so. Both parents would read and discuss *Discipline Without Spanking or Shouting* as soon as possible.

In a 45-minute phone conversation with the preschool teacher, she expressed great frustration about Billy's conduct. She was eager for any advice I might give. She confirmed that he resisted orders, engaged in yelling and namecalling, violated the rules at will, and got into frequent fights with the other children. She was beginning "to hate" him and felt terrible because of it.

We examined her rules, her corrective procedures, and her verbalizations. She made use of a time-out chair and supervised time-out room. She had gotten into the habit of giving frequent scoldings.

She argued, pleaded, threatened, and gave lengthy explanations to Billy to explain her frustrations with him. She tried to argue him into obedience.

Because she has an assistant, I asked her to devote full attention to Billy during the first fifteen minutes of each day. During the first two or three minutes after his arrival at school, it was important to find something positive to say to him. She was advised to catch him doing good and to ignore minor misbehaviors including backtalk. When clear violations of rules occurred, she would make use of the time-out chair. If he failed to comply with the time-out procedure, she should carry him, if necessary, to the isolation room and stay there only until calm was restored. During the rest of the day she would proceed as usual except she would stop talking so much, stop lengthy explanations, and use "please" and "thank you" when appropriate.

I also de-emphasized her guilt feelings and complimented her for her willingness to continue working with a difficult child. I told her I would follow up with another conversation in one week. If no progress occurred within two weeks, I would agree he should be withdrawn from school.

Final Comment: One week after the second office visit, mother reported a general improvement of her son's behavior at home. In my followup call to the teacher, she indicated that his fighting and namecalling were reduced, her own attitude was much improved, and, although there was still a long way to go, she felt she was getting on top of the situation. It is expected that three to four months of additional work with the parents on parenting skills and disciplinary practices will be needed to restore stability to this household.

Case Study #2

Client: Doris, age 16, adopted in infancy.

Chief Complaint: Hatred of school, constant arguments with mother, frequent long crying spells, and social isolation.

Background Overview: Doris is the only child of Mr. and Mrs. T. During her early childhood her Air Force father was often gone for long periods of time. Consequently, her mother was primarily responsible for her care. The parents are currently separated and the father has been living out-of-state for approximately three years. Mother refuses to divorce him because of financial reasons. Doris has an intense dislike for her father, but maintains periodic contact whenever she needs expensive material items.

Doris describes herself as dumb and ugly. She has few friends, no talents, and "never really does anything wrong" like other kids, except at home. She admits to frequent temper tantrums and arguments with her mother. She cries "every single Sunday night" and can't wake up Monday mornings until her mother "nags her to death."

Mother describes Doris as "really a good girl" who was taught to be kind and gracious. However, since the seventh grade, she has become very difficult to live with. She whines, complains and cries constantly. She bites her fingernails and overeats. Mother has tried to solve her problems by advising her, befriending her, changing schools, and making decisions for her. Mother's approach to discipline depends upon begging, pleading, scolding, and excessive grounding. She also withholds money privileges from Doris.

Both Doris and her mother agree they needed help to improve their personal relationships. In addition, Doris wants to overcome her hatred of school but doesn't think "that's really possible." She also recognizes she suffers from extremely low self-esteem.

Procedures and Recommendations: To begin with, we set a few short term goals. 1) Every day Doris and her mother would set aside time to talk about anything she wanted to. Mother would listen, not offer any advice and would ask only those questions needed to clarify what Doris was saying and feeling. 2) Mother agreed to let Doris decide whether or not she would go to school between this appointment and the next. On any day she opted to stay home, nothing was to be said about it. Doris agreed not to go anywhere else during that day or evening. 3) Mother would buy an alarm clock for Doris, who agreed to get herself up each morning or be late to or absent from school. 4) Mother would try to stop yelling and would not ground Doris for anything between appointments unless all three of us agreed on the merits of doing so. 5) After discussing a way to "gut it out" for the next three school days no matter what happened, Doris hesitantly agreed to try and we shook hands on the agreement. 6) Concerning her crying "every single Sunday night:" I told her I expected she would probably cry as usual this Sunday. However, when she did so, I wanted her to cry much harder and shed more tears in an hour than ever before. She laughed and asked, "Are you kidding?" I replied, "Not at all. If you really cry hard enough, you might find it easier to get up the next day."

Final Comment: Doris got up by herself and went to school the next three days. She cried Sunday, but couldn't cry as hard or as long as she usually did. Future sessions with her alone focused on self-esteem, improving social relations, and becoming involved in organized after-school activities. Separate sessions with Mother dealt with her own guilt and dependency needs as well as more effective discipline and parenting practices.

Concluding Statement

We tend to think that the approach to discipline is highly complex and requires excessively detailed explanations. In point of fact, it's fairly easy to outline a basic healthy discipline approach for any child of any age. *The key ingredient: parents who are self-disciplined, who have developed self-control and who approach their children not as possessions but as beings of equal worth.* Such parents will perceive most of their child's behavior as trial and error learnings, creative explorations, and testing of the environment to determine results. They will use a problem solving approach and are aware that their own behavior may be a part of the problem.

We need to help more parents understand that they must go beyond looking for "three easy steps to discipline." Discipline is really a day-to-day-dynamic process, not a magical bag of tricks. Discipline is an integral part of every aspect of parenting. The orderly or disorderly routine and general climate in any home set the stage for effective or harmful approaches to discipline. The special needs of the adopted child, the foster child, or the child who presents a behavioral difficulty are best addressed through overall parenting practices which include but go beyond any specific approach to discipline.

In my judgment, one of the major problems for parents living with difficult children is the heavy reliance upon all forms of punishment as a standard for dealing with problem behavior. This practice and its underlying attitude lead to power struggles, to angry clashes, and violates the spirit of loving parental guidance. In fact, I believe that the combined effect of punishment, neglect, and impulsive discipline procedures are the major causes of most maladaptive behavior in our society.

Resources to Read and Recommend

Although this brief paper can serve to help start a more effective approach to discipline, it is clearly only an overview of some basic and elementary ideas. Any parent who is having problems with one or more children would do well to increase his or her awareness, knowledge, and understanding of parenting skills and practices. The art of parenting may not be easily taught but it can clearly be improved. Listed below are several sources that I have found helpful. These cover the years from preschool through adolescence. They are representative of many other excellent resources which are now available to parents, therapists, counselors, teachers, and other adults who work with, help, train, or advise children.

The first six are available in bookstores or libraries.

1. Dinkmeyer and McKay, *The Parent's Handbook* (S.T.E.P.), American Guidance Service, 1982.

Probably one of the best known and most thorough approaches to the training of parents based upon Adlerian principles. A workbook for use alone or in courses taught throughout the nation.

2. Katherine C. Kersey, *Sensitive Parenting,* Acropolis Books Ltd., 1983.

A highly readable, rational and humane approach to parenting. Covers all the major bases in a lucid and understandable fashion.

3. Saf Lerman, *Parent Awareness,* Winston Press, 1980.

An easy to read, anecdotal, question and answer format applicable to all ages but especially relevant for younger children. Lerman combines her own teaching experience with a variety of approaches to parenting. She is an excellent proponent of nonhitting ways of discipline.

4. Karen Pryor, *Don't Shoot the Dog,* Bantam Books, 1984.

Karen Pryor has produced an enjoyable, readable, and understandable exposition of Behavioral Training based upon her work with dolphins and people. She presents persuasive arguments and illustrations to demonstrate the superiority of shaping behavior by positive reinforcement and, at the same time, demonstrates the drawbacks to punishment.

5. Stanley Turecki, M.D., *The Difficult Child,* Bantam Books, 1985.

The first approach I know of written especially for parents who live with the temperamentally difficult child. Turecki describes eight characteristics which are present at birth in these children and which require special management approaches in order to achieve effective discipline.

6. Wycoff and Unell, *Discipline Without Shouting or Spanking,* Meadowbrook Books, 1984.

I was extremely pleased when I read the prepublication manuscript of this incisive little book for parents of pre-schoolers. Describes overall principles and then focuses on specifics concerning what and what not to do to prevent, correct, and modify a variety of potential problems.

The following booklets were written by me and self-published. They are not available in bookstores. Information about them and my personal newsletter HUMANETHIC may be obtained by writing to me at 3629 Mossman, Wichita, Kansas 67208.

1. *Some Ways of Thinking about Human Behavior* (36 pages)

2. *Jottings* (48 pages)

3. *People Are Not for Hitting* (78 pages).

Contributors

Josephine Anderson earned an MSW at Western Reserve University. She then went on to work for 20 years in various aspects of adoption. During the past decade, Josephine has presented parent and staff training workshops dealing with techniques of therapy and parenting pertaining to the unattached child.

"Jophie" is currently living and working with the programs and service projects of a nondenominational Christian community called Koinonia Partners. As an extension of Koinonia's commitment to the well-being of children, she will provide staff and parent training related to adoptive and foster care placements of unattached children.

Josephine is the foster parent of eight children, many of whom are being prepared for adoptive family life.

Margaret Beyer has a Ph.D. in Clinical/Community Psychology from Yale University. Formerly the Director of the D.C. Coalition for Youth, Marty is a therapist, trainer and consultant, designing programs to serve delinquent and neglected children in the Washington, D.C. area.

Marty's consulting service includes designing community-based programs for young people and providing support groups for staff in therapeutic foster care and other services. Marty works with judges in the Family Division of D.C. Superior Court, and child care workers in a variety of public and private organizations.

Earl T. Braxton is Director of Three Rivers Training and Development Institute in Pittsburgh, Pennsylvania. The institute specializes in training staff to work with difficult adolescent population and working with high stress occupations.

Dr. Braxton has a Ph.D. in Organizational Psychology from the Union Graduate School. He did his post doctoral work in group and family therapy at Yale University, where he also served as a lecturer in the Department of Psychiatry.

Dr. Braxton has written and trained extensively in the area of working with angry and hostile children and adolescents. His published works include: "Structuring the Black Family for Survival and Growth," "The Psychological Destruction of Black Males" and numerous articles on adolescents.

David M. Brodzinsky is Vice Chair for Graduate Studies in Psychology, Rutgers University. He serves as a consultant for Diversified Health Services, Philadelphia, and is a member of the New Jersey Adoption Advisory Committee.

Dr. Brodzinsky has taught developmental psychology on undergraduate and graduate levels. He has received numerous, grants and fellowships for research on various aspects of adoption. Dr. Brodzinsky's findings have been an important contribution to the understanding of the adoptive relationship for families, and children.

David reviews journals for the *Journal of Applied Developmental Psychology and Youth and Society*. He acts as editorial consultant for the National Institute of Mental Health and a number of other professional journals. David is married and resides in New Jersey.

Foster W. Cline is a physician, a child psychiatrist, an author, and a lecturer. Dr. Cline is the Director of Evergreen Consultants in Human Behavior, a multi-disciplinary group of professionals, where people throughout the world come for treatment of individual and family problems. He is popular as a psychiatric consultant to school systems and pupil personnel teams across the continent and throughout the world.

Dr. Cline is a prolific author. He has written four books, some twenty professional papers, and numerous articles.

Foster along with the professionals of Evergreen Consultants has provided field clinical experience for therapists and students enrolled at a number of Colorado institutions. Participants at his workshops can immediately envision themselves doing more successful things with young people.

Paulette Donahue received her MSW from the University of Pittsburgh. Paulette has a private clinical practice specializing in family therapy and marriage counseling. Paulette has done consulting work in Mental Health and provides on-going therapy groups around interpersonal relationships, communication skills and assertiveness training.

Since 1978, Paulette has provided a consulting service to the PACO (Parents and Adopted Children's Organization) of Western PA and has presented workshops focusing on the challenges special needs children present in adoptive placements.

Ms. Donahue is the author of the self-help book, *Take the Bull By the Horns*.

Kathryn S. Donley is Executive Director of New York Spaulding for Children and the original director of Spaulding for Children in Michigan.

For the past 25 years Kay's involvement with adoption has been in the capacity of child welfare worker, supervisor and administrator. Eighteen of those have been in specialized adoption services. Through the years she has become convinced that "given thoughtful assistance these families will make it through."

Kay has made many presentations nationally and internationally and is widely regarded for her insight and sensitivity for adoptive children and their families. Kay has written a large number of articles on special needs adoption and the subject of disruption.

Maris H. Blechner is a social worker, educator and adoptive parent. She received a Masters in Education from Queens College, City University of New York and an MSW degree from Hunter College, New York.

Ms. Blechner has been active for 17 years in New York's Child Advocacy Program and for 5 years was Director of a Special Needs Adoption Program for the city of New York.

Currently Maris is serving as a consultant and trainer on child welfare issues.

Vera I. Fahlberg, M.D. a writer, lecturer and pediatrician serves as Psychotherapist and Medical Director of Forest Heights Lodge, a residential treatment center for emotionally disturbed boys. She also serves as a consultant to the foster care program for the state of Colorado and has been a foster parent herself.

Vera has done numerous workshops around the United States and abroad. She has also presented conferences from Israel to Australia. Vera's work with children and their families is indicative of her sensitivity and caring. She has trained hundreds of professionals in adoption and foster care expanding their knowledge around placement issues for children.

Dr. Fahlberg is the author of a multi-volume work titled *Putting the Pieces Together* and co-author of *Preparing Children for Adoption*.

M. Jerome Fialkov is an Assistant Professor of Child Psychiatry at the University of Pittsburgh School of Medicine and Medical Director of the Children's Psychiatric Treatment Center of Mayview State Hospital. He is the consulting psychiatrist to the Westmoreland County Children's Bureau and

Westmoreland County Juvenile Service Center in Greensburg, Pennsylvania.

Eric D. Cohen is currently a Resident in Psychiatry at the Western Psychiatric Institute and Clinic, University of Pittsburgh. As of July 1986, he will be a Fellow in Child and Adolescent Psychiatry, at that Institution. He received a B. A. degree at Brandeis University and his medical degree at the Albany Medical College of Union University.

Joyce Forsythe is director of Family Development Services in New Rochelle, New York. She has long been interested in working with adoptive children and their families. Her involvement includes helping to found a nationwide parent support movement, the Council on Adoptable Children, and a pioneer placement agency for special needs children, Spaulding for Children. More recently she directed the Project for Building Family Stability, a program for designing a therapeutic model for working with emotionally handicapped adopted children, sponsored by the North American Council on Adoptable Children and later by Spaulding of New Jersey.

Joyce is now completing a book entitled *Helping Families Help Themselves*. Joyce and her husband Peter have five children, three of whom are adopted.

Charlotte Goodluck graduated from Smith College School for Social Work in 1973. Charlotte is an enrolled Navajo. She was raised in a bi-cultural setting both on and off the reservation.

While working on an Arizona project recruiting Indian families, Charlotte helped to place over 100 Indian children within tribal contexts. She has worked for the Family Resource Center, Region VIII, and the American Indian Law Center focusing on the implementation of the Indian Child Welfare Act and the Adoption Assistance and Child Welfare Act.

Ms. Goodluck has been a consultant, trainer and author of several publications within Indian child welfare. She is currently Vice President of the New Mexico Indian Child Welfare Association.

Dr. Hamlin is a graduate of Georgetown University School of Medicine. He completed his residency in General Psychiatry at Georgetown and a Child Psychiatry fellowship at Children's Hospital National Medical Center in 1980.

Dr. Hamlin is founder and former director of the Department of Child and Adolescent Psychiatry at Howard University Hospital. He is the founder and director of the Institute for Child and Family Psychiatry, Inc., Silver Springs, Maryland and he also founded and serves as chairman of the Foundation of the Institute for Child and Family Psychiatry, Inc., which is a nonprofit research, training and advocacy organization. Dr. Hamlin is an Assistant

Clinical Professor of Psychiatry at the Children's Hospital National Medical Center and the George Washington University Department of Psychiatry and Behavioral Sciences.

Mary Howard is an Associate Professor of Sociology at Brooklyn College of The City of New York. She received her Ph.D. from the University of Oregon.

Dr. Howard has written on social issues and social policy. The focus of her articles has been on adoptees' search and reunion experiences. She is an adoptee, and for the last 10 years Dr. Howard has been studying, writing, researching and lecturing on various aspects of adoption.

At present Mary is pursuing an interest in documentary photography. She is married and has one child.

Missy Behrents Iski received an M.A. in guidance and counseling from the University of Tulsa. At present she is Director of the Girls Residential Treatment Center/Shadow Mountain Institute and has played a central role in developing a sexual abuse treatment program for the Shadow Mountain facility.

Missy is currently being trained as a puppeteer with *Kids on the Block* to provide child sexual abuse prevention for the public school system.

Ms. Iski has led seminars on sexual abuse and provides on-site group consultation to clinicians on a regular basis.

Ann M. Jernberg is the founder and director of The Theraplay Institute. She has written *Theraplay: A New Treatment Using Structured Play for Problem Children and Their Families* as well as numerous articles and chapters in other books on a number of clinical subjects.

For 12 years Ann was director of Mental Health Services for the Chicago Head Start program as well as consultant to Head Start programs in New York, Michigan, Indiana and Virgin Islands. Dr. Jernberg has worked as staff psychologist at Michael Reese, Billings Hospital, and chief psychologist on a part-time basis for the La Porte County Comprehensive Mental Health Center.

Some of the Theraplay Institute programs include research in the areas of bonding and attachment; national and international training of Theraplay therapists; and serving as a therapeutic resource for prospective adoptees and their parents.

Patrick J. Koehne received his masters degree from the University of North Carolina. He continued his training in the areas of family therapy, clinical hypnosis, Transactional and Gestalt therapies. Patrick has a private practice as a Psychotherapist in Fayetteville, North Carolina.

Mr. Koehne also acts as a consultant for several county departments of social services specifically addressing challenged children. In his private practice he offers a family system approach in his work with families of special needs adoption.

Patrick and his wife Patricia are the parents of three older adopted children.

Dorothy LePere is in private practice specializing in the pre-school and school-aged child. She has conducted children's workshops around divorce issues and leads adoptive parent groups for the Texas Department of Human services.

Dorothy has served as a consultant and led a special project to train adoption workers for the Region VI Adoption Resource Center. Prior to this endeavor she worked in child protective services.

Ms. LePere is the author of *Large Sibling Groups: Adoption Experiences.* Dorothy is married and has one child.

Carolyne Rodriquez is currently Director of The Texas division of the Casey Family Program at Austin, a private children's agency providing long-term foster care. She has also given training on issues related to child welfare, adoption and foster care nationally and internationally and has developed specific knowledge on stepparenting and divorce.

Carolyne has been Director of the Texas Foster Care Project which resulted in state wide improvements in the foster care system. Ms. Rodriquez is the author of *An Evolutionary Reveiw of Foster Parent's Roles in the Foster Care System and co-author of Moving In, Moving Out, Moving On: Assessing and Planning Issues for Adolescent Independence.* She is married and has four step-children.

Reuben Pannor is director of Community Services, Vista Del Mar Child-Care Service, Los Angeles, California.

In 1984 Mr. Pannor was awarded the Koshland Award as the outstanding social work practioner in California for his work in Adoptions. He also received recognition for his work with teenage fathers from the Fatherhood Forum for Southern California.

Mr. Pannor's published articles are numerous. He is the author of *The Unmarried Father: New Approaches for Helping Unmarried Young Parents; The Adoption Triangle: The Efffects of the Sealed Record on Adoptees, Birthparents and Adoptive Parents,* Pannor, Baran and Sorosky.

Mr. Pannor is married and the father of three children.

Evelyn A. Nerlove is a consultant and group therapist at Vista Del Mar Child-Care Services in California. She is the author of several publications, the most recent being *"Who is David?,''* the story of an adolescent adoptee struggling with his feelings about his adoption and birthparents.

Alvin L. Sallee is Academic Department Head and Associate Professor Department of Social Work, New Mexico State University. He chaired the task force which wrote the New Mexico Adoption Act and is himself an adoptive parent.

Elaine S. LeVine is Associate Professor of Counseling and Educational Psychology at New Mexico State University, currently on leave for full time clinical practice. She has conducted extensive research on vulnerable children such as the adopted, abused and neglected, children of divorce and the gifted.

The authors have just completed a new text book entitled, *Listen to Our Children: Clinical Theory and Practice.*

Barbara T. Tremitiere has an MSW from the University of Pittsburgh and is currently Director, Adoption Services, Tressler-Lutheran Service Associates, a multi-service and nonprofit agency in York, Pennsylvania. Barb has published several articles and is a co-author of the *Team Training Manual* (North American Council on Adoptable Children).

Since 1967, Barb has been instrumental in developing the focus on the group home study process. Barb has travelled extensively in providing training and consultation for social workers, adoptive and/or foster parents, adult adoptees, and interested community persons.

Barb is a parent of 15 children—12 of whom are adopted special needs children.

John E. Valusek is a lecturer, author and consultant in human awareness/ human relations. He is a psychology staff member of Cooperative Urban Teacher Education program of Kansas (a student-teacher training program which prepares teachers for inner city schools). He has also acted as a Psychotherapist at Family Psychological Center, Pennsylvania.

For over a decade, Dr. Valusek has been engaged in a personal campaign to establish a new national ethic of nonviolence based upon the idea: People are not for hitting and children are people, too. He has presented his ideas on nationally televised programs and throughout the country via lectures and speaking engagements.

Dr. Valusek is the author/publisher of three booklets: *Some Ways to Thinking about Human Behavior; Jottings;* and *People Are Not for Hitting.* He is co-author of a college level workbook *Learning To Learn.*

Index

Abuse, 8, 9. *See also* Sexual abuse

Abused children, 91. *See also* Neglected children; Sexually abused children

Academic performance: of adopted vs. nonadopted children, 322; of neglected children, 101, 105

Accommodation process, 264

Acosta, R., 239

Acting-out behavior, 117

Activation therapy, 51–52, 140–141

Adolescent problems: options for dealing with, 160–163; reasons for, 156–160; signs of, 157–158; stress-reduction strategies for, 328–330

Adolescents: developmental issues in, 323–325; examples of group experiences for, 311–317; identity issues in, 250–252, 312, 325; impact of divorce on, 304; pregnancy in, 102, 232; relationship-building skills for, 107–108; self-image in, 110n, separation in, 186; sexuality in, 323–324; sexually abused, 261, 263–265, 267; support groups for, 306, 314–317, 328–329, team therapy for, 306

Adopted children: adjustment of, 320–323; experiences of, 271–272; rejection and loss in, 297–298; special-needs, 200, 203, 281, 288–290; unique needs of, 333–337. *See also* Adolescents; Children

Adopted-child syndrome, 52

Adoption: attitudes toward, 28–29; definition of, 53; disruption of, 5, 151–156; history of, 27, 297; intraracial, 29, 127; inter-country, 67; interracial, 55–56, 74–75, 123, 127, 250; Native American issues regarding, 217–227; number of children available for; 14; open, 298, 328; placement process for, 167–179, 272–273; post-placement support following, 72; relative, 28; resistance to, 8–9; single-parent, 151, 303; special-needs, 27, 36, 72, 284–290; unrelated, 28

Adoption agencies, 72

Adoption Assistance and Child Welfare Act of 1980, 190–191, 193, 217

Adoption home studies: restructuring of, 36–37; shifts away from use of, 29

Adoption policy needs, 253–254

Adoption process: regulation of, 53; stresses of, 123

Adoption subsidy, 54–55

Adoptive child syndrome, 246

Adoptive parents: Black, 234–236; changing profile of, 28–29; characteristics of, 30–33, 311–312; fantasies regarding adoptive children by, 69; group therapy for, 45–47, 311–314; infertility of, 80–81, 154; preparation of, 29–30

Adoptive parents group. *See* Parents groups

Adult development stages, 286

Advertisements, 233

Advocacy, 192

Alcohol abuse, 198. *See also* Substance abuse

Allergies, 210–211

American Indians. *See* Native Americans

Anderson, Josephine, 62, 79

Anger: causes of, 114–115, 337; expression of, 113–114; forms of, 115–117; management skills for dealing with, 106; in neglected children, 101–102, 109n; parental, 344–345; regarding loss of foster parents, 6

Anxiety: bonding and level of, 210; effect on family of, 206–207

Assessment of adoptive children, 282–290

Attachment: dealing with previous and forming new, 112, 191–192; definition of, 168–169; mother-infant, in adoptive families, 121–132; in neglected children, 102; process of, 57–58. *See also* Mother-infant attachment

Attachment enhancement: case examples of, 277–278; feedback relevant to, 273–275; intervention techniques for, 275–277

Attachment theory, 213

Behavior: acting-out, 117; effects of sugar reduction on, 211; expectations of, 91

Bellak, L., 43

Berlin, Irving N., 218

Berman, Lauren C., 298, 306, 308

85–86; problems regarding, 81–82
Grief work: case examples of, 83–85; explanation of, 65–66, 275–276; goals of, 82–83
Griffith, E.E.H., 239
Gross, S.F., 320
Group therapy: for adolescents, 306, 314–317, 328–329; for adults, 37, 45–47, 69–72, 311–314; for children, 47–49; for sexually abused children, 265–267. *See also* Support groups; Therapy
"A Guide to the Genogram Family Systems Training" (Pendagast and Sherman), 284
Guided imagery, 292–293
Guilt, 263

Hamlin, Willie T., 231
Handicapped children: adoption of, 32–33; disruption rate for, 321. *See also* Special needs children
Hartman, Ann, 306
Holding therapy: case example of, 94–96; containment, 139–140; foundation for, 89, 91, 207; preparation for, 91–92; process of, 92–94, 141
Holmes, Thomas, 21–22
Homosexuality, 263
Honeymoon, 66–67, 113
Hoopes, Janet L., 250
Howard, Mary D., 243
HUMANETHIC, 349

Identity: in adolescents, 250–252, 312, 325; confusion over, 251; disruptions in formation of, 327; infancy to age two, 247–248; life cycle and, 246–247; limits of research regarding, 245–246; policy considerations regarding, 253–254; in preschool-age children, 248–249; in school-age children, 249–250; searchers vs. nonsearchers for, 252–253; theories of, 243–245;
Identity crisis, 324–330
Imagery, 292–293
Incest victims: characteristics of, 262; group therapy for, 265–267. *See also* Sexual abuse
Indian Child Welfare Act of 1978 (P.L. 95–608), 216, 217, 220–222, 226, 227
Indian Health Services, 216–217
Indians. *See* Native Americans
Infants: identity issues in, 247–248; impact of divorce on, 300; narcissism in, 326;

separation from biological parents, 123, 182. *See also* Mother-infant attachment
Infertility: as grief for adopting parents, 80–81; reversal of, 154
In-home counseling for birth family, 104–105. *See also* Counseling
Initiative, 248–249
Institutional rearing, 9, 124
Intellectual delays, 7–8
Intelligence testing, 197–198
Inter-country adoptions, 67
Interracial, 55–56
Interracial adoption, 74–75, 123; identity issues in, 250; Native American children in, 217–227; quality of attachment in, 127–132. *See also* Black children
Intraracial adoption, 29, 127
Iski, Missy Behrents, 259

Jernberg, Ann M., 271
Jewett, Claudia, 132, 169, 297
Joining process, 111–115, 119

Kadushin, Alfred, 35, 36, 132, 319, 320, 321
Kagan, R.M., 233
Kelly, Joan B., 299, 303
Kennell, J.H., 132, 169
Kirschner, David, 52
Klaus, M.H., 132
Koehne, Patrick J., 281
Koller, T.K., 275
Korean children, 67, 74–75
Kubler-Ross, Elisabeth, 169

Lankton, Stephen, 283–284
Laqueur, H.P., 314
Latin American Parents Association, 70
Lawton, J.J., 320
Le Pere, Dorothy W., 297
Learning disabilities, 8, 211–212
Lefley, H.P., 239
Legal termination of parental rights, 194–200
Letter writing therapy, 266–267
LeVine, Elaine S., 319
Life books, 67–68, 306
Life cycle, 246–247
Life Pie, 284–285
Love, 262
Lying-cheating-stealing syndrome, 87
McWhinnie, A.M., 328
Magical thinking: description of, 69; in preschoolers, 184–185; in teenagers,